SHĀṬIBĪ'S PHILOSOPHY OF ISLAMIC LAW

A REVISED AND ENLARGED VERSION OF

ISLAMIC LEGAL PHILOSOPHY

MUHAMMAD KHALID MASUD

KITAB BHAVAN

NEW DELHI-110002

KITAB BHAVAN
Publishers, Distributors, Exporters & Importers
1784, Kalan Mahal, Darya Ganj,
New Delhi - 1100 02 (India)

Phone : (91-11) 23277392, 23274686,
: (91-11) 23263383
Mob : +91-9953098606

Website : www.kitabbhavan.net
Email : info@kitabbhavan.net
nasri@vsnl.com

First Published in India : 1997
Reprint : 2022

ISBN - 10 : 81-7151-234-8
ISBN - 13 : 978-81-7151-234-8

Book Code No. : S00122

Batch ID : SPRFNS130722

Printed & Published in India by :
Moonis Ali Nasri for Kitab Bhavan
1784, Kalan Mahal, Darya Ganj,
New Delhi - 1100 02 [India]

"God made this blessed righteous Sharī'a accommodating and convenient and thus won the hearts of human beings and invoked in them love and respect for law. Had they had to act against convenience they could not have honestly fulfilled their obligations."

ABŪ ISḤĀQ AL-SHĀṬIBĪ

"The *Sharī'a* is all Justice, Kindness, Common Good and Wisdom. Any rule that departs from justice to injustice . . . or departs from common good (*maṣlaḥa*) to harm (*mafsada*) . . . is not part of *Sharī'a,* even if it is arrived at by literal interpretation".

IBN QAYYIM

CONTENTS

PREFACE

Abū Isḥāq al-Shāṭibī's (d. 790/1388) concept of *maṣlaḥa* forms the basis of his philosophy of Islamic law, the doctrine of *maqāṣid al-sharī'a*. There are frequent references in modern Muslim writings to Shāṭibī's doctrines and their relevance to the problems of modern Islamic legal theories. Some of Shāṭibī's works, hitherto existing only in manuscripts, have been published. Studies on Shāṭibī's idea of *maṣlaḥa* and some other aspects of his thought have also appeared in Arabic language. Shāṭibī's *al-Muwāfaqāt* has been translated into Turkish and Urdu languages. Nevetheless, no exclusive study of Shāṭibī's legal philosophy appears to have been made in any European language. The present study that first appeared under the title *Islamic Legal Philosophy* in 1977, was the first attempt in this regard, and to our knowledge, it still remains so.

In his doctrine of *maqāṣid al-sharī'a*, Shāṭibī not only develops the concept of *maṣlaḥa* as the basis of rationality and extendibility of Islamic law to changing circumstances, but also presents it as a fundamental principle for the universality and certainty of Islamic law. *Maṣlaḥa,* initially a concept attributed to Mālik and his school, was developed later by Shāfi'ī (e.g. Ghazālī), Ḥanbalī (e.g. Ṭūfī) and other jurists and criticised on various grounds. Certain theological and philosophical considerations had limited the legal validity of the concept of *maṣlaḥa*. The legal theorists, even Mālikī jurists, therefore tended to deal with it as an expedient rather than an independent principle. Shāṭibī's penetrating analysis of such doctrines and his definition of this concept in the context of *maqāṣid al-sharī'a* freed it from such limitations:

Contrary to the opinion of some of the reviewers of the first edition of this book, Shāṭibī's contribution cannot be fully appreciated by narrowing it down as a Mālikī doctrine. As the title of Shāṭibī's book *al-Muwāfaqāt* (An agreement between the legal theories and principles of the Mālikī and Ḥanafī school) also indicates, Shāṭibī's treatment of *maṣlaḥa* was not limited to the Mālikī school. The present study has therefore used sources from different schools of law, including modern writings on the subject to understand Shāṭibī's legal theory.

After defining the problem—the question of the adaptability of Islamic legal theory to social changes—as a context of the present study in which Shāṭibī's doctrine of *maqāṣid* is analysed, the first four chapters provide necessary information about the background and set up for the development of this doctrine. The first chapter outlines the history of political, social, economic and legal developments in Granada in Shāṭibī's period. The second chapter reconstructs Shāṭibī's biography from the available information. The third chapter analyses Shāṭibī's legal opinions and responses to the questions actually posed to him. This chapter shows the gradual development of Shāṭibī's attitude to social changes and the challenges to Islamic legal theory. The fourth chapter provides an analytical summary of the contents of Shāṭibī's four volume *al-Muwāfaqāt* in which this doctrine is elaborated. This chapter also overviews the reception of the book among Muslim jurists and thinkers in modern times. The following nine chapters offer a detailed summary and analysis of Shāṭibī's discussion of *maṣlaḥa, dalāla, taklīf, ta'abbud, niyya, 'āda, bid'a, ijtihād, khilāf* and *sharī'a*, the ten technical terms of fundamental significance in his legal philosophy.

The present book is an outcome of continuous research work spreading over more than twenty years. It grew out of my doctoral thesis written at the Institute of Islamic Studies, McGill University, Montreal, Canada, and submitted to the Faculty of Graduate Studies in 1973 under the title: "Shāṭibī's Philosophy of Islamic Law - An analytical study of Shāṭibī's concept of *maṣlaḥa* in relation to his doctrine of *maqāṣid al-sharī'a* with particular reference to the problem of adaptability of Islamic legal theory to social change". A revised version of this thesis was published in 1977

The present is a completely revised edition. Not only the title has been changed, but the chapters have also been rearranged. The book has also been revised and updated as much as possible in the light of new information available about Shāṭibī's life and works.

Since its first publication, the book has been reviewed in several eminent journals. Their comments and observations have been very useful in improving the present revision. Of course, it still remains a book written by a non-English speaking person, and hence may still contain expressions unfamiliar to the English. I have however tried to meet the main demands of reviewers' criticism.The book was criticised on three general points. Firstly, the title was criticised to be too general for a focused study. In response to this criticism I have changed the title to reflect its specified focus. Secondly, it was observed that the historical portion of the study was weak and did not utilise the latest historical studies of the period. Since my objective was not to write a history of the period, and my argument was that the historical background was necessary to understand the need and development of Shāṭibī's philosophy, I did not feel obliged to consult all the available recent historical studies. Further, the present studies do not affect my argument, and since I have already consulted most of the important original sources available, I feel justified in not referring to all the recent historical studies of the period. The third point was made about the nature of this study. One of the reviewers pointed out that "the book is a study with an underlying purpose". The reviewer was however kind enough to clarify that the study was neither "tendentious", nor did it disregard scholarly objectivity.

Referring to certain statements in the Introduction and concluding remarks about the utility and relevance of Shāṭibī's doctrine to the solution of legal problems in modern Muslim society, the reviewer found the study with an underlying purpose and cautioned that "there are dangers to scholarship in research linked to a search for material wherewith to lay the foundation of a twentieth-century renaissance in Islamic thought". There is certainly wisdom in this caution, but since this caution has relevance to modern sociology of knowledge, it deserves a detailed comment.

Firstly, as we have explained in the introductory chapter, the frame of reference for this study is the question whether Islamic law is immutable or adaptable to social change. The conservative Muslim as well as a number of non-Muslim scholars e.g. Goldziher and Schacht view Islamic law to be immutable. The modernist Muslim and a few non-Muslim scholars regard Islamic law adaptable to social changes. While the conservatives oppose legal reforms as interference in Divine law, the non-Muslim scholars support them arguing that it was a religious law and that reform and change were modern concepts and cannot be justified by medieval or pre-modern Islamic legal history or theory. These scholars do not consider Islamic law a law in the proper sense. The modernists, including a few non-Muslim scholars, on the other hand, treat Islamic law as law and find it adaptable in theory as well as in practice.

I placed this study in the context of this debate and chose to study Shāṭibī who belongs to medieval period. I found Shāṭibī engaged in similar debates. A detailed analysis of Shāṭibī's doctrine was expected to help in a better understanding of the nature of Islamic law, if placed in the context of this debate.

Secondly, an underlying purpose in a study could be dangerous if evidence is studied selectively and partially and the opposing view is completely dismissed. It should not however mean that the study should have no purpose or objective at all. Relevance of research with contemporary environment does not necessarily mean disregard of scholarly objectivity.

Thirdly, modernists' quest for justification for the continuity of present modern renaissance with past is often resented by European scholars because they consider modernity essentially a result of Western impact. There is no denying the fact that both these views could be subjective in their extreme form. It is, however, more dangerous to favour only one of these views.

A transliteration table for Arabic words is included. The Arabic affix *al-* is usually ommitted in case of proper names. English translations of Arabic terms are not yet standardized or universally accepted. I have therefore supplied Arabic terms in parenthesis. A glossary of terms is given at the end of the book.

MUHAMMAD KHALID MASUD

TRANSLITERATION TABLE

CONSONANTS

ء	'
الف	a
ب	b
ت	t
ث	th
ج	j
ح	ḥ
خ	kh
د	d
ذ	dh
ر	r
ز	z
س	s
ش	sh
ص	ṣ
ض	ḍ
ط	ṭ
ظ	ẓ
ع	'
غ	gh
ف	f
ق	q
ك	k
ل	l
م	m
ن	n
و	w
ه	h ـه -*a* (-*at* in construct state)
ى	y
ال	*al*- and *'l*. (generally omitted in front of proper names)

VOWELS

Long

آ = ā
أو = ū
إى = ī

Short

ـَ = a
ـِ = i
ـُ = u

Doubled:

يّ iyy (final form ī)
وّ uww (final form ū)

Diphthongs:

أَو : aw ; أَى : ay

INTRODUCTION

The relationship between legal theory and social change is one of the basic problems of the philosophies of law.[1] "Law" having its semantic association with natural laws, is assumed to be fixed, determined, certain, permanent and, therefore, unchanging. Yet, it always faces the challenge of social change which demands adaptability from it. Most often the impact of social change is so profound that it affects legal concepts as well as institutions and thus creates a need for a fresh philosophy of law. The problem of social change and legal theory is of particular significance in Islamic legal philosophy. Islamic law is generally defined as religious, sacred and hence immutable. How does such a law face the challenge of change?

The above question has brought to the fore the problem of the adaptability of Islamic law which has been widely discussed, yet remains debatable. The problem has been generally formulated in the form of the following question: Is Islamic law immutable or is it adaptable to the extent that the change and modernization sought can be pursued under its aegis?

Broadly speaking, there have been two points of view in answer to this question. One view, which is shared by a large number of Islamicists such as C.S. Hurgronje and J. Schacht, and by most traditionalist Muslim jurists, maintains that in its concept, and according to the nature of its development and methodology, Islamic law is immutable and hence not adaptable to social changes. A second view, which is upheld by a few experts on Islamic law such as Linant de Bellefonds and by the majority of Muslim reformists and jurists such as Subḥī Mahmaṣānī, contends that such legal principles as the consideration of *maṣlaḥa* (roughly translated, human good), and *ijtihād* (independent legal reasoning) and the history of the adaptability of Islamic law sufficiently demonstrate that Islamic law is adaptable to social change.

Before any general conclusions be drawn regarding the adaptability of Islamic law, the problem requires a great deal of spade work. For a clear analysis, the primary task is to study the various aspects and levels of this problem which should be distinguished sharply from one another and yet be studied in conjunction with one another. Furthermore, since Islamic theory has developed through the writings of various jurists having different historical backgrounds, the problem of adaptability requires to be studied in specific reference to individual jurists in their historical settings.

An analysis of the concept of Islamic law, on the other hand, requires a detailed study of the essential ideas in Islamic legal theory especially those pertinent to the question of adaptability. *Maṣlaḥa* is one such idea. This concept is of fundamental significance to the proponents of the adaptability view. They argue that Islamic law aims at the *maṣāliḥ* (plural of *maṣlaḥa*) of man, hence logically, it should welcome any social change that serves this purpose. Furthermore, with such an objective in view, Islamic law cannot be rigid and inert in regard to social change.

Among the very few jurists who treated the concept of *maṣlaḥa* as an independent principle of legal theory, Abū Isḥāq Ibrāhīm b. Mūsā al-Shāṭibī (d. 790/1388) made one of the more significant contributions. In his *al-Muwāfaqāt*, Shāṭibī presented a doctrine of *maqāṣid al-sharī'a* (the purpose or ends of law) which comprises an exposition of the various aspects of the concept of *maṣlaḥa* as a principle of legal theory. Shāṭibī is therefore a valid choice for a study the requirements of which we have discussed above.

The choice of Shāṭibī is further prompted by the fact that in their support of the adaptability-view, it is largely Shāṭibī upon whose arguments the modern reformists have relied in facing the challenge of social change to Islamic legal theory.

Shāṭibī sought an answer to such a challenge in the principle of *maṣlaḥa*. A discussion of Shāṭibī's answer is, however, unwarranted unless we first explain what the 'immutability' of Islamic law means.

Presuming that the interaction between social change and legal theory must have been at work in Islamic law before Shāṭibī as well, it may be rightfully suggested that to define the key terms of this study in order to evaluate Shāṭibī's contribution to the philosophy of Islamic law his views must be studied in comparison with those of his predecessors. Unfortunately, a general history of Islamic legal philosophy is yet to be written.

On the other hand, an attempt to establish the views of Shāṭibī's predecessors by surveying the original sources is also beyond the scope of this study. The literature available on *uṣūl al-fiqh*, belonging to the pre-Shāṭibī period, is enormous and there is no way to estimate how much more material was lost or has yet been discovered. There is, in addition, the problem of the differences in the legal doctrines among various schools of law due to the various theological and philosophical predilection of the *uṣūl* writers. Such extra-legal considerations are reflected in the treatment of legal theory. A survey of the philosophy of law, therefore, would demand an investigation of all these aspects which is impossible within the limited scope of this volume.

It is with these limitations in view that in attempting to formulate an understanding of the key terms of the problem of the adaptability of Islamic legal theory to social change, this chapter is divided into two parts. The first part proposes to make an analysis of the findings of recent scholarship on this problem. This choice is made mainly in consideration of the fact that in the modern period (since the beginning of the nineteenth century) the question of adaptability of legal theory to social change has been asked more pointedly than ever before. Hence, the formulation of the problem can be expected to be clearer than in earlier periods of the history of Islamic law. In the second part, we shall offer working definitions of the key terms of the problem.

I

In the nineteenth century when most of the Muslim peoples, directly or indirectly, came to be ruled by Western powers, a number of attempts were made to reform the laws of the Muslim peoples. Whether they were attempts to codify or to modify the Muslim laws, the strong religious reaction among the Muslim peoples against such legislative attempts made the reformists aware of the complexities of the problem of change in the Islamic law.

The early colonial policy of non-interference in personal and religious laws, particularly in India, in fact, tended to support the conservatives' view of the immutability of Islam law.[2] One of the solutions was to avoid interference in personal and religious matters. This solution required either that the courts should be entrusted entirely to the traditional jurists, or that the judges should be assisted by specialists trained in the traditional Muslim laws. The situation led to a series of translations of the traditional texts and their codification along Western patterns. This was the beginning of legislative modernism in Islamic law. The early legislative modernism, however, added a new dimension to the problem. Most of the translators and jurists were lawyers such as Van Den Berg and M. Morand and their attempts at translations and codifications were meant for judges in modern courts. More significantly, most of them were foreigners and non-Muslims. Perhaps naturally they tended to treat the whole body of Islamic law as though it were Western law. At the extreme of their reform efforts, they excluded from the body of Islamic law what they considered as not belonging to Law. The underlying conception in these attempts was that Islamic law, like other laws, could be changed, reformed and codified by government legislation according to social needs. Confronted with orthodox conservative opposition, these men spelled out their views more explicitly by questioning the idea of the immutability of Islamic law.[3]

This view of Islamic law was strongly criticised by Islamicists, especially by Snouck Hurgronje[4] and G. Bergsträsser.[5] Hurgronje pointed out that it was a mistake to treat Islamic law like Western law and that Islamic law was a 'doctrine of duties', i.e. ethics, and not law in the proper sense. By its nature it was religious law, and as such it was immutable.[6]

Consequently, from that time, as J. Schacht also reported in his lecture on the status of scholarship on Islamic law,[7] there appeared two approaches to the study of Islamic law: one, that of the lawyers, the other that of the Islamicists. An implicit controversy between these two approaches continues even today on the problem of legal theory and social change. Whereas the lawyers have been inclined to regard Islamic law as adaptable to social change, the Islamicists have stressed the immutable character of Islamic law.

The arguments of the advocates of the immutability of Islamic law can be summed up in the following three general statements:

1. Islamic law is immutable because the authoritarian, divine and absolute concept of law in Islam does not allow change in legal concepts and institutions. As a corollary to this concept, its sanction is divine and hence it cannot change.

2. Islamic law is immutable because the nature of its origin and its development in its formative period isolated it from the institutions of legal and social change—the courts and the state.

3. Islamic law is immutable as it did not develop an adequate methodology of legal change.

The advocates of the adaptability view disagree with the above conclusions, yet their arguments also turn around these three aspects of Islamic law: concept, history and methodology.

It is, therefor, possible to accept these three aspects as general landmarks in surveying the problem of social change and legal theory. The following discussion is, therefore, arranged according to these three aspects. We have limited our review in the following section mainly to recent western studies, as in its essence the conservative traditional view on the subject of immutability does not differ from the Western view.

1. THE CONCEPT OF LAW

The argument that the Islamic concept of law is absolute and authoritarian and hence immutable, has been advanced from two points of view. First, with regard to the source of Islamic law it is contended that source of Islamic law is the will of God, which is absolute and unchangeable. The second point of view springs from the definition of Islamic law; there it is demonstrated that Islamic law cannot be identified as law in the proper sense, rather it is an ethical or moral system of rules. The first view, thus, treats the problem of the concept of law in terms of distinction between reason and revelation. The second view deals with it in terms of distinction between law and morality.

The arguments in regard to the first view take into account two subject matters: (i) law and theology, and (ii) law and epistemology.

J. Schacht has very forcefully argued in his article, "Theology and Law in Islam", that there has always been a close connection between Islamic law and theology; and that certain isolated instances of separatist trends are only accidental. He has demonstrated this connection by the fact that the schools of law and their eponyms showed their interest both in law and in theology.[8] Further, a certain symbiosis of the schools of law and the schools of theology existed throughout the history of Islamic law.[9] Malcolm H. Kerr also observes that the concept of Islamic law is very firmly grounded in theology.[10]

The connection between law and theology, however, must not be understood in the sense that law was theological so as to be a counterpart of 'Divine Law' or 'Canon Law' as in Christian teachings. 'Islam', as Schacht put it, 'is a religion of action rather than of belief'.[11] Hence a 'Theology' in the Christian sense could not be conceived of in Islam. The argument asserting the theological foundations of the concept of Islamic law is advanced simply to stress that the law's source is Divine will, and not human reason.

C.H. Toy has put this idea more neatly by comparing the Greek and the Semitic concepts of law. He found that the Semites conceived law as absolute, revealed by God, whereas the Greeks worked out the idea of natural law. The absolute law of the Semites is external, imposed on man from without, by God, while the Greek conception is of an inward law which is part of man's nature.[12]

It appears that arguments holding Islamic law to be theologically grounded are advanced in the sense in which Toy speaks about the Semitic concept of absolute law. The evidence that the advocates of the immutability view present to prove their point confirms our observation.

The first evidence they advance concerns the divinity of the sources of Islamic law. It is argued that Islamic law seeks its basis in Divine Revelation through the Prophet; it is embedded in the Qur'ān and *ḥadīth*. Being divine, or divinely inspired, these sources are believed to be sacred, final, eternal and hence immutable. It is in this sense that some scholars have understood Islamic law as divine law. Among them N.J. Coulson,[13] H.A.R. Gibb,[14] H.J. Liebesny,[15] M. Khadduri,[16] H. Lammens,[17] G. Makdisi,[18] and particularly J.N.D. Anderson[19] have expressed this view.

One cannot fail to notice an ambivalence in the argument of these scholars. If one description or definition implies certain positive point contrary to their argument, they would qualify that description by another definition. This attitude has prevented them from looking at the evidence that would have led them to appreciate Islamic law differently. There are a number of scholars who treat Islamic law differently.

Leon Ostrorog,[20] S.G.V. Fitzgerald[21] and some others have disagreed with the view of the scholars mentioned above. They argue that the strictly legal materials in these 'revealed' sources are limited and, indeed, negligible. Furthermore, this material is more concerned with the religious and moral teachings than with matters strictly pertinent to law. The whole body of Islamic law cannot, therefore, be called revealed and sacred when the amount of legal material existing in the revealed sources is very little.

The second evidence advanced by the advocates of the immutability view takes the question of the sources of law in a more abstract sense. It contends that Islamic law has its source in the Will of God. Since Gibb has expressed this view more succinctly, we quote him as follows:

> The conception of law in Islam is thus authoritarian to the last degree. 'The law, which is the constitution of the Community, cannot be other than the Will of God, revealed through the Prophet'. This is a Semitic form of the principle that 'The will of the sovereign is law', since God is the sole Head of the Community, and therefore sole Legislator.[22]

The concept of the Will of God has theological implications, which render it entirely absolute and immutable. The reason for this situation Gibb finds in the nature of the development of Muslim theology. Because of its stress on monotheism, Islamic theology refused to admit any limitations whatsoever upon the Powers and the Will of God. But the frame of reference of these theological discussions was Aristotelian logic rather than metaphysics. Consequently, the theology was forced into extreme positions; one such position is that there could be no agent of any kind in the universe except God, since the existence of an agent implies the possibility of an action independent of God, and, therefore, a theoretical limitation upon the absolute power of God.[23] This conclusion was extended by Ash'arī theologians even to 'human acts'; man was not considered a free agent of his acts. This, apparently, would also imply a denial of moral and legal responsibility on the part of man. It would also imply that nothing can be qualified as good or bad by itself, because the creation would have no intrinsic value. The knowledge of good and bad can only be had through revelation and not through human reason. This point leads us to the other subject matter of the concept of law, its epistemology.

The arguments by the Western scholarship in respect to epistemology of Islamic law have referred to two aspects of the problem, (a) the possibility and method of knowing the law, and (b) the role of human reason.

Gibb has brought these points clearly to the fore. He argues that Islamic law is thought of, not as a product of human intelligence and adaptation to social needs and ideals, but of divine inspiration and hence immutable. The Qur'ān and Ḥadīth are not the basis of Islamic legal speculation but only its sources. The real foundation of the law is to be sought in the attitude of mind which determined the methods of utilizing these sources. The ultimate reason of such a mental attitude is metaphysical; an *a priori* conviction of the imperfection of human reason and its inability to apprehend by its sole powers the real nature of the good, or indeed, of any reality whatsoever.[24] As a corollary of the above concept of the epistemology of law, no primary role is allowed to independent human reason in law making.

Schacht has pointed out that as a consequence of such an epistemological attitude a number of irrational elements have survived in the Islamic law.[25] R. Brunschvig also speaks of the irrationality of Islamic law in this special sense.[26] G.F. Hourani's distinction between two theories of values in Islam refers to *maṣlaḥa* as a rational and ethical concept.[27]

The principle in Islamic legal theory that implies the employment of reason in knowing and interpreting law is *maṣlaḥa*. In fact, both Grunebaum[28] and Hourani[29] have classified it as a rational principle. This classification has been nevertheless, disputed by scholars like Schacht.[30]

The second view, in regard to the concept of Islamic law - dealing with it in terms of the opposition between law and morality - is concerned with its definition. Since law and morality or ethics have a great deal in common, they are often liable to be confused. Hence, any attempt to define law necessarily starts by distinguishing one from the other, law from morality. In defining Islamic law, Islamicists conclude that it is a system of ethical or moral rules. This conclusion must be understood in reference to the separation of law from morality. By defining Islamic law as 'ethics' it is certainly never implied that it is a branch of philosophy; nor is it 'morality' in the sense of having its source in mores and social customs only.

The main aim of the argument in describing Islamic law as ethical law was to refute the modern lawyers' approach to Islamic law as being law in the modern sense. The second aim was to maintain the position that being a system of ethics, Islamic law is not capable of change through legislation. Snouck Hurgronje was the first scholar to advance this argument. He defined, in very clear terms, Islamic law as a 'Doctrine of Duties'.[31] Th. W. Juynboll[32] and others agreed with Hurgronje. G.-H. Bousquet carried this argument to the extent of affirming that Islamic law is idealistic and casuistic, based on imaginative, non-discursive and often rationally absurd hypotheses.[33]

Gibb's elaboration on this point is very succinct. To maintain that Islamic law was a system of ethics would naturally imply that it was a system based on human reason. Gibb explained that it was an ethical system only in contradistinction to a legal system; yet it was not a rational or philosophical system as it sought its basis in revelation. The main points in his argument that distinguish Islamic law as an ethical system in contrast to a legal system were the following:

(a) The classification and categories of actions in Islamic law are moral, not juridical. The five categories of obligatory, recommended, indifferent, reprehensible and forbidden which are to cover all human actions, are moral and ethical.[34] The ethical nature of the categories of action does not mean that there did not exist any legal subject matter in Islamic law. As a matter of fact, Schacht maintained, the legal subject-matter can be distinguished from other subjects but what is meant by the all-inclusiveness of these five moral categories is that even legal subject-matter is classified as an ethical and religious duty.[35]

(b) Islamic law speaks of 'duties', not of 'rights'. In other words there is much more emphasis on what one ought to do rather than upon what one is entitled to claim as a right. The term *ḥuqūq* even though it means 'rights' in a sense, nonetheless, does not contradict the point. In Islamic law, *ḥuqūq* are divided into those belonging to God and those belonging to men. Subsequently, the latter are subordinated to the former, and this, in fact, renders them into religious and ethical duties rather than rights in the strictest meaning.

(c) Penalties and sanctions in Islamic law are religious and moral, not civil and legal. The term used for a penalty, even in matters belonging to penal law, is *ḥudūd Allāh* (the limits of God) which stresses the fact that a certain offence has been committed against God and that it is His right to impose penalty.[36]

Schacht explains further that the other category of penalty called *ta'zīr*, according to which a *qāḍī* (judge) may punish at his discretion any act which, in his opinion, calls for punishment, in fact, did not belong to the Islamic legislation which appears in the Qur'ān and in the tradition of the Prophet.[37] What is implied in this explanation is that the concept of civil penalty which the term *ta'zīr* might convey, originally did not belong to the concept of Islamic law.

To sum up this discussion on the concept of law we find some ambiguity in Western scholars' analysis. Firstly their perspective appears to be biased. They begin by saying that Islamic law is not law in the proper sense. Obviously 'proper sense' here is defined from the Austinian perspective, and therefore, call Islamic law a doctrine of duties. They do not, however, accept the implications of this conclusion because characterising Islamic law as ethical and moral would imply that it is rational and systematic.

Apart from this bias, the Western analysis is ambiguous from the point of view of the referent as well: to whom are they referring as Islamic law: *dīn*, *sharī'a* or *fiqh*? In the Qur'anic usage, *Dīn* is the essence and is common in all revealed religions. *Sharī'a*, on the other hand, has differed from one religious community to the other. *Fiqh* is an interpretation of *sharī'a* by jurists, muftīs and qāḍīs, and thus a product of human reason. There is no doubt that Muslim thinkers are also not clear on this point, yet very few of them claim divine origin of *fiqh*. Furthermore a distinction must be made among the various expressions of law in Islam as are found in books of *kalām* and *fiqh*, and as found in the *fatāwā* and judgements of the *qāḍīs*. If we have in mind the law as practised in Courts, then we cannot limit our observation to *fiqh* books and conclude that Islamic law is jurists' law, and is not law in the proper sense. Furthermore, we have to investigate the range of subjects covered by courts of Islamic law to determine the scope of Islamic law applicable in courts. Only then we can conclude whether the subject matter of Islamic law could be categorised as juridical or not.

Lastly, to characterise Islamic law as a religious and moral system, not a legal system, because its sanctions and penalties are moral and religious, is indeed begging the question. Firstly this statement is inaccurate as most penalties, e.g. in case of murder, theft, robbery etc. cannot be described as moral reprimands. Secondly when a legal system sanctions a certain action as penalty, even though it may be a moral reprimand in its essence, it becomes legal. The various punishments under *ta'zīr*, if adopted in statutes, become law.

Besides being Eurocentric and ambiguous, this analysis is basically weak on two points. Firstly, it does not conceive the possibility that a legal system can develop within a religious social order. Secondly, this analysis is essentially based on a study of doctrines and theories, and does not take into account the law in practice i.e. the legal institutions and legal systems as they functioned in Muslim society in various periods of history. This point leads us to the second section where we will review the recent studies on the history of Islamic law.

2. THE HISTORY OF ISLAMIC LAW

A comprehensive history of Islamic law is yet to be written. In general, those scholars who took a historical approach for understanding the nature of Islamic law have pointed out the following as its characteristics: 1) its idealistic nature, 2) its religious nature, 3) its rigidity, and 4) its casuistic nature. All four characteristics are related to one another and are presented as reasons for the Law's immutability.

The arguments about the divine nature of Islamic law refer to the following four areas: i) the origins of Islamic law; ii) Islamic law and state legislation; iii) the role of the institution of the *qāḍī*, iv) the establishment of the schools of Islamic law, and v) Islamic Law in practice.

i) THE ORIGINS OF ISLAMIC LAW

The traditional Muslim point of view maintains that Islamic law began with the Divine Revelation in the Qur'an and with Prophet Muḥammad's decisions. These decisions as preserved in the large corpus of *ḥadīth* literature were the foundation of Islamic law.

I. Goldziher's study of the *ḥadīth* literature from the point of view of its historicity questioned the authenticity of the larger part of this literature.[38] J. Schacht[39] and R. Brunschvig[40] brought this criticism to bear upon that part of the *ḥadīth* literature that concerned Islamic law. Schacht argued that a large number of legal *aḥādīth* were, in fact, legal doctrines of the early scholars of Islamic law which were projected back to the Prophet in the form of *ḥadīth, ḥadīth* being the most acceptable method of establishing a point. Such a criticism of *aḥādīth* has been severely criticized in a number of recent *ḥadīth* studies.[41]

Some scholars also found that there existed in Islamic law a considerable foreign element coming especially from Roman law.[42] As the ancient schools of law developed in areas where Roman law had been applied before the advent of Islam, these scholars concluded that the origins of Islamic law must be sought in Roman law. This view has been a point of controversy among a number of scholars.[43]

Schacht connected the existence of the foreign elements to the *Sunna*. He argued that the ancient scholars, in fact, had assimilated local administrative practices and foreign legal elements into a series of doctrines which they had Islamicized by incorporating them into the *Sunna*.[44] The need for projection backward to the Prophet, Schacht has argued, was not felt until Shāfi'ī (d.820) very forcefully presented the thesis of the traditionists and established the sole authority of the Prophet in opposition to the authority of "living tradition".

The bearing of these studies on the origins of the law and upon the problem of the law's immutability lies in their conclusion that Islamic law originated from a pious and religious motivation. This motivation became stronger as the religious element in the law was threatened by the attempts of government in the early 'Abbāsī period to control Islamic law. To save Islamic law from government control, Muslim jurists stressed its religious and divine nature so as to raise it above any human tampering.

Goldziher's and Schacht's criticism on the authenticity of the *hadīth* literature have been questioned in a number of recent studies but since most of these studies are not directly relevant to the question of the law's origins, they do not concern us here. Two studies are, however, relevant to our discussion.

Fazlur Rahman[45] disagreed with Schacht's conclusion that the *Sunna* of the Prophet was a late concept that emerged in consequence of the development of the *hadīth* movement. Using literary, philological and historical evidence, F. Rahman showed that, contrary to Schacht's argument, the *Sunna* of the Prophet could not have been a late concept. According to F. Rahman, therefore, the origin of Islamic law is to be sought in the early period of Islam.

S.D. Goitein,[46] although he has insisted that his conclusions do not differ from those of Schacht, suggested that the origins of Islamic law may be dated to the year 5/627. Goitein draws his conclusions from a Qur'anic verse which, he says, establishes Muhammad's role as law-giver. From the verse he concluded that the idea of Islamic law was not the result of post-Qur'anic developments but was given by Muhammad himself.

Besides these differences in determining the historic beginnings of Islamic law, all of the above arguments agree upon the religious nature of its origins.

ii) ISLAMIC LAW AND STATE LEGISLATION

Gibb observed that in Islam the law preceded the state, both logically and in terms of time, and that the state existed for the sole purpose of maintaining and enforcing the law.[47] Gibb argued that in the Umawī period the formulation of the Revealed Law was left in the hands of theologians. The advent of the 'Abbāsī Caliphs brought this scholastic law, for the first time, to the test of practice.[48] Schacht's investigation of the early development of Islamic law explains the above observation historically.[49] As was mentioned above, Schacht concluded that Islamic law began with the activities of the jurists due to religious motives; it was not created by state legislation. This phenomenon resulted in the jurists' conviction of the independence of Islamic law from state control. Certain historical events in the eighth century solidified this attitude further.

In the early 'Abbāsī period the administration of justice was in a chaotic condition because of the lack of unity in juridical doctrines. Ibn al-Muqaffa' (d.727), a secretary in the 'Abbāsī government, strongly recommended that the caliph control this diversity of opinions by state legislation.[50] The jurists reacted to this suggestion by insisting that the law was superior to the state, and hence not subject to state legislation.[51]

Whether Islamic law maintained this independence in actual practice is a matter dealt with in the next section. What concerns us here is the Western scholars' approach to this problem. It may indeed be true that the jurists refused to let Islamic law be subject to state legislation, but the jurists' refusal does not warrant to conclude that there was no state legislation in Islamic legal history. Unfortunately, not only that the laws promulgated by the Muslim rulers were not considered a proper subject for the study of the history of Islamic law, but by implication it was also assumed that no such laws existed. This assumption was made the basis of a further conclusion that Islamic law was theoretical and divorced from social realities.

H. Lammens and others have argued that, being severed from state legislation, Islamic law became divorced from social realities.[52] G.-H. Bousquet concluded that the idea of successive adaptations to changing circumstances was strange to its system.[53]

Claude Cahen, however, has disagreed with such conclusions. He argues that the problem for the early jurists was not to derive the ideal of Muslim government but rather to institute a very loose filtering which would reserve to them the right of the bestowal upon the regime as a whole of its certificate of 'good Muslim'. He concluded that "it would be supremely unjust...to regard the work of the 'Abbasi jurists as abstract and turning the back on reality."[54]

iii) ROLE OF THE INSTITUTION OF QĀḌĪ

J. Schacht observed that the institution of *qāḍī* evolved out of the pre-Islamic institution of the *ḥakam* (arbitrator). Like the *ḥakam,* the early *qāḍī* was bound by the precedents of local tradition and decided cases, not through some formal methods of reasoning, but according to his own discretion.[55]

However, looking at the history of Islamic law, e.g. as gleaned from the biographies of the *qāḍīs*, one notices a very intensive and creative role of the muftis and *qāḍīs* in the formation of Islamic law in the early period. Even Schacht, who otherwise characterises Islamic law as a jurists' law, observed the significance of *qāḍīs*' contribution. He argues that the decisions of the Umawī *qāḍīs* were assimilated into the body of Islamic law.[56] He nevertheless states that the role of *qāḍī* was not recognised to be that of making or interpreting the law, but, essentially, only of applying it. One may ask who defined this role of the *qāḍī*? State or jurists? Schacht is not clear on this point. As mentioned above, he finds jurists incorporating the interpretations of the Umawī *qāḍīs* into Islamic law. Regarding the *qāḍīs* in the 'Abbāsī period, he observes that in the 'Abbāsī period the office of the *qāḍī* was connected with Islamic law. He concludes that *qāḍī* in this period was separated from the general state administration, being subject to Islamic law only.[57]

This conclusion does not agree with Schacht's early remarks that the *qāḍīs* had no role in the interpretation and formation of Islamic law. Schacht's characterisation may apply to the period of *taqlīd,* when after the establishment of the schools of law, the role of a *qāḍī* was reduced to the application of the teaching of one of these schools. *Taqlīd* might have developed, however, as a legal necessity rather than a theological or religious obligation, because in the latter case the office of *qāḍī* would not be unpopular among the jurists.

Analyzing the causes of the widespread dislike of the office of *qāḍī* among the jurists, N.J. Coulson concluded that the rejection of the office could not be fully explained by such factors as the fear of sudden political disfavour or as pious motives, such as I. Goldziher, H.F. Amedroz and É. Tyan had suggested. Accordingly to Coulson the real cause of dislike of the office was its impracticable and idealistic nature as conceived by the traditionist jurists.[58]

Coulson, however, observed a significant distinction in the attitudes of the jurists toward the institution; the distinction between the attitude of the practical lawyers and the attitude of the idealist traditionists. He stresses that this distinction was real and vital in the history of Islamic law.[59] For lawyers Islamic law consisted of enforceable legal rules; for traditionists it was a code of moral and religious duties. The former regarded the office of *qāḍī* as essential and honourable; the latter wished to avoid it at all costs. The attitude of the lawyers was a continuation of the outlook of the early Umawī *qāḍīs* who, as legal secretaries, were responsible to the governor. The other attitude was the result of the growing influence of the religious concept of law in the eighth century, extending to the office of the *qāḍī*. The morally-inclined *qāḍīs* began to feel that their allegiance lay to religion rather than to the interests of the state.

As a result of this dichotomy there developed two trends of law; the 'religious law' as expounded by the jurists and the 'positive law' as administered by the courts. An example of the latter is the development of *'amal* (juridical practice), as court law in the Mālikī school.[60]

H. Toledano has observed that *'amal* became "an instrument for modifying and adapting the *sharī'a* to meet the practical needs of the society, and the judges in Morocco were filling the same role as their predecessors in the first two centuries of Islam".[61]

iv) THE ESTABLISHMENT OF THE SCHOOLS OF LAW

As a result of the rapid legal activity from the late Umawi period until the end of the second century, there emerged several schools of law which were consolidated to the extent that adherence to one of these schools was common and also necessary. This adherence was required not only of common man but also of the *qāḍī* and the jurist. This requirement was called *taqlīd*.

The effects of *taqlīd* on the growth of Islamic law were fateful. It reduced legal activities to the confines of particular schools. On the one hand, the procedure of legal reasoning became mechanical and, on the other hand, the whole body of Islamic law was cast into a rigid mould, not allowing further independent growth.[62]

The phenomenon of *taqlīd* has been considered by a number of scholars as a factor responsible for the belief in the immutability of Islamic law.

Taqlīd might have led to the stagnation of Islamic law and rendered juridical reasoning mechanical, but it cannot be concluded with certainty without an analytical study of the judgements of *qāḍīs* and *muftīs* in this period. However theoretically speaking, *taqlīd* does not mean immutability. The enormous literature on Islamic law produced in this period is not an indication of stagnation.

v) ISLAMIC LAW IN PRACTICE

Most studies on Islamic law have noticed the development of two trends in the history of Islamic law but they term it as a gap between theory and practice. Only a few scholars such as J. Kramers have noticed two system of law existing side by side in Islam: *'droit de l'Islam'*, the laws in practice, and *'droit islamique'*, the law in theory.[63]

The cleavage between theory and practice has been observed under three aspects: (i) between Islamic law and the customs of the Muslim people; (ii) between Islamic law as elaborated in Texts and as practised in the courts; (iii) between different kinds of subject matters in reference to their application.

Although custom was not recognized, theoretically, as a source of Islamic law,[64] yet scholars have observed that custom not only played an important role in the growth of Islamic law but also that it always co-existed with the law.[65]

As for the cleavage between the jurists' law and the court law, scholars have observed that the administration of justice was not completely subject to the textual Islamic law. An evident example of this was the introduction of the courts of *naẓar fi'l-maẓālim* where decisions were reached through individual discretion and *siyāsa*. The jurisdiction of the *qāḍī* was limited, and even there interference by the governor and other government officials in the *qāḍī's* decision, and his jurisdiction was so frequent that, in fact, the applicability of *sharī'a* law in courts was more and more restricted. Consequently, the 'positive law' applied in the courts grew separately from the religious law.

As mentioned above, the '*amal* tradition is an example of the positive law. As a matter of fact, it was assimilated into Mālikī law as a doctrine that had a regulative force. The judges were required to follow it even when it ran contrary to the dominant opinion of the school.[66]

Customary law and the law of the courts that responded to actual social facts and that were adaptable to social changes ought to have influenced Islamic law. This influence, as observed by the scholars, did operate, but it varied according to the various subject matters of Islamic law.

A.L. Udovitch believes that Bergsträsser was the first scholar who pointed out this distinction.[67] He distinguished three broad categories of the subject matters of the Islamic law:

1. Ritual, family and inheritance laws, which though they accepted certain changes based on custom, yet remained as a whole closest to Islamic law.

2. Constitutional, criminal and fiscal laws - an area where Cahen believed the jurists to be very flexible[68]—were constantly being adapted to social changes. In fact, Bergsträsser observed that this category of Islamic law diverged farthest and in some cases completely from the classical formulation of Islamic law.[69]

3. Commercial laws, or to use Schacht's terminology, the laws of contract and obligation, fell somewhere between the two extremes. Schacht,[70] in one of his early statements agreed with Hurgronje[71] who maintained that Islamic commercial law remained for the most part a dead letter. Goetein and Udovitch, on the contrary, have concluded on the basis of commercial documents that commercial laws also conformed with the textual Islamic law.[72]

These observations indicate that there existed an Islamic law parallel to the one found in jurists' books. This law was not always in conflict with the textual law. In fact both interacted with each other, and mostly the jurists incorporated the laws developed in its counterpart system. The jurists may not recognise custom, court judgements and state legislations theoretically but they never denied their existence. To treat this difference as a gap between theory and practice means agreeing with the jurists to recognise only the textual law as Islamic law. Nevertheless, even described as a gap, this legal activity shows dynamism, not the immutability of Islamic law.

3. THE QUESTION OF METHOD

The significance of the question of method with reference to the immutability of Islamic law has been generally recognized by all scholars. Systems of law tend to be perfect and permanent; hence a sense of immutability gathers around the concept of law. But changing social needs challenge such an attitude. Various systems of law devised methods to meet such challenges.For instance, Roman Law resolved this problem by distinguishing between *jus civile* which was strict and *jus honorarium* which was elastic.[73] In Common Law the flexibility was achieved through Equity.[74]

The question of method in Islamic law has generally been discussed in reference to the classical theory of the 'four sources of Islamic law'.[75]

Modern scholarship also discusses the question of method in reference to the sources of Islamic law. É. Tyan[76] and Ch. Chehata[77] observe that Islamic law did evolve methods to adopt legal theory to changes. Chehata spoke about the principle of *istiḥsān* as being the counterpart of Equity in Common Law.[78] Tyan pointed out three such methods: *istiḥsān, istiṣlāḥ,* and *siyāsa shar'iyya* (administration of justice according to the spirit of Islamic law). All of these methods were devices to incorporate social changes into Islamic law where the strict requirements of Islamic law would not allow it.

Schacht contended that Islamic law did not and could not evolve such methods,[79] mainly because by its very nature Islamic law was not a need of them. Islamic law was not an official law like other laws. Official law came to be by the authority of secular legislators, but Islamic law did not recognize it. Hence Islamic law was a 'sacred law' par excellence; perfect, immutable, and not in need of change. Schacht maintained that principles such as *istiḥsān*, *istiṣlāḥ* and *'amal* were not used as principles of change but rather to interpret and justify the already existing rules of Islamic law. Moreover, if ever they were used to adopt certain changes they were meant to build a protective zone around that particular change lest it affect the whole of the theory.[80]

Malcolm H. Kerr, in his study of Islamic reforms in the nineteenth century, has confirmed Schacht's conclusions. Kerr chose to study the principle of *maṣlaḥa* ("welfare, benefit, utility")[81] because it was considered by the upholders of the dynamism in Islamic law as a principle of adaptability.[82] He concluded that although theoretically a liberal principle, the *maṣlaḥa* in actual application succumbed to the theological and idealistic limitations imposed upon it by the Islamic legal theory.

The relevant concept of legal theory and their application have not been sufficiently studied to warrant any definite conclusion. Particularly studies about *maṣlaḥa* suffer from a basic defect that they study it from the perspective of sources of Islamic law theory and do not treat it as an independent principle. The present study is an attempt to fill this gap. It studies the question of adaptability in Islamic legal theory with special reference to the concept of *maṣlaḥa*, particularly as expounded by Abū Isḥāq al-Shāṭibī. The study argues that even in theory Islamic law favours adaptability.

Before proceeding to a discussion of Shāṭibī's philosophy of Islamic law, let us define our understanding of the key terms used in this study.

II

'Adaptability/Immutability'

It is clear that the above views have the following questions as a starting point: Does Islamic law in fact change? Further, is Islamic law changeable? Scholars provide different answers to these questions. The immutability-view claims that Islamic law does not change, adding that in fact it cannot change. The 'immutability', to them, therefore, means that the rulings pronounced by Islamic law are static, final, eternal, absolute and unalterable. The adaptability-view, on the contrary, maintains that Islamic law changes and that, in fact, it has changed, and more-over, it can be changed further. This view also stresses that law can be changed and modified to fit new social conditions. In other words, 'adaptability', in the specific context of the above controversy, is not simply a contrary term to 'immutability', but it consists of an additional meaning, i.e. a distinct implication of modifying to meet new conditions.

One may also note that the term 'adaptability' has been used by modern scholars in two senses. For the purpose of clarity the two uses of the term must be distinguished. One use of the term means 'the possibility of *expanding* the already existing body of law'. In the second sense it means 'the *openness* of this body of law to *change* (according to social conditions)'. The former sense of the term is hardly in question here. With the exception of a few literalists, 'adaptability' in the first sense has been always allowed by the jurists on the basis of analogy. In fact, as mentioned elsewhere, the need and method of analogy arose from this meaning of 'adaptability'.

In this study we are, therefore, concerned with the second sense of 'adaptability'. The other use of the term is secondary, but complementary.

'Social Change'

The term 'adaptability' is, thus, immediately concerned with social change.

Social change, here, is obviously not a technical term which implies 'transformation of society' or 'social control'.[83] This term is rather used in a general sense to signify that the change in question has happened in society in response to social needs. A legal change that interacts with such social change or recognizes the social needs, demonstrates the adaptability of a particular legal system.

'Islamic Law'

In the above controversy neither of the views disputes the fact that social change occurred in Islamic history and that legal changes did take place accordingly, but whereas the adaptability-view connects these changes to the nature of Islamic law, the other view does not. The immutability-view asserts that these changes took place only in practice but were not recognized by the theory of Islamic law. The question is then obviously not about the historicity of legal changes, but about the theory of Islamic law regarding these changes. The difference of the two views is confined, therefore, to the theoretical aspect of the question. Since the two hold opposite views on this point, it is worth investigating whether they mean the same thing when they say 'Islamic law', or not.

The adaptability-view refers to *fiqh* as Islamic law, and even *Sharī'a* is understood as *fiqh*. The immutability-view is not so monolithic. In reference to the concept of law, Islamic law is identified with *Sharī'a*, but even here the arguments about its ethical and moral nature are made in reference to *fiqh*. In the arguments contending that the law is divine and the will of God, obviously it is not the *fiqh* which is meant. In discussions of the nature of the law and practice what is implied by Islamic law is *fiqh*. The contrast between theory and practice is made in reference to *fiqh*.

The reason for this apparent inconsistency and ambiguity is that the immutability-view believes that *Sharī'a* and *fiqh* are inseparably connected, *Sharī'a* being the law, and *fiqh* the science of knowing the law. This explanation, however, does not remove the ambiguity.

To explain this ambiguity we may borrow Kerr's formula of the levels of meaning. He observed the following four levels of meaning implicit in the discussion of jurists theory: (1) Divine Will, the sole metaphysical reality; (2) the spiritual relationship between man and God; (3) the normative relationship between man and man, and (4) the non-normative relationship of man and nature.[84]

In reference to these four levels we may say that *Sharīʻa* belongs to the first level, and *fiqh* covers both the second and third levels. The third and fourth levels concern social change. Now social change would usually have immediate effect on the third level; its effects on the second level are not immediate, however. In respect of the question of adaptability, therefore, the *fiqh* at level three is more significant than at level two. (see Table 1.)

TABLE 1

FOUR LEVELS OF MEANING

LEVEL	RELATIONSHIP	EXPRESSION
First level	Divine Will	*Dīn* *Sharīʻa*
Second level	Spiritual Relationship between God and Man	*Sharīʻa* *Fiqh* (*ʻibādāt*)
Third level	Normative Relationship between Man and Man	*Fiqh* Society Custom/Social practices (*Muʻāmalāt*) (Social change/legal change)
Fourth level	Normative Relationship between Man and Nature	Habits/Social behaviour (*ʻĀdāt*) (Social Change)

In view of this explanation, both positions involve ambiguity in some sense. The adaptability-view confuses the first and third levels by equating *fiqh* with *Sharīʻa*. The immutability-view also confuses the two levels. A distinction in these levels can help in demarcating *Sharī'a* from *fiqh* and also in distinguishing among various subject matters of *fiqh*.

The question whether *Sharī'a* or *fiqh* can be called law is another source of ambiguity. The question stems from the fact that the English term 'law' has a special sense which is not conveyed by the Islamic terms. The adaptability view believes that *fiqh* may be called 'law'. This position is taken by Linant de Bellefonds.[85] He has argued that the theocratic and religious nature of Islamic law has been stressed in an exaggerated manner, by referring to its teachings on *'ibādāt* (rituals, worship) and by comparing it with Western concepts of law. He maintained that even if the theocratic nature of its origins be admitted, it was not prevented from becoming a juridic system so long as its precepts were sanctioned by a secular authority. Implicit in his argument is the view that *fiqh* became law as much as and whenever it was sanctioned by governors and administrators.

The opposite view contends that *Sharī'a*, though not law in the proper sense, is the law of Islam. *Fiqh* is a science that deduces rules of law from the *Sharī'a*. Accordingly *Sharī'a* is known through the *fiqh*. It shows that there are different answers to the question of location of Islamic law. In the abstract sense *Sharī'a* is a metaphysical reality known through the Qur'ān and the sayings of the Prophet. The question whether everything contained in the Qur'ān and *ḥadīth* is law takes us back to *fiqh*, as that is where the law is spelled out. Hence for practical purposes, even in this position, *fiqh* comes to stand for Islamic law.[86]

'Islamic Legal Theory'

Now, coming to the question of the legal theory and social change, can we consider *fiqh* to be the legal theory?

Most probably not. In the preceding discussion, to consider *fiqh* as legal theory is possible but only in a limited sense. *Fiqh* cannot stand for legal theory in the sense of principles and methods, because the branch of the Islamic legal sciences that concerns such matters is *uṣūl al-fiqh*.

Uṣūl al-fiqh is the formal science in which Muslim jurists have dealt with legal theories, the principles of interpretations of the legal texts, methods of reasoning and of deduction of rules and other such matters. Thus, this study proposes to mean *uṣūl al-fiqh*, when it speaks of 'Islamic legal theory'.

'Legal Positivism'

In examining Shāṭibī's attempt to free legal obligation from theological determinism, we will interpret such an outlook as a 'positive' element in his legal philosophy. Since our use of the term 'positivism', differs apparently from Analytical School of Jurisprudence to-day, it needs to be elaborated.

'Positivism' refers to the well-known doctrine which explains the evolution of human thought in three stages: theological-metaphysical - positive. The third stage, positive, seeks to separate philosophical thinking from theological and metaphysical modes of thought, and stresses observable phenomena. Historians of legal philosophy, such as Huntington Cairns, attribute this development to the tendency of jurisprudence towards complete independence.[87] Jurisprudence has shown this tendency by breaking with theology in the sixteenth century and culminating in the recent trend which is called 'legal positivism' or the Analytical School of Jurisprudence.[88]

Recent exponents of 'legal positivism', such as H.L.A. Hart, have excluded considerations of morality and justice from the concept and definition of legal obligation.[89] Hart has, however, made a significant observation at this point. He admits that the origin of the rules of law may be found in the ideas of morality and justice but this does not prevent legal obligation from separating itself from morality in actual enforcement of law.[90]

This observation will help us in understanding the distinction that Shāṭibī suggests in defining legal obligation in reference to *ta'abbud*. In Shāṭibī's philosophy *ta'abbud* (non-extendibility of a rule of law) applies only to *'ibādāt* (rituals) whose cause and effect are not known by human experience. There is, therefore, an attempt to separate positive matters from metaphysical ones.

The suggestion that there is an element of "positivism" in Shāṭibī's legal thinking is advanced as described above. His attempt to free legal theory from theology and morality will be interpreted as a step towards positivism. Shāṭibī's distinction between *'ādāt* and *'ibādāt* on the basis of observability of *maṣāliḥ* in the former is understood as an attempt to separate positive law from religious elements. Shāṭibī's doctrine of *maqāṣid* provides a system and structure for the consideration of *maṣlaḥa*, so that it is no longer an abstract and discretionary principle but becomes a more exact and positive principle.

Having defined our terms of analysis, we now explain the steps of our arguments according to which the chapters are divided.

Our framework of discussion in this study consists of two sets of arguments. One part of the argument is that Shāṭibī's concept of *maṣlaḥa* in relation to his doctrine of *maqāṣid al-sharī'a* was the product of the need of his time to adapt Islamic law to the new social conditions. For this part the argument comprises the following steps: 1) A broad picture of the social changes in fourteenth-century Granada (chapter one) shows the extent to which the political, religious and economic developments in this period brought a basic change in Granadan society, and influenced Shāṭibī's life (chapter two). 2) We also study how the legal system was affected by these social changes. These observations are substantiated with an analysis of the actual *fatāwā* in this period. (chapter three). Since these *fatāwā* are answers to the actual questions arising out of new social conditions, we are to able to assess to what extent the need for legal change was connected with the developments as already observed. 3) This enables us to observe how Islamic legal theory dealt with the problem, i.e. what legal concepts and methods were used and whether, in this respect, there was a departure from the legal tradition. In chapter four we have analysed Shāṭibī's *al-Muwāfaqāt* in detail. Summarising its contents, we have also traced its impact on juridical thought, particularly in the modern period.

This leads us to the second part of the argument in our study. Shāṭibī's concept of *maṣlaḥa* is an attempt to justify the adaptability of Islamic legal theory of social needs. In this regard, the assumptions and premises of our argument are drawn from the above discussion. These assumptions are as follows: First, to determine the adaptability of Islamic law one must examine whether a certain method or concept, proposed as a theoretical justification of the adaptability, succeeds in freeing the concept of legal obligation from the theological determinism that it has received from having its origin in the absolute Will of God. To verify this hypothesis, Shāṭibī's concept of *maṣlaḥa* will be examined in this frame of reference. The analysis is undertaken in reference to the development of this concept in *uṣūl al-fiqh* (chapter five). The purpose of this analysis is to assess the direction in which Shāṭibī wanted this concept to lead. In the subsequent chapters we have studied the following concepts in Shāṭibī's philosophy: *dalāla* (chapter six), *taklīf* (chapter seven), *ta'abbud* (chapter eight), *niyya* (chapter nine), *'āda* and *bid'a* (chapter ten), *ijtihād* (chapter eleven), *khilāf* (chapter twele), and *sharī'a*(chapter thirteen). All these concepts, together, constitute Shāṭibī's doctrine of the purpose of law.

NOTES AND REFERENCES

1. See W. Friedmann, *Law in a Changing Society* (London: Pelican, 1964), 19. In Chapter One, Friedmann surveys the history of this problem in Western legal philosophy.
2. In 1897, in a case (Calcutta, 25:18) before the Privy Council the appellants sought a revision of the decision of a lower court of law. The appellants contended that the decision which was based on the *Hidāya* was not in accordance with the Qur'an on this point. The Privy Council confirmed the decision of the lower court and declined to go beyond *Hidāya*. Their Lordships explained: "It would be wrong for the Court on a point of this kind, to attempt to put their own construction on the Koran in opposition to the express ruling of commentators of such great antiquity and high authority". Quoted by A.J. Robertson, *The Principles of Mahomedan Law* (Rangoon, 1911), 5.
3. See, for instance, M. Morand, *Introduction à l'étude du droit musulman algérien* (Algiers, 1921), 108-112.

4. For example, L.W.C. van den Berg's translation of *Minhādj at-ṭālibīn,* (Batavia, 1862-1884), was strongly criticized by Hurgronje in his review article in *Revue de l'histoire des religions,* XXXVII (1898), 1-22 174-203; available to us in G. H. Bousquet and J. Schacht (editors), *Selected Works of C. Snouck Hurgronje* (Leiden, 1957), 214-255.
5. G. Bergsträsser's work, *Grundzüge des islamischen Rechts,* published by J. Schacht in Berlin, 1935. Cf. J.H. Kramers, "Droit de l'Islam et droit islamique" in *Analecta Orientalia: Posthumous Writings and Selected Minor Works of J.H. Kramers*, Vol. 2 (Leiden: Brill, 1956), 67.
6. *Selected Works, op. cit., 256.*
7. J. Schacht, "The Present State of Studies in Islamic Law", in *Atti del Terzo Congresso di Studi Arabi e Islamici* (Naples, 1967), 621-622.
8. J. Schacht, "Theology and Law in Islam", in G.E. Von Grunebaum (ed.), *Theology and Law in Islam* (Wiesbaden, 1971.), 4 ff.
9. *Ibid., 7.*
10. M. H. Kerr, *Islamic Reform* (California, 1966), 56.
11. Schacht, "Theology and Law... ", *op. cit.,*10.
12. C.H. Toy, "The Semitic Conception of Absolute Law", in Carl Bezold (ed.), *Orientalische Studien Theodor Nöldeke,* Vol. 2 (Giessen, 1906), 804. Toy's attribution of natural law to Indo-European people (p. 798) and of external absolute law to Semites has been confirmed by Hajime Nakamura in "The Indian and Buddhist Concept of law", published in E.J. Jurji (ed.), *Religious Pluralism and World Community* (Leiden: Brill, 1969), 131-174.
13. N. J. Coulson, *A History of Islamic Law* (Edinburgh: Edinburgh University Press, 1964) 1, 2.
14. H.A.R. Gibb, "Constitutional Organization", in M. Khadduri and H.J. Liebesny (eds.), *Law in the Middle East,* Vol. I (Washington, 1955), 4. Also in Gibb and H. Bowen, *Islamic Society and the West,* Vol. I, part 2 (Toronto: Oxford University Press, 1957), 114.
15. H.J. Liebesny, "Religious law and Westernization in the Moslem Near East", in *The American Journal of Comparative Law,* Vol. II (no.4, 1953), 492.
16. M. Khadduri, "From Religion to National Law", in J.H. Thompson and R.D. Reischauer, (editors), *Modernization of the Arab World* (Princeton: Nostrand, 1966), 38.
17. H. Lammens, *Islam, Belief and Institutions* (London, 1929), 82.
18. G. Makdisi, "Remarks on Traditionalism in Islamic Religious History" in Carl Leiden (ed.) *The Conflict of Traditionalism and Modernism in the Muslim Middle East* (Austin: University of Texas, 1966), 77.
19. J.N.D. Anderson, *Islamic Law in the Modern World* (New York: New York University Press, 1959), 17.
20. Leon Ostrorog, *The Angora Reform* (London: University of London, 1927), 19.
21. S.G. Vesey-Fitzgerald, "Nature and Sources of Sharī'a", in *Law and the Middle East, op. cit.*, 87.
22. Gibb, *Mohammedanism* (New York: Oxford, 1962), 99.
23. Gibb, *Studies on the Civilization of Islam* (Boston, 1968), 204-206.
24. *Mohammedanism,* 90f.
25. Schacht, *Introduction to Islamic Law* (Oxford, 1966), 202-203.
26. R. Brunschvig, "Logic and Law in Classical Islam", in G.E. Von Grunebaum, (ed.), *Logic in Classical Islamic Culture* (Wiesbaden, 1970), 9f.
27. G.F. Hourani, "Two Theories of Value in Medieval Islam", *Muslim World*, Vol. 50 (1960), 269-278. See also chapter 5.
28. Von Grunebaum, "Concept and Function of Reason in Islamic Ethics", *Oriens,* Vol. 15 (1962), 15.
29. G.F. Hourani, "Two Theories of Value in Medieval Islam", 273, and *Islamic Rationalism* (Oxford: Clarendon, 1971), 8-14.
30. Schacht, *The Origins of Muhammadan Jurisprudence* (Oxford, 1959), 111.
31. Hurgronje, *op. cit.,* note 6.

32. Th. W. Juynboll, *Handbuch des Islamischen Gasetzes* (Leiden: Brill, 1910), 22f.
33. G.-H. Bousquet, *Précis de droit musulman* (Alger, 1947), 44.
34. Gibb, *Islamic Society and the West,* 188.
35. Schacht, *Introduction,* 200-201.
36. *Ibid.*, 176f.
37. *Ibid.*, 207.
38. "Closer acquaintance with the vast stock of *ḥadīths* induces sceptical caution rather than optimistic trust regarding the material brought together in the carefully compiled collections. We are unlikely to have even as much confidence as Dozy regarding a large part of the *ḥadīth*, but will probably consider by far the greater part of it as the result of the religious, historical and social development of Islam during the first two centuries." Goldziher, *Muslim Studies,* translated by C.R. Barber and S. M. Stern, Vol. 2 (London: George Allen and Unwin, 1971), 19.
39. Schacht, *Origins of Muhammadan Jurisprudence*, 4.
40. R. Brunschvig, "Polémique medievals autour du rite de Malik", *Al-Andalus,* 15 (1950), 377-435.
41. See for instance Muhammad Mustafa Azami, *Studies in Early Hadith Literature: With a critical Edition of some Early Texts* (Indianapolis: American Trust Publications, 1978), M.M. Azami, *On Schacht's Origins of Muhammadan Jurisprudence* (Riadh, 1985); F. Rahman, *Islamic Methodology in History* (Karachi, 1965).
42. This point has been subject of controversy among scholars of Islamic law. The following studies on this subject are noted by S.D. Goitein [in "The Birth-Hour of Islamic Law?" *Muslim World,* Vol. 50 (1960), 23]:
J. Schacht, "Foreign Elements in Ancient Islamic law", *Journal of Comparative Law,* (1950), 3-4, 9-16; A. D'Emilia, "Roman Law and Muslim Law, a Comparative Outline", in *East and West,* Vol. IV/2 (1953); Fitzgerald, "The Alleged Debt of Islamic Law to Roman Law", *Law Quarterly Review,* (Jan. 1951), 81-102; C.A. Nallino, "The Impossibility of the Influence of Roman Law on Muslim Law" (trans. Hamidullah, *Voice of Islam,* Karachi, 1963, 1/2, 63-67).
43. See S. Vesey-Fitzgerald, "The Alleged Debt of Islamic To Roman Law", *Law Quarterly Review* 67 (1951) 81-102; M. Hamidullah, "Influence of Roman Law on Muslim Law", *Hyderabad Academy Journal,* 6 (1943).
44. Schacht, *Introduction,* 19ff.
45. F. Rahman, *Islamic Methodology in History*, 5-21.
46. S.D. Goitein, *op. cit.*, 102. See also David Ṣ. Powers, *Studies in Qur'an and Hadith, The Formation of the Islamic Law of Inheritance* (Berkeley, 1986).
47. Gibb, "Constitutional Organization" *op. cit.*, 3.
48. *Mohammedanism, op. cit.*, 102.
49. Schacht says that "during the greater part of the first/seventh century, Islamic law, in the technical meaning of the term, and therefore, Islamic jurisprudence, did not yet exist", article "*Fiḳh*" in *E.I.* (2nd edition) Vol. 2, 887-8.
50. Schacht, *Introduction,* 55.
51. *Ibid.*, 56.
52. H. Lammens, *Islam ..., op. cit.*, 92.
53. G.-H. Bousquet, *Precis..., op. cit.*, 50.
54. Claude Cahen, "Body Politic" in Grunebaum, *Unity and Variety in Muslim Civilization* (Chicago: University Chicago, 1955), 139.
55. Schacht, *Introduction,* 24f.
56. *Ibid.*, 25.
57. *Ibid.*, 4.
58. N.J. Coulson, "Doctrine and Practice in Islamic Law", *BSOAS,* Vol. 18/2 (1956), 211.
59. *Ibid.*, 226.
60. Cf. J. Berque, " 'Amal" in *E.I.* (2nd edition) Vol. 1, and H. Toledano, "*The Chapter on Marriage from Sijilmāsī's Al-'Amal al-Muṭlaq: A Study in Moroccan Judicial Practice* (Ph. D. Thesis, unpublished, presented to Columbia University, 1969), Introduction.

61. Toledano, *op. cit.*, ii.
62. Coulson, *History of Islamic Law*, 80f.
63. J. Kramers, "Droit de l'Islam et droit islamique", *op. cit.*, 63-64.
64. Schacht, *Introduction*, 62.
65. *Ibid.*, 76ff.
66. For details, see Toledano, *op. cit.*, ii-vii.
67. Abraham L. Udovitch, *Partnership and Profit in Medieval Islam* (Pirnceton: Princeton University Press, 1970), 7.
68. Cahen, *op. cit.*
69. Udovitch, *op. cit.*
70. Schacht, "Islamic Law", *Encyclopedia of Social Sciences* (Old Edition), Vol. 8, 348.
71. Hurgronje, *Selected Works*, 260.
72. Udovitch, *op. cit.*, 10.
73. Schacht, "Classicisme, traditionalisme et ankylose dans la loi religieuse de l'Islam, in R. Brunschvig and other, (editors) *Classicisme et déclin culturel dans l'histoire de l'Islam* (Paris, 1957), 141.
74. Y. Linant de Bellefonds, "Immutabilité du droit musulman et réformes législatives en Égypte", *Revue internationale de droit comparé*, Vol. 7 (1955), 10f.
75. See Chapter five.
76. É. Tyan, "Méthodologie et sources du droit en Islam", *Studia Islamica*, Vol. 10 (1959), 84f.
77. Chafik Chehata, "Logique juridique et droit musulman", *Studia Islamica*, Vol. 23 (1965), 5-26.
78. Chehata, "L'équité en tant que source du droit hanafite". *Studia Islamica*, Vol. 25 (1966), 123-138.
79. Schacht, "Classicisme...", *op. cit.*, 142.
80. *Ibid.*, *Introduction...*, 61ff.
81. M.H. Kerr, *op. cit.*, 55.
82. *Ibid.*, 56.
83. In maintaining this distinction, we are relying on Amitai Etzioni and Eva Etzioni, *Social Change, Sources, Patterns and Consequences* (New York: Basic Books, 1964), Introduction, p. 7f.
84. M.H. Kerr, *Op. cit.*, 21ff.
85. Y. Linant de Bellefonds, *Traité de droit musulman comparé* (Paris: Mouton, 1964), Vol. 1, 46-46.
86. In our opinion the real expression of Islamic law was made in decrees, judgements and fatāwā for which *fiqh* remained the main source. Regrettedly studies of Islamic law have not explored that area sufficiently. For the purpose of the present study, therefore, we understand fiqh as Islamic law, yet we also include fatāwā and *qaḍāya* in it for this purpose.
87. Huntington Cairns, *Legal Philosophy from Plato to Hegel* (Baltimore: John Hopkins, 1967), 2f.
88. The exact definition of 'legal positivism' has been a subject of debate among recent philosophers. Lone L. Fuller and others contrast "legal positivism" with "natural law" philosophies. H.L.A. Hart regards such a use of the term as a cause of the confusion in modern discussions of separation of law from morals. See the following: H.L.A. Hart, *The Concept of Law* (Oxford: Clarendon, 1965), 253-54, and *Law, Liberty and Morality* (New York: Vintage, 1963), 2: Lone L. Fuller, *The Morality of Law* (New Haven: Yale, 1970), the chapter: "A Reply to Critic".
89. Hart, *The Concept...*, Ch. 8, section 2; Ch. 9, section 3.
90. Hart, *Law, Liberty and Morality*, Ch.1.

CHAPTER ONE

SHĀṬIBĪ'S PERIOD

As stated earlier, one part of the argument of the present study is that Shāṭibī's philosophy of Islamic law did not originate in a vacuum, but that it was born in answer to the challenge of social change and the needs of his time to adapt legal theory to the new social conditions. The fact is that the fine texture of Shāṭibī's legal philosophy cannot be properly studied without an adequate knowledge of the historical setting in which it evolved. Lack of such an appreciation is the major cause for the difficulty faced by modern scholars in studying Shāṭibī's complex and dense system of legal thought.

Granada,[1] where Shāṭibī lived, underwent very significant, sometimes unprecedented, changes in the fourteenth century in which Shāṭibī flourished. Shāṭibī's legal thought reflects a deep awareness of these changes.

The fourteenth century was a period of peace and quiet for the Muslim world after the turmoils of the thirteenth century. Two major Mongol dynasties, the Ilkhānīs and the Golden Horde had been converted to Islam. The Mamlūks who had withstood the Mongol invasion had stabilized their rule in the fertile crescent and in Egypt. In North Africa as well, conditions were rather stable. Banū Marīn had emerged as powerful successors to the Muwaḥḥidūn. In Spain, Banū Naṣr had succeeded the Muwaḥḥidūn. They maintained their rule by keeping a delicate balance of alliance with the Christian kingdoms in Spain and with the Banū Marīn in Africa.

This political stability provided the much-needed peace for the intellectual activities essential to re-evaluating the tradition in the light of the multitudinous changes brought about by the turmoils of the thirteenth century. These changes had affected the political, financial, commercial, social and religious domains. A number of social changes that had taken place needed somehow to be accommodated within the tradition.

The intellectuals of the community who had either personally experienced these changes or were affected through the experience of others received a lasting impact on their minds. This is no doubt the reason why we find that a number of distinguished works dedicated to the re-evaluation, systematization and readjustment of the tradition appeared in this period. In

North Africa, Ibn Khaldūn (784/1382) worked on a philosophy of history.[2] In Syria, Ibn Taymiyya (728/1328) reviewed the entire tradition of political and legal theory.[3] In Persia, Al-Ījī (756/1355) resystematized Sunni theology.[4] In Spain, Shāṭibī was occupied with the philosophy of Islamic law.

Consolidation of political power by Sulṭān Muḥammad V al-Ghanī Bi'llāh in Granada strongly affected the growth and development of almost all the social institutions in Granada. It particularly affected the status and role of *fuqahā'*, and hence of *sharī'a* in the Granadan society. New educational system, judicial structure, penetration of Ṣūfī *ṭarīqa*s and spread of liberal thought all supported by the political system were such factors as were consequential for the intellectual activities of the people of Granada. The economic developments in this period were in fact so significant that they were to change the course of history in this region. The rise of the Mediterranean trade, shift from rural to urban economy, introduction of copper dinar and other such factors deeply affected the pattern of life in Granada. New forms of business partnerships, contracts and dealings demanded new concepts of legal obligation.

I

POLITICAL DEVELOPMENTS

With the decline of the Muwaḥḥidūn, the political situation in the Andalus (Muslim Spain) fell into a chaotic condition.[5] Two warlords appeared in this period: Ibn Hūd in Murcia and Ibn al-Aḥmar in Arjona. Ibn Hūd revolted against the Muwaḥḥidūn in 625/1228 in Murcia.[6] He received investiture from the 'Abbāsī caliph Al-Mustanṣir Bi'llāh (623-640/1226-1242) in Baghdad. Once established as Sulṭān, he assumed the title Al-Mutawakkil Bi'llāh. Important cities such as Almeria, Malaga, Granada, Seville and the greater part of Eastern Andalus fell to him.

Ibn al-Aḥmar (Muḥammad b. Yūsuf... b. Naṣr b. Qays al-Khazrajī al-Anṣārī), a soldier who fought on the borders of Andalus, earned his fame mainly by his campaigns against the Christians. In 629/1232 he declared independence and quickly captured Seville, Cordova and Granada from Ibn Hūd.

In 634, he declared himself the Sulṭān of Andalus, and assumed the title of al-Ghālib Bi'llāh. Thus was founded in Granada the dynasty of the Banū Naṣr, also called Banū Aḥmar. The dynasty ruled Granada by a delicate balance of truce and war with its Muslim and Christian neighbours.

Shāṭibī's contemporary Muḥammad V al-Ghanī Bi'llāh was chosen as 8th Naṣrid Sulṭān at the age of sixteen[7] after the assassination of his father Yūsuf in 755/1354. The affairs of the state were completely in the hands of his chamberlain (*ḥājib*), the Qā'id Abū Na'īm Riḍwān.[8] Other important offices of the kingdom were held by the following notables: the office of *shaykh al-ghuzāt* by Yaḥyā b. 'Umar; *qāḍī al-jamā'a* by Abu'l-Qāsim Sharīf al-Sabtī; *kātib al-sirr* by Ibn al-Khaṭīb. In order to pay attention to the internal state of affairs, Sulṭān Muḥammad V first sought peace with his neighbouring powers. He sent Ibn al-Khaṭīb and Abu'l Qāsim al-Sabtī to the Marini ruler. The Castillian king, Pedro who had confirmed his truce of 751/1350 made with Muḥammad V's father,[9] also renewed this pact with Granada. As we shall see in the sequel, these alliances proved very useful to the Sulṭān in his struggle for power after he was dethroned by his brother in 760/1359.

Muḥammad V had two brothers whom Riḍwān had imprisoned in Alhamra to clear Sulṭān Muḥammad's path to throne. Their mother sought the help of Ra'īs Muḥammad, the *Shaykh al-Ghuzāt*, the head of a contingent of soldiers.[10] Ra'īs killed Riḍwān and proclaimed Muḥammad V's brother, Ismā'īl, as Sulṭān and himself as his regent. Ibn al-Khaṭīb and other supporters of Riḍwān were imprisoned. Sulṭān Muḥammad V escaped to Guadix. There he received a visit from Abu'l Qāsim al-Sabtī, his former *qāḍī* who had joined the Marini court during this crisis. Abu'l Qāsim was sent by Abū Sālim, the Marīnī Sulṭān, who invited Sulṭān Muḥammad V to Fez to express his gratitude for the refuge he had received at the Naṣrī court when he fled from his brother Abū 'Inān. Muḥammad V accepted the invitation. Abu'l Qāsim then proceeded to Granada to negotiate the safe conduct of the Sulṭān to Fez as well as the release of other prisoners, including Ibn al-Khaṭīb.[11] The mission succeeded and Muḥammad V along with his supporters arrived in Fez in 761/1361. He received a warm welcome from the Marīnī Sulṭān. This event shows also the immense political influence of the Mālikī *fuqahā'* in this region, a point to which we will return shortly.

In 762/1361 in Fez, during a revolt, the Marīnī Sulṭān Abū Sālim lost his life.[12] Sulṭān Muḥammad could no longer stay in Fez. To regain his throne Muḥammad V required the help of the *amīrs* of Ronda and Malaga. The castle of Ronda which belonged to Andalus had been taken by the Marīnī regent 'Umar b. 'Abd Allāh. Muḥammad V succeeded in regaining[13] the possession of Ronda and Malaga. Alliance of Ronda and Malaga in favour of the Sulṭān assured his capture of Granada. At the same time, King Pedro of Castille, Sulṭān Muḥammad V's ally, attacked Granada. Ra'īs Muḥammad, who saw himself pressed from both sides, decided to surrender himself to Pedro, who killed him treacherously. Thus ground was prepared for the recapture of Granada; Muḥammad V finally remounted the throne in 763/1362.

In his second reign Muḥammad V was no longer a youth, and the incident of deposition had been an instructive experience. He determined to make himself independent of internal as well as external powers.[14] He decided to undermine the office of *wazīr*. He succeeded in routing 'Alī b. Yūsuf b.

Kumātha, whom he had been obliged to accept as his *wazīr* during his stay in Ronda. He sent Ibn Kumātha on a mission to the Marīnī court to get rid of him. Ibn Kumātha tried, in vain, to instigate the rulers of Castille, Barcelona, and of Tunis against Muḥammad V, but he was finally captured in Castille and sent to prison in Fez.[15] After a while, Ibn al-Khaṭīb, his former secretary, joined Muḥammad V. Following lengthy secret talks and promises, Muḥammad V accepted him as *wazīr*.[16] Ibn al-Khaṭīb soon prevailed upon the Sulṭān who charged Ibn al-Khaṭīb with the responsibility of almost all the affairs of the government.

The office of the *shaykh al-ghuzāt* was confirmed for 'Uthmān 'Alī who had deserted Ra'īs Muḥammad. He appointed successively Abū'l-Ḥasan 'Alī b. Badr al-Dīn and 'Abd al-Raḥmān b. Abī Sa'īd, both from Banū Marīn, to the office of *shaykh al-ghuzāt*. Almost all of the military campaigns against the Christians were from then onward led by the Sulṭān himself.[17]

The office of *qāḍī al-jamā'a* was given to Qāḍī Abū'l Ḥasan al-Nubāhī, and the office of *kātib al-sirr* to the *faqīh* and poet Ibn Zumruk, a disciple of Abū Isḥāq al-Shāṭibī. In 767/1366 Muḥammad V decided to lead a series of campaigns against the Christians to establish himself as a *ghāzī*, the defender of Islam.[18] Some fortresses close to Malaga and Ronda were taken back from the Christians. Jaen was recaptured. The campaigns in the years 770/1369 and 771/1370 were carried out as deep into Christian territory as the neighbourhood of Seville. These campaigns brought a huge amount of booty to the Muslims.

The success of these campaigns was partially due to internal troubles in the Christian kingdoms, which did not allow them to attend to the defence of their borders. In this way Muḥammad V's period remained generally safe from Christian attacks. In fact, Christian kingdoms were in a defensive position against the attacks of Granada.

The same was true for his neighbours in Africa. Muḥammad V was no longer threatened by powerful neighbours. But this situation was partially accidental and partially due to his skilful manoeuvres respecting the political affairs of the African rulers.[19]

From the above survey it can be noted that the strength of the Banū Naṣr depended on two things: first, maintaining a balance between their neighbours by alternating peace treaties and court intrigues; second, by controlling the internal sources of power.

This state of affairs had a social as well as an intellectual impact upon Granadan society. The treaties with neighbouring Christian and Muslim kingdoms allowed an exchange of scholars and mystics on both sides.[20] The social impact of this situation is evident from the fact that the Granadan Muslims generally came to accept Christian dresses.[21] These changes must have been a challenge to the Mālikī *fuqahā'* who were known for strict adherence to their tradition.

POLITICAL SYSTEM

The Granadan political structure, as we have noted above, consisted of three major offices directly responsible to the sulṭān: *shaykh al-ghuzāt, wazīr* and *qāḍī al-jamā'a*. A brief analysis of these offices reveals the powerful hold of Mālikī jurists and Mālikī law on the political structure in Granada.

Shaykh al-Ghuzāt

The chief of the *ghāzīs* (warriors for the faith) actually was the office of the head of the armies, both regular soldiers and mercenaries. This office, according to Gaudefroy Demombynes, was "comparable to that of the *amīr al-'umarā'* in the late 'Abbāsī period."[22] The peculiar tribal structure and allegiance to the chief provided the *shaykh al-ghuzāt* with absolute power.

The office of *shaykh al-ghuzāt* was introduced by al-Ghālib Bi'llāh (1230-1272) the founder of the Banū Naṣr dynasty, to replace the power of the Banū Ashqīlūla who had been responsible for the establishment of the Naṣrī dynasty but who had soon fallen into the custom of revolting against the Banū Naṣr on frequent occasions. To counterbalance their power the Banū Naṣr welcomed the Marīnī clans left behind in Andalus by the Marīnī Sulṭān Manṣūr. The first *shaykh al-ghuzāt* was appointed from among these Marīnīs.

The *shaykh al-ghuzāt* was given vast powers as is evident from a *ẓahīr* (investiture)[23] conferred upon Yaḥyā b. 'Umar by Sulṭān Abu'l Ḥajjāj Yūsuf (733-755/1334-54). The titles mentioned in the investiture include 'Pillar of Power', 'The supermost Head of Defence', 'The Bond of the Kingdom' etc. 'Uthmān b. Abī'l 'Ulā' was the most powerful and illustrious *shaykh al-ghuzāt* in Naṣrī history. The holders of this office often came into conflict with the Marīnī and Naṣrī Sulṭāns and were even responsible for the assassination of Sulṭān Muḥammad IV. Sulṭān Muḥammad V's *shaykh al-ghuzāt* also had plotted against him.

Muḥammad V decided to break the power of the *shaykh al-ghuzāt*. Consequently, within a year he struck upon Shaykh 'Uthmān and banished the entire family from the political scene.[24] He appointed other individuals from Banū Marīn to perform the necessary functions, but he reduced their powers by taking two steps: first, he led most of the campaigns against the Christians himself, thus taking the credit of *ghazw* and *jihād* away from the *shaykh al-ghuzāt*. Second, he sent the *shaykh al-ghuzāt* on campaigns against the Banū Marīn,[25] thus discrediting them as *ghāzīs* since they fought against Muslims and their own kith and kin. One may notice that a re-interpretation of the role of Sulṭān in *jihād* helped to reduce the power of this office. It indicates a possible vigorous activity of the interpretation of Mālikī jurisprudence in Granada.

Wazīr

The *wazāra* was the second most powerful office in the Naṣrī political structure. Ibn Sa'īd observed that the institution of *wazāra* in Umawī Andalus consisted of a group of notables who assisted the caliph by counsels and aided him in administration. One of them whom the caliph appointed his deputy was called *ḥājib*. This office became hereditary and continued within certain families. The designation of *wazīr* was lower than that of *ḥājib*.[26]

During the Naṣrī period the emergence of the institution of *shaykh al-ghuzāt* had overshadowed the powers of the *ḥājib*. Moreover, the office of *ḥājib* and *wazīr* were often combined. Some *wazīrs* even claimed to be regents of the minor sulṭāns whom they succeeded in bringing to the throne. Such *wazīrs* enjoyed the highest powers. Instances of such *wazīrs* are Ibn al-Ḥakīm al-Lakhmī during the reign of Muḥammad al-Makhlū', Ibn Maḥrūq in the period of Muḥammad IV, Qā'id Riḍwān in the time of Abū'l Ḥajjāj Yūsuf and Ibn al-Khaṭīb during the reign of Muḥammad V. Under the *wazīr* were *kuttāb* (secretaries) who held the various offices of civil administration. The *wazīr* also commanded the *shurṭa* or the city police.[27]

Early Naṣrī *wazīrs* such as Abū Marwān b. Ṣanādīd, who was the ruler of Jaen, and the Qā'id Abū 'Abd Allāh al-Ramīmī, who was the son of the ruler of Almeria, both *wazīrs* of Ghālib Bi'llāh, had powerful family connections. The later *wazīrs* were, however, men of learning, having no such powerful connections. This is why the *wazīrs* depended for their support on diplomatic influence. Their powers were often temporary. Whenever their plots failed, it proved easy to break their power. The *wazīrs* were frequently imprisoned, expelled or assassinated.

The following incident illustrates the significance of the office of the *wazīr* not only in the internal political structure but also in affecting the foreign relations. The Marīnī Wazīr 'Umar b. 'Abd Allāh, who was responsible for a series of dethronements and bloodshed during 762-767/1361-66 expelled the Marīnī prince 'Alī b. Badr al-Dīn and his *wazīr* Mas'ūd b. Masā'ī. They were welcomed in Granada by Sulṭān Muḥammad V. He even appointed 'Alī as *shaykh al-ghuzāt*. In the meanwhile Sulṭān 'Abd al-'Azīz took all powers into his hands after killing 'Umar b. 'Abd Allāh. He was apprehensive of prince 'Alī. He requested the Naṣrī Sulṭān to send the prince and his *wazīr* back to Fez. The Sulṭān refused, but Ibn al-Khaṭīb whom Sulṭān 'Abd al-'Azīz had taken into his confidence, prevailed upon Muḥammad V, yet the latter only agreed to imprison them. The Marīnī Sulṭān accepted but did not like this move. Ibn al-

Khaṭīb, apprehensive of the intrigues against him at the Naṣrī court, was planning to escape. Sulṭān 'Abd al-'Azīz welcomed him at the Marīnī court. Now Sulṭān Muḥammad V requested Sulṭān 'Abd al-'Azīz to send Ibn al-Khaṭīb back again to Granada, but he refused. This disagreement soured their relations to the extent that from that point on both the Banū Marīn and the Banū Naṣr spent their efforts in staging intrigues against one another.

Muḥammad V released the Marīnī prince and his *wazīr* and sent the prince as pretender to the Marīnī throne. He even marched toward the Marīnī borders and captured Ceuta to stress his support for the pretender. He succeeded finally in staging a revolt and establishing his own choice on the Marīnī throne.[28] Thus Sulṭān Muḥammad V was able to solve an almost century-old problem. His successes against the Marīnīs brought further security to his rule as well as to the Granadan society in general.

Qāḍī al-Jamā'a

Qāḍī al-jamā'a (the Judge of the community of Muslims) was counterpart of the office of *qāḍī al-quḍāt*, the chief justice in the Islamic East. This was the most respected office in the political structure. The *qāḍī al-jamā'a* was responsible for the administration of justice, the inspection of markets and for regulating commercial contracts. The *qāḍī al-jamā'a* was also sometimes the chief *Khaṭīb* of Granada.[29]

No executive powers such as the command of soldiers, police, etc., belonged to the *qāḍī*. It was rather supposed to be the duty of the Sulṭān to support a *qāḍī*'s judgement with his executive powers.[30] The Sulṭān and often the *wazīrs* as well, interfered in the administration of justice; yet symbolically, the *qāḍī* enjoyed the highest prestige in the political structure. In spite of the absence of executive powers, the chief *qāḍī* had vast influence in the affairs of the state as he was responsible for the appointment of a significant number of functionaries in the administration of judicial and religious affairs. The real basis of the *qāḍī*'s power lay in his being part of a sort of 'religious elite' which had grown in strength in the Umawī period and proven itself indispensible ever since.[31]

Qāḍī al-Nubāhī's success in prosecuting the powerful *wazīr* Ibn al-Khaṭīb, is one of the recurrent examples of the powers of *qāḍīs* in the political structure of Muslim Spain. As stated earlier, Sulṭān Muḥammad V was enraged by Ibn al-Khaṭīb's defection to Morocco. From certain accounts it appears that there existed a rivalry between Nubāhī and Ibn al-Khaṭīb. Ibn al-Khaṭīb, as Ibn Khaldūn has noted, enjoyed the highest powers after the collapse of the office of the *shaykh al-ghuzāt*.[32] He interfered with Qāḍī al-Nubāhī in many cases. It is evident from certain stories recounted by Ibn al-Khaṭīb in his *A'māl al-a'lām*[33] and *al-Katībat al-kāmina*, that Ibn al-Khaṭīb went beyond the limits of politeness in ridiculing Nubāhī in the court. Publicly insulting the *qāḍī al-jamā'a* must have undermined the office of *qaḍā'*. This derision was not without the Sulṭān's approval.[34] The Sulṭān must have encouraged the *wazīr* for such a derision to weaken the office of *qāḍī al-jamā'a*. It was only after Ibn al-Khaṭīb had left for Morocco that Nubāhī could accuse Ibn al-Khaṭīb, in public, of heresy and burn his books. In this accusation, of course, he, too, was encouraged by the Sulṭān. The Naṣrī Sulṭān sent Nubāhī to Morocco to bring Ibn al-Khaṭīb back to Spain but he finally prevailed in having him killed in Morocco.

This is how the Sulṭān eventually succeeded in removing a *wazīr* who had become too powerful and, by using the *qāḍī* to his advantage, he also achieved his designs to make himself independent of the offices of the *qāḍī* and *wazīr* both.

By these means the Sulṭān was able to stabilize his rule as absolute king and help Naṣrī dynasty to withstand the forces of decline for many years to come. This political system, however, did not allow political institutions to become strong and powerful enough to work even with weaker sulṭāns who succeeded Sulṭān Muḥammad V.

Politically, the *qāḍī al-jamā'a* had been a very influential office yet the Sulṭān was able to use it to consolidate his own power. This was possible because the religious authority of the *fuqahā'* on which the power of the *qāḍī* depended had been already weakened. Let us now examine how it happened.

II

THE POLITICAL POWER OF THE *FUQAHĀ'*

The historians of Muslim Spain do not forget to point out the power of the *fuqahā'* (the *'ulamā'*, the jurists), in the political affairs as a trait of Muslim history in Spain.[35] The various opinions about the significance of *fuqahā'* are not immediately relevant to our purpose. Nevertheless, in general, we learn that scholars have suggested three reasons for the political significance of the *fuqahā'*.

First, some scholars such as Ibn Khaldūn[36] and Goldziher[37] argue that it was the conservatism of the Spanish Arabs that encouraged the spread of Malikism and that eventually conferred significance on the *fuqahā'* since they were the bastions of this tradition.

The second reason, as suggested by López Ortiz,[38] Hussain Monés[39] and others,[40] was the need for the legitimization of their rule as was always felt by the Muslim rulers of Spain. López Ortiz argues that because of their breakaway from the 'Abbāsī caliphs, the Banū Umayya in Spain needed the support of religion to justify their caliphate. Mālik b. Anas, being an antagonist of the 'Abbāsīs, was the ideal choice for them.[41] Monés furthers this argument more strongly in the case of Hishām I (788-796) and Ḥakam I (796-822).

Contrary to the claim made by historians of Hishām I's piety, Monés argues that Hishām, in fact, chose religion for rather political reasons. Hishām felt weak in the struggle against the rightful claimant to the throne, Sulaymān, who enjoyed the support of the Syrian contingents of the army.[42] Thus from political necessity on the part of the Umawī rulers there arose a class of *'ulamā'* and *fuqahā'* who played a continuously important role in political affairs.

The third factor, suggested by L.E. Provençal[43] and Roger Idris,[44] was the establishment of a kind of 'religious aristocracy'— composed of *fuqahā'* and *'ulamā'*— who comprised of the intellectual as well as the social elite in the capital by the time of Ḥakam I (180-206/796-822). When Ḥakam tried to reduce their influence, they staged two insurrections in Cordova.[45] In these revolts the *fuqahā'* had the support of a number of aristocrats in the court as well as the people in the suburbs of Cordova. These revolts did not succeed but Ḥakam was forced to recognize the power of the *fuqahā'*.

We cannot agree that any one of these factors alone can sufficiently explain the influence of the *fuqahā'*, particularly in the Naṣrī period. Nevertheless, the third factor probably clarifies the phenomenon better than the others.

It is difficult to characterise the generality of the Spanish people as primitive and conservative. There is much evidence to the contrary. Especially in the Naṣrī period the Spanish people were quite flexible in accepting their Christian neighbours' way of life, particularly with regard to dress and recreational activities.[46] Conservatism was also absent from their ever-changing practices in trade and commerce.[47] There was conservatism, of course, in the intellectual attitude and academic activities of the elite. The latter, however, was probably the result, not the cause, of the conservatism of the *fuqahā'*.

Similarly it is hard to maintain that the rulers' alliance with the *fuqahā'* was based on the former's need for religious legitimacy. In a society where the rule of the usurper can be justified in the political theory by equating *de facto* with *de jure*,[48] the need of a religious institution for that purpose is not very great.

In the case of the Naṣrī claim to the legitimacy of their rule, stress fell upon their Arabness rather than on an any religious doctrine. The tension between Arabs and Berbers has been a salient feature of Muslim Spanish history. The two Berber dynasties, the Murābiṭūn and the Muwaḥḥidūn, had pushed the Arabs aside. With the decline of the Muwaḥḥidūn, the Arab element rose again, as the rise of Banū Hūd and Banū Naṣr manifested. These Arab tribes were supported by the local Spanish element and by the Arab aristocrats. They did not trust the Berbers; they sought Berbers' help only temporarily. While Berbers were inclined more toward religion and piety,[49] as expressed by their zeal for *jihād* and *taṣawwuf,* the Banū Naṣr laid stress on genealogical nobility.[50] The founder of the Naṣrī dynasty was called Marwānī by a contemporary historian.[51] This shows that the Banū Naṣr in all probability wanted to present themselves as a continuation of the Banū Umayya. Later, however, they linked themselves with the Khazraj tribe of Madina. Ibn al-Khaṭīb established the proof of their genealogy from earlier sources,[52] and Ibn Zumruk recited eulogies narrating the merits of the Khazrajīs in the days of the Prophet.[53] This very fact that they stressed their descent from the *Anṣār* would have been detrimental to their cause if they had been seeking religious support for their legitimacy, in view of the commonly accepted orthodox view that the Caliph must be from the Quraysh. The nature of the argument shows how much significance the Banū Naṣr gave to the religious aspect of the legitimacy of their rulership.

The foregoing discussion was necessary to show that the need of legitimacy existed but that it was not sought from the *fuqahā'* as religious leaders. The rulers needed the support of the *fuqahā'* because the latter, through strong family relations and land holdings, had established themselves in Spain as a political power. We need not go into these details; what interests us here is their strength as a political group. We will briefly review the factors of their strength.

The high status the *fuqahā'* enjoyed in Andalus is evident from the fact that the appellation '*faqīh*' (singular of *fuqahā'*) had acquired a sense of nobility. Ibn Sa'īd points out in his narrative of the Andalusian society that:

> The appellation of '*faqīh*' is most honourable for them, so much so that if they want to make an honourable mention of their grand *amīr (sulṭān)*, they call him '*faqīh'*. At present a *faqīh* in the West is what a *qāḍī* is in the East. They even sometimes call the *kātib* (secretary) a grammarian and a linguist *faqīh* because it is the highest appellation for them.[54]

Fuqahā' achieved political power mainly by controlling vital offices in the political system, institutions of learning and intellectual movements. The strong conservatism of Spanish *'ulamā* is reflected by the fact that several books on and against *bid'a* (innovation, heresy) were written largely by the Mālikī jurists of Spain.[55] As we shall see in the following chapter, Shāṭibī was also accused of *bid'a* by them.

It was through the operation of these factors that the *fuqahā'* could preserve Mālikī tradition in its conservative mould and hence maintain their power.

RELIGIOUS AND JUDICIAL OFFICES

The highest religious and judicial office was that of *qāḍī al-jamā'a*, the appellation of the chief *qāḍī* in Granada. The historians stress that it was the noblest office in the political structure. The evidence for the truth of the claim is to be found in the generous salaries, the ceremonial investitures, and the lengthy formal decrees of appointment given to *qāḍīs*. The *qāḍī al-jamā'a* also enjoyed a wide range of prerogatives.[56]

Beside the administration of justice, the *fuqahā'* were officially attached also to courts as *muftīs* (jurisconsults), *mushāwars* (consultants) and *wuththāq* (formularies and notaries).[57] The administration of religious and trust properties was also in their hands. Whenever a ruler made a donation for a special purpose, he appointed a *faqīh* to supervise it. The appointments of Abū 'Abd Allah al-Ḥaffār (811/1408).[58] and Ibn al-Qabbāb (779/1378)[59] were of such nature.

The inspection of trade and commerce was also the domain of the *fuqahā'*. They were responsible for fixing prices and for the quality and weight of commodities in the market.[60] The particular teachings of Islamic law against *ribā* (usury) and *qimār* (speculation) prohibited a number of transactions which thus required the supervision of experts in the law, i.e. the *fuqahā'*.[61] These prohibitions also extended to transactions involving money exchange and minting. The *fuqahā'* were therefore required also to supervise the minting of coins. The important offices in the mint such as *nāẓir al-sikka* were held by the *fuqahā'*.[62]

The office of chief *khaṭīb* was next to that of *qāḍī al-jamā'a* in importance in the capital city of Granada as well as in other cities and towns in the kingdom. Often both offices of *qāḍī* and *khaṭīb* were held by one person.[63] Since in Islamic history the *sikka* (coin) and *khuṭba* (Friday sermon) which became the vehicle of the announcement of the ruler's name, had become the formal signs of claim to rulership or to allegiance of one ruler to another, the *khaṭīb* had also become a kind of political office.[64] Attached to the office of *khaṭīb* were a number of other religious offices such as that of the *mu'adhdhin*, etc. All the above-mentioned offices were lucrative, and often tracts of land, commensurate with their ranks, were attached to these offices.[65] This land ownership also contributed to the political power of these office holders.

THE INSTITUTIONS OF LEARNING

Ibn Sa'īd, who visited Andalus in the early Naṣrī period, depicts the conditions of learning in the following words:

> As to the conditions of the Andalusians in respect of the art of sciences, the truth of the matter is that they are the most eager people in this regard.... The scholars enjoy the noblest rank among the elite as well as the common people.... Despite the fact that the Andalusians do not have schools (*madāris*) to help them in seeking knowledge, they rather study (learn) all the sciences in mosques on paying fees. Thus they read in order to learn, not in order to earn a stipend.[66]

Ibn Sa'īd praised the Andalusian system as conducive to learning in contrast to the system of the *madrasa* in the Muslim East where the interest of the student was monetary rather than academic.

This conclusion of Ibn Sa'īd stands in contrast to that of Ibn Khaldūn who praised the system in the East saying that the system of *madrasa* encouraged learning and made it possible to study even for those students who could not afford to pay fees to individual teachers. On the other hand, the system in the West limited the spread of learning and eventually resulted in the decline of the sciences.[67]

Neither Ibn Sa'īd nor Ibn Khaldūn mentions one significant fact, that learning itself could not have been the sole aim of all the students. The majority of them graduated, thereupon to be given various offices in the administration. The factor that must be emphasized here is that the teachers—who were mostly *fuqahā'*—had more influence in the system of the West in comparison to the East.

The institution of learning in the Andalus was completely in the hands of the *fuqahā'*. They were absolutely independent in choosing the materials of teaching, in the manner of teaching and the assessment of the achievement of the pupils. Shāṭibī, dealing with the question of learning, in fact, discouraged the method of learning from the books without a teacher.[68]

This system was advantageous to the *fuqahā'* in two ways. First, it established their influence and supremacy over the people. The *fuqahā'* could not have had this advantage in the *madrasa* system, because in that system they could not be as independent as they were without the *madrasa*. Because of the absence of an institutionalized system of higher learning pupils had to depend on the teachers if they were to get diplomas of graduation. Second, the Andalusian system made possible the preservation of tradition and strict adherence to it, as well as the control of any ideas or movements that might oppose the tradition.

The *fuqahā'* in the West were certainly aware of these advantages when they opposed the establishment of *madāris*.[69] The institution of the official *madrasa* was introduced quite late in Spain. Provençal mentions that the first *madrasa* was established by the Qā'id Riḍwān (d. 760/1359), the *ḥājib* of Abū Yūsuf al-Ḥajjāj (733-755/1333-1354).[70] This move was strongly opposed by a number of scholars. Two main arguments were advanced in this respect: First, that it was *bid'a* (innovation), hence prohibited; second, that it suppressed the freedom of the *'ulamā'* and hence the independence of *'ilm* (scholarship).[71]

After the establishment of *madrasa*s, the *'ulamā'* and *fuqahā'* gradually lost their independence. The change did not, however, immediately affect their aristocratic status; but their control over intellectual movements, especially their resistance to *taṣawwuf,* certainly relaxed. It was after the establishment of *madāris* that *taṣawwuf* and Ṣūfi *ṭarīqas* gained a wider following in Granadan society.

CONTROL OF INTELLECTUAL MOVEMENTS

The Mālikī *fuqahā'* had hitherto opposed the movements of rationalist philosophy and *taṣawwuf* from entering into Andalus. The following brief analysis of the factors of their success until thirteenth century would help understand the changes in the fourteenth century.

(1) RATIONALIST PHILOSOPHY

Ibn Sa'īd says that:

> They (the Andalusians) take part in every science except philosophy and astronomy. These are specially enjoyed by the elite, but they do not show this (interest) in public for the fear of the common people. Because as soon as it is stated that 'so and so studies philosophy' or 'practices astronomy', he is at once declared *zindīq* (heretic), and his days are numbered (*qayyadat 'alayhi anfāsuhū*). If someone slipped into skepticism (*zalla fī shubhatin*) the people would stone him to death or would burn him alive long before his case was brought to the Sulṭān.[72]

Ibn Sa'īd's observation is supported by stories that frequently refer to an aversion of philosophy. Ibn Khaldūn narrates that his teacher 'Ābilī used to teach philosophy to Ibn 'Abd al-Salām in secret.[73] The condemnation of the study of philosophy was a very common theme in the literature written by *fuqahā'*.[74] This antagonism had grown to such an extent that even Ghazālī's works were condemned being philosophical.[75] One of Shāṭibī's teachers, Sharīf Tilmasānī, was forced on one occasion by his students to use a certain book by Ghāzalī. He dreamt the same night that he was soiling his books in filth.[76]

The outstanding case in Shāṭibī's lifetime was the condemnation of the *wazīr* Ibn al-Khaṭīb. We need not recount the event which has been mentioned earlier. Qāḍī Nubāhī was asked to bring charges against Ibn al-Khaṭīb.[77] He declared the latter as heretic because of his indulgence in philosophy and other such matters. Qāḍī Nubāhī's attitude to philosophy can be learnt from the following passage in his book pertaining to the administration of justice and the biographies of *qāḍī*s:

> If something relating to the philosophical schools contradicting *sharī'a* or something similar to that is found in someone's handwriting, then the practice (*ḥukm*) in this respect is to study the written material. If it is clearly the opinion of the writer and (something) to which he agrees, even though he may deny it verbally, the case will be decided on the basis of the written material. ...Even if this writing is found only quoting these philosophical schools without relating the statement to the writer... Who could be worse than the man who possesses such books? ...Such books must be burnt and the man must be punished.. "[78]

Towards the middle of 773/1372, Qāḍī Nubāhī announced his *fatwā* about the books composed by Ibn al-Khaṭīb, relating to beliefs and morals. These books were burned in the presence of the *fuqahā'* and *mudarrisīn* (teachers) and others from the same class as the *fuqahā'*. "This happened because the afore-mentioned books contained articles that necessitated this action."[79] Sulṭān Muḥammad V, assisted by Qāḍī Nubāhī and Ibn Zumruk finally succeeded after a few years' struggle to have Ibn al-Khaṭīb charged in the Marīnī court as a heretic. He was treacherously killed in prison and then burnt.[80]

Ibn al-Khaṭīb's tragic death illustrates the extent to which the *fuqahā'* could go in their apposition to philosophy. The case of Ibn al-Khaṭīb also provides evidence to the fact that the reason for opposing philosophy and such trends was to preserve the supremacy of the *Sharī'a*, the basis of their religious authority. These facts are found in Nubāhī's letter to Ibn al-Khaṭīb which has been preserved in *Nafḥ al-ṭīb*. Nubāhī charged Ibn al-Khaṭīb saying:

> This unfortunate office tenure [Qāḍī Nubāhī's period of *qaḍā'* during Ibn al-Khaṭīb's *wazāra*] endured the nonsense resulting from your ridiculing the rules of *Sharī'a*, and your scorn at matters of religion... Some of such cases are the following:

> Ibn al-Zubayr was sentenced to death on account of heresy (*zandaqa*) despite your disdaining such a decision. Ibn Abī'l 'Aysh was detained (*muthaqqaf*) in prison on account of his heterodox statement. He cohabited with his wife after pronouncing the formula of triple divorces, because he claimed that the Prophet himself commanded him to mate with her. You sent one of your men to secure the escape of Ibn Abī'l 'Aysh from the prison with no consideration of others. Another of such cases was that one young man related to you was prosecuted on the charge of murder. I could not do anything but imprison him according to the requirements of religion and the decision of *Sunna*. You detested this judgment. You imprisoned the plaintiff and immediately released the above-mentioned young man.[81]

For a fuller understanding of the contents of this letter it must be pointed out that Ibn al-Khaṭīb was very much distrustful of the *fuqahā'*. His reasons for this attitude were the *fuqahā*'s general ignorance of the Arabic language, lack of piety and too much concern for mundane matters. He wrote a few treatises combining satire and criticism on the practices of the *fuqahā'*.[82] The main targets of his writings were Qāḍī Ibn al-Ḥasan al-Nubāhī and Qāḍī Ibn al-Qabbāb. It is evident from Nubāhī's letter that Ibn al-Khaṭīb did not agree with the *fuqahā'* in condemning heretics to death. His interference in the implementation of court decisions was considered as ridicule of the *Sharī'a*.

Ibn al-Khaṭīb's boldly favourable attitude towards philosophy and pure thought was made possible, among other factors, by the introduction of Razism into Western Malikism in the thirteenth century. Fakhr al-Dīn al-Rāzī was responsible for raising the status of *kalām* to bring it closer to philosophy,[83] but his influence also meant the revival of an interest in philosophy - a forbidden science among the conservative orthodoxy. Razism was introduced to Malikism mainly through *uṣūl al-fiqh*. This made the acceptance of Razism easier, and the resistance to pure philosophy grew weaker and weaker.

In Eastern Malikism this impact manifested itself in two works on *uṣūl al-fiqh* which were in many ways based on *al-Maḥṣūl,* Rāzī's work on *uṣūl al-fiqh*. One of these works was by Ibn Ḥājib (d. 646/1248, Alexandria), *Muntahā al-su'l wa'l amal fī 'ilmay al-uṣūl wa'l-jadal*. The second was the work by Ibn Ḥājib's pupil Shahāb al-Dīn al-Qarāfī (d. 685/1282), *Tanqīḥ al-fuṣūl.*[84] Both soon became very popular *uṣūl* texts of the Mālikī school. Ibn Ḥājib's work gained currency even in his life time. Consequently he had to prepare its abridged version.[85] This abridged work on *uṣūl* along with another short work on *furū'* were called *Mukhtaṣar aṣlī* and *Mukhtaṣar far'ī* respectively since they were used as texts in *madāris*.

Ibn Ḥājib's *Mukhtaṣars* were introduced into the Muslim West by one of his well known disciples, Nāṣir al-Dīn al-Mishdhālī (d. 731/1331).[86] He was one of the three Western scholars who travelled to the East and served as an agent for the influence of Razism on Mālikī thought. The other two were Ibn Zaytūn and al-Ḥaskūnī.[87] In the West more attention had been paid to the study of *fiqh* and Arabic grammar, but under the influence of these scholars *kalām* began to be given equal attention.

Philosophy was also making inroads, but it was still a taboo. Some stories, told by the biographers of this period, indicate that philosophy and other rational sciences were eagerly sought after by certain individuals, but in secret. Such secretly perused texts included those by Ibn Sīnā and Fārābī.[88] Among the above-mentioned scholars Mishdhālī seems to be critical of Razism, although he retained his interest in philosophy. Abū Manṣūr al-Zawāwī and Sharīf Tilimsānī, both Shāṭibī's teachers and in Mishdhālī's circle of influence, show this critical attitude towards Rāzī and exhibit favour towards the perapetic school of Islamic philosophy.

Such trends were encouraging freedom of thought and general intellectual activities. Yet, what probably accelerated the spread of movements of free thought the most was the rise of Ṣūfī *ṭarīqas*. Even Mālikī *fuqahā'* seemed to have failed in their resistance to *taṣawwuf* and encouraged a relaxed attitude towards the strict legalistic tradition of Malikism. We turn now to examine this development.

(2) *TAṢAWWUF*

The absolute supremacy of *Sharī'a,* the palladium of the power of the religious authority of the *fuqahā'*, was threatened by philosophy and *kalām* insofar as these two sciences undermined the authority of *Sharī'a* as the only guide to life. *Taṣawwuf,* however, probably presented a more direct threat to *fuqahā'* than any other movement of thought. Their emphasis on piety, religiosity and moral commitment appealed to intellectuals as well as to the common people. The rise of *taṣawwuf* in their midst was, therefore, naturally considered a threat by the Mālikīs in the West.

In addition to this consideration, certain other events heightened this feeling of danger. In the twelfth century when Malikism had been re-established by the Murābiṭūn, the *fuqahā'* had begun to purge Andalus of *ṭasawwuf*. Among the Ṣūfīs denounced by the *fuqahā'*, the following three were prominent: Abū Bakr Muḥammad from Cordova, Ibn al-'Ārif from Almeria and Ibn Barrajān from Seville. They were persecuted, and all three died in prison. Ibn Barrajān had criticized the Mālikī *fuqahā'* very severely for their neglect of *ḥadīth*. He succeeded in gathering enough supporters in Almeria to form an opposition directed primarily against the *fuqahā'*.[89] Another such uprising against the ruling class and the *fuqahā'* was led by another *ṣūfī* Abū'l Qāsim Ibn al-Qaṣiyy, a disciple of Ibn al-'Ārif (1088-1141). This insurrection took place in Algraves region (Southern Portugal) in 1141. Ibn Qaṣiyy was killed in 546/1151.[90]

Viewing *taṣawwuf* in the perspective of these uprisings, the *fuqahā'* naturally considered *taṣawwuf* a threat to Malikism and to themselves as a class. One significant victim of this opposition to *taṣawwuf* was al-Ghazālī's book, *Iḥyā' 'ulūm al-dīn*. One of the earliest reactions to Ghazālī's *Iḥyā'* was that of Abū Bakr al-Ṭurṭūshī (d. 520/1125) who wrote a treatise refuting Ghazālī's *Iḥyā'*.[91] Ibn al-'Ārif was the first to interpret Ghazālī's *Iḥyā'* in the West.[92] Along with the persecution directed against him came the suppression of *Iḥyā'*. In 1142 'Alī b. Yūsuf b. Tāshufīn who had persecuted Ibn Barrājān and other Ṣūfīs ordered that all copies of *Iḥyā'* be burnt in public.[93] Qāḍī 'Iyāḍ (544/1149) also issued a *fatwā* in favour of burning the *Iḥyā'*. Abū'l Ḥasan ibn Ḥirzihim prohibited the study of the *Iḥyā'* and ordered that all of its copies be burnt.[94]

Like other movements of free thought *taṣawwuf* continued to be considered dangerous both by rulers and *fuqahā'* until Muwaḥḥidūn toppled this alliance. Although the religious views of the Muwaḥḥidūn, because of their stress on the Qur'ān and *Sunna*, did not allow absolute freedom to pure thought, yet Malikism definitely lost its supremacy. Especially in Ya'qūb al-Manṣūr's (580-590/1184-1193) reign, a sort of war was declared on Malikism. He patronized Ibn Ḥazm's school on the one hand and Ibn Rushd's philosophy on the other.[95] The Muwaḥḥidūn could not, however, destroy the power of the *fuqahā'* in Spain. It grew stronger. The best illustration is the fact that the Muwaḥḥid Sulṭān Manṣūr, under the pressure of Mālikī *fuqahā'*, was forced to expel Ibn Rushd from Cordova.[96]

During this period another movement was gaining force. It grew much stronger in the period of the decline of the Muwaḥḥidūn. We refer to the establishment of Ṣūfī *ribāṭ*s. As G. Marçais[97] has pointed out, originally *ribāṭ* was a military institution, but mystic movements which began in eleventh century and bloomed in the thirteenth century in North Africa, changed the nature of the *ribāṭ*. The volunteers for *jihād* in the *ribāṭ*s were also connected with *ṣūfī ṭarīqas*. The *ribāṭ,* thus, was no longer only a military post but also a place for ascetics and travellers. By the thirteenth century the *ribāṭ*s were also transformed into *zāwiya*s or centres for certain *ṣūfī ṭarīqas*.[98] By that time every *ribāṭ* had a resident *ṣūfī-shaykh*. This phenomenon had an effect on the *fuqahā'* intellectually as well as socially.

Spain had resisted *taṣawwuf* successfully but in thirteenth and fourteenth centuries we find travellers and biographers mentioning the emergence of a number of *zāwiyas*, notable Ṣūfīs and a number of works on *taṣawwuf*. Ibn Baṭṭūṭa mentions, among other such centres of Sufism in Muslim Spain, two *zāwiyas* in the vicinity of Granada: *Zāwiyat al-Maḥrūq*, and *Rābiṭat al-'Uqāb*.[99] Two of the significant works on *taṣawwuf* in the fourteenth century were written by Spanish Ṣūfīs; Abū Isḥāq Ibrāhīm b. Yaḥyā al-Anṣārī (751/1350) of Murcia's *Zahrat al-akmām* and Abū 'Abd Allāh Muḥammad b. Muḥammad al-Anṣārī al-Mālaqī's (754/1353). *Bughyat al-sālik fī ashraf al-masālik fī marātib al-ṣūfiyya wa ṭarā'iq al-murīdīn*.[100]

This phenomenon affected the intellectual as well as the social status of the *fuqahā'*. The emphasis on piety and simple living in their personal lives by Ṣūfīs was in sharp contrast to the aristocratic way of life of the *fuqahā'*. This difference in life syle might have made Ṣūfīs more popular than the *fuqahā'* among the common people. This rising influence of Ṣūfīs among the people and especially among the Berber mercenary volunteers for *jihād*, was also recognized by the rulers who, to establish their piety and influence among the warrior tribes, began to give attention to Ṣūfī *shaykhs* and *ribāṭs*.[101] The *fuqahā'* also acknowledged this change, and some of them began to drift towards *taṣawwuf*. This trend is evident from a number of *fatwās* which mention the popularity of sufism among the *fuqahā'*.[102]

The impact of *taṣawwuf* on *fiqh* can be seen in two principal ways. First, the Ṣūfīs did not abolish the *Sharī'a*, but they undermined the importance of *fiqh* by their emphasis on principles of personal moral commitment (*wara'* and *zuhd*) to one's obligations. The *fuqahā*'s treatment of obligations was rather legalistic. Second, instead of limiting themselves to the *fiqh* books, the Ṣūfīs appealed to the Qur'ān and the Sunna. Both of these aspects affected the *fiqh* tradition. The most obvious influence can be seen in the discussions on *uṣūl al-fiqh* in this period. The *fuqahā'* had to make concessions to both principles. Qarāfī discussed *zuhd* and *wara'* as one of the bases of *fiqh*.[103] Ibn 'Abd al-Salām's legal theory is also illustrative of this accommodation.[104]

The influence of *taṣawwuf* had grown very strong by the thirteenth century. At the same time with the passing away of the Muwaḥḥidūn, Malikism was also rising again. But this rise of Mālikism could no more be a continuation of the past tradition. Malikism now faced many challenges, social as well as theoretical. Hence in this period *fiqh* and *taṣawwuf* both are actively present on the scene, and both are alive with a rejuvenating spirit. The Banū Marīn and Banū Ḥafṣ who had succeeded the Muwaḥḥidūn, realizing the force of both movements, took steps toward combining the two.[105] They encouraged the *fuqahā'* to concede to *taṣawwuf*. They also began to endow the *ribāṭ*s with large trusts.

The *fuqahā'*, realizing the situation, soon accommodated themselves with *taṣawwuf*, but they still held to the supremacy of *Sharī'a*. A typical example of this rapprochement was the formation of a new *silsila* (chain of a *ṭarīqa*) that combined the Ṣūfīs and the *fuqahā'*. Abu 'Abd Allāh al-Maqqarī (758/1356), a famous jurist, is also noted for his work on *taṣawwuf, Al-ḥaqā'iq wa'l-raqā'iq.*[106] Ibn 'Abbād Rundī (792/1389), the famous Shādhilī Ṣūfī, was one of Maqqarī's disciples of whom he was very proud.[107]

Maqqarī, along with his lectures on *fiqh,* also initiated his pupils into his *silsila* of *taṣawwuf*. The initiation was done with a symbolic act in which the *shaykh* placed a morsel of food into the mouth of the disciple. A most significant indicator of the new conjunction between *fuqahā'* and Ṣūfīs is to be seen in the names comprising this *silsila.*

Maqqarī - Abū 'Abd Allāh al-Musfir - Abū Zakariyyā al-Maḥyāwī - Abū Muḥammad al-Ṣāliḥ - Shaykh Abū Madyan - Abū'l-Ḥasan b. Ḥirzihim - Ibn 'Arabī - Ghazālī - Abū'l Ma'ālī - Abū Ṭālib al-Makkī - Abū Muḥammad al-Ḥarīrī [sic] - Junayd - Saqaṭī - Ma'rūf al-Karkhī - Da'ūd al-Ṭā'ī - Ḥabīb al-'Ajamī - Ḥasan al-Baṣrī - 'Alī b. Abī Ṭālib - Rasūl Allāh.[108]

This chain has been subjected to criticism by some scholars mainly because of gaps in the chain between Abū'l Ma'ālī and Makkī. Paul Nwiya, after comparing the presentation of this chain as given by Shāṭibī with those given by others, maintains that it belongs to the Shādhilī Order which became better known after Ibn 'Abbād.[109] The chain comprises four parts: the first part consists of Maqqarī and Musfir both primarily *fuqahā'* it is connected with the second part comprising a chain from Maḥyāwī to Abū Madyan - primarily Ṣūfīs. They are connected again with the third part consisting of mainly *fuqahā'*; starting with Ibn Ḥirzihim to Abū'l Ma'ālī. They are then connected with the traditional chain of early Ṣūfīs, through Abū Ṭālib al-Makkī.[110]

Nwiya's suggestion about the connection of this chain with the Shādhiliyya, together with his conclusion that Ibn 'Abbād's reanimation of the Shādhiliyya was a revival of the early sufism of Muḥāsibī, also partly explains the compromise of the Ṣūfīs with the *fuqahā'* in order to exclude the more comprehensive and radical type of sufism, such as that of Ibn 'Arabī which the *fuqahā'* considered a threat to the supremacy of *Sharī'a.*

Having found this compromise possible, the *fuqahā'* eased their opposition to *taṣawwuf* as such. There was yet another aspect of *taṣawwuf* which continued to threaten their status. This threat can be seen in three ways. First, *Ṭarīqa-taṣawwuf* required total submission to the *shaykh*. This was one of the subjects of Shāṭibī's disputations with his contemporary scholars. This submission undermined the religious authority of the *fuqahā'*. One event (probably an anecdote) illustrates this tension:

> Qāḍī Abū'l Qāsim al-Sabtī had two sons. One, Abū'l 'Abbās Aḥmad became *qāḍī*. The other, Abū'l Ma'ālī chose the path of *'qawm'* (Ṣūfīs). He never used or ate anything at his brother's house. After many years he visited Zāwiya Maḥrūq in the outskirts of Granada. He saw Shaykh Abū Ja'far Aḥmad al-Maḥdūd and asked him if he could explain a mystery that had been worrying him. The mystery was that he had a torch that always showed him light, but suddenly he lost it. The *Shaykh* asked the first person entering the *Zāwiya* to answer that question. This person who appeared to be an illiterate villager answered that Abū'l Ma'ālī lost this torch as punishment for some of his actions. After a number of questions it was revealed that Abū'l Ma'ālī had taught someone the Divine name of *al-Laṭīf* which he was not permitted to do. A curse fell on him as a consequence. He became *qāḍī al-jamā'a* and died a worldly man.[111]

The second and the most critical impact of *taṣawwuf* was its potential intrusion into the realm of *'ibādāt*. A number of Ṣūfī practices like *dhikr* and *samā'* were treated almost like *'ibāda,* a religious obligation. Their stress on *tark ḥuẓūẓ* (asceticism) led sometimes to abandonment of rights and facilities allowed by *Sharī'a*. Shāṭibī, in his *fatāwā* and other writings analysed these terms and practices. In his *fatāwā* he declared such practices as *bid'a* leading to *kufr,*[112] because it amounted to treating these practices as *'ibādāt* which they were not. As a matter of fact an exposition of the terms *'ibādāt, ta'abbud, ḥuẓūẓ* and *bid'a* is vital in Shāṭibī's philosophy of Islamic law.

In the thirteenth century the celebration of the Prophet's birthday was introduced into the Muslim West. This celebration took place in mosques. The poets wrote and recited poems for the occasion. Various forms of *dhikr* and *samā'* were also part of the celebration. A significant factor in this development was the patronage that rulers provided for this celebration.[113] The *fuqahā'* could scarcely afford to offer strong resistance to these ceremonies in view of the wide popularity of this 'innovation' among all groups of people. The situation forced them, therefore, to revise their stand on *bid'a*. Shāṭibī, nevertheless opposed this practice as we shall see in a subsequent chapter on his *fatāwā*.

The third aspect of the threat was economic. Generous donations and trust properties were given to *zāwiyas* and *ribāṭs*.[114] This wealth attracted a number of devotees as well as travellers. Ibn Baṭṭūṭa came across Ṣūfīs in these centres from almost all corners of the Muslim world.[115] *Fuqahā'* were appointed for the supervision of the expenses of such donations, although the supervision and maintenance of such properties was left to the *shaykh* of the *zāwiya* and his associates.

Some *fuqahā'* were critical of Ṣūfī ṭarīqas. According to them the Ṣūfī centres were attracting and encouraging idleness in the society. For many devotees asceticism meant to forsake all worldly occupations and to spend one's life in some *zāwiya*. The finances of the *zāwiya* made it possible to live in such a manner. This practice, however, was creating a large number of unproductive elements in the society who were living on the labours of others. For the already stringent economy of Granadan society this was a very heavy burden.

This economic burden becomes very significant as we shall see that the Granadan economy was in the process of changing from an agricultural to a commercial and mercantilistic economy. Even the rural areas could no more support the maintenance of such a burdensome institution as the Ṣūfī *zāwiya* or *ribāṭ* had become. The problem became acute in the days of Shāṭibī. A distinct economic view of the matter, in contradistinction to the older political and theological view, that had motivated the *fuqahā'* to oppose Sufism now came to be.

The inhabitants of a small town Qanālish,[116] an agricultural town on the borders of Aragon, sought a *fatwā* concerning the *shar'ī* opinion about a *zāwiyat al-ghurabā'* in their vicinity. The Chief Qāḍī Al-Balfīqī answered vaguely, justifying the existence of such an institution. The Chief Muftī Ibn Lubb countersigned the *fatwā*. The people of Qanālish, however, mounted a protest against the *fatwā* accusing both *muftīs* of subjecting the people to an unnecessary burden.[117]

The same *istiftā'* was then sent to Shāṭibī and Abū 'Abd Allāh al-Ḥaffār. Ḥaffār's *fatwā* spelled out the economic aspect in more detail. A few excerpts from this *fatwā* are worthy of notice:

> This band of people who claim their connection with *taṣawwuf*, has caused the severest harm to religion in this period and in this part of the world. Their evils have spread throughout the Muslim world and especially in the fortresses, towns and villages which are farther from the capital... They are more dangerous to Islam than the infidels....
>
> They have no virtue... None of them knows how to clean himself or to make ablution.... In the name of religion they only know how to sing, to utter nonsensical statements and to encroach upon others' property unlawfully...

What made this band of people adopt this way of life which is so dangerous for the religion? Was it that they needed things basic for the human being, e.g. food, drink, clothing and such things, and they did not know any trade or craft to live from? Or if they knew a trade, did they find it hard to toil to earn their livelihood?... The devil seduced them and suggested to them this path which was full of fun and pleasure. They deceive the ignorant with the practice of *dhikr*... wearing patched clothes... as these were the signs of the virtuous people of this path...

A certain scholar said that the people in a city must be like the parts of body. As every part of a body has a particular use and none of them is futile... so are the inhabitants of a city. The soldiers guard the city, the *fuqahā'* and judges protect the law (*Sharī'a*) and also teach it... Therefore one who is of no use in a city whereas he is capable of being so ... must be expelled from the city.

A philosopher (*ḥakīm*) taught his disciples to be like bees in a beehive... They do not let any idle members stay there. They would drive it out of the hive, because it would cramp their space, would use their honey and would spread idleness, and abandonment of trades....

It is incumbent upon whoever can do so to restrain these people who are like a gangrenous sore in the side of religion. He must obstruct the way to this group for those who are inclined towards it. He must expel them from these places. (If he does so) he is a warrior of faith (*mujāhid*) in this respect.[118]

The following section examines the economic conditions and developments which shaped such opinions of the jurists.

III

ECONOMIC DEVELOPMENTS[119]

Muslim Spain under Banū Naṣr was reduced to the Southern part of Spain. The Naṣrī kingdom extended in the South to the shores of the Mediterranean Sea and the Strait of Gibraltar. For a certain period even the African seaport of Ceuta came within Naṣrī territories. In the North were the principalities of Jaen, Cordova and Seville. In the East it extended to the principality of Murcia and its Mediterranean shores. In the West lay the principality of Cadiz and La Frontera. The kingdom was divided into three provinces (*kūrāt*): Gharnāṭa (Granada), Al-Mariyya (Almeria) and Mālaqa (Malaga). The kingdom was crossed in the middle by the lofty mountains of the

Sierra Nevada. The depressed areas were traversed by the river Genil (Shanīl), a tributary of Guadalquivir, and the river Derro. The land was a combination of plains and valleys with thick forests.

The difference between the present geographical conditions and those described by historians is confusing. Today this part of Spain is dry and arid,[120] but the historians vie with each other in praising the fertility and the greenery of this region. The following description by Ibn al-Khaṭīb is typical of other historical geographical descriptions:

> God Almighty has distinguished this country of ours by endowing it with lofty hills and fertile plains, sweet and wholesome food, a great number of useful animals, plenty of fruits, abundance of waters, comfortable dwellings, good clothing... a slow succession of the seasons of the year.[121]

The city of Granada, situated north of the Sierra Nevada, was the capital of the kingdom. By the city flowed the rivers Genil and El Derro. Granada was surrounded by approximately 300 small towns (*qurā*).[122]

POPULATION

Granada in this period attracted a great number of immigrants. Fleeing from the various Spanish territories which had been conquered by Christians, or having been persecuted by Christians, the Muslims came to Granada. In addition, a large number of Berbers kept coming constantly from Africa: they came as Ṣūfīs, mercenaries, students or simply as fortune seekers.

We have no way of knowing the exact number of the population as the sources generally do not mention it. Nevertheless, the growing burden of the population in this small kingdom can be seen in the educated guesses in the secondary sources. According to Imamuddin, in the days of al-Ghālib Bi'llāh (1230-1272) the population in the city of Granada was 150,000.[123] Seybold estimated the figure in the later period as approximately 500,000.[124] Over and above the rising numbers, the ethnic diversity of the population also affected the economy of the kingdom.

The bulk of the population in Granada and other cities was composed of Berbers and Arabs, both usually soldiers and hence fief holders. Spaniards who were mostly cultivators thus worked for both. The Berbers were disliked by the Arabs who considered themselves culturally more advanced than Berbers, as well as by Spaniard Muslims who inhabited most of the rural areas.

ECONOMY

Generally speaking, prior to the eventful impact of the change in Mediterranean trade, the economy of the kingdom had two aspects: urban and rural. The economic activity in rural areas consisted of agricultural and pastoral occupations. In the urban areas the crafts and commerce were the main productive economic activities. Urban economic activity was largely concentrated on luxury goods, hence the actual burden of production fell upon the rural economy. Village life was severe. This situation forced a number of villagers to go to the cities, which were already few in number. This meant the availability of cheap labour, but since the production of luxury goods had a limited number of consumers, city life also was becoming highly expensive. The impact of the Mediterranean trade, however, as we shall see below, shifted the burden of production from rural to urban economy.

PROSPERITY

There was a marked difference in the standards of living even among city dwellers. The aristocrats who also owned the sources of production lived a luxurious life. Their wealth was distinctly evident in the ornaments and jewellery worn by the women of this class. [125] Their jewellery consisted of such precious stones as emeralds and rubies, and their dresses were embroidered with gold and silver. It was, in fact, the prosperity of this section of the population which so much impressed travellers such as Ibn Baṭṭūṭa who described Granada as the most prosperous kingdom in the West.[126]

FINANCIAL CONDITIONS

The revenue of the kingdom consisted mainly of taxes collected from lands. According to one secondary source, the yearly income of the kingdom was 1,200,000 ducats.[127] The permanent deposits in the treasury consisted, of course, of precious stones and diamonds,[128] but the expenses of the kingdom were met by the revenue.

The major source of revenue was land tax, called *kharāj*. It was usually 1/9 or 1/10 of the produce, but we learn from Shāṭibī's *fatāwā* that another 1/5 was also levied as rent of land.[129] Since land was scarce and irrigation facilities were not commonly available, the most fertile lands around Granada were procured by the Sulṭān. These lands were called *mukhtaṣṣ* and were leased at very high rentals. Because of the nature of the lands they were eagerly sought by the people.

In addition to *kharāj*, the other sources of revenue consisted of the customs duties collected from incoming and in-transit commercial shops in the ports of the kingdom of Granada. Another frequent source of revenue was the proceeds from raids carried out in the enemy territory which brought back prisoners, slaves, and movable properties, etc.

The taxes were collected in kind, but latterly, more emphasis was given to collection of revenue in cash. There was a complex system of tax collection. The tax collectors, called *musharrif* were responsible to one of the important *kātib*s of the Sulṭān, called *ṣāḥib al-ashghāl.*[130] The taxes were collected in the name of the *makhzan* (treasury, replacing the old term *bayt al-māl*) which applied to both Islamic and non-Islamic taxes. Even the trust properties belonging to mosques were not exempted. The provincial and local administration as well as tax collection was in the hands of a *qā'id* in each district.[131]

The expenses of the kingdom were very high. The major expenditure was the tribute paid to the kingdoms of Castille and Aragon. According to Imamuddin,[132] the amount of such tribute in Ghālib Bi'llāh's days was 250,000 ducats. The second major expenditure was the salaries and compensation paid to the soldiers and mercenaries. In addition, large amounts were also paid to the Banū Marīn to recompense the expenses incurred in the preparation for war against the enemies of Granada. Since in both modes of expenditure the terms were cash, the country was geared to a money economy.[133]

Money and Currency

The Naṣrī currency was similar to that of the Muwaḥḥidūn both in type and value. The basic units of money were the Dīnār and the Dirham. Dirhams were usually silver currency and varied in value and fineness.[134] The Dīnār remained comparatively stable, the quality and quantity of gold helping to stabilize its monetary value.[135] From the legal documents it appears[136] that three types of Dīnārs were in currency: the golden Dīnār, the silver Dīnār and the Dīnār 'Aynī (copper). The golden Dīnār was usually of 2 grams in weight containing 22 carats gold. Its monetary value was equal to 5 to 7 silver Dīnārs or 75 silver Dirhams. The Banū Naṣr struck silver Dīnārs in square shape in contradistinction to the round shape of the golden Dīnār and the *dobla* (a well-known non-Muslim gold piece). Contrary to the conjectures of early scholars of numismatics,[137] the silver and 'Aynī (copper) Dīnārs were not debased coins; but as studies of documents of contracts in the Naṣrī period show, they seem to have been introduced by the Naṣrī rulers according to fixed monetary values, while the gold piece was accepted in the market according to the current price of gold.

We have here the evidence of a money economy in the form of copper Dīnār. The reason for this development was most probably the rapid growth of trade between Granada and foreign principalities. This trade is discussed at a later point in this section. What concerns us here is a plausible explanation of the copper Dīnār by the fact that because of the need for gold for trade a kind of currency based on credits to the treasury could have been introduced in the form of the copper Dīnār. Such a development could also be interpreted to mean that because of commercial needs the internal money was devalued.[138]

Agriculture

Spain had been known for highly developed agricultural methods and ample fertile land,[139] but in the Naṣrī period the extent of Muslim Spain was reduced to Southern Andalusia. The nature of the soil and climatic conditions did not allow a scale of cultivation that permitted self-sufficiency in the production of grains. Often it proved necessary to import grains from North Africa.[140]

The soil seemed to be conducive, however, for the growth of durable plants. Andalus produced a variety of fruits which were eagerly sought at home as well as in foreign markets. For export purposes, however, the cultivation of olives and mulberry trees became very common in the fourteenth century. Even though manufactured with primitive methods, olive oil was also exported. Mulberry leaves used in rearing silk-worms had also gained commercial value. As we shall see in a subsequent chapter, extensive dealings in olive and mulberry leaves led to newer forms of contracts that called for continuous *ijtihād*. The *fatāwā* by Shāṭibī and other jurists in Granada reflect this complexity.

As mentioned earlier the *mukhtaṣṣ* lands, the best lands of Granada, were leased to cultivators who used to pay dues in kind. In the fourteenth century. It appears that these lands began to be rented to those tenants who would pay the rent in cash. These tenants hired seasonal labour for cultivation.[141] By the fourteenth century land had become critically scarce. Evidence of this fact is found in the *fatāwā* literature where various forms of ownership and complex methods of the division of the property and produce are noted.[142]

The ever-growing population and the continuous loss of territories to the Christians were also responsible for the fact that extraordinary forms of ownership appeared in the distribution of cultivable land. A small tract of land might be co-owned by a number of persons.[143] Not only that, but the practice of division and subdivision of property extended even to a tree and its branches; a tract of land was divided among its owners by the number of trees; or a tree, when it was owned by more than one, was divided by its branches.[144] The extraordinarily intense cultivation even forced the people to use or rent the areas of land around their houses for agricultural and commercial purposes.[145] Besides the seasonal crops, fruit cultivation was a major occupation. A highly developed system of irrigation made higher level lands useful for orchards.[146]

In general, however, it appears that the pressure toward a cash economy was forcing even the rural agricultural economy to change into a certain type of economy, which for lack of a better term, we may call 'mercantile' economy. It must, however, be made clear that our use of the term 'mercantile' should not be confused with its technical use in a special sense which refers to the sixteenth century 'mercantile policies' in certain European countries.[147] We are using this term in its simple sense to mean a type of economy that lays stress on trade and commerce, and where money as wealth becomes important in preference to land.

Some of the indicators of the rise of this type of mercantilism are the following: The use of seasonal labour and contract workers who received their wages in cash or kind at the end of the contract[148] period was replacing the older system of semi-serfdom for the peasants. Forms of co-operative cultivation and production where partner contributed money in place of land were also current. Evidence for this development is found in the specific cases of rearing of silkworms[149] and of production of cheese.[150]

Industries

The existence of gold, precious stones, amber and metals such as copper and iron[151] in the kingdom of Granada encouraged various industrial activities. These industries had become a major base of the Naṣrī economy. Louis Bertrand tells us how the people in Granada enjoyed "up to a certain point, industrial wealth."[152]

Among others the major industrial centres were Granada, Malaga and Almeria in which the following industries flourished: Weaponry, Silk, Pottery, Leather, Cotton and other textiles.[153] The most profitable industry was silk. The cities that were busy in the silk industry were Jubiles, Granada, and Almeria. In Almeria there were about 800 looms for brocaded silk and about 1,000 for embroidered silk. Similarly there were looms for other kinds of silk among which the following were well known in the foreign markets: *Usqulāṭūn,* Georgian, Isphania, *'Unābī, Ma'ajir al-Mudahash.*[154]

In the fourteenth century, because of the growth of the Italian silk industries, the Granadan silk industry suffered heavily.[155] Nevertheless, the market demand for raw silk material ensured that this industry in Granada remained profitable.[156]

Crafts

The crafts were usually connected with luxury commodities. Many artisans coming from other parts of Spain, had settled in the kingdom of Granada. This influx advanced not only the development of crafts but also turned the craft-industries toward the production of luxury goods. These crafts concentrated on jewellery, golden silk embroidery, decorative pottery and fancy leather among other things.[157]

Trade and Commerce

The most significant phenomenon in the economic history of the Islamic West in the fourteenth century was the quick development of a commercial economy. The coastal cities developed significantly along with the growth of their political influence. This is evident in the case of Ceuta, Malaga, Ronda and Almeria. The Alliance of Ronda and Malaga with Muḥammad V al-Ghanī Bi'llāh meant his remounting the throne of Granada.[158] His capture of Ceuta meant a greatly increased influence on Marīnī political affairs.[159]

Besides political influence, these cities also experienced a rapid growth of the textile, metal, leather, dairy, flour-milling, and ceramic industries and other crafts. The produce was largely meant for foreign markets. The main cause of the quick development of a commercial economy in this area, according to S.M. Batsieva, was the economic upsurge in the Mediterranean countries in the thirteenth and fourteenth centuries. The cause of that development was the sudden growth of manufacturers in Italy.[160] Trade, however, necessarily required relations with foreign nations. The overseas trade of the Italian cities reached its zenith in the fourteenth century. This trade was carried further by the maritime cities of Catalonia, Provence, Constantinople, Alexandria and others. This activity created a wide Mediterranean market which made possible the enormous upsurge of production there and which was conducive to the appearance of mercantilism in Italy.

The emergence of vigorous trade patterns around the Mediterranean made possible a wide sale of agricultural produce in the foreign market. This, in turn, affected the Granadan economy by producing a stimulus to commercialize agriculture. López Ortiz, studying the *fatāwā* literature of this period, concluded that in Granada, the agricultural production was moving towards a mercantilized economy.[161] Among the materials that Florence, Naples, Catalonia and Provence imported were raw leather, processed leather, olive oil, cotton, silk, wax, etc. The main importer of Granadan raw silk was Florence.[162]

Almeria and Malaga, the main seaports of Granada, were situated on the sea trade route connecting the maritime cities in Western Spain and in West Africa with Naples in Italy. This sea route connected with another sea trade route starting from Seville and going through Murcia, Valencia, Barcelona and ending in Marseilles. In terms of land trade Granada was connected with a number of trade routes that spread throughout Spain and which were also connected with the maritime cities. Granada was connected with the land trade routes in Africa through Ceuta which was under her suzerainty at that time. These land routes led to Fez, Tlemcen, and Algiers.

The significance given to the safety of these trade routes by the rulers can be seen in the mutual trade pacts between the kingdom and its neighbours in that period. The Banū Naṣr frequently signed trade pacts with their neighbours; or one should perhaps rather say that every treaty included a condition of mutual agreement on the safety of trade routes and merchants. In 684/1285 in a treaty with Castille the condition read that the Muslim merchants going to Castille would be exempted from taxes.[163] The treaty with Aragon, signed in 695/1300, provided that the cities in the territories of both parties to the treaty would be open to the merchants from both territories and that their lives and merchandise would be safeguarded.[164] In 721/1321 in the renewal of this treaty an additional condition provided that the boats (ships), shores and ports of each party would be safeguarded.[165] Such security pacts with Christian neighbours were essential for the Banū Naṣr as the major part of their trade consisted of exports to Italy by these trade routes. As mentioned above, Naples, Catalonia and Provence were the main importers of Granadan commodities.

Money lending

A natural result of the mercantilistic activities was the growth of a strong and widespread money-lending class. This money-lending class operated both in Christian and Muslim territories. Most probably the intermediaries in such transactions were Jews. In the literature of that period they were called "transgressors and unjust".[166] These money lenders controlled the markets where agricultural products were brought for auction. They worked also as intermediaries in auctions.[167] They were also responsible for the exchange of currencies. There is also an indication in a *fatwā* that they even determined the values of different currencies.[168]

A peculiar and typical product of this economic and political milieu was *al-fakkāk*. The term, originally meaning to separate, disjoin, and redeem,[169] probably under the influence of the Qur'anic legal term *fakk-u-raqaba*[170] (to liberate someone), came to be used also in commercial legal transactions to mean the redemption of pledges and of debts.[171] Most probably this Andalusian term *al-fakkāk* etymologically springs from that usage. In Andalus this term was applied to an intermediary who was paid by the relatives of a prisoner in the enemy territory to buy the liberty of the prisoner by paying the required amount to the enemy.[172]

To grasp the situation it must be pointed out that despite the truces, payments of tribute, and promises of protection, the Granadans found themselves often invaded by armed bands which cut down fruit trees, carried off crops and cattle and took prisoners. These events were so common that Muslim fraternities along the lines of the French fraternities such as the *Ordre de la Merci* were established to ransom Muslim prisoners and slaves in Christian territory.[173]

Ibn Baṭṭūṭa witnessed such an incident in Spain. He relates the story that on the coast of Marbella four galleys of a Christian band appeared, and after killing a fisherman, captured eleven horse riders who were travelling to Malaga a little distance ahead of Ibn Baṭṭūṭa. When he reached Malaga and arrived at the main mosque, he found the Chief Qāḍī Ṭanjālī already busy talking to a number of jurists and a notable businessman in Malaga. They were collecting a sum to buy back the freedom of the captives.[174]

From the legal literature of this period, it appears that the institution of *al-fakkāk* was an already established practice.[175] Under Muslim influence the Castillians also called such intermediaries *Alfaqueques*. In Castille they were supposed to be responsible for the administration of the property of the prisoners of war.[176]

In Andalus, however, although the institution may have originated from pious and selfless interests, yet by the fourteenth century it was more of a commercial nature than any thing else. The *fatāwā* indicate that *al-fakkāk* used to contact interested persons on both sides and earned a commission from both parties. *Al-fakkāk* bargained about the prices for ransoms, etc., devalued the currencies, and earned profits from such transactions.[177]

In the light of this and other descriptions of the institution of *al-fakkāk* in the sources, it may be rightly assumed that *al-fakkāk* belonged to the money-lending class. The assumption gains weight since the sources indicate that *al-fakkāk* also traded in silk, advanced money on anticipated earnings and dealt in debased currencies.[178]

We dwelt longer on the description of economic conditions in Granada in Shāṭibī's period. The reason for this emphasis will become clear when we discuss Shāṭibī's *fatāwā* that deal with the problems arising from these extensive and complex economic activities. The impact of the economic conditions on the legal theory was such, that, as we shall point out in this study at several places, Shāṭibī and other jurists had to appeal to broader principles of Islamic law because precedent and analogy were no longer sufficient. This point calls for a brief analysis of the legal system in Granada at that time.

IV

LEGAL SYSTEM

The data available for this section is particularly scanty. Since a description of the legal system and legal developments, however cursory it may be, is helpful to complete the picture of social changes which is the object of this chapter, this section makes such an attempt.

This section deals first with the legal system and second with legal developments in the fourteenth century. Reference has already been made to the institutions of *qaḍā'* and *futyā* and the place of Malikism in the legal system. Not to repeat what has already been said, we will briefly recapitulate the main points relating to the legal system.

1. Mālikī *fiqh* was recognized as the law of the kingdom.

2. Mālikī *fiqh* was applied on three levels:

   (a) On the level of *futyā*, strictly religious matters including those of exegesis and theology were referred to *muftīs*, and except for cases of heresy, such matters were beyond the courts' jurisdiction. The opinion of the *muftīs* was called *fatwā*, and its implementation largely depended on the individual conscience.

   (b) On the level of the courts (*qaḍā*), the decision of the judge (*ḥākim*) was called *ḥukm*. Although the judge had no executive powers, yet in contradistinction to *fatwā*, the *ḥukm* was enforced by government agency. The *qāḍī* was assisted by a concilium of *fuqahā'* called *mushāwarūn*.[179]

   (c) On the level of the notaries (*wuththāq*), the Mālikī *fiqh* was applied to register and validate various kinds of contracts and other types of legal documents. These *wuththāq* were usually *faqīh*s and were often appointed also as *muftī*s and *mushāwar*s.

3. In matters of procedure the litigants sought *fatāwā* of the *muftī*s in favour of their claims and presented them in the court. The judge reached his decision after consulting the *mushāwar*s in his court. The *qāḍī*'s decision was final in the sense that neither he nor any other judge could revise this decision; in the opinion of some scholars the decision stood as it was even if the witnesses changed their testimony. In certain matters an appeal could be made to the Sulṭān against the decision of the court.[180]

4. Since Mālikī *fiqh* covered all matters relating to religion, ethics, family, property, etc., and the *muftī* could be consulted even on matters which were also in the *qāḍī's* jurisdiction, a confusion between the jurisdictions of a *muftī* and a *qāḍī* always existed. The function of the notaries added to the confusion. The notaries were sometimes given limited jurisdictions such as the attestation of a witness or a contract, yet they could not decide a case.

In short, the essential problem of the Granadan legal system lay in the confusion of the function of *fatwā* and *ḥukm*. The Egyptian Mālikī jurist Qarāfī (d. 684/1285), whose influence, as has been mentioned earlier, was felt deeply on Mālikī *fiqh* in Andalus, wrote the following treatise on this problem: *Al-Iḥkām fī tamyīz al-fatāwā 'an al-aḥkām.*[181]

Qarāfī disagreed with the usual distinction made between *fatwā* and *ḥukm* by considering the former as only *ikhbār* (statement) and the latter as *ilzām* (binding).[182] On the contrary, he maintained that both are *ikhbār 'an ḥukm Allāh* (statement about God's command) and both are "binding". According to him a *fatwā* is a statement which implies either *ilzām* or *ibāḥa* (permission), and the *ḥukm* is a statement which implies either *ilzām* or *inshā'* (prescriptive action).[183] In respect of subject matter, the *ḥākim* has jurisdiction only in *al-umūr al-ijtihādiyya* (the matters which were not agreed upon among the Mālikī scholars) and *al-maṣāliḥ al-dunyawiyya* (matters relating to this world); the *ḥukm* has no jurisdiction in *'ibādāt* (ritual and worship) and *ijmā'*.[184] Qarāfī, however, could not remove the confusion completely as he maintained that both *fatwā* and *ḥukm* form part of the function of the *imām* (in this case the Sulṭān)[185] but where he made the *muftī* responsible to God, he did not define to whom *ḥākim* was responsible.

LEGAL DEVELOPMENTS

Beside the confusion that existed in the functional aspect of Mālikī *fiqh* certain new developments had added to this uncertainty. We will briefly mention two of them.

The legal status of Andalus

Mālikī *fiqh*, in certain cases, maintains that the legal status of a territory changes according to its political condition; whether it is on peace terms with another territory or at war. In the fourteenth century Andalus was constantly at war or on peace terms with her Christian neighbours. It even had the status of a vassal state to the principality of Castille. A number of questions in the *fatwā* literature show the confusion that this situation created in the application of Islamic law.[186]

Diversity of laws

The diversity of laws had a number of causes. In many cases the diversity came about because of the differences in the local practices which were recognized in Andalusian Mālikī tradition as a source of law. The diversity of laws was also caused by other factors such as the use of the principle of *murā'āt al-khilāf*. These aspects have been discussed in chapter twelve.

It seems that Ibn al-Khaṭīb became painfully aware of the weakness of the legal system and tried to reform it. He criticised Qāḍī al-Nubāhī in his treatise *Khal' al-rasan*. He also wrote the following books on legal theory: *Sadd al-dharī'a fi tafḍīl al-sharī'a,*[187] *Alfiya fī uṣūl al-fiqh*[188] and *Muthlā al-ṭarīqa fī dhamm al-wathīqa.*[189] In his *Muthlā al-ṭarīqa* he strongly criticised the institution and practice of notaries (*wuththāq*). He condemned them for their ignorance of the Arabic language and of *fiqh*. His essential criticism of this practice was on the basis of *wara'* (moral responsibility) that was completely neglected by the legalistic and formalistic trends in the legal practice.[190]

The little information we possess on the actual legal developments in the Andalus should perhaps be supplemented by comparison with Christian Spain. It is quite probable that developments similar to those in neighbouring areas took place in the Andalus, since both countries underwent the same kind of socio-economic changes. For an understanding of legal developments in Christian Spain it is quite revealing to notice the various stages through which *Fuero*, an important Spanish legal institution, went.

The institution of *Fuero* existed before the arrival of the Muslims in Spain. It survived under Muslim rule and later became a stronghold of resistance to the renaissance of Roman law in Spain in the thirteenth and fourteenth centuries. *Fuero,* deriving its name from *Lex fori,* tribunal justice,[191] came to stand for the legal practice of townships and thus took the name of *Fuero Juzgo.*[192] *Fuero Juzgo* also called *Liber Judiciorum* and *Lex Barbara Visigothorum*, was a compromise between Visigothic and Roman law, developed during the seventh century.[193] *Fuero Juzgo* was medley of legal rules which included, among others, subjects such as the following: rules for visiting the sick, and the graves of the dead, heretics, etc.[194] Under Muslim rule these Fueros incorporated some Muslim elements as well.[195]

In the thirteenth century the administration was faced with the profusion of all kinds of laws in Spain. The excessive diversity became threatening to the fabric of the state.[196] The progress of trade also demanded a system of uniform laws. By the middle of the thirteenth century a movement for the reform of laws emerged. A long contest between the supporters of Fueros and the supporters of legal unity began. Two weapons were used to reform Fueros: (1) Exposing the shortcomings of the Fuero system and (2) the renaissance of Roman law.[197] Three Castillian kings Ferdinand III (1199-1252), Alfonso X (1221-84) and Alfonso XI (1311-50) are known as staunch supporters of these legal reforms to bring about the uniformity of law.[198] In the days of Alfonso the Learned another development was also taking place. In Southern France there arose a school which both there and in Bologna supplanted the glossators (medieval commentators on Roman civil law). Instead of seeing in Roman law a multitude of texts to be examined and interpreted, those of the new trend sought to do two things:

(a) systematize Roman law in accordance with the rigid method of Aristotle and in the light of Christian doctrine, and

(b) to ascertain what reasons could have motivated its rules. The trend thus marked the beginning of a philosophy of law.[199]

Many scholars from Spain travelled to Bologna to study and teach Canon Law. In Spain, the University of Salamanca became an important centre for the study of Roman and Canon law.[200]

The above description indicates that factors such as the diversity of laws and the need for reform of local legal practices to bring about the uniformity of laws led scholars to investigate the motive and purpose of law. The attempts of these scholars had very far-reaching effects on the evolution of law in Europe in later centuries. Although this evolution came about two centuries after Shāṭibī, it is not irrelevant to refer to it briefly as it helps in understanding the direction to which the legal philosophy was led by the legal developments in Shāṭibī's period.

As a result of the continuous concern for the philosophy of law in Spain there emerged a group of prominent legal philosophers who are now known as 'Spanish Theologian Jurists'. Two of these jurists are usually described in the following manner: Vitoria (Fransisco de Vitoria who died in 1546 in Salamanca), "the expounder of the law of nations" and Suárez, "the philosopher".[201] Francis Suárez was born in Granada in 1548 and died in Lisbon in 1617. His influence on the later development of the philosophy of law is well-known. His legal philosophy had its pivotal point in the exposition of the end of law which, according to Suárez was the "common good of the community".[202]

The similarity between the legal developments in Muslim and Christian Spain is worth noting. Shāṭibī investigated the purpose of law and he found the concept of *maṣāliḥ al-'ibād* (the good of the people) to be the objective of law. Suárez's philosophy of law also focused on common good. The theological approach by the Spanish jurists to define the objectives of law and to stress on the uniformity of law is close to Shāṭibī's approach and criticism of *khilāf* in Maliki law.

Unfortunately the similarity in the legal developments in Muslim Spain with that in Christian Spain did not go beyond this point. There is similarity in the socio-economic factors that led to an investigation of the philosophy of law in both Muslim and Christian Spain. Jurists' conclusions about the objectives of the law were the same. Yet whereas in Christian Spain these investigations continued and were responsible for the shaping of the modern concept of law in Europe, among the Muslims this attempt seems to have stopped with Shāṭibī.

NOTES AND REFERENCES

1. Not to speak of secondary sources, even the primary sources on the Naṣrī Granada are often confusing. The confusion of the secondary sources is partly due to their indiscriminate use of the primary sources which are often conflicting. For a general history of the period a critical study of the primary sources is indispensable. The two contemporary historians on whom the later sources have depended are Ibn al-Khaṭīb and Ibn Khaldūn. Not only did these two men belong to different courts which were often enemies to each other, but Ibn Khaldūn also had a particular philosophy of history that stresses the role of tribes and families. These differences make their narratives of the same period conflict with one another. Furthermore, the attachments of the two historians to these courts also fluctuated. These changing loyalties affected their narratives. Ibn al-Khaṭīb revised, added and suppressed much information at various stages of writing the history of this period.

   Only to avoid confusion, we have chosen Ibn al-Khaṭīb's *al-Iḥāṭa fī akhbār al-Gharnāṭa* (Cairo: Maṭba' Mawsū'āt, 1901), as the basic text mainly because this was written before Ibn al-Khaṭīb had been prejudiced against Muḥammad al-Ghanī Bi'llāh. For the events after 771/1369, mainly for the story of Ibn al-Khaṭīb's persecution, we have relied upon the information in al-Maqqarī, *Nafḥ al-ṭīb* (ed. M.M.'A. Ḥamīd, Cairo: Sa'āda, 1949), which derives its information mainly from Ibn Khaldūn's *Kitāb al-'ibar* (Bayrut, 1959). We have also used Qāḍī al-Nubāhī's *al-Marqabat al'ulyā,* (Cairo, 1948) to supplement *Nafḥ al-ṭīb*. Secondary sources have been used only complementarily.
2. See Muhsin Mahdi, *Ibn Khaldūn's Philosophy of History* (Chicago: Phoenix, 1964).
3. See Henri Laoust, *Contribution à une étude de la méthodologie canonique d' Ibn Taymiyya* (Cairo: IFAO, 1939) and *Essai sur les doctrines sociales et politiques d' Ibn Taymiyya* (Cairo: Institut Français d'Archéologie Oriental, 1939).
4. See Josef van Ess, *Die Erkenntnislehre des 'Aḍudîn al-Îcî: Übersetzung und Kommentar des ersten Buches seiner Mawâqif* (Wiesbaden: Steiner, 1966).
5. Ibn al-Sa'īd, an African traveller, who visited Andalus at that period described the capricious political attitude of the populace as follows:

   > Their attitude toward a sultan can be described by the fact that whenever they find a horse rider who distinguishes himself among his peers...they rush to his side and appoint him their king without any consideration for the future...or sometimes there is in the kingdom a soldier of the officer rank (*qā'id*) who has earned fame for his campaigns against the enemy...They offer him the rulership in one of the fortresses..." Quoted by al-Maqqarī, *Nafḥ al-ṭīb, op. cit.,* Vol. I, p. 201.

   Another evidence of this political confusion is the story narrated by Ibn al-Khaṭīb saying that the Andalusian territories were in the hands of robbers and warlords whose alliance Ibn Hūd sought in order to become the Sulṭān of al-Andalus. See *al-Iḥāṭa,* 2, p. 91.
6. Ibn al-Khaṭīb: *al-iḥāṭa,* 2, pp. 90-91. Huici Miranda is of the opinion that Ibn Hūd's insurrection personified Spanish Muslims against the Berber Al-Muwaḥḥidūn. See article "Gharnāṭa" in *Encyclopedia of Islam* (Leiden: 1965), Vol. II, p. 1014.

7. Ibn al-Khaṭīb (*al-iḥāṭa*, 2, p. 59) mentions that Muḥammad was born on 22 Jumāda al-ākhira in the year 739/1338.

8. *Ibid.*, p. 4.

9. *Ibid.*, p. 9.

10. Ibn al-Khaṭīb attributes this revolt to the negligence of Riḍwān. *Ibid.*, p. 11.

11. Ibn Khaldūn, *Kitāb al-'Ibar*, Vol. 7, p.637.

12. Ibn Khaldūn provides more details of this event. For him the cause of this revolt was the faqīh Ibn Marzūq - a scholar and *ṣūfī* connected with the *ribāṭ* of Abū Madyan. Ibn Marzūq was so influential that Abū Sālim had left almost all of his affairs in Ibn Marzūq's hands. This antagonized other officers at the court. Consequently, 'Umar b. 'Abd Allāh, the Wazīr at the court conspired with Garcia Antoine, the Andalusian Christian who was at the head of the mercenary soldiers. Abū Sālim was killed. Soon after 'Umar b. 'Abd Allāh, apprehending the plan of Garcia, succeeded in assassinating him and thus became the virtual ruler. Ibn Khaldūn, *Kitāb al-'ibar*, Vol. VII, pp. 648ff.

13. Ibn al-Khaṭīb gives no detail, and mentions the name of 'Umar b. 'Abd Allāh in derogatory terms (*khabīth:* wicked), *al-Iḥāṭa*, p. 14. But Ibn Khaldūn, giving the details, takes the credit to himself. He narrates that 'Umar b. 'Abd Allāh was his friend, and that he advised 'Umar to surrender Ronda to Sulṭān Muḥammad V (*Kitāb al-'ibar*, p. 694). Ibn al-Khaṭīb, in *A'māl al-a'lām fī man būyi'a qabl al-iḥtilām* (ed. Lévi-Provençal. Bayrut, 1956, p. 314) however, takes credit for this event to himself by mentioning the same reasons that Ibn Khaldūn gives. Interestingly enough at another place Ibn Khaldūn mentions that 'Umar b. 'Abd Allāh, who, after killing Abū Sālim had taken over the Marīnī throne, was looking for a proper candidate for the throne from the Marīnī family. He found the Marīnī prince Muḥammad, then in the custody of the Castillians, to be the most proper choice. Since Muḥammad V was on good terms with the Castillians, 'Umar b. 'Abd Allāh promised him the surrender of Ronda if he would procure the release of the prince from Castille (*Kitāb al-'ibar*, Vol. 7, p. 659).

14. Ibn al-Khaṭīb mentions this in reference to two offices: in case of the Wizāra, he says: "His prudence demanded to neglect this office entirely, even though it was essential in the political and financial administration [This resolution was made] to avoid the evils that had come out of it before...". (*al-Iḥāṭa*, II, p. 15). He repeats the same reference in case of Shaykh al-ghuzāt (p. 20).

15. *Al-Iḥāṭa* II, p. 17.

16. *Ibid.*

17. *Ibid.*, p. 48 ff.

18. The details of these campaigns are provided by Ibn al-Khaṭīb, *al-Iḥāṭa*, II, PP. 48-59.

19. See Ibn Khaldūn, *Al-'ibar*, vol. 7, pp. 695 ff.

20. 'Abbādī, in his comments on Ibn al-Khaṭīb's *Mi'yār al-ikhtibār* (*Mushāhadāt Lisān al-Dīn Ibn al-Khaṭīb fī bilād al-maghrib wa'l Andalus*, Iskandariya, 1958, p. 99, n.2) notes that this exchange was well known. Many Spanish Christians knew Arabic; similarly, many Andalusian Muslims knew the Castillian and Aragonese languages. Frequent debates and disputations on religious and academic subjects took place. Ibn al-Khaṭīb states that a Muslim scholar Muḥammad b. Lubb al- Kan'ānī, wandered in Spanish lands debating with priests. Another, Muḥammad Raqūṭī went to Murcia to teach Jews and Christians. 'Abdullāh b. Sahl was well known in mathematics. His fame reached as far as Toledo, and many scholars came to Baeza to study with him.

21. 'Inān, *Nihāyat al-Andalus* (Cairo: Maṭba'at al-Miṣr, 1958) p. 432; *Nafḥ al-ṭib*. Vol. I, p. 207.

22. Gaudefroy-Demombynes, "Histoire des Benou'l-Aḥmar", *Journal Asiatique*, vol. xii (1898), p. 340: n. 61.

23. This *Zahīr* is mentioned by Ibn al-Khaṭīb in his *al-Iḥāṭa* in those parts which still remain in MS. preserved in the historical section of Gayangos Collection. We are quoting it here from the excerpts in an article by Muḥammad Kamāl Shabāna, "Shuyūkh ghuzāt al-maghāriba fī andalus kamā arrakha lahum Ibn al-Khaṭīb fi *al-Ihāta*" in *al-Baḥth al-'ilmī*, (December-January, 1968), pp. 134-136.

24. Ibn al-Khaṭīb, *al-Iḥāṭa,* Vol. II, p.20.
25. For details see the notice of Muḥammad al-Ghanī Billāh in Ibn al-Khaṭīb, *al-Iḥāṭa,* Vol. II, pp. 48-59.
26. As quoted by Maqqarī, *Nafḥ al-ṭīb,* Vol. I, p. 202.
27. 'Inān, *Nihāyat al-andalus,* p. 426.
28. For the details of this event see Ibn Khaldūn, *Kitāb al-'ibar,* Vol. VII, pp. 695 ff.
29. *Ibid.*
30. Abu'l Ḥasan al-Nubāhī, *al-Marqabat al-'ulya*, p. 49.
31. Roger Idris, "Réflexions sur le Malikisme sous les Umayyades d'Espagne", *Atti del Terzo Congresso di studi Arabi i Islamici* (Napoli, 1967), p. 399.
32. Ibn Khaldūn, *op. cit.*, p. 694.
33. Ibn al-Khaṭīb, *A'māl...* pp. 78-79.
34. *Al-Katībat al-kāmina fī man laqaynāhu bi al-andalus min shu'arā' al-mi'at al-thāmina,* ed. Iḥsān 'Abbās, (Bayrut: Dār al-Thaqāfa, 1963) pp. 146-152.
35. See for instance: R. Dozy, *Histoire des musulmans d'Espagne,* Vol. I (Leiden, 1932), pp. 286ff; and Lévi-Provençal, *Histoire de l'Espagne musulmane,* Vol. I (Paris, 1950) pp. 149ff.
36. Ibn Khaldūn, *Muqaddima* (Cairo, 1320 A.H.), p. 425.
37. I. Goldziher, "The Spanish Arabs and Islam", Translation from Spanish by J. de Semogyi, *Muslim World,* Vol. LIII (1963), p. 13 and *passim.*
38. Quoted by J.T. Monroe, *Islam and the Arabs in Spanish Scholarship* (Leiden, 1970), p. 233.
39. Hussain Monés, "Le role des homme de religion dans l'histoire de l'Espagne musulmane jusque'à la fin du Califat", *Studia Islamica,* XX (1964), 49ff.
40. Among many others see the recent thesis in Jamīl Abū'l Naṣr, *A History of the Maghrib* (Cambridge, 1971), p. 11.
41. Monroe, *Islam and the Arabs in Spanish Scholarship*, p. 233.
42. Monés, 50 ff.
43. Provençal (*Histoire de l'Espagne musulmane*, p. 149) says: "Dès cette époque, en effet, on vit se constituer, principalement dans la capitale..., une sorte d'aristocratie, à la fois religieuse et intellectuelle, composée par les fakihs ou juristes-theologiens malikites".
44. Roger Idris, "Réflexious sur le Malikism sous les Umayyades d'Espagne," p. 399.
45. For details see Dozy, *Histoire des musulmans d'Espagne*, p. 288 ff.
46. See above note no: 21.
47. See the subsequent chapter on Shāṭibī's *Fatāwā.*
48. E.I.J. Rosenthal, *Political Thought in Medieval Islam* (Cambridge, 1962), p. 44.
49. Salāwī, *al-Istiqṣā'* (Dār al-Bayḍā', 1954), Vol. III, p. 101, recounts that a Granadan envoy was punished by the Marini Qāḍī for drinking.
50. The genealogical superiority is very often expressed in the eulogies of the court poet Ibn Zumruk. This aspect is officially expressed particularly in *finā' al-aswad* in al-Ḥamrā' of which the following inscription is very indicative:

فيـا وارث الانصـــار لا عـــن كلالـــة   تـراث جـــلال يســـتخف الرواسـيا

'Inān has noted that there may be some epigraphical errors in Arabic as the local workmen, especially during renovation, were not proficient in the language. For details see 'Inān, *al-Āthār al-andalusiyya al-bāqiya* (Cairo, 1956), p. 170, and *Nafḥ al-ṭīb* (Cairo: 1302 H), vol. 4, p. 308.
51. Ibn Sa'īd, *al-Mughrib fī ḥulā al-maghrib,* Vol. I (Cairo. Dār al-Ma'ārif, 1953), p. 57 and Vol. II, (1955), p. 109. For an explanatory note on the authors of this work see Shawqī Ḍayf's (the editor) introduction.
52. Ibn al-Khaṭīb, *al-Iḥāṭa*: vol. II, p. 60.

53. See for instance two of Ibn Zumrak's eulogies preserved by al-Maqqarī, *Nafḥ al-ṭīb,* Vol. VII, pp. 96-107 and Shīhāb al-Dīn al-Maqqarī, *Azhār al-riyāḍ,* (Cairo, 1939), vol. 2, pp. 33, 37, 94. The following verses illustrate our point:

وخص انصاره الاعلين صفوته   واسكنوا من جوار الله اعلاه
انصار ملته اعلام بيعته   مناقب شرفت اثنى بها الله
لا غرو ان فقت الملوك سياده   اذ كان جدك سيد الانصار
السابقون الاولون الي الهدى   والمصطفون لنصرة المختار
ورثت هذا الفخر يا مالك الهدى   عن كل من آوى النبى ومن نصر
من شاء يعرف فخرهم و كما لهم   فليتل وحى الله فيهم والسير
ابناؤهم ابناء نصر بعدهم   بسيوفهم دين الاله قد انتصر

54. Ibn Sa'īd, as quoted in *Nafḥ al-ṭīb*. Vol. I, p.206.
55. See Maribel Fierro, "The Treatises against Innovations (*Kutub al-bid'a*)", in *Der Islam*, vol. 69 (1992), pp. 204-246. Out of eleven books she discusses, six are written by Mālikīs, four of them in Spain.
56. See for instance the Ẓahīr of Qāḍī Ibn 'Āṣim for his appointment as Qāḍī. This Ẓahīr is preserved by al-Maqqarī, *Nafḥ al-ṭīb,* Vol. VIII, p. 262-268.
57. 'Inān, *Nihāyat al-Andalus,* pp. 426f.
58. Aḥmad Bābā, *Nayl al-ibtihāj,* (Cairo: 'Abbās b. 'Abd al-Salām, 1351 A.H.) p. 282.
59. *Al-Iḥāṭa, op. cit.,* Vol. I, p.71
60. Al-Maqqarī, quoting Ibn Sa'īd, says that the inspector of the market, on his mount, passed through the market. A balance was carried by one of his assistants in which he weighed the bread as its weight and price were fixed. A small child or a charming girl was sent to buy the bread. This bread was weighed and inspected. The same process was followed for meat and other merchandise. See *Nafḥ al-ṭīb*, vol. I, pp. 203 ff.
61. The rules of Islamic law in this respect were based on the Qur'anic verses prohibiting usury and speculative transactions. For instance the verse: "O ye who believe! Devour not usury, doubling and quadrupling (the sum lent). Observe your duty to Allah, that ye may be successful" (3: 129), and "O ye who believe! Strong drink and games of chance and idols and divining arrows are only an infamy of Satan's handiwork, leave it aside in order that ye may succeed." (5: 90).
62. See Abū'l Ḥasan 'Alī b. Yūsuf al-Ḥakīm, *al-Dawḥat al-mushtabika fī ḍawābiṭ dār al-sikka,* Ed. Ḥusayn Mu'nis (Madrid, 1960), pp. 52-53.
63. For instance see the notice of Qāḍī Ibn 'Ayyāsh in al-Nubāhī, *al-Marqabat al-'ulyā*, pp. 20-21.
64. This point is explained by R. Levy in *The Social Structure of Islam* (Cambridge, 1957), pp. 291-293.
65. Although it is difficult to find specific evidence on the number and quality of these tracts of land, yet, the large number of fatwās requested about *aḥbās* which were attached to mosques and the fuqahā's complaints when these lands were made subject to tax are indicative of the point we are making. For such *fatāwā* see Wansharīsī, *al-Mi'yār al-mughrib* (Fas, 1314-15 A.H.), Vol. VII, 68 ff.
66. See *Nafḥ al-ṭīb,* Vol. I, p. 205.
67. Ibn Khaldūn, *Muqaddima, op. cit.,* pp. 407 f.
68. Shāṭibī, *al-Muwāfaqāt* (Cairo: Raḥmāniya, n.d.), Vol. I, p.97.
69. Paul Nwiya [*Ibn 'Abbād de Ronda* (Beyrouth, 1961), p. XXVII] mentions Ābilī, Ibn 'Abd al-Salām and Qarāfī among those who opposed the establishment of *madāris*. They regarded such institutions as *bid'a*.

70. Lévi-Provençal, *Inscriptions arabes d'Espagne* (Leyde: Brill, 1930), p. 158ff, particularly see n. 1, where Ibn al-Khaṭīb is quoted calling this *madrasa* as *bikr al-madāris*.
71. Nwiya, *op. cit.*
72. *Nafḥ al-ṭīb,* Vol. I, p. 205.
73. Muhsin Mahdi, *Ibn Khaldūn's Philosophy of History,* p. 35, n. 2.
74. See al-Nubāhī, *op. cit.,* p. 201.
75. Qāḍī 'Iyāḍ (d. 544/1149) and Ibn Ḥirzihim issued a *fatwā* giving orders to burn Ghazālī's *Iḥyā' 'ulūm al-dīn*.
76. *Nayl*, p. 261.
77. Iḥsān 'Abbās, Introduction to Ibn al-Khaṭīb's *al-Katībat al-kāmina*, p. 10f.
78. Nubāhī, *al-Marqabat al-'ulya*, p. 201.
79. *Ibid.*
80. *Ibid.*, p. 202.
81. *Nafḥ al-ṭīb,* Vol. VII, p. 49 ff.
82. Among them the following has been edited and studied by Abdel Magid Turki, in his article "Lisān al-Dīn Ibn al-Ḥaṭīb (713-76/1313-74), Juriste d'après son oeuvre inéditè, Muṯlā al-Ṭarīqa fi Ḏamm al-Waṯīqa [*Muthlā al-ṭarīqa fi dhamm al-wathīqa*], *Arabica*, Vol. XVI (1969), pp. 155-211 and 280-311.
83. E. Sharqāwī, *Religion and Philosophy in the Thought of Fakhr al-Dīn al-Rāzī* (unpublished thesis, McGill University, 1970), pp. 285f.
84. Brockelmann, *G.A.L.* I, p. 667 and *SI,* 921.
85. Makhlūf, *Shajarat al-nūr al-zakiyya,* Vol. I (Cairo, 1930-31), pp. 167-168.
86. *Ibid.*, p. 218.
87. Muhsin Mahdi, *op. cit.*, p. 30 n. 3.
88. *Ibid.*, p. 35, n. 2.
89. P. Nwiya, *op. cit.*, p. XVIII.
90. J. Spencer Trimingham, *The Sufi Orders in Islam* (Oxford, 1971), p. 46.
91. Brockelmann, *G.A.L. S.I,* P. 830. Margaret Smith, *Al-Ghazālī, The Mystic* (London: Luzac, 1944), in Chapter XIII mentions critics of al-Ghazālī and omits al-Ṭurṭūshī whose refutation of *Iḥyā* is one of the most significant contributions towards a criticism of al-Ghazālī. The reason why she omitted this work is probably her statement about the co-operation between al-Ghazālī and al-Ṭurṭūshī. She said, "..al-Ghazālī in consultation with Abu Bakr Turtushi, a well-known authority on law and tradition (d. 520/1126), addressed letters of advice to Yūsuf (bin Tāshufīn), urging him to govern with justice..." (p. 21). She made this statement on the authority of De Slane's translation of Ibn Khaldūn's statement in this connection. The original statement by Ibn Khaldūn, however, as we quote below, does not imply a co-operation between al-Ghazālī and al-Ṭurṭūshī. Ibn Khaldūn's sentences are as follows:

وخاطبه الامام الغزالى والقاضى ابوبكر الطرطوشى يحضانه على العدل والتمسك بالخير

(*Kitāb al'ibar, op. cit.*, Vol. VI, p. 386).
De Slane's translation [*Histoire des Berberes,* Vol. II, (Paris, 1972), p. 82] is as follows: "L'imam El-Ghazzali et le cadi Abou Bekr-et- Tertouchi lui addresserent aussi des lèttres de conseils et l'engagerent de la manière la plus pressante à gouverner avec justice..."
92. A.M.M. Mackeen, "The Early History of Sufism in the Maghrib prior to Al-Shadhili (d. 650/1256)" in the *Journal of the American Oriental Society,* Vol. 91 (1971) p. 402.
93. Muḥammad al-Zabīdī al-Murtaḍā, *Ithāf sādat al-muttaqīn,* commentary on *Iḥyā' 'ulūm al-dīn,* written in 1193 A.H. (Cairo, 1893), Introduction, Vol. I, p. 10.
94. *ibid.*, p. 27.
95. Ambroxio Huici Miranda, "The Iberian Peninsula and Sicily", in *The Cambridge History of Islam,* Vol. II (Cambridge: Cambridge University Press, 1970), p. 427.
96. R. Arnaldez, "Ibn Rushd", *E.I.* new edition, p. 910, referring to D.B. Macdonald's view on this point.

97. George Marçais, "Note sur les ribats en Berbérie" in "*Mélanges René Basset,* Vol. II, (Paris, 1925), p. 399. Particularly, see his article "Ribāṭ" *E.I.* (1st ed.), Vol. III, pp. 1150-1152.
98. H.A.R. Gibb, Introduction to *Travels in Asia and Africa* 1325-1354 (London, 1963), p. 34.
99. Ibn Baṭṭūṭa, *Tuḥfat al-Nuẓẓār fī gharā'ib al-amṣār wa 'ajā'ib al-asfār*, Vol. II, Ed. 'Awāmiri Bek and Jād al-Mawlā (Cairo, 1934), p. 294.
100. 'Inān, *Nihāya,* p. 449.
101. For instance Ibn Qabbāb was appointed to supervise a trust donated by the Sulṭān to a Zāwiya.
102. See *al-Iḥāṭa,* I, 71, and Wansharīsī, *Mi'yār* IX, 31-36.
103. Shihāb al-Dīn al-Qarāfī, *al-Furūq,* Vol. IV (Cairo: Dār Iḥyā Kutub al-'Arabiya, 1346 A.H.), p. 210.
104. Ibn 'Abd al-Salām, *Qawā'id al-aḥkām fī maṣāliḥ al-anām* (Cairo: Istiqāma, n.d.)
105. S. Trimingham, *op. cit.*, p. 50.
106. Maqqarī, *Nafḥ al-ṭīb,* Vol. VII, *op. cit.*, pp. 232-249 gives long extracts from this work.
107. *Ibid.*, p. 261.
108. *Ibid.*, p. 189-90.
109. P. Nwiya, *Ibn 'Abbad de Ronda,* op. cit., pp. XXXIX and XLI relates a similar chain from Ibn Qunfudh. He observes certain historical defaults in this chain, and provides a detailed criticism on this point.
110. It is curious to note that in the third patch Ibn al-'Arabī (Qāḍī Abū Bakr) and Ibn Ḥirzihim are juxtaposed with Ghazālī. Ibn Ḥirzihim, as has been pointed out above, is known for his *fatwā* against Ghazālī's *Iḥyā',* and Qāḍī Ibn 'Arabī's commentary bears a general trend of opposition to Sufism.
111. *Nafḥ al-ṭīb,* Vol. VII, p. 124-125 quoting from *al-Fatḥ al-munīr.*
112. Shāṭibī's *fatwā* issued in 786/1384, preserved by Wansharīsī, *op. cit.*, Vol. XI, p. 34.
113. In the Muslim East the practice of celebrating the Prophet's birthday started earlier, but in the Muslim West, according to Salāwī, it was started by the Marīnī ruler, Abū Yūsuf Ya'qūb in 691/1291, from whence it came to Andalus. (Salāwī, *al-Istiqṣā', op. cit.*, Vol. 3, p. 290). Ibn Khaldūn, *op. cit.*, pp. 864, 881 and 885 mentions how on three such occasions poems were recited. These celebrations lasted for a few days. Verses from the Qur'an were recited, and animal sacrifices were offered. Cf. Maqqarī, *Azhār al-riyāḍ* (Cairo, 1939), Vol. I, p. 245. Some fuqahā' considered this a *bid'a,* and opposed it. Shāṭibī, in a *fatwā,* refused the validity of a will which wished to dispose of one third of the property for the purpose of the Prophet's birthday celebration. Wansharīsī, *op. cit.*, Vol. IX, p. 181.
114. Trimingham, *op. cit.*, p. 50.
115. Ibn Baṭṭūṭa, *op. cit.*, p. 294.
116. See for the description of this rural town now called Canales in Ibn al-Khaṭīb, *Khaṭrāt al-ṭayf fī riḥlat al-shitā' wa'l ṣayf* in A. M. 'Abbādī, *Mushāhadāt, op. cit.*, p. 33 and 'Abbādī's note no 4.
117. See Wansharīsī, Vol. IX, p. 31.
118. *Ibid.*, pp. 34-36.
119. The best contemporary sources of information on the economy and geography of this period, in our opinion, are Ibn al-Khaṭīb's following two treatises: *Khaṭrāt al-ṭayf fī riḥlat al-shitā' wa al-ṣayf and Mi'yār al-ikhtibār fī dhikr al-ma'āhid wa'l diyār,* edited and published by A.M. 'Abbādī, in *Mushāhadāt Lisān al-Dīn ibn al-Khaṭīb, op. cit.* The above must be supplemented with the study of *fatāwā* of this period (i.e. 14th century) by López Ortiz, "Fatwas granadianas de los siglos XIV y XV", *Al-Andalus,* Vol. VII (1941), pp. 73-127.
120. Lévi-Provençal, "Al-Andalus", $E.I.^2$, pp. 486-492.
121. Quoted in Maqqarī, *Nafḥ al-ṭīb,* Vol. I, p. 124, translation Pascual de Gayangos, *The History of the Mohammedan Dynasties in Spain,* Vol. I (Cairo: 1902), p. 17.
122. Ibn al-Khaṭīb, *al-Iḥāṭa,* Vol. I, p. 32.

123. Imamuddin, *A Political History of Spain,* p. 294.

124. Cf. Seybold, "Granada", in *E.I.* (1st edition), Vol. II, p. 176.

125. *Al-Iḥāṭa, op. cit.*, I, p. 38.

126. H.A.R. Gibb, *Ibn Baṭṭūṭa,* p. 319.

127. 'Inān, *Nihāyat al-andalus,* p. 430. 'Inān does not indicate his source but probably he derives this information from Prescott, *History of Ferdinand and Isabella the Catholic* on which he relies for most of his data of this period.

128. A detailed description of the reserves of the Nasrid treasury are given by 'Abd Allāh Muḥammad b. al-Ḥaddād al-Wādī Āshī as quoted by Muḥammad Kamāl Shabāna, "al-ḥālat al-iqtiṣādiyya bi'l-andalus khilāl al-qarn al-thāmin al-hijrī" in *al-Baḥth al-'ilmī,* Rabāṭ, Vol. III (August, 1966), p. 137. Unfortunately, Shabāna's reference to the original source is not clear.

129. For this information we have relied on López Ortiz's above-mentioned study. See particularly pp. 95-97.

130. *Nafḥ al-ṭīb,* Vol. I, p. 202.

131. López Ortiz, *op. cit.*, p. 96.

132. Imamuddin, *op. cit.*, p. 294.

133. López Ortiz. *op. cit.*, p. 95.

134. Antonio Vives, "Indicacion del Valor en las Mondedas Arabigo - Españolas" in D.E. Saavedra. (Ed.) *Homenaje* à D. Fransisco Codera, (Zaragoza, 1904), p. 522. Also, see D.G. Codera y Zaidin, *Tratado de Numismatica Arabi-Española*, (Madrid, 1879), p. 231.

135. See H.W. Hazard's analysis of the metrology of the coins of North Africa (which partly includes Spain as well) in *The Numismatic History of Late Medieval North Africa,* (American Numismatics Society, New York, 1952), pp. 48-49. Hazard says that Zirid dīnār was 4. 11 - 4.35 grams in weight and 22-24 milimeters in diameter. The Muwaḥḥidūn introduced double dīnārs averaging 4.55 grams and 27-32 milimeters, whereas their normal dīnār averaged 2.27 grams and 19-22 milimeters. The Nasrid dinar seems to have been better than its predecessors. Two specimens registered in M.H. Lavoix, *Catalogue des monnaies musulmanes de la Bibliothèque Nationale*, Vol. V (Paris, 1891), pp. 328-329, provide the following data:
    (1) Catalogue no: 780: Yūsuf b. Muḥammad (1333-1354), gold; weight 4.65 grams, diameter 31 milimeters.
    (2) Catalogue no: 781: Muḥammad V al-Ghanī Billāh (1354-1359 and - 1362-1391), gold: weight 4.70 grams; diameter 32 milimeters.

136. Luis Seco de Lucena, in *Documentos Arabigo-Granadinos,* Instituto des Estudios Islamicos, (Madrid, 1961), studied a number of documents of a judicial nature belonging to fifteenth century Granada. In his analysis he found very interesting data bearing on the social and economic conditions of that period. We have derived our information from Lucena's analysis of currency in these documents as given by him on pp. XLVI-XLVIII.

137. Most probably Lucena is here referring to Antonio Vives, *op. cit.*, and Fransisco Codera, *op. cit.*

138. See López Ortiz, *op. cit.*, p. 94f.

139. See such statements by early historians and geographers as quoted extensively by Maqqarī, *Nafḥ al-ṭīb*, Vol. I, pp. 124-194, but particularly pp. 136-138, where the description by Rāzī, the geographer, is quoted at length.

140. "Andalus" $E.I.^2$, p. 491.

141. López Ortiz, *op. cit.*, pp. 97, 106f.

142. *Ibid.*, p. 106ff.

143. *Ibid.*

144. *Ibid.*, p. 109.

145. *Ibid.*, p. 103.

146. In the days of Muḥammad V, the irrigation system was further improved. See Imamuddin, *op. cit.*, p. 294.

147. On this point we are relying on E.F. Heckscher, "Mercantilism" in H.W. Spiegel, *The Development of Economic Thought* (New York: Science Books, 1966), pp. 32-41.

148. López Ortiz, *op. cit.*, p. 114.
149. *Ibid.*, pp. 114ff.
150. *Ibid.*, p. 110.
151. Ibn al-Khaṭīb, *al-Iḥāṭa,* Vol. I, p. 15.
152. Louis Bertrand and Charles Petrie, *The History of Spain,* trans. W.B. Wells (New York, 1934), p. 204.
153. Ibn al-Khaṭīb, *Mufākharāt mālaqa wa salā,* in 'Abbādī, *Mushāhadāt... op. cit.*, pp. 77-90.
154. *Nafḥ al-ṭīb*, Vol. I, 154.
155. S.M. Batsieva, "Ibn Khaldūn et son milieu social", *Atti del Terzo Congresso,*, p. 138.
156. 'Inān, *op. cit.*, p. 429.
157. *Ibid.*, p. 428.
158. Ibn Khaldūn, *Kitāb al-'Ibar*, vol. 7, p. 694f.
159. *Ibid.* p. 695 ff.
160. Batsieva, p. 138.
161. López Ortiz, *op. cit.*, p. 95.
162. 'Inan, *op. cit.*, p. 428.
163. *Ibid.*, p. 97.
164. *Ibid.*, p. 100.
165. *Ibid.*, p. 110.
166. López Ortiz, *op. cit.*, p. 101.
167. *Ibid.*, p. 98.
168. *Ibid.*, p. 94f.
169. Dozy, *Supplement aux dictionnaires Arabes, Vol. II (Paris, 1967), p. 275.*
170. Al-Qur'an, 90: 12-13: "What would make thee know what is an uphill task? The freeing of a slave or captive."
171. Lane, *Arabic English Lexicon,* (London: 1874), Vol. 6, p. 2431.
172. E.N. Van Kleffens, *Hispanic Law until the End of the Middle Ages* (Edingburgh, 1968). p. 105, no. 3, refers to the Hispanic legal term "alfaqueques" meaning the administrator of the property of the prisoners of war.
173. L. Bertrand, *The History of Spain,* p. 200. This observation is supported by Ibn Baṭṭūṭa's narration of such an attempt by the notables in Malaga (see note 174 below). Ibn al-Khaṭīb also praised the people of Maḷaga for the purchase of freedom of such prisoners. See *Mi'yār al-ikhtibār, op. cit.*, p. 78.
174. Ibn Baṭṭūṭa, *Tuḥfat al-nuẓẓār ... op. cit.*, pp. 290-292.
175. See al-Wansharīsī, *op. cit.*, Vol. II, p. 127.
176. See above note 172.
177. López Ortiz, *op. cit.*, p. 95.
178. *Ibid.*, p. 95.
179. 'Inān, *Nihāyat al-Andalus*, pp. 426f.
180. See the story of the litigant in case of *ḥabs*, in *Al-Mi'yār,* vol. 7, pp. 70-74.
181. Shihāb al-Dīn al-Qarāfī, *Al-Iḥkām fi tamyīz al-fatāwā 'an al-aḥkām.* (Edited by) 'Abd al-Fattāḥ Abū Ghudda. (Ḥalab: Maṭbū'āt Islāmiyya, 1967).
182. *Ibid.*, p. 18.
183. *Ibid.*, p. 20.
184. *Ibid.*, pp. 22-23.
185. *Ibid.*, p. 32.
186. This conclusion is drawn from the following sources: López Ortiz, *Fatawa Granadinas... op. cit.*, p. 91; Wansharīsī, *al-Mi'yār...op. cit.*, Vol. II, p. 166; Vol. V, 186f.
187. *Nayl*, p. 265.
188. *Shajara*, p. 230
189. This treatise was studied by Abdelmagid Turki, see above note 82.
190. Ibid., pp. 280, 284 and *passim.*
191. E.N. Van Kleffens, *Hispanic Law until the End of the Middle Ages,* p. 124.
192. *Ibid.*, p. 154.

193. *Ibid.*, p. 74.
194. *Ibid.*, p. 77.
195. *Ibid.*, p. 79.
196. *Ibid.*, p. 145.
197. *Ibid.*, p. 146.
198. *Ibid.*, p. 147.
199. *Ibid.*, pp. 176-78.
200. *Ibid.*
201. Henry Lacerte, *The Nature of Canon Law according to Suárez* (Ottawa: University of Ottawa Press, 1964), p. 3.
202. *Ibid.*, pp. 20ff.

CHAPTER TWO

SHĀṬIBĪ'S LIFE AND WORKS

We know virtually nothing about Shāṭibī's family or his early life.[1] His full name is reported as Abū Isḥāq Ibrāhīm b. Mūsā b. Muḥammad al-Lakhmī al-Shāṭibī. The most we can learn by deduction from his name is that he belonged to the Lakhmī Arab tribe. We know also that his immediate family came from Shāṭiba (Xativa or Jativa). This latter *nisba* has misled some scholars to maintain that Shāṭibī was born or lived in Shāṭiba before coming to Granada.[2] This is not possible because Shāṭiba was taken by the Christians a few decades ago, and, according to the chronicles, the last Muslims were driven out of Shāṭiba in 645/1247.[3]

Shāṭibī grew up in Granada and acquired his entire training in this city which was the capital of the Naṣrī Kingdom. Shāṭibī's youth coincided with the reign of Sulṭān Muḥammad V al-Ghanī Bi'llāh, a very eventful period in the history of Granada. For various reasons explained in the preceding chapter, the city had become a centre of attraction for scholars from all parts of North Africa. It is not necessary to list here all the scholars who visited Granada or who were attached to the Naṣrī court, names such as Ibn Khaldūn[4] and Ibn al-Khaṭīb[5] are sufficient to illustrate our point.

It appears that, according to normal practice, Shāṭibī started his education in Arabic language, grammar and literature. He began his studies with Abū 'Abd Allāh Muḥammad b. 'Alī al-Fakhkhār al-Ilbīrī[6] who was known as 'the master of grammarians' (*Shaykh al-nuḥāt*) in Andalus. Shāṭibī stayed with him until the latter's death in 754/1353. Shāṭibī's notes about al-Fakhkhār in the *Ifādāt* illustrate clearly that he received a thorough training in matters pertaining to the Arabic language.[7] His second teacher in the Arabic language was Abū'l Qāsim al-Sharīf al-Sabtī (760/1358), author of the well-known commentary on the *Maqṣūra* of Ḥāzim.[8] He was called "The Bearer of the Standard of Rhetoric".[9]

The famous Andalusian *faqīh* Abū Sa'īd ibn Lubb began his lectures in the Madrasa Naṣriyya in 754/1353.[10] Most probably he succeeded al-Fakhkhār on the latter's death. Ibn Lubb was well versed in *fiqh* and was recognized for his "rank of *ikhtiyār* (decision by preference) in respect to *fatwā*"[11] Shāṭibī's training in *fiqh* was almost entirely completed with Ibn Lubb.

Shāṭibī owes much to this man, still as we shall discuss later in this chapter, he entered into controversy on a number of issues with Ibn Lubb also.

We need not recount the names of all of Shāṭibī's teachers;[12] it seems he benefited from all the well-known scholars in Granada as well as those who visited Granada on diplomatic missions. Among such scholars mention must be made of Abū 'Abd Allāh al-Maqqarī[13] who came to Granada in 757/1356 on a diplomatic mission sent by the Marīnī Sulṭān Abū 'Inān.[14] Maqqarī had an eventful career. Sulṭān Abū 'Inān chose him as his chief Qāḍī, but soon Qāḍī Abū 'Abd Allāh al-Fishtālī succeeded in having him deposed. Maqqarī was sent to Granada from where he refused to return to Fez. The Naṣrī Sulṭān arrested and sent him back. Abū'l Qāsim al-Sabtī and Abū'l Barakāt Ibn al-Ḥājj al-Balfiqī, both qāḍīs in Granada, followed him to Fez to secure his release. Nevertheless, Maqqarī was tried by al-Fishtālī and convicted.[15]

Maqqarī's academic tastes were versatile. He is the author of a book on Arabic grammar. He was known as holding the rank of "*muḥaqqiq*"[16] (expert on the application of general principles of the [Maliki] school to particular cases). Maqqarī seems to have acquainted Shāṭibī with Razism in *uṣūl al-fiqh*. He started to compose an abridgement of Fakhr al-Dīn al-Rāzī's (606/1209) *al-Muḥaṣṣal.*[17] He is also the author of a commentary on the *Mukhtaṣar* of Ibn Ḥājib who introduced Razism into Mālikī *uṣūl al-fiqh*. Maqqarī is also responsible for initiating Shāṭibī into Sufism - a special *silsila* we have described in the preceding chapter. Maqqarī is known for his book *al-Ḥaqā'iq wa'l-raqā'iq fī al-taṣawwuf.*[18]

Mention must also be made of Shāṭibī's two more teachers who introduced him to *falsafa* and *kalām* and other sciences which are known in the Islamic classification as rational sciences (*al-'ulūm al-'aqliyya*) as opposed to the traditional sciences (*al-'ulūm al-naqliyya*). Abū 'Alī Manṣūr al-Zawāwī[19] came to Granada in 753/1352. Ibn al-Khaṭīb praises him highly for his scholarship in traditional as well as rational sciences. He appears to have run into frequent controversies with jurists in Granada. He was accused of various things. Finally in 765/1363, he was expelled from the Andalus.[20] Shāṭibī mentions Zawāwī quoting his teacher, Ibn Musfir, saying that in his commentary on the Qur'ān, Rāzī relied on four books, all written by the Mu'tazilīs; in *uṣūl al-dīn,* he used Abū'l Ḥusayn's *Kitāb al-dalā'il*, in *uṣūl al-fiqh,* his *al-Mu'tamad*, in *uṣūl al-tafsīr,* he relied on Qāḍī 'Abd al-Jabbār's *Kitāb al-tafsīr* (?) and in *uṣūl al-'Arabiyya,* and *bayān* on Zamakhsharī's *Kashshāf.*[21] This comment seems to imply that Zawāwī and his teacher saw in Rāzī a continuation of Mu'tazilī *kalām*.

Al-Sharīf al-Tilimsānī (d. 771/1369) also seems to have been critical of Razism. He studied with Ābilī and specialized in the rational sciences. Ibn Khaldūn mentions that Tilimsānī secretly taught Ibn 'Abd al-Salām the books of

Ibn Sīnā and Ibn Rushd.[22] Tilimsānī was well-versed in both the traditional and the rational sciences. Contemporary scholars laid stress on his attainment of the rank of *mujtahid*.[23] Ibn 'Arafa lamented Tilimsānī's death as the demise of the rational sciences.[24]

From the above account of his notable teachers it may be concluded that Shāṭibī's training must have been quite thorough in both the traditional and the rational sciences. His main interest, however, as we shall see from the list of his works, was in the Arabic language and *uṣūl al-fiqh*, particularly the latter.

We do not find any allusion to Shāṭibī's career or to his profession. Three conjectures, however, can be made. First in Shāṭibī's account of the accusations brought by people against him, on one occasion it can be deduced that he was an *imām* and also a *khaṭīb* in a certain mosque. During his period of trial, it can be assumed that he was dismissed from these posts.[25] The second conjecture can be made on the basis of the *fatwā*s asked from him, that he was a *muftī*. Since he is never called *al-mushāwar*, it is difficult to maintain if he was officially appointed to this office. He, however, had a number of disciples. From this, a third conjecture can be made, that he taught in the *madrasa* of Gharnāṭa. Among his disciples, Ibn 'Āṣim is noteworthy. He became the chief *qāḍī* of Granada. He is known for his *Tuḥfat al-ḥukkām*, a compendium of rules compiled for the *qāḍī*s. He also wrote an abridgement of Shāṭibī's *al-Muwāfaqāt*.[26]

Shāṭibī died on the eighth of Sha'bān in 790/1388.[27] This date is mentioned in a verse written by one of Shāṭibī's disciples at the end of his abridgement of Shāṭibī's *al-Muwāfaqāt* entitled *Nayl al-munā*:

حتى غدت حياته منقضيه

فى عام تسعين الى سبع مائة

"Until his life came to an end in the year of ninety in seven hundred"[28]

SHĀṬIBĪ'S INTERESTS

As we have seen in the preceding chapter, *fiqh* was a very profitable and hence popular subject, but interest in *uṣūl al-fiqh* was rare in the Andalus.[29] What induced Shāṭibī to interest himself in *uṣūl al-fiqh* was his feeling that the weakness of *fiqh* in meeting the challenge of social change was due largely to its methodological and philosophical inadequacy. This weakness struck Shāṭibī very early in his education.

(1) *UṢŪL AL-FIQH*: SEARCH FOR A PHILOSOPHY OF LAW

Shāṭibī's occasional autobiographical remarks explain how he got interested in *uṣūl al-fiqh*. He writes in his book *al-I'tiṣām*:

> Ever since the curiosity of my intellect was aroused for understanding (things) and ever since my anxiety was directed towards knowledge, I always looked into its [the *Sharī'a*'s] reasons and legalities; its roots and its branches. As far as the time and my ability permitted I did not fall short of a science among the sciences, nor did I single one out of the others.
>
> I exploited my natural capacity, or rather plunged into this tumultuous sea... so much so that I feared to destroy myself in its depths... until God showed His kindness to me and clarified for me the meanings of *Sharī'a* which had been beyond my reckoning...
>
> From here I felt strong enough to walk on the path as long as God made it easier for me. I started with the principles of religion (*uṣūl al-dīn*) in theory and in practice and the substantive laws based on these principles. (It was) during this period (that) it became clear to me what were the *bid'a* and what was lawful and what was not. Comparing and collating this with the principles of religion and law (*fiqh*), I urged myself to be in the company of the group whom the Prophet had called *al-sawād al-a'ẓam* (the majority).[30]

One of the most perplexing problems for Shāṭibī was the diversity of opinions among scholars on various matters. Use of the principle of *murā'āt al-khilāf* made the problem even more complex. This principle as we shall see subsequently,[31] was employed to honour differences of opinion by treating them all as equally valid. Because of this attitude, diversity of opinions was proudly preserved even from the earliest days of Mālikī *fiqh*. Shāṭibī himself recalled that the diversity in the statements of Mālik and his companions used to occupy his mind frequently.[32]

Studying with Abū Sa'īd b. Lubb, Shāṭibī faced such perplexities very often. He states:

> I once visited our master, Abū Sa'īd b. Lubb, the *mushāwar*, along with my friends... He said, "I wish to inform you about one basic principle on which I relied in such and such a *fatwā*, and (to explain) why I intended for leniency in that". We knew about his *fatwā*... We used to dispute with him on his answer... He said, "I want to tell you a useful rule in issuing a *fatwā*. This rule is authentically known (as practised) by the scholars. The rule is not to be hard on the one who

came asking for a *fatwā*". Before this meeting various aspects in the statements of Mālik and his companions used to confuse me. But now God cleared my mind in the light of this discourse.[33]

This satisfaction, however, did not last long. Shāṭibī's indulgence in the problem of *murā'āt al-khilāf* shows that Ibn Lubb's clarification was not satisfactory. Shāṭibī felt that the body of the law was without spirit, its formalism would remain devoid of reality unless the real nature of the legal theory was investigated.[34] Shāṭibī's *al-Muwāfaqāt* was dedicated to such an investigation.

(2) *BID'A*: AN ANALYSIS OF SOCIAL AND RELIGIOUS PRACTICES

Sometimes during his career Shāṭibī was accused of introducing innovations (*bid'a*). The exact date of this period of trial cannot be known. The inquisitive mind of Shāṭibī must have led him to discussions and controversies with other *fuqahā'*. Most probably the period of trial occurred during the time he was writing his book *al-Muwāfaqāt*, as he corresponded with scholars about a number of subjects.

Shāṭibī's verses in reference to this trial indicate how he felt about these accusations. He says:

بليت ياقوم، والبلوى منوعة

بمن ادار به حتى كاد يرديني

دفع المضرة، لاجلبا لمصلحة

فحسبي الله في عقلي وفي ديني

O my people! you put me to the ordeal (*balayta*)
Whereas an ordeal shakes violently
The one who whirls with it, until it seems to destroy him.
(You condemn me) for preventing wrong, rather than
[praising] for attaining good (*maṣlaḥa*).
May God suffice me in my reason and religion.[35]

Shāṭibī recounts the story of this ordeal in *al-I'tiṣām* in the following words:

I had entered into some of the common professions (*khuṭaṭ*) such as *khiṭāba* (preaching) and *imāma* (leading the prayers). When I decided to straighten my path, I found myself a stranger among the majority of my contemporaries. The custom and practice had dominated their profession; the stains of the additional innovations had covered the original tradition (*Sunna*)... [36]

> I wavered between two choices; one to follow the *Sunna* in opposition to what people had adopted in practice. In that case I would inevitably get what an opponent to the [social] practice would get, especially when the upholders of this practice claimed that theirs was exclusively the *sunna*.... The other choice was to follow the practice in defiance of the *sunna* and the pious ancients. That would get me into deviation [from the true path]... I decided that I would rather perish following the *sunna* and to find salvation...
>
> I started acting in accordance with this decision gradually in certain matters. Soon the havoc fell upon me; blames were hurled upon me... I was accused of innovation and heresy.[37]

Shāṭibī, at this point, enumerates the following charges that were laid against him:[38]

> (1) Sometimes I was accused of saying that invocation (*du'ā*) serves no purpose... That was because I did not adhere to the practice of invocations in congregational form after the ritual prayer (*ṣalāt*).
>
> (2) I was accused of *rafḍ* (extreme Shī'ism) and of hatred against the companions... That was because I did not adhere to the practice of mentioning the names of the pious Caliphs in the *khuṭba* (Friday sermon)...
>
> (3) I was accused of saying that I favoured rising against the *a'imma* [the rulers]...That was because I did not mention their names in the *khuṭba*.
>
> (4) I was accused of affirming hardship in religion... That was because I adhered to the well-established tradition regarding legal obligations and duties in *fatwās*, while they ignored it and issued *fatwās* in accordance with what was convenient to the enquirer... [cf. Ibn Lubb's above statement.]
>
> (5) I was accused of enmity against the *awliyā' Allāh* (friends of God)... That was because I opposed certain innovating sufis who opposed the *sunna*...

Shāṭibī was accused of *bid'a* (heresy) mainly because he opposed the practices of the *fuqahā'*. Particularly, one of the controversial problems was mentioning the name of the Sulṭān in the *khuṭba* and praying for him towards the end of the ritual prayers. Shāṭibī declared this practice as *bid'a*. His action shook the foundations of the political power of the religious elite. On this issue, it is interesting to note that he was opposed by all the *qāḍīs* in Spain and North Africa as well as by some dignitaries holding government offices.[39]

Shāṭibī's above account of his trial for *bid'a* refers to the controversies that brought him into conflict with other scholars. These controversies, some of which are discussed in the following section, led Shāṭibī to write *al-I'tiṣām* in which he expounded and clarified the doctrine of *bid'a*.

DISPUTATIONS

The Granadan society was changing rapidly and its impact on Islamic Law was quite conspicuous. As discussed in the preceding chapter, introduction of new educational system, changes in the authority pattern of Granadan jurists, permeation of *taṣawwuf* and theological philosophy in the West and many other factors had produced a wide range of changes which agitated the minds of scholars of this period. Shāṭibī took keen interest in these developments and wrote to scholars disputing their opinions and practices on certain matters and raising fundamental questions about the goals and ends of Islamic law. A few of such disputations are discussed below.

(1) *TAṢAWWUF* AND *FIQH*

Shāṭibī was much worried not only by the fact that *taṣawwuf* comprised a number of rituals which he considered *bid'a* but also by the fact that *taṣawwuf* was having an adverse effect upon *fiqh* and *uṣūl*. He did not oppose the Ṣūfīs if they followed their peculiar practices individually or as a requirement of *taṣawwuf*. He opposed them when certain Ṣūfīs and *fuqahā'* suggested under the influence of *taṣawwuf*, that these practices were obligatory in a religio-legal sense. The following two issues became very prominent in this regard.

(1) The obligation of freeing the *Sirr*

A certain scholar sent an epistle to Shāṭibī in which under the rubric, "What is obligatory for a seeker of the Hereafter to observe and do", he wrote the following:

> If a certain thing distracts someone from his prayers even for a while, he must free his inner self [*sirr*] from this distraction by getting rid of it, even if these distractions number as many as fifty thousand.[40]

Shāṭibī strongly objected to this statement. He disputed its obligatory claim. He argued that if freeing the inner self were a universal obligation, it would lead to absurdity because it demands that people should get rid of their property and abjure their towns, villages and families since these were the things that constituted distractions. He added that poverty was the major source of distraction, especially if people are occupied with the worries of supporting large families.[41]

(2) Submission to a Shaykh

With the introduction of *ṭarīqas*, Sufism passed into a new phase. In the previous phase, more significance was attached to books on *taṣawwuf*.[42] In the new phase, the initiation into *taṣawwuf* without a *shaykh* was considered forbidden. Such an emphasis on submission to a *shaykh* generated a debate among the scholars.

According to Shāṭibī submission to a *shaykh* led to a belief in the superiority of the *shaykh* to all other religious leaders. It was rather a claim to religious authority which only befitted Prophet Muḥammad.[43] According to some *ṣūfīs*, including Qushayrī, Ṣufism was nothing more than spiritual *fiqh* (*fiqh al-bāṭin*)[44] It was, therefore, questionable for Shāṭibī that one should submit oneself totally to a *shaykh* to be initiated into a discipline; the discipline could be known from books.

Shāṭibī composed a query in which he summarized the arguments of both parties and sent it to a number of scholars in North Africa. Three of the responses to this query have come down to us. Those of Ibn al-Qabbāb (d. 779/1377) and Ibn 'Abbād of Ronda (d. 792/1389) were preserved by Wansharīsī in his *al-Mi'yār al-mu'rab*. They are reproduced by Paul Nwiya in *al-Rasā'il al-ṣughrā* of Ibn 'Abbad[45] and commented and elaborated in his well-known work *Ibn 'Abbad de Ronda*.[46] The third answer was written by Ibn Khaldūn in *Shifā' al-sā'il li tahdhīb al- masā'il,* available in two editions by Ṭāwīt Ṭanjī[47] and by Khalifé.[48]

Ibn 'Abbād maintained that, on the whole, the (submission to a) *shaykh* is an essential fact in the journey on the path of *taṣawwuf*; no one can deny that".[49] He, however, distinguished between two kinds of *shaykhs: shaykh al-tarbiya* (educator) and *shaykh al-ta'līm* (instructor). The former is not essential for every "traveller", while the latter is necessary for everyone. He also pointed out that reliance on the "educator" *shaykh* is the approach of the modern (*muta'akhkhirīn*) Ṣūfīs, while the ancients relied on the "instructor" *shaykh*.[50]

Ibn 'Abbād stressed that the initiation to the mystic state (*ḥāl*) exclusively belonged to special individuals. No one could open its doors except those whom God had chosen for that purpose.[51]

(3) Invocation after the Prayers

The mention of the ruling Sulṭān or Khalīfa as a symbol of legitimacy had long been accepted in practice. Al-Muwaḥḥidūn gave the practice much more significance by making some additions. Especially the Muwaḥḥid Caliph 'Abd al-Wāḥid al-Rāshid (630-640/1232-1242), fearing the dissensions among various groups of the family and in order to check a general decline of al-Muwaḥḥidūn, re-established Mahdī's (Ibn Tūmart) institutions which had been discontinued by al-Manṣūr (580-595/1184-1199) and al-Idrīs Ma'mūn (620-630/1229-1232).[52] One of such institutions was the invocation of the name of the ruling caliph after the prayers in congregational form. This was an innovation, but it gradually became so much established that opposition to it was considered a political as well as a religious offence, punishable by death.[53]

Contrary to the claim by the other *fuqahā'* about the consensus on the acceptance of this practice, Shāṭibī argued that it was a *bid'a* and that scholars had always expressed their dissent against this practice. When this practice was introduced into Spain in the twelfth century, some of the Maliki *fuqahā'*, namely Abū 'Abd Allāh b. Mujāhid (d. 574/1178) and his disciple Abū'l 'Imrān al-Mīrtalī, opposed it at the risk of their lives.[54]

The practice continued even after the Muwaḥḥidūn, obviously for political reasons. Most probably it was Shāṭibī who publicly opposed this practice by disregarding it whenever he was leading the prayers. This public act of defiance raised havoc for Shāṭibī. The issue became a subject of heated discussion; Shāṭibī, however, did have some followers. From a letter written by Shāṭibī to one of his followers, it appears that an *imām* who rejected this practice in favour of Shāṭibī's position was deposed from *imāma* and was denied all other privileges and was put to trial.[55]

The first two refutations written against Shāṭibī were the following: one by the Qāḍī of Andalusia, Abū'l Ḥasan al-Nubāhī, *Mas'alat al-du'ā ba'd al-ṣalāt,*[56] the other by the *muftī* and *Mushāwar* of Granada and Shāṭibī's teacher Abū Sa'īd ibn Lubb. His treatise was titled as *Mas'ala al-'ad'iya ithr al-ṣalāt.*[57]

Shāṭibī's disciple Abū Yaḥyā ibn 'Āṣim (d. 813/1410) wrote a treatise refuting Ibn Lubb and supporting Shāṭibī.[58] Muḥammad al-Fishtālī, the Qāḍī al-Jamā'a in Fez wrote a refutation of Ibn 'Āṣim, supporting Ibn Lubb, entitled *Kalām fī'l-du'ā ba'd al-ṣalāt 'alā al-hay'a al-ma'hūda.*[59] Ibn 'Arafa (d. 803/1400), the Qāḍī of Tunis, also entered into the discussion when he was asked for a *fatwā* on this issue by someone in Granada.[60]

SHĀṬIBĪ'S WORKS

The following is a list of Shāṭibī's works known to us. They belong mainly to two fields: Arabic grammar, and jurisprudence.

1. *SHARḤ 'ALĀ AL-KHULĀṢA FĪ AL-NAḤW*

A commentary on Ibn Mālik's, *Alfiyya* in four parts.

Mentioned in:

(i) Al-Maqqarī, *Nafḥ al-ṭīb*, VII, 275; (ii) Kaḥḥāla, *Mu'jam al-mu'allifīn*, I, 118; (iii) Sarkīs, *Mu'jam maṭbū'āt al-'Arabiyya*, 1090; (iv) *Fihris al-Azhariyya*, IV, 255; (v) *Nayl*, 48; (vi) Al-Makhlūf, *Shajarat al-nūr al-zakiyya*, 231; (vii) al-Ziriklī, *al-A'lām*, I, 71.

MS. (1) Al-Azhariyya / 1487 / 10806. Beginning:

اللهم انا نحمدك على ما علمت ونشكرك على ما انعمت

Four volumes containing Parts I, II, III and V, are written in old naskh. Copyist's name: 'Umar b. 'Abd Allāh al-Manzarāwī. The completion of the third part by the copyist is dated 868 and of the fifth as 872 A.H. Each page contains 27 lines, 27 cm.[61]

(2) Al-Khazāna al-Malikiyyah bi'l Rabāṭ, no. 276.

(3) **Editing** of the MS is in progress at the Umm al-Qurā University, Mecca.[62]

2. *'UNWĀN AL-ITTIFĀQ FĪ 'ILM AL-ISHTIQĀQ*

Mentioned in:

(i) *Nayl*, 48; (ii) *al-A'lām*, I, 71; (iii) *Shajara*, 231; (iv) Kaḥḥāla, *Mu'jam*, I, 118; (v) *Iḍāḥ al-maknūn* [Al-Baghdādī, *Iḍāḥ al-maknūn* (Cairo, 1945)], 127.

3. *KITĀB UṢUL AL-NAḤW*

Mentioned in:

(i) *Nayl*, 49; (ii) *al-A'lām*, I, 71; (iii) *Shajara*, 231.

Shāṭibī mentions both of the above books (i.e. nos. 2 and 3) in his *Sharḥ al-alfiyya* but Aḥmad Bābā recalls reading elsewhere that Shāṭibī destroyed both of those works in his life-time.[63]

4. *KITĀB AL-MAJĀLIS*

A commentary on the chapter of sale (*buyū'*) in the *Ṣaḥīḥ* of al-Bukhārī.

Mentioned in:

(i) *Nayl,* 48; (ii) *Shajara*, 231; (iii) Sarkīs, *Mu'jam,* 1090; (iv) *al-A'lām,* I, 71.

5. *A MEDICAL TREATISE*

MS. University of Leiden: 139r-140r: CCO 1367; Warn/Or. 331-(3b).

The University of Leiden holds this MS.[64] The treatise is not mentioned by any major authorities on Shāṭibī. The catalogue, however, attributes this treatise to Shāṭibī and, significantly enough, it describes it as having been written down by his (Shāṭibī's) pupil (?) Ibn al-Khaṭīb.[65]

The probability that Shāṭibī was the author of this treatise is heightened by the following points. Among Shāṭibī's teachers, there is mention of one al-Shaqūrī.[66] We have no further information about him. From other sources we know that a family from Shaqūra was known as a family of physicians. Among them Abū Tamām Ghālib al-Shaqūrī and Abū 'Abd Allāh al-Shaqūrī are known as the authors of medical treatises.[67] We also know that Ibn al-Khaṭīb was associated with both of these men. He is also the author of certain medical treatises.[68]

From these facts, it might conceivably be argued that Shāṭibī, having been taught by one of these Shaqūrīs, had education in medicine and hence could be the author of a medical treatise.

6. *AL-IFĀDĀT WA'L-INSHĀDĀT/INSHĀ'ĀT*

Mentioned in:

(i) *Nafḥ,* VII, 187-192, 276-301; X, 139-140; (ii) *Nayl,* 48; (iii) Sarkīs, *Mu'jam,* 1090; (iv) *al-A'lām,* I, 71; (v) Kaḥḥāla, *Mu'jam,* I, 119; (vi) *Shajara,* 231; (vii) Nwiya, *Ibn 'Abbād,* 252.

Published:

Al-Ifādāt wa'l Inshādāt, edited by Abū'l Ajfān and published by Mu'assat al-Risāla, Beirut, in 1983.

CONTENTS

This is Shāṭibī's notebook, completed towards the end of 759/1358. The book consists of 101 notes including citations of verses called *inshādāt*. Shāṭibī has noted in this book comments, called *ifādāt*, from his teachers and other scholars dealing with the subjects of law and linguistics. Similarly he cites verses that he heard from his teachers or the poets themselves. This notebook is a valuable source of information that provides insights into the system of education of Shāṭibī's time, about his teachers and their method of teaching and the subjects taught.

7. *FATĀWĀ*

1. **Preserved in:**

   Al-Wansharīsī, *al-Mi'yār al-mu'rab wa'l- jāmi' al-mughrab 'an fatāwā 'ulamā' Ifrīqiya wa'l-Andalus wa'l-Maghrib* (Fas, 1314-15 A.H.), I, 22, 24, 229, 267-68; II, 230, 401-403; III, 163; IV, 146; V, 17-19, 50-51, 186-189, 192; VI, 254, 179; VII, 68-74; VIII, 235; IX, 163-165, 181, 478; X, 31-37, 82-83, 87, 88-91, 96-98, 107-III; XI, 6, 7, 8, 11, 16, 19, 28, 201-11.

2. **MS.** mentioned in M. Casiri, *Bibliotheca Arabico Hispana* Escurialensis, I, 460/No: 1, 096.

   Mentioned in: *Nayl, pp.* 49f.

3. **Published:** *Fatāwā al-Imām al-Shāṭibī*, (256 pages). Edited and published by Muḥammad Abū'l Ajfān in 1987.

CONTENTS

Shāṭibī's 60 fatāwā in this collection relate the following subjects: Knowledge, *Ijtihād, Ṣalāt, Ṣawm, Zakāt,* Vows, Slaughter, Marriage, Sales, Rent and Lease, Partnership and Association, Trust, Penalties, Inheritance, Questions about *Ḥadīth* and *Da'wa*, Land Revenue, Innovations in Religion.

Abū'l Ajfān the compiler of this collection has consulted the following sources: (1) "*Al-Ḥadīqat al-mustaqilla al-naḍara fī'l fatāwā al-ṣādira 'an 'ulamā' al-ḥaḍara*" (MS) (2) "*Taqrīb al-amal al-ba'īd fi nawāzil al-ustādh Abī Sa'īd*" [Ibn Lubb]" (MS) (3) "*Fatāwā Ibn Ṭarkāt al-'Akkī*" (MS) (4) *Al-Mi'yār al-mu'rab wa'l jāmi' al-mughrab 'an fatāwā 'ulamā' Ifrīqiyya wa'l Andalus wa'l Maghrib,* 13 volumes (Bayrut: Dār al-gharb al-Islāmī, 1403 A.H); (5) "*Al-Mi'yār al-jadīd al-mu'rab 'an fatāwā al-muta'akhkhirīn min 'ulama' al-Maghrib*" (Fas, n.d.), (6) "*Ruwāt al-a'lām*" (MS)

A study of Shāṭibī's *Fatāwā* is presented in chapter three.

8. *KITĀB AL-I'TIṢĀM*

Published

(a) Partly published in *al-Manār*, XVII (1333/1913).[69]

(b) Published in Maṭba' Muṣṭafā Muḥammad, probably in 1915 edited by Muḥammad Rashīd Riḍā, the editor of *al-Manār*. It is based on an incomplete MS. from the library of Shanqīṭī.

(c) By the same publisher without date edited by Muḥammad Sulaymān.

(d) Reprint of Riḍā's edition by Dār 'Umar b. al-Khaṭṭāb, Alexandria, without date.

CONTENTS OF THE BOOK

This book in two volumes focuses on *bid'a*, its definition and doctrine. The following aspects of the subject have been discussed in ten chapters: Definition of *bid'a*, justification of condemning *bid'a* and its scope, the arguments in favour of *bid'a*, the types of *bid'a*, rules and regulation of *bid'a*, the scope and areas of *bid'a*, distinction between *bid'a*, *istiḥsān* and *al-maṣāliḥ mursala*, *bid'a* and sects, causes of deviation, and the right path.

Shāṭibī clarifies that *bid'a* relates only to the area of *'ibādāt* or rituals. Since *'ibādāt* are known by revelation, not by reason, they are not extendible. However, if an ordinary social practice not falling in the area of *'ibādāt* is preformed as a religious obligation, it enters the domain of *bid'a*. There is no good or praiseworthy *bid'a*; all *bid'as* are condemnable. However their levels of condemnation vary depending upon their deviations from the objectives of Islamic law, and whether they are true or relative *bid'a*. Thus there are only two types of *bid'a*: forbidden and reprehensible. *Bid'a* has led to heresies and heretic sects. Shāṭibī discusses these sects and the causes of heresy. Deviations are generally caused by two factors: ignorance of Arab usage in the interpretation of the Qur'ān and Sunna, and ignorance of the objectives of Islamic law.

9. *AL-MUWĀFAQĀT*

The original title was *'Unwān al-ta'rīf bi asrār al-taklīf* (An exposition of the reasons of obligation). An epitome of this work was done by Qāḍī Abū Bakr b. 'Āṣim (d. 829 A.H.)[70]

Published

(i) First published in 1302/1884 in Tunis by the government press, edited by Ṣāliḥ al-Qā'ijī, 'Alī al-Shanūfī and Aḥmad al-Wartatānī.

(ii) Reprint of the first part of the above in Kazan in 1327/1909 with an introduction in Turkish by Mūsā Jārūllāh. This edition is no longer available but Mūsā Jārullāh's introduction is now available in Turkish translation of *Al-Muwāfaqāt*.

(iii) Third (in fact, the second complete) print from 1341/1923 in Maṭba' Salafiyya, Cairo, edited by Muḥammad al-Khiḍr Ḥusayn, the rector of Al-Azhar, and partly by Muḥammad Ḥasanayn al-'Adawī, the Administrator of the Religious Department, Government of Egypt.

(iv) Fourth print from Maṭba' Muṣṭafā Muḥammad (n.d.), edited with extensive notes by Shaykh 'Abd Allāh Dirāz.

(v) Fifth print from Maṭba' Muḥammad 'Alī, Cairo, in 1969, edited by Muḥammad Muḥiy al-Dīn 'Abd al-Ḥamīd.

(vi) Reprint of 'Abd Allah Dirāz edition from Beirut, n.d. [probably 1970]

TRANSLATIONS: Translation into Turkish by Dr. Mehmed Erdoğan,: *El-Muvâfakât Islâmî ilimler Metodolojisi* (Istanbul: 1z Yayincilic, 1990). 2 Volumes published.

An Urdu translation by 'Abd al-Raḥmān Gīlani (Diyal Singh Trust, Lahore, 1992) has also came to our knowledge.

An analysis of the contents of *al-Muwafaat* is given in a subsequent chapter, where we also discuss the impact of this book on Islamic legal thought. The next chapter presents a detailed analysis of Shāṭibī's *Fatāwā*.

NOTES AND REFERENCES

1. Our main source on Shāṭibī's life is Aḥmad Bābā (d. 1036/1626), the author of *Nayl al-ibtihāj*. For details on his life and works see M. Cheneb, "Aḥmed Bābā" in *E.I.*, (1st ed.), Vol. I, 191-2; Lévi Provençal, "Aḥmad Bābā", *E.I.*, (2nd ed.) Vol. I, 279-280; J.O. Hunwick, "Aḥmad Bābā and the Moroccan Invasion of the Sudan (1591)", *Journal of Historical Society of Nigeria*, II (1962), 311-28; same author, "A New Source for the Biography of Aḥmad Bābā al-Tinbuktī (1556-1627)", *Bulletin of the School of Oriental and African Studies*, XXVII (1964), 568-593; Muḥammad Makhlūf, *Shajarat al-nūr al-zakiyya* (Cairo, 1349 A.H.), Vol. I, 298.
Nayl al-Ibtihāj (referred to as *Nayl* subsequently) is available to us in two editions; in

Maghribī script, (Fās: Maṭba' Jadīda, 1317 A.H.); second edition, printed on the margin of Ibn Farḥūn, *Al-Dībāj al-mudhahhab* (Cairo 1351). (Henceforth the reference *Nayl* will refer to the latter edition). The question of Aḥmad Bābā's sources for *Nayl* has been dealt with by scholars with varied competence. To my knowledge the best review available is still that by Cherbonneau (*J.A.* 1853) which is mainly a re-enumeration of the sources which Aḥmad Bābā himself mentions towards the end of *Nayl* (p. 361).

In addition to *Nayl*, we have used the following sources for this chapter:

(1) Ignaz Goldziher, *Streitschrift des Gazali gegen die Batinijja - Sekte* (Leiden, 1916), pp. 32-34, where he mentions *al-Muwāfaqāt* (2) D.S. Margoliouth, "Recent Arabic Literature" in *J.R.A.S.* (London, 1916), pp. 397-98, where he reviews *al-I'tiṣām*. Among the biographical notices are: Brockelmann, *Supp. II*, 374-75; Muhammad Makhlūf, *Shajarat al-nūr al-zakiyya*, p. 231; Ismā'īl Pāshā Baghdādī, *Īḍāḥ al-maknūn*, supp. to *Kashf al-ẓunūn* (Cairo: Bahiyya, 1945), Vol. II, p. 127; Maḥmūd Ḥasan al-Tonkī, *Mu'jam al-muṣannifīn* (Beirut, 1344 A.H.), Vol. IV, pp. 448-454; 'Abd al-Muta'āl al-Ṣa'īdī, *Al-Mujaddidūn fi'l-Islām* (Cairo, Namūdhajiyya, n.d.), pp. 307-12; Fāḍil b. 'Āshūr, *A'lām al-fikr al-islāmī fī tārīkh al-maghrib al-'arabī* (Tunis: Najāḥ, n.d.), pp. 70-77; Yūsuf Iliān Sarkīs, *Mu'jam al-maṭbū'āt al-'Arabiyya wa'l-mu'arraba*, Vol. I, (Cairo, 1928) p. 1090; Khayr al-Dīn al-Ziriklī, *al-A'lām*, Vol. I (2nd ed., 1954), p. 71; Kaḥḥāla, *Mu'jam al-mu'allifīn* (Dimashq, 1957), Vol. I, pp. 118-19.

2. I. Goldziher, [*Streitschrift*, p. 32] said that Shāṭibī "dem aus Xativa stammenden, später in Granada lebenden". The same mistake was carried over by Brockelmann, *G.A.L.S.* II, p. 374; "aux Xativa, gest. in Granada". Asin Palacios was also misled by the *nisba*, as he stated that Shāṭibī lived in Shāṭiba, see Asin Palacios transl. by M.L. de Celigny. "Un précurseur Hispano-Musulman de San Juan de la Cruz". *Étude Carmelitaines*, 1932, p. 121-22, *vide* P. Nwiya, *Ibn 'Abbad de Ronda* (Beyrouth, 1961) p. 173, n.2.

3. Lévi-Provençal, "Shāṭiba", *E.I.* 1st ed. (Brill, 1938), Vol. IV, p. 337.

4. Ibn Khaldūn's *Shifā' al-sā'il li tahdhīb al-masā'il*, ed. by Muḥammad b. Ṭāvīt al-Ṭanjī (Istāmbūl, 1957) was written in response to a query sent to scholars in the West of whom the names of Ibn Qabbāb and Ibn 'Abbād are confirmed by Wansharīsī. The attribution of this treatise to Ibn Khaldūn has been doubted by scholars. See: Ṭalbī, "*Ibn Khaldūn*", *E.I.* (2nd edition), (Leiden, 1971) vol. III, p. 828. Ṭanjī, the editor of this work, however, argues in detail in favour of such attribution. He is of the opinion that it was Shāṭibī whose *taqyīd* (query) is referred to in this treatise. See his Introduction, p.ṭ. See also *Nafḥ al-ṭīb*, IV, 195-201.

5. Ibn al-Fakhkhār al-Ilbīrī, Abū 'Abd Allāh al-Maqqarī, Abū 'Abd Allāh al-Tilimsānī and Abū'l Qāsim al-Sabtī are some of their common teachers. Cf. Maqqarī [*Nafḥ al-ṭīb*, (Cairo: Maṭba' Sa'āda, 1949), VII, 187] gives an extract from al-Shāṭibī's *Ifādāt* where al-Shāṭibī mentions Ibn al-Khaṭīb among others who attended with him al-Maqqarī's lectures in 757 A.H. See Shāṭibī, *Al-Ifādāt wa'l Inshādāt* (Beirut: Al-Risāla, 1983), p. 127.

Ibn Zumruk (also spelled Ibn Zamrak) whom Ibn al-Khaṭīb patronized and who later replaced Ibn al-Khaṭīb when the latter defected to Tlemcen, was a close friend of al-Shāṭibī (See *Nafḥ al-ṭīb*, X, 139)

Shāṭibī (*al-I'tiṣām*, ed. Rashīd Riḍā, (Cairo, 1915), Vol. II, 84), quotes an extract saying "As narrated by one of our contemporary writers" which exactly corresponds with *al-Iḥāṭa*, (Cairo, 1901), Vol. I, p. 75. Various dates have been suggested for the year when *al-Iḥāṭa* was completed. For instance Mahdī, [*Ibn Khaldūn's Philosophy of History* (Chicago, 1964), p. 35, n. 5] suggests 763/1361-62. This date is not possible because (1) Ibn Al-Khaṭīb enumerates among the works of Ibn Khaldūn, already completed, a treatise on logic which he wrote for Sulṭān Muḥammad V of Granada. We know that Ibn Khaldūn's stay in Granada was in 764-65. Hence the date of *al-Iḥāṭa* must be after 765/1363. (2) Secondly, *al-Iḥāṭa* recounts the events in the year 771/1369 (op. cit. Vol. II, p. 58), which places the date of its completion after 771/1369. It is because of the second evidence that we believe that *al-Iḥāṭa* must have been finally completed in 771/1369.

6. Maqqarī, *Nafḥ al-ṭīb*, Vol. VII, p. 275.: *Shajara, op. cit.*, Vol. I, p. 228.
7. *Nafḥ al-ṭīb*, Vol. VII, pp. 2756-278; 297-301.
8. Kaḥḥāla, *Mu'jam, op. cit.*, Vol. VIII, p. 252.
9. *Shajara, op. cit.*, Vol. I, p. 233.
10. *Nayl*, p. 219.
11. *Shajara*, p. 230.
12. *Nayl*, p. 47.
13. *Nafḥ al-ṭīb*, Vol. VII, p. 134.
14. *Al-Iḥāṭa*, Vol. II, p. 139.
15. *Nayl*, p. 250.
16. *Shajara*, p. 232.
17. *Nafḥ al-ṭīb*, Vol. VII, p. 206.
18. *Ibid.*, pp. 232-249.
19. *Nayl*, p. 245, 346; *Shajara*, I, p. 234. Zawāwī was alive until 770 A.H.
20. *Nayl*, p. 346.
21. This extract from Shāṭibī's *al-Ifādāt* is quoted by Aḥmad Bābā in *Nayl*, p. 349 and by P. Nwiya, in *Ibn 'Abbād de Ronda*, p. XXXIX, n. 2.
22. Muhsin Mahdi, *op. cit.* p. 35, n. 2; *Nayl*, p. 256.
23. *Nayl*, p. 256.
24. *Ibid.* p. 258.
25. Shāṭibī, in a letter to his friend, implies that dismissal from the office of *imām* or *khaṭīb* of mosque was usual after one had opposed *bid'a* practices. See Wansharīsī, *al-Mi'yār al-mughrib*, Vol. XI, p. 109.
26. Leon Bercher, (ed. Transl. and Comment. on) Ibn 'Āṣim al-Mālikī al-Gharnāṭī, *Al-'Acimiyya ou Tuh'fat al-ḥukkum fi nukat al-'uqoud wa'l ah'kam*, (Alger, 1958), Introduction, p. III.
27. *Nayl*, p. 49. Abū'l Ajfān, *Fatāwā al-Imām al-Shāṭibī*, (Tunis, 1987), p. 48.
28. See Abū'l Ajfān, *Fatāwā al-Imām al-Shāṭibī*, quoting on the authority of Shanqīṭī.
29. The lack of interest in uṣūl al-fiqh is observed by Ibn Sa'īd as quoted by Maqqarī in *Nafḥ al-ṭīb*, Vol. I, p. 9.
30. *Al-I'tiṣām*, Vol. I, p. 9.
31. See chapter twelve.
32. *Nayl*, p. 221.
33. *Ibid.*
34. *Al-Muwāfaqāt*, Vol. I, p. 22.
35. *Nayl*, p. 49.
36. *Al-I'tiṣām, op. cit.* p. 9f.
37. *Ibid.*, p. 11.
38. *Ibid.*, p. 11 ff.
39. *Ibid.*
40. *Al-Muwāfaqāt*, Vol. I, p. 102.
41. *Ibid.*, p. 103.
42. Ibn Khaldūn, *Shifā' al-sā'il, op. cit.*, describes the controversy between those who attached significance to books and those who favoured the necessity of *Shaykh*, in the form of an interesting dialogue. See pp. 79-85.
43. *Al-I'tiṣām, op. cit.*, p. 208.
44. Ibn Khaldūn, *Shifā' al-sā'il, op. cit.*, p. 11.
45. P. Nwiya (Ed.), *Ar-Rasā'il as-Ṣugrā*, (Beiruth: Imprimérie Catholique, 1958), pp. 106-115, and Appendice C, pp. 125-138.
46. P. Nwiya, *Ibn 'Abbad de Ronda*, pp. 209-13.
47. Ṭāvīt Ṭanjī. *op. cit.* Our references to *Shifā'* are based on this edition.
48. P. Khalifé. (ed.) Ibn Khaldūn, *Shifā as-sā'il litahzīb al-masā'il* (Beyrouth, 1958).
49. Ibn 'Abbād, *Ar-Rasā'il as-Ṣugrā* (ed. P. Nwiya) *op. cit.*, p. 106.
50. *Ibid.*, p. 107.
51. *Ibid.*, p. 109.

52. A. Bel, " 'Abd al-Wāḥid al-Rāshid", *E.I.* (1st ed.) Vol. I. p. 66.
53. *Al-I'tiṣām,* op. cit. Vol. II, p. 237.
54. *Ibid.*, pp. 237-8.
55. Al-Wansharīsī, *Al-Mi'yār,* Vol. XI, p. 109.
56. Lévi-Provençal, introduction to Al-Nubāhī, *Al-Marqabat al-'ulyā, p.ṭ.*
57. *Shajara, op. cit.*, p. 231.
58. *Ibid.*, p. 247.
59. *Nayl, op. cit.*, p. 266.
60. Wansharīsī, *Al-Mi'yār,* Vol. VI, pp. 258ff.
61. *Fihris maktabat al-Azhariyya,* V (Cairo, 1946), p. 255; also see 'Abd al-Ḥafīẓ Manṣūr, *Fihris makhṭūṭāt al-maktabat al-Aḥmadiyya bi Tūnis,* (Bayrūt: Dār al-Fatḥ, 1969), pp. 316-319.
62. Se *Fatāwā*, p. 44, n. 103.
63. *Nayl*, p. 49.
64. Voorhoeve, *Handlist of Arabic Manuscripts,* Library of University Leiden, (Lugduni: Batavorum, 1957), p. 238.
65. *Ibid.*
66. *Nayl*, p. 47.
67. See Renaud, "Un medecín du royaume de Granade: Muhammad aš-šaqūrī," *Hespéris* Vol. XXXIII (1946), pp. 31-64.
68. Renaud, "Deux ouvrages perdus d'Ibn al-Haṭīb: Identifiés dans des manuscrits de Fes - Conclusion sur Ibn al-Haṭīb medecín", *Hesperis,* XXXIII (1946), pp. 213-225. Also *Nayl*, pp. 264-265.
69. These extracts from *al-I'tiṣām* were mistaken for extracts from *Al-Muwāfaqāt* by I. Goldziher, and the same mistake was carried over in Brockelmann.
70. *Shajara*, I, p. 247.

CHAPTER THREE

SHĀṬIBĪ'S *FATĀWĀ*

We have argued in the preceding chapters that the political, social, religious, economic and legal developments in the fourteenth century Granadan society demanded fresh interpretation of Islamic laws. The spread of Ṣūfī ṭarīqas had contributed to idleness and an exaggerated ideal of Islamic piety that constricted the concept of legal obligation. The influence of Razism increased the influence of the Shāfi'ī and Ash'arī schools of thought. The establishment of the *madrasa* system promoted education and widened its scope. The economic changes, especially the new developments in the Mediterranean trade, challenged the Andalusian Mālikī legal concepts and theories on trade and commerce. In a number of situations, the new trade practices came into apparent conflict with the prevailing doctrines of Islamic law. A study of Shāṭibī's *fatāwā* reveals how Islamic legal theory responded to social changes.

The impact of his *fatāwā* was so conspicuous that Shāṭibī's biographers e.g. Aḥmad Bābā and others never forget to refer to them and to highlight Shāṭibī's innovative legal reasoning.[1] The significance of his *fatāwā* is also demonstrated by the fact that his *fatāwā* were collected in the famous *fatāwā* collections like: "*Al-Ḥadīqat al-mustaqillat al-naḍrah fī'l fatāwā al-ṣādirah 'an 'ulamā' al-ḥaḍara*"; "*Taqrīb al-amal al-ba'īd fi nawāzil al-ustādh Abī Sa'īd; Fatāwā Ibn Ṭarkāt; Al-Mi'yār al-Jadīd*" "*Rawḍāt al-a'lām*",[2] and *Al-Mi'yār*[3]. In 1941 López Ortiz[4] studied Shāṭibī's fatāwā along with those of his contemporary muftīs. Like Aḥmad Bābā, Ortiz also noted Shāṭibī's use of the principle of *maṣlaḥa* in his fatāwā. Ortiz particularly remarked about Shāṭibī's "skill of an economist from the fiscal point of view".[5] In 1984, Muḥammad Abū'l Ajfān made a very comprehensive analytical study of Shāṭibī's *fatāwā*. Commenting on the importance of Shāṭibī's *fatāwā* Abū'l Ajfān observed:

> Shāṭibī's *fatāwā* reveal the salient features of his contemporary social and economic life. For instance they tell us about the system of endowments and how the caretakers of the mosques received grants from the income of these endowments. They tell us about some of the agricultural phenomena, some cases of the industrial and commercial practices, and even about the trade relations with the enemy at war.[6]

These studies of Shāṭibī's *fatāwā* stress their significance not only as a source of social and economic history of that period, but also underscore Shāṭibī's fine legal reasoning to solve the problems caused by these social changes.

In this chapter we shall study Shāṭibī's *fatāwā* with the following questions in mind:

(1) Which areas of Islamic law were affected by these changes?
(2) In which areas did the Islamic law adopt these changes?
(3) What were the legal principles employed by Shāṭibī to reject or accept various social practices?

We have used the term "social change" to refer to changes in social practices resulting from the political, religious, economic and legal developments, and therefore they include economic, social, religious and political changes in the Granadan society.

Shāṭibī's *fatāwā*, studied in this chapter, are available in the following sources, the location of which has been indicated in the notes respectively: (1) Al-Wansharīsī *Al-Mi'yār al-mu'rab...*, (2) *Al-Muwāfaqāt*, (3) *Al-I'tiṣām*, (4) *Nayl al-ibtihāj*, and (5) *Fatāwā al-Imām al-Shāṭibī.*

We have not analysed all the *fatāwā* in these sources. The total number of *fatāwā* studied in this chapter is 40 and they have been distributed in the following categories. The number of *fatāwā* is also indicated in each category.

(i) Exegesis (questions about clarifying the meanings of Qur'ān and Ḥadīth): 1
(ii) Theological matters (questions about creeds, definition of a Muslim and dealings with non-Muslims and apostates): 2
(iii) Ritual and worship (cleanliness, rituals, prayers): 12
(iv) Family (marriage, divorce, inheritance): 5
(v) Property (objects of property, *waqf*): 5
(vi) Taxes (*zakāt, kharāj*): 3
(vii) Contracts and Obligations (sale, hire and lease, society): 11
(viii) Procedure (witness): 1.

EXEGESIS

Responding to a request, Shāṭibī explains in a *fatwā* the meaning of an *ḥadīth qudsī*,[7] in which God is quoted showing His affection and closeness by becoming the ears, hands and feet of a person who endeavours to approach Him. Shāṭibī finds this *ḥadīth* implying anthropomorphism. Without denying the authenticity of the *ḥadīth*, he explains how the apparent anthropomorphic implications can be removed by the method of *ta'wīl* (interpretation).[8]

Strictly speaking, 'exegesis' is not a *fiqhī* subject matter; the *fiqh* books generally do not include discussion on this subject. Yet exegesis often finds a place in *fatāwā*. Questions about exegesis arise out of certain texts that are interpreted and understood in a manner bringing them into conflict with the teachings of Islamic law. The question reflects the spread of Sufism in the Andalus. Shāṭibī is very careful to not to accept new developments in this area.

THEOLOGICAL MATTERS

Again discussions about theology are not one of the subjects treated in *fiqh* books, yet it is a very common subject in *fatāwā*. It may be argued that since a larger part of the provisions of Islamic law are applicable only to Muslims, the question "Who is a Muslim?", even though a theological question, is quite relevant to Islamic law. In addition to the above, Shāṭibī's two *fatāwā* reveal other aspects of the relevance of dogma to *fiqh*. A dogma may sometimes impose restrictions on certain acts.

Shāṭibī was asked about a person who interpreted Qur'anic terms to his own advantage, claiming that commands about worship were metaphoric. He also insisted that direct knowledge of God was possible and that books did not provide true knowledge.It appears that this question came from a court where this person was accused of *kufr* and five witnesses testified to his various statements and acts of unbelief. Shāṭibī declared that the person was a *kāfir*, and that he must be sentenced to death (*wājib al-qatl*). This person rejected and ridiculed the *Sharī'a* and its transmission and mocked the names of God.[9] He added that the statements of this person echoed the beliefs of Bāṭiniyya, Zanādiqa and Ibāḥiyya who were unanimously declared *kuffār*.

This *fatwā* appears to disagree with Shāṭibī's view on heresy. As Fazlur Rahman has pointed out, Shāṭibī analyses in detail the doctrines of heretic sects and categorically states that "it is not possible to locate absolutely the capital errors of these sects so that they may be stigmatized as *kuffār*."[10] Shāṭibī is quite clear, Rahman observes further, that erroneous beliefs and practices can and must be exposed but that it is impossible to locate absolutely the holders of these practices.[11]

Shāṭibī clarifies that even the *ḥadīth* speaking about seventy two sects apparently counts them within Islam, yet "the *ḥadīth* means those sects whose innovations (*bid'a*) do not exclude them from Islam."[12] Shāṭibī argues that it is impossible to define and identify *firqa nājiya* (the saved sect who is absolutely on the right path).

The other *fatwā* related to this subject matter concerned the wax industry. For their Christian customers, the Muslim artisans manufactured wax candles resembling hands in prayer. This resemblance apparently violated the teachings of Islam about strict monotheism that forbade any representation of the human figure in sculpture or paintings, since such an attempt would resemble God's act of creation. Shāṭibī dismissed the objection and declared this industry lawful. Quoting earlier Mālikī jurists, Shāṭibī argued that what was forbidden was the representation of the complete figure; a figure without its head in particular had been previously permitted in Mālikī *fatāwā*.[13]

RITUAL AND WORSHIP

We see here Shāṭibī distinguishing between *'ibādāt* and *mu'āmalāt* with reference to *bid'a* which is applied only in case of *'ibādāt*. Any change in practice leading to restriction or expansion of the area of *'ibādāt* already defined by *Sharī'a* is termed *bid'a* and condemned. *Bid'a* in the area of *'ibādāt* implies belief in the innovator as Lawgiver beside God. A number of new practices, mostly under the influence of Ṣūfism were introduced in this domain in Al-Andalus. These new practices were considered *'ibādāt*. In his response to an inquiry about these practices, Shāṭibī condemned them on two grounds: first, that they were *bid'a* (innovation) and second, that these practices were imposed as religious obligations, whereas the right of imposing such an obligation belongs only to God. The practices condemned by Shāṭibī in this regard included the following:

(a) Reciting in congregation the Qur'ānic chapter *Yāsīn* on the occasion of bathing the deceased in preparation for burial.[14]

(b) The practice of the group of people called *ṣūfiyā* who assembled in some *zāwiya*, performing *dhikr* (chanting the names of God or some such formula), singing and reciting poetry.[15]

(c) Congregational recital of the *Ḥizb*[16] (certain prayer formulas).[17]

(d) Recital of certain books in congregation in the mosques.[18]

(e) Congregational invocation after the regular prayers (*ṣalāt*).[19]

(f) The practice of insisting on the completion of the recital of the Qur'ān in the month of Ramaḍān.[20]

(g) Saying loudly the *takbīr*s (the formulae declaring the greatness of God) on the eve of 'Īd prayers.[21]

(h) Shaking hands and embracing each other after 'Īd prayers.[22]

(i) Adding certain sentences in the *adhān* (call to prayer).[23] In *al-I'tiṣām*, Shāṭibī refers to the practice of adding the following in the call for morning prayers: "The day dawned, praise be to God".[24]

(j) *Taṣbīḥ al-qabr*: It had become the practice of the people in Al-Andalus that after the burial of the deceased, they gathered for seven days and recited the Qur'ān loudly in congregation. Shāṭibī considered this custom equivalent to *ma'tam* (mourning) which was forbidden in Mālikī *fiqh*.[25]

Whereas the above ten responses emphatically rejected those religious practices as *bid'a,* there were two other practices in regard to which Shāṭibī showed flexibility. In Mālikī *fiqh* uncleanliness (*najāsa*) is a legal qualification (*ṣifa ḥukmiyya*) in opposition to the sensory (*ḥissiyya*) or rational (*'aqliyya*) qualification.[26] Cleanliness (*ṭahāra*) can be determined only on legal bases. *Khamr* (wine) and *mayta* (corpse) are unclean accoridng to the Qur'ān.[27] Accordingly if either of these two happens to fall into something, it makes that thing unclean, and that uncleanliness cannot be removed in a sensory or rational sense.

In practice, however, the earthenware used for wine, was used for other purposes, after washing. Shāṭibī was asked whether this practice was Islamically justified.[28] In another case he was asked about the use of a book or the Qur'ān polluted by some unclean thing (in another similar *fatwā* this "unclean thing" was the ink polluted by the dead body of a mouse).[29]

Ibn al-Sirāj and other *muftīs* declared these things unclean and their usage not permissible; the earthenware to be disposed of and the Book to be buried.[30]

Shāṭibī, however, had a different view. In the case of the earthenware, he held that if it was enamelled or glassware, it could be washed with water in an ordinary manner. Otherwise, it should be washed thoroughly with hot water. If hot water is not available, then it might be washed with cold water that should be allowed to soak for a while. Its cleanliness would then be decided by ascertaining that water standing in it does not change its colour, flavour or smell.[31]

In the case of books, Shāṭibī advised that if water would not harm or efface the writing, the books should be cleaned with water; otherwise it should be mended by other means, and the book allowed to stay as it was.[32] Shāṭibī refers to the practice of the companions of the Prophet who let the bloodstains of Caliph 'Uthman stay on the Qur'ān that he was reading at the time of his murder.

One can see here Shāṭibī trying to avoid hardship on people because utensils and books both were expensive. He allowed their re-use after proper cleaning.

FAMILY

Someone repudiated his wife with regular expression of the formula of divorce, and after some time he also pronounced *ẓihār* (another form of repudiation by expressing the formula: "You are for me as the back of my mother"). Afterwards, however, he neither expressed repudiation nor revoked it. Shāṭibī was asked about this case: whether the divorce had come into effect or not. Treating *ṭalāq* and *ẓihār* as two distinct acts, Shāṭibī advised that in the Mālikī school one declaration of repudiation was revokable (*raj'ī*), not irrevocable (*bā'in*). Hence, in this case, since the declaration of repudiation was not repeated, the marriage was not yet dissolved.[33] Marriage was still valid but the man had to pay penalty (*kaffāra*) for *ẓihār*.

The other three cases under this category concerned inheritance. Whereas the above case of divorce does not appear to have emerged from the changing conditions of the society, the following three were quite possibly related to these changes.

A certain Muslim committed apostasy. Soon after, his father died. Since an apostate is not entitled to inherit from his Muslim father, this person enquired whether he could lawfully inherit his father if he re-converted to Islam. The people in town, feared that if he did not return to Islam he would be harmful to the town. Shāṭibī denied the son the right of inheritance on the ground that the cause of the transfer of the deceased person's property to the other inheritors was the eligibility of the inhenitor at the time of the "death of the owner", not at the time of the "disposal of the property", hence the right of inheritance belongs to whoever was rightful heir at the time of death. Since, due to his apostasy, the son had lost his right of inheritance the right cannot be restored to him by his reconversion to Islam after his father's death. This view was unanimously accepted. Shāṭibī adds that although in his days a *muftī* was required to adhere to the views of early Mālikī jurists, yet he was not ready to allow a thing by choosing one of the conflicting doctrines (*khilāf*). He would rather search for the popular practice (*mashhūr*) or a better Mālikī view. If there was no option available, he would not give a *fatwā*. He nevertheless suggested that if the other heirs wished, they might give the son some part of the inheritance as a gift; or alternatively he could be granted assistance from *Bayt al-māl*.[34]

An opposite opinion in favour of the son was possible but Shāṭibī insisted that the common practice of the Mālikī school be adhered to. It appears that a strict attitude was adopted to discourage apostasy, the growth of which is conceivable under the changing circumstances.

In another case of inheritance, the heirs of a cloth merchant claimed that some cloth, the kind of which was used by women, that lay in his wife's house was part of the inheritance. The wife claimed that her husband gave the cloth to her; hence it was her property, not legacy. Shāṭibī advised that the wife's statement could not be accepted without witness. Lacking evidence or witness, the heirs' claim would be accepted. Nevertheless the heirs should be asked to declare under oath that they did not know that the cloth belonged to the wife. Shāṭibī, however, explained that this case was neither comparable nor analogous to the dispute of husband and wife regarding household articles.[35]

Shāṭibī took a similar stand in another case of inheritance, where the wife claimed that the house in which she and her husband had lived had been given to her by her husband as a marriage gift (*shawār*).[36] In both cases Shāṭibī also referred to the customary practice that house and household articles are used by the wife, but the proprietary rights belong to the husband unless he specifically makes such things gifts to the wife.

We may say that in this section Shāṭibī relied on local custom and local consensus of Mālikī *fuqahā*. He found them more suitable to the *maṣlaḥa* of the community.

PROPERTY

Some of the cultivated land around Granada along the river Manṣūra was quite steep. For the purpose of irrigation small dams had to be built and the users had to take turns using water. These turns were strictly determined and were often passed on to the heirs as transferable rights. At times, however, some heirs either gave up cultivation or allowed their land to become barren, so that they had no use for the water. They, therefore, began to sell their portion of water to the actual users.

OBJECTS OF PROPERTY

A dispute arose out of such a situation, and Shāṭibī was asked about it. He emphatically declared that the water was not an object of property, and that its use could not be owned by any person. He, however, distinguished between two kinds of water; such water as is in rivers and in desert ponds was not the object of property, while those waters which were either purchased with or belonged to a land, which itself was private property could become the object of property. Yet no exclusive right of ownership could be claimed on the waters of rivers by virtue of the building of dams, a builder of dam has right only to the extent of his needs.[37]

ḤABS (waqf)

The question on this subject was most probably asked by Abū 'Abd Allāh al-Ḥaffār, who was appointed as supervisor of *awqāf*. [38] Someone willed that one third of his estate be demarcated as *waqf* (trust) for the purpose of celebrating the birthday of the Prophet. Shāṭibī, in his response to the inquiry about this will, resolved that such a will was unlawful and hence could not be executed. The reason for its unlawfulness, according to Shāṭibī, was that the celebration of the Prophet's birthday was an innovation and hence unlawful.[39]

The other two responses relating to *waqfs* indicate the confusion in the practice of *waqf* as well as the juridical strictness in abiding by the rules of *waqf*.

For the maintenance of mosques certain *aḥbās* (trust properties) were attached to them. The officer in charge of these *aḥbās* decided to rearrange the distribution of income among various mosques, so that the income of some of the mosques be increased. Shāṭibī was consulted; he explained that the income of the mosques could be increased either from *bayt al-māl* or from *aḥbās*. Whereas there were some restrictions in the case of *aḥbās*, there was nothing against such an increase from *bayt al-māl*. This view is based on the distinction between the different objectives of *bayt al-māl* and *ḥabs*; whereas the essence of the latter is *ta'yīn* (specification), the basis of the former is *'adam ta'yīn* (non-specification). Because of *ta'yīn*, the increase from *aḥbās* would become problematic. Re-arrangement of the distribution of trust income was not possible if it was definitely known that the trust was specified for a certain mosque or a certain purpose. It would be possible only if it were known that a certain number of *aḥbās* were specified for mosques but that the mosques were not specified individually. Shāṭibī, however, explained that, formerly, these *aḥbās* had been specified, but later, due to negligence, or because they were considered analogous to *bayt al-māl*, these specifications became confused. Then the share of each mosque was decided at the discretion of the officer in charge. In fact, it was not permissible to combine various trusts in order to increase the income of mosques.[40]

Shāṭibī took a similar view in another case of *aḥbās*. Someone bought the trees on a tract of land that was adjacent to a *ḥabs* property. A doubt passed through his mind that this tract of land might be the *anqāḍ* (the demolished and unused parts of an estate) of that *ḥabs*. In Mālikī *fiqh*, the act of sale of a *ḥabs* property is legally void and if this act were knowingly committed, it was punishable by the court.[41] Yet it was common practice in the Andalus to sell the *anqāḍ* of a *ḥabs* and, often the *ḥabs* and *milk* (ordinary property) were confused or joined deliberately, to share the income of such a sale. The person concerned asked Shāṭibī what to do.

Shāṭibī replied that the practice of combining *ḥabs* and *milk* is like mixing *ḥalāl* (lawful) and *ḥarām* (forbidden). As for the sale of *anqāḍ* the legal view was not as categorical as on *ḥabs* itself. The Mālikī scholars had different opinions. Yet Shāṭibī explained that this difference of opinion, in fact, emerged from the different bases of analogy. Ibn Mawwāz made the *anqāḍ* analogous to *'arāḍī sulṭān* or *arāḍī bayt al-māl* (crown land) and therefore, permitted flexibility in the sale and long-term lease of *anqāḍ*. Shāṭibī differed on this point on the basis of his distinction between *bayt al-māl* and *ḥabs*. He advised the person in question to go to the court for the cancellation of the sale contract; otherwise, he should appeal to the Sulṭān. This person accordingly appealed to the Sulṭān after securing *fatāwā* from 'Abd Allāh Ibn al-Ḥaffār and Ibn 'Allāq which were endorsed by Shāṭibī. The Sulṭān accepted the opinion of the *muftīs* and referred the case to the *qāḍī* concerned. Despite the Sulṭān's orders, the upholders of the practice prevailed upon the *qāḍī*. They shouted and condemned the plaintiff for opposing the practice. The *qāḍī*, for fear of disturbances, gave a verdict in favour of continuing the practice.[42]

TAXES

In the three *fatāwā* pertaining to taxes, Shāṭibī departed from the traditional viewpoint. In fact, López Ortiz interpreted this departure as the skill of an economist.[43] Two of these *fatāwā* concerned *kharāj* and one was about *zakāt*.

In view of the deteriorating financial conditions, the Sulṭān levied a few additional taxes. One of these new sources of revenue was a tax levied on the building of walls in or around Granada. The *muftī* of Granada, Ibn Lubb, declared such taxes unlawful, because they were not provided for in the *sharī'a*.

Shāṭibī disagreed with Ibn Lubb. He viewed taxation from the point of view of *maṣlaḥa* (public weal). His idea was, and he quoted Ghazālī and Ibn al-Farrā' in his support, that the safeguarding of public interest was essentially the responsibility of the community. In situations when they could no longer carry out this responsibility, the community might transfer it to the public treasury and contribute from their wealth for this purpose. With this aim in view, the public treasury is in constant need of such contributions. Especially in circumstances similar to those found in Shāṭibī's period, when the treasury had to pay a heavy tribute to the enemy. The levying of new taxes was, therefore, quite in order.[44]

Shāṭibī applied this criterion even to *zakāt*. According to *al-Mudawwanat al-kubrā*, *zakāt* on merchandise for sale could be levied only after the merchandise was sold and after one year had passed; it was to be levied on the price earned from the merchandise.[45] Accordingly the artisans did not pay any *zakāt* on their products, because first, only a few of these products would be sold immediately and the rest would remain as potential income not yet taxable. Second, the condition of allowing one year to pass would be hard to meet if the investment in these products was an on-going process.

Shāṭibī viewed this practice in the light of the changing economic conditions, which gave these artisans ample opportunity for production and yet allowed them to avoid *zakāt*. Shāṭibī, therefore, opined that the products of the artisans should be taxed, as they were potentially sold merchandise.[46]

CONTRACTS AND OBLIGATIONS

One very conspicuous impact of the changing economic conditions can be seen in the area of contracts and obligations. The demand for raw material in foreign markets generated extensive trade activities within Andalus and with neighbouring principalities. On the other hand, these trade demands were confronted with the rising number of population and the scarcity of resources within al-Andalus. It was quite understandable that such a situation necessitated freedom of contracts to meet social demands.

In practice, as we shall see below, a number of new and complex forms of contracts emerged, but they did not always satisfy the stipulations of Islamic law. Islamic legal theory did not lay down any general principles of contract and obligation; yet its insistence on avoiding *ribā* (unjustified enrichment) and *gharar* (hazard, risk) put restrictions on a number of sales and associations. Despite such restrictions, the scholars of Islamic law have observed that Islamic commercial law showed much flexibility and that custom played an important role.[47] We should keep this observation in mind as we turn now to the responses which Shāṭibī made to inquiries about contracts.

CONTRACT OF SALE

Shāṭibī was asked about a widespread commercial practice among Muslims in the Andalus who traded commodities such as weapons with the Christians. Such trade was prohibited by the Mālikī scholars for obvious reasons. But in the particular case of the Andalus, the Muslims were forced to trade such commodities for food and clothing. The question was whether special concessions might not be granted to the Muslims of Andalus because of their peculiar circumstances. The second question was whether that prohibition applied also to the sale of candles to Christians, because those candles were used to invoke prayers against Muslims. The third problem was whether the *'aṭṭārs* (pharmacists) and general merchants were obliged to abide by that prohibition.

In his response, Shāṭibī, first of all, denied any special concession to al-Andalus. Cities (or countries) could not be classified on these bases; even the *hādin* (the inhabitant of a country which was on truce terms with another) or *ḥarbī* (at war) territories could not claim such concessions. The only distinction that the Maliki jurists maintained concerned the sale of food commodities. They allowed such sales to a *hādin* but not to a *ḥarbī*. Shāṭibī did not allow such contracts of sale with Christians even on the basis of dire need for food articles in Andalus. As to the question about candles, if they were known to be used against Muslims, their manufacture and sale would both be unlawful. Prohibitions, however, could not be imposed on the *'aṭṭārs*, because they were merely salesmen; they did not know for what purpose their merchandise might be used. They had among their customers both Muslims and Christians.[48]

It is obvious from this response that Shāṭibī did not allow the sale of arms and other such articles which would eventually be used against the Muslims; yet this did not mean that trade with Christians was to be stopped altogether. The circumventing method of permitting the *'aṭṭārs* to make such contracts of sale shows that the jurists did allow consideration for the dire needs of the people, even though as a general principle they would deny it.

Someone asked Shāṭibī if the common practice among the saffron merchants to mix the yellow stigma of saffron with the white style of its pistils was not *ghashsh* (adulteration), analogous to the mixing of saffron with yellow colouring powder. Shāṭibī agreed that adulteration of saffron with yellow colouring powder was not permitted, but he disagreed with the analogy made to the practice of mixing the stigmas and styles of saffron. Rather, in his opinion, such 'mixing' was analogous to the 'mixing' of fig seeds with figs and raisin stems with raisins. In fact the matter comes down to the question of cutting the stigma of the saffron to remove it from its styles. In common practice, to do this is considered inconvenient. Since failure to cut the stigma does not make much difference in weight and its removal is not considered necessary, this practice should not be regarded as adulteration.[49]

Shāṭibī was consulted in another case of sale contract. Someone handed his merchandise over to a sales agent on the basis of a suggested price. A buyer offered a different price. The agent informed the owner, and the latter agreed to that price. The agent, however, asked the buyer to raise the price to which the latter agreed. Thus the agent sold the merchandise for more than the price agreed upon between him and the owner. Shāṭibī was asked if such a sale contract was valid. He responded that, since the stipulation of a contract of sale i.e., the offer (*ījāb*) and acceptance (*qubūl*) had been fulfilled, the contract was valid and it could not be revoked. As to the question of the agent charging price higher than the one consented to by the owner, this fact did not invalidate the contract, because the owner's acceptance and bid to sell at the particular price was commonly understood as "sell it at this price if there be no higher offer", not as "sell it at this price only and do not accept higher offers".[50]

CONTRACT OF LEASE AND PARTNERSHIP

Beside the cases mentioned above in the category of sales, the rest of the cases pertaining to contracts overlap with the categories of lease and partnership. Two of the cases are even related to the category of 'joint ownership'. We have juxtaposed all these cases here, without imposing our own classification. The purpose of such a treatment is to indicate the confusion in the original treatment of the cases.

With the exception of one which concerns the 'joint ownership of food', the rest of the cases in this category are related to agricultural contracts. For a fuller explanation of the context of the problems in these cases a few remarks about the Mālikī law on agricultural contracts must be made.

In broad terms the agricultural contracts are considered analogous to 'contracts of sale', and in a specific sense they are 'contracts of the sale of usufruct' (*ijāra*). Having inherited the confusions and uncertainties from the sale contracts in the early development of Mālikī theory and practice in Medina, Mālikī *fiqh* has become very complicated in regard to such questions. First confusion arose between two types of contracts for *kirā' al-arḍ* (the lease of land): *musāqāt*, the lease of a plantation of fruit trees, and *muzāra'a*, the lease of a field. Early Mālikīs maintained distinctions between the two and regarded *muzāra'a* as valid only if the fields were situated in the middle of the plantation.[51] Later, however, it seems that this stipulation was no longer observed, and *muzāra'a* came to be closer to a contract of partnership and *musāqāt* to that of hire of services. The second source of confusion was the prohibitions that concerned *ribā al-faḍl* (inequality in exchange of the same stuff), which implied the prohibition of the lease of one agricultural property for another and *gharar* (hazard, risk) or *juzāf* (undetermined quantities) which invalidated most agricultural contracts since the object of the contract, e.g. wages, was often undetermined. The third source of confusion was the failure to distinguish among contracts for hiring of services, contracts of lease of land and contracts of partnership. All three are treated as contracts of lease but the stipulations are often borrowed from other types of contract of sale. Furthermore, the stipulations of *ijāra*, that the period of time must be determined and the task be defined, were often ignored in *muzāra'a* and *musāqāt*.

Santillana marked out the following four basic types of contracts of *muzāra'a* in Mālikī *fiqh* involving situations where:

(a) The land, the labour, the seed, the animals and the tools of cultivation are shared by both parties (i.e. the landowner and cultivator), the produce to be shared by both.

(b) The land is common, one party provides the seeds, the other party provides the labour and the animals.

(c) One party provides the land and the seeds, the other the labour and the animals.

(d) One party provides the land and part of the seed, the other provides the other part of the seed and the labour as well as the animals.[52]

These types of arrangements indicate that *muzāra'a* in Mālikī *fiqh* is a contract of partnership (since it is also called *shirka fī al-zar'*), rather than a contract of sale; yet in regard to the distribution of the produce there is much similarity to a contract of sale of usufruct or to a contract of hire and lease. We turn now to the specific responses.

The *mukhtaṣṣ* lands belonging to *bayt al-māl* were leased to cultivators with the stipulation that every thing needed for cultivation would be provided by the cultivator himself and, furthermore, that he had to pay 1/5 plus 1/10 (or 1/9) of the produce if the land was provided with irrigational or other facilities. When Shāṭibī was asked about this practice, he declared such contracts invalid because the contract confused two distinct obligations; the obligation to pay 1/5 which was the rent on the land and the obligation to pay 1/10 which was the tax on land.[53]

López Ortiz further observed that such contracts were not even valid instances of *muzāra'a* according to Mālikī *fiqh* since the landowner did not contribute anything more than land.[54]

Another source of confusion was the practice of hiring the farm labour. The regular types of contract of *muzāra'a* did not allow this. If the hire of labourers was considered to be hire of services, then it was restricted by two stipulations:

(a) the wages could not be paid from the produce of the land, and

(b) an uncertainty existed in the payment of the wages.

These questions were raised in the case of contracts of labour and partnership regarding the collection of olives and the rearing of silk worms.

In the case of picking olives Ibn Sirāj (d. 848 H.) responded to an *istiftā* that the contract for the hire of labour to collect olives could be considered *musāqāt* if the olives were not yet ripe. The contract would then consist of taking care of trees, irrigation, etc. The labour could be contracted for in this case on the promise of payment of 1/4 or so of the produce. But if the olives were ripe and the task was only to collect them, such a promise of wages would make the contract invalid because the task was uncertain and the price of the amount of olives undeterminable.

Shāṭibī argued that if the task were to collect the olives by picking them from the branches or by shaking the trees, the contract was invalid and the wages unlawful. However, if the task were to collect olives that were already on the ground, a contract for the hire of labour may be allowed because in this case the labourer could guess how much he would eventually receive in wages.[55]

In the case of rearing silkworms, Ḥaffār (d. 811 H.), drawing an analogy with the *musāqāt*-type of contract, argued that a contract could be made only when the mulberry trees had grown leaves. The owner of the trees would contribute his share of leaves (1/2, 1/3, 2/3 or whatever had been agreed upon). The partner would also contribute his share of leaves. The owner of the silkworms would pay wages to the other in proportion to his share of leaves. In other words, this would be a case of partnership, and each of the partners would contribute his known share. The common practice, on the other hand, was to contract before the appearance of the leaves and to pay the wages from the leaves or from silkworms.

Shāṭibī responded that, in principle, the wages were not to be paid from the produce, but if the case were made analogous to *muzāra'a* by equal partnership in leaves, silkworms, etc., such payment could be allowed because, in that case, the labour would stand equal to half of the partner's share of leaves.[56]

A more complex case of partnership was the practice of pooling milk to make cheese. Shāṭibī explained that, in principle, the mixing of milk in unequal quantities to make cheese could not be allowed because it resembled *muzābana* (a contract for barter of dried dates for fresh dates). The practice may also be associated with *gharar* and *ribā* which are prohibited. Yet the mixing of milk could be allowed by consideration of *tashīl* (convenience) and *raf' al-ḥaraj* (removal of hardship). The consideration of *ḥaraj* becomes relevant in this case because it would be inconvenient to produce cheese individually by keeping every partner's share of milk separate.[57]

A peculiar case of partnership had to do with the produce of a tree owned by more than two persons. The question was asked whether it was permissible to distribute the produce equally. Shāṭibī did not allow such distribution because the matter of the tree was actually a case of partnership and not of joint ownership. Hence the distribution of the produce must be according to known shares. Shāṭibī suggested that to make such a distribution convenient the branches of that tree should be marked for every partner and then the produce be divided accordingly.[58]

CONTRACT FOR HIRE OF SERVICES

Shāṭibī was asked whether it was allowed for an *imām* (leader of prayers) to live on income from the *ḥabs* of a mosque, without any other vocation. Shāṭibī responded that the office of *imām* was a vocation, and if the person in question performed his duties, it was lawful for him to live on such income.[59]

An interesting case was the emergence of the appointment of *mu'īn al-dhabḥ*. In the meat market a person was hired by the butchers to supervise the killing of animals and to keep accounts of animals, meat and skins. He was paid partly by the butchers and partly by the sale of the meat. Shāṭibī was asked whether such an appointment was lawful.

Shāṭibī replied that if the consideration governing the appointment of *mu'īn al-dhabḥ* was to safeguard *maṣlaḥa* (public interest) in the observance of *sharī'a* rules about the killing of animals, then in view of *fasād al-zamān* (corruption of contemporary conditions) or the ignorance of religious teachings, such an appointment could be allowed. If such considerations did not exist and the person was not qualified to carry out the rules, his appointment would fall into the category of reprehensible things. Furthermore, such a practice would impose upon the people hardships in those matters in which God had allowed convenience. The Prophet Muḥammad used to eat meat brought by *badawīs* after simply saying the name of God.[60]

Abū 'Abd Allāh Ḥaffār asked Shāṭibī if an increase in his salary received from the *bayt al-māl* was lawful. Shāṭibī replied that it was lawful only on two conditions:

(i) that the amount of work had increased and,

(ii) that the increased wages were commensurate with the increased work.

When Ḥaffār received that answer he wrote again saying that he had been receiving that increase already for thirty years and that the practice of the community had allowed him to do so. He asked Shāṭibī what to do. Shāṭibī answered that he was not obliged to return the overpayment; what deserved consideration in this case was the morality of receiving such an increase, not whether the practice of the community allowed it or not.[61]

PROCEDURE

Shāṭibī was asked about the legal nature of *lawth* (incomplete circumstancial evidence leading to presumption of guilt in case of homicide), in a case where there was one eye witness of the murder and two witnesses of the culprit's confession. According to Mālikī law the requirements of proof in such a case are the following:

(i) the confession of the culprit, and

(ii) two eye witnesses of the murder,

(iii) one witness on the basis of *qasāma* (declaration on oath by several persons), and

(iv) strong circumstantial evidence.[62]

The evidence in the above case did not fulfil the requirements completely, but it was evidence of presumption. Shāṭibī was asked whether it was *lawth*. He responded that *lawth* could be described as accepting weaker evidence that could prove harm. Accordingly, the evidence in this case would be regarded as *lawth*. Shāṭibī, however, explained that the difference of opinion among Mālikī jurists on the effectiveness of *lawth* is based, in fact, on the principle that the efficacy of *lawth* depends largely upon the discretion of the judge (*nāẓir al-qaḍiyya*).[63]

CONCLUSION

To conclude this chapter, we may recapitulate the above with reference to the questions that we raised in the beginning of this chapter. A fuller statistical analysis of the *fatāwā* is given in a tabulated form. Brief answers to the questions are attempted below:

The first question concerned the subject matter of Islamic law that was confronted by the impact of social change. Out of the 40 cases 34 implied social change. Among them the following categories are included:

Theological matters:	2	Ritual and worship:	11
Family:	3	Property:	4
Taxes:	3	Contracts and obligations:	11

Only in two categories, i.e. exegesis and court procedure, cases did not imply social change.

The second question concerned the adaptation to social change by the jurists. Out of the 40 cases Shāṭibī accepted social change in 14 and rejected in 23.

Table 2: Social Change and Legal Theory

The following table shows, in detail, Shāṭibī's attitude towards the acceptance of social changes in his fatāwā.

Subject matter	Number of cases	Number of cases implying social changes		Related to the general social conditions			Shatibi's attitude			Acceptance Percentage (approx)
		Yes	n/a	yes	no	n/a	accepted	rejected	n/a	
1. Exegesis	1	-	1	1	-	-	-	-	1	-
2. Theological matters	2	2	-	2	-	-	-	1	1	50%
3. Ritual/worship	12	11	1	10	2	-	1	11	-	8%
4. Family	5	3	2	3	-	2	3	2	-	60%
5. Property	5	4	1	4	-	1	-	4	1	-
6. Taxes	3	3	-	3	-	-	3	-	-	100%
7. Contract and obligation	11	11	-	11	-	-	3	-	-	55%
8. Procedure	1	-	1	-	1	-	-	-	1	-
TOTAL:	40	34	6	34	3	3	14	23	3	
PERCENTAGE:	100	85	15	85	7.5	7.5	35	57.5	7.5	

The subject matters in which Shāṭibī rejected adaptation to social change most often were ritual and worship, family and trust. He showed flexibility with respect to theological matters and taxes. In contracts and obligations, he accepted and rejected cases almost equally, although he accepted adaptability more often than he rejected it.

As to the third question, whether these changes were related to the general social conditions or not, it may be seen that out of 40 cases, 34 were related to such conditions; two cases of ritual and one case of procedure were not the result of such conditions, whereas the rest of the cases were posed by social changes.

The fourth question concerns the method of adaptation to or rejection of adaptation to social change by the jurists. Broadly speaking, in rejecting adaptation of law to several social changes two different principles are invoked by Shāṭibī. In cases relating to theological matters, ritual and worship, and trust, he rejects adaptability of law to the social changes by declaring these changes *bid'a* (innovations). It is obvious that these matters particularly concern religion or relate primarily to a matter between man and God. It is very important to note that Shāṭibī does not invoke this principle in other matters. Apparently a social change affecting the above mentioned subject matters implied, for Shāṭibī, the imposition of a new obligation or the rejection of an earlier obligation in the name of religion. This must have led him to an investigation of the philosophical question of religious authority -- to whom did it belong? An analysis of Shāṭibī's concept of *bid'a* can provide us with an answer to this question in the particular context of our dissertation. To this we shall turn in chapter ten.

The second principle employed in rejecting social change, especially in cases of contracts and obligation, was that of 'unjust enrichments' and 'risk'. This principle can be understood as the negative side of the principles such as *tashīl* (convenience), *'adam al-ḥaraj* (removal of hardship) and *maṣlaḥa* (public good) on the basis of which he accepts social changes especially in matters of taxes and contracts. Whereas the latter served public good positively, the former guarded it by opposing what is harmful to public good.

The use of such general principles as *tashīl* and *maṣlaḥa* was prompted because of the failure or confusion of the regular methods of interpretation usually employed by the jurists. Among such regular methods the following were used in these *fatāwā* but found insufficient.

First is the method of analogy. This method is used in three ways:

(a) Seeking proximate analogy with a precedent that has some affinity with the case in question.

(b) Seeking new analogy to refer to a precedent which was not usually employed to make analogy, e.g. the case of the production of producing cheese was made analogous to producing olive oil.

(c) To adjust the case in a way to suit the requirements of analogy. As in the case of rearing silkworms, analogy was sought with *muzāra'a* by restructuring the form of the contract. This method of analogy forced the jurists to be casuistic, and even then the results were not very satisfactory. Consequently, they had to refer to general principles.

Second was the method of abandoning strict adherence (*taqlīd*) to Mālikī *fiqh* in order to borrow from other schools. This method, though employed by other jurists, was rejected by Shāṭibī as it led to a diversity of legal practices and also because it did not help to solve the problems. The method still depended on analogy.

The third method which was used in contracts was to subdivide the contract into different moments and parts so as to find suitable analogies applicable to each.

In short the usual *fiqh* methods generally proved to be insufficient to meet the new changes, and, hence, the jurists turned to general principles. An obvious result of such a trend was that more attention was paid to *uṣūl al-fiqh* in order to investigate the foundations, objectives and purposes of Islamic law.

Not only did lengthy discussions go on between various jurists about such matters as *qiyās, ikhtilāf,* and the role of custom, but the question of *mashhūr madhhab* and such subject matters were also discussed, indicating the interest of the jurists in legal theory.

Another important factor stimulating the interest in legal theory was the fact that the nature and form of contracts, which have a fundamental significance in every legal system were changing in that period. The factor of labour, and especially of seasonal labour, had brought a new dimension to the problem of wages. The new forms of contracts did not fit into the old framework of agricultural contracts for lease of land. The *fuqahā'* who still considered hired labour a *shirka fi'l-zar'* found contracts considered in this way too complicated and too unjust to be convenient for any of the parties.

The above analysis reveals how the impact of social change was felt in the *fatāwā* in this period. It has further shown that the older legal concepts failed to answer the problems raised by the social changes. We have also seen that because of this failure, Shāṭibī and other jurists resorted to general principles such as *maṣlaḥa*. The failure of older legal concepts and resort to general principles caused the jurists to reflect on basic matters of legal theory.

Finally, the above analysis has shown that in practice a change in method and substance of *fiqh* had taken place. Such a change logically called for a theoretical justification of the adaptation of law to social changes. Shāṭibī sought this justification in the principle of *maṣlaḥa*. There were, however, certain theoretical and methodological objections raised by the jurists against using *maṣlaḥa* as a method of legal reasoning. These objections have been outlined in chapter five. Shāṭibī's analysis of *maṣlaḥa* cannot be fully understood without a general understanding of such objections.

As a general conclusion of this chapter we may point out that the underlying theme in Shāṭibī's *fatāwā* is the question of the philosophy of law. With the exception of *'ibādāt*, in almost all the cases he gives more weight to public interest and common good than to the strict adherence to law.

Shāṭibī developed this teleological approach in his legal theory of *maqāṣid* that he presented in his book *al-Muwāfaqāt*. Next chapter offers a study of *al-Muwāfaqāt* enalysing its contents, and describing its influence on Islamic legal thinking.

NOTES AND REFERENCES

1. Aḥmad Bābā, *Nayl al-Ibtihāj* (Cairo: 'Abbās, 1351 H.), p. 49.
2. See for details Abū'l Ajfān, *Fatāwā al-Imām al-Shāṭibī* (Tūnis: Author, 1987), pp. 101-107. This work will be referred to later as *Fatāwā*. Abū'l Ajfān has catalogued 60 *fatāwā* by Shāṭibī in this book.
3. These *fatāwā* are recorded by Al-Wansharīsī, *Al-Mi'yār al-mu'rab wa'l-jāmi' al-mughrib 'an fatāwā ahl Ifrīqiya wa'l Andalus wa'l Maghrib* (Fās, 1314-1315 A.H.) at the following places:
Vol. I, 22, 24, 229, 267, 267-68; Vol. II, 230, 401-403; Vol. III, 163; Vol. IV, 146; Vol. V, 17, 18, 19, 50-51, 186-89, 192; Vol. VI, 256-279; Vol. VII, 68-69, 70-74; Vol. VIII, 238; Vol. IX, 163-165, 181, 478; Vol. XI, 31-37, 82-83, 87, 88-91, 96-98, 107-111; Vol. XII, 6, 7, 8, 11, 16, 19, 28, 201-211.
4. López— Ortiz, "Fatwas Granadinas de los siglos XIV y XV", *Al-Andalus*, VII (1941), pp. 85, 89, 93, 97, 102, 109, 114, 120, 123.
5. *Ibid.* p. 97.
6. See *Fatāwā*, p. 100.
7. *Ḥadīth qudsī*, in contradistinction to the *ḥadīth nabawī*, represents those sayings of the Prophet in which the actual "word of God" is related by Muḥammad, whereas *ḥadīth nabawī* represents the sayings of the Prophet. See *Shorter Encyclopedia of Islam*, article "Ḥadīth", p. 117.
8. *Al-Mi'yār*, Vol. XI, 96f, *Fatāwā*, p. 178.
9. *Al-Mi'yār*, Vol. II, 401-403., *Fatāwā*, p. 189 ff.
10. F. Rahman, *Islamic Methodology in History* (Karachi, 1965), 166.
11. *Al-I'tiṣām*, Vol. II, 208ff. Rahman's reference to Shāṭibī (*al-I'tiṣām*, III, 178) needs to be corrected. According to our text of *al-I'tiṣām* the quotation is located at Vol. II, p. 251.

12. *Al-I'tiṣām, op. cit.* Vol. 2, p. 293.
13. *Al-Mi'yār, op. cit.*, Vol. XI, 87; *Fatāwā*, p. 211 f.
14. *Al-Mi'yār*, Vol. I, 267; *Fatāwā*, p. 209.
15. *Al-Mi'yār,* Vol. XI, 31-33; *Fatāwā*, p. 193.
16. Most probably the practice of *ḥizb* was introduced into the Andalus by the Shādhiliyya. The most well-known *ḥizb al-baḥr*, which was supposed to be chanted while crossing the sea, is attributed to Abū'l Ḥasan al-Shādhilī. See D.B. MacDonald, "Ḥizb", *E.I.* (2nd ed.), Vol.III, 513-14.
17. *Al-Mi'yār*, Vol. XI, 88; *Fatāwā*, p. 206.
18. *Al-Mi'yār*,, Vol. IX, 88; *Fatāwā*, p. 211.
19. *Al-Mi'yār*, Vol. IX, 88; *Fatāwā*, p. 127 f.
20. *Al-Mi'yār*, Vol. IX, 1; *Fatāwā*, p. 207 f.
21. *Al-Mi'yār*, Vol. IX, 89; *Fatāwā*, p. 200 f.
22. *Al-Mi'yār*, Vol. IX, 89; *Fatāwā*, p. 213.
23. *Al-Mi'yār*, Vol. I, 229, *Fatāwā*, p. 207.
24. *Al-I'tiṣām*, Vol. I, 207.
25. *Al-Mi'yār,* Vol. I, 267; *Fatāwā*, p. 209.
26. Ibn 'Arafa (d. 803 A.H.), *Ḥudūd Fiqhiyya, vide* Abū 'Abd Allāh Muḥammad al-Raṣā', *Sharḥ al-Ḥudūd al-Fiqhiyya* (Tunis, 1305 A.H.), 12-13.
27. The *fiqhī* conclusion on the prohibition of *khamr* is based on the following verses: 2: 219; 5:90-91. "O you who believe, intoxicants (*khamr*) and games of chance are only an abomination of Satan's handiwork, so be ye away from it so that ye may be successful". The prohibition of *mayta* is based on the following verses: 2:173; 5:3; 16:115. "Verily He hath forbidden unto you what dieth of itself.."
28. *Al-Mi'yār*, Vol. I, 22; *Fatāwā*, p. 124.
29. *Al-Mi'yār*, Vol. I, 25; *Fatāwā*, p. 125.
30. *Al-Mi'yār*, Vol. I, p. 25.
31. *Ibid.*, 22.
32. *Al-Mi'yār,* 25.
33. *Al-Mi'yār*, Vol. IV, 146; *Fatāwā*, p. 141.
34. *Al-Mi'yār*, Vol. IX, 163; *Fatāwā*, p. 175 f.
35. *Al-Mi'yār*, Vol. IX, 478; *Fatāwā*, p. 139 f.
36. *Al-Mi'yār*, Vol. III, 163; *Fatāwā*, p. 140 f.
37. *Al-Mi'yār*, Vol. VIII, 238; *Fatāwā*, p. 163.
38. *Al-Mi'yār*, Vol. VII, 74.
39. *Al-Mi'yār, Fatāwā*, p. 203 f.
40. *Al-Mi'yār*, Vol. VII, 68; *Fatāwā*, 165.
41. Ibn 'Āṣim, *Tuḥfat al-ḥukkām*... Ed. by L. Bercher. (Alger, 1958), 174. See also Bercher's note: 873, p. 386.

ومن يبيع ما عليه حبسا   يرد مطلقا ومع علم أسا

42. *Al-Mi'yār*, Vol. VII, 70-74.
43. See n. 5.
44. *Al-Mi'yār*, Vol. VII, 85; *Nayl,* 49; *Mi'yār*, Vol. XI, 101-107; *Fatāwā*, p. 187.
45. *Al-Mudawwanat al-kubrā*, Vol. I, (Baghdad, 1970), 268. Saḥnūn asked Ibn Qāsim about a case where someone inherited certain merchandise, which he decided to sell; would there be *zakāt* on this merchandise. Ibn Qāsim said no, because:

لاتكون هذه السلعة للتجارة حتى يبيعها، فاذا باعها استقبل بالثمن حولا من يوم باعها لانه يوم باعها صارت للتجارة

On p. 294, Mālik states about *zakāt* on fruit as follows:

فليس فيها زكاة ولا فى اثمانها حتى يحول على اثمانها الحول من يوم تقبض اثمانها

46. López Ortiz, *op. cit.*, 97.
47. Udovitch, *Partnership and Profit in Medieval Islam* (Princeton, 1970), pp. 7f., 9, 10.
48. *Al-Mi'yār*, Vol. V, 186-187; *Fatāwā*, p. 144.
49. *Al-Mi'yār*, Vol. V, 19; *Fatāwā*, p. 149.
50. *Al-Mi'yār*, Vol. V, 192; *Fatāwā*, pp. 143-144.
51. D. Santillana, *Istituzioni di diritto musulmano malichita*, Vol. II (Rome, 1938), 306. See also *Mudawwana*, Vol. VI, 21.
52. Santillana, *loc. cit.*
53. López Ortiz, *op. cit.*, 97. *Fatāwā*, pp. 153-54.
Shāṭibī's *fatwā* is understood better in the context of the following two stipulations of *musāqāt*, mentioned by Ibn 'Āṣim:
(i) لاتصح (المساقاة) مع كراء
(ii) والدفع للزكاة ان لم يشترط بينهما بنسبة الجزء فقط
Ibn 'Āṣim, *Tuḥfa, op. cit.*, 162, 164.
54. López Ortiz, *op. cit.*
55. *Ibid.*, 109. *Fatāwā*, p. 151.
56. *Al-Mi'yār*, Vol. V, 50. *Fatāwā*, p. 154.
57. *Al-Mi'yār*, Vol. 5, 187; *Fatāwā*, pp. 156-160.
58. López Ortiz, *op. cit.*, 102; *Fatāwā*, p. 162.
59. *Al-Mi'yār*, Vol. VII, 68; *Fatāwā*, p. 172.
60. *Al-Mi'yār*, Vol. IX, 98. Slightly different version in *Fatāwā* p. 137-8.
61. *Al-Mi'yār*, Vol. VII, 74; *Fatāwā*, pp. 167 ff.
62. Ibn 'Āṣim, *op. cit.*, 226.
63. *Al-Mi'yār*, Vol. II, 230; *Fatāwā*, p. 173.

CHAPTER FOUR

AL-MUWĀFAQĀT

In his introduction to *al-Muwāfaqāt*, Shāṭibī narrates that he had initially titled this book as *'Unwān al-ta'rīf bi asrār al-taklīf* because he discussed in this book the underlying reasons of legal obligations. He later changed it to the present title consequent upon his teacher's dream that he told Shāṭibī. He saw in his dream that Shāṭibī was carrying a book that he had written. On enquiry Shāṭibī explained that it was *al-Muwāfaqāt* whose unusual title alluded to the agreement that Shāṭibī sought between the schools of Ibn Qāsim and Abū Ḥanīfa.[1] This is a very significant statement about *al-Muwāfaqāt* to which we shall return soon. We would like presently to note in this story that scholars had begun to show interest in the book during Shāṭibī's life.

An immediate influence of *al-Muwāfaqāt* can be noticed by the fact that Shāṭibī's disciple Abū Bakr Muḥammad b. Muḥammad b. 'Āṣim (d. 829 A.H), the author of a well known Mālikī text *Tuḥfa*, wrote an abridgement of *al-Muwāfaqāt* entitled *Nayl al-munā fī ikhtiṣār al-Muwāfaqāt*.[2] Another of his disciples from Wādī Āsh versified *al-Muwāfaqāt* with the title *Nayl al-munā min al-Muwāfaqāt*. He begins his book with these verses:

> Praise be to God who by His grace
> Posited the secrets of His wisdom in the laws
> He prepared human reason for the changes
> According to the commands of obligation.

After explaining the purpose of revelation, Prophet Muḥammad's merciful prophecy and admiring the persuit of knowledge, he says:

> I found comfort in books of knowledge
> I abstained myself from all things other than knowledge.
> (The books are) the springs of sweet water
> The most notable among them is *al-Muwāfaqāt*, by our master, the most learned, our guide Abū Isḥāq al-Shāṭibī.
> This is a book of best objectives. The seeker has no targets beyond it.
> He had titled it as *al-'Unwān*
> But changed it to another title after a dream.
> I have studied it partly with him

> I have my reservations on some points.
> My disagreement however, is very little.[3]

Andalusian scholar Al-Ḥafīd Ibn Marzūq (842/1438) described *al-Muwāfaqāt* as "the most acceptable book".[4] It appears, however, that Shāṭibī and his book became a subject of debate in Andalus in fifteenth century and remained so for a long time. Al-Mawwāq (897/1491) the last of the *muftī*s of Granada, wrote *Sunan al-muhtadīn* in which he criticised Shāṭibī's views, especially with reference to his differences with Ibn Sirāj and Ibn Lubb.[5]

Aḥmad Bābā (1036/1626) a sixteenth century biographer of Shāṭibī, admired the book in the following words:

> The most valuable book in jurisprudence (*uṣūl al-fiqh*). It is unique. It is an evidence of his (Shāṭibī's) leading position in sciences, especially in the science of *Uṣūl*.[6]

Muḥammad Makhlūf (d. 1941), a modern biographer of Mālikī scholars, appreciated *al-Muwāfaqāt* in words that echo Aḥmad Bābā's comments: "A great book without any precedent, the most noble writing".[7]

Shaykh 'Abdullāh Dirāz (d. 1958), the editor and commentator of *al-Muwāfaqāt*, wrote:

> Thus the science of *uṣūl* continued to lack discussion of a significant part [intent of the lawgiver]... Until God, may He be praised and exalted, appointed Abū Isḥāq al-Shāṭibī in the eighth century of Hijra to make amends for this deficiency, and to erect this great edifice....[8]

Abū Zuhra (d. 1974) praises the book very highly saying:

> Abū Isḥāq Ibrāhīm b. Mūsā al-Shāṭibī (d. 780 H.), a Mālikī jurist, carried all the burden and fulfilled this heavy task, or almost did it, in his book *al-Muwāfaqāt*. He explained the objectives of Islamic law clearly, and linked them with the rules expounded by the theorists. He discussed the sources of law in the light of these objectives and ends. Thus, he broke new grounds in jurisprudence and that is the road that must be followed from now on.[9]

Shaykh al-Fāḍil b. 'Āshūr (d. 1970) assesses the contribution of *al-Muwāfaqāt* in the following words:

> With this writing Shāṭibī erected a lofty pyramid for the Islamic civilization. It made possible to watch from this tower the roads and ways leading to the achievement of perpetuation and protection of

religion. Few scholars before him discovered it. The searchers for the philosophy of Islamic law depend on him. The advantages of this book appeared surprisingly in the present and preceding centuries when after its awakening, the world of Islam faced the problem of integrating the religious law with the new events of contemporary life. Shāṭibī's *al-Muwāfaqāt* was the refuge to which people resorted...[10]

We can see appreciation of the book gradually increasing during the last centuries. In the twentieth century the book has been used so extensively by modern scholars that one can say without exaggeration that the book has contributed immensely towards the making of modernists' conception of Islamic law, particularly the concept of *maṣlaḥa* which is its essential ingredient.[11]

The significance of *al-Muwāfaqāt* in modern legal thinking may be seen in the fact that in Egypt, Muftī Muḥammad 'Abduh used to advise scholars and his students to study *al-Muwāfaqāt* in order to understand the true philosophy of "Islamic law making".[12] In Pakistan, Abū'l A'lā Mawdūdī, in his programme to introduce Islamic law in Pakistan, recommends the translation of *al-Muwāfaqāt,* among other books on the philosophy of law, into national languages, "So that our law experts may acquire a deeper insight into, and gain a correct understanding of, the spirit of Islamic fiqh".[13]

As noted in the preceding chapter, since its first publication in 1884 in Tunis, five editions of *al-Muwāfaqāt* have so far appeared, all edited and annotated by well-known scholars such as Mūsā Jār Allāh (d. 1942).[14] Muḥammad al-Khiḍr Ḥusayn and 'Abd Allāh Dirāz.

Evidence for the merit of Shāṭibī's lengthy work may be drawn not merely from the number of editions it has undergone but, more importantly, from the rank which *al-Muwāfaqāt* soon attained among works on Muslim law. It came to transcend even the limits of the Sunni schools of law. With few exceptions, all modern Muslim authors on legal matters and theories frequently refer to Shāṭibī as an authority.The works of the following eminent authors adequately substantiate this point: Abū Zuhra, Ma'rūf Dawālībī, Muḥammad Iqbāl, Muḥammad Khuḍrī, Yūsuf Mūsā, Muṣṭafā Zarqā', Abū Sinna and Abū 'Abd Allāh 'Umar.[15]

Furthermore, some modern authors grant to Shāṭibī a rank as high as that of *mujaddid* (religious reformer believed to appear at the turn of each century). Rashīd Riḍā (d. 1935) counts him among the *mujaddids* of the 8th/14th century and regards his contribution equal to that of Ibn Khaldūn.[16] Fāḍil Ibn 'Āshūr[17] and 'Abd al-Muta'āl al-Ṣa'īdī[18] also express the same opinion, but Ṣa'īdī adds that Shāṭibī ranks alongside Shāfi'ī in significance, because his exposition of the goal and spirit of Islamic law made it possible for Islamic law to escape the impasse into which the strict adherence to the limits defined by

Shāfi'ī in *uṣūl al-fiqh* had led. This is a very significant comment that needs to be elaborated.

Shāfi'ī's *uṣūl al-fiqh* paved the way for juridical theology[19] which defined *uṣūl* in terms of sources and limited the method of legal reasoning to *qiyās*. This method led to an impasse in solving modern legal problems in the absence of precedents. Shāṭibī sought a way out of this impasse by means of his doctrine of *maqāṣid al-sharī'a*.

Notwithstanding its influence and significant contribution to modern legal thought very few scholars have studied the book exclusively. Two reasons can, perhaps, be suggested in this regard. One, as 'Abd Allāh Dirāz, the commentator on *al-Muwāfaqāt*, remarks, is the fact that Shāṭibī's thought is too difficult and too complex to be easily penetrated.[20] Margoliouth also referred to confusion and subtlety in Shāṭibī's views.[21] This complexity is not due to any abstractness of thought or to any bizarreness in his style, nor in his choice of words. His style is lucid, and his discussion is systematic and clear. The difficulty in understanding Shāṭibī lies, rather, in the fact that a study of his thought demands not only a sufficient knowledge of the development of *uṣūl al-fiqh* prior to him, but also a fair acquaintance with the development of the doctrines of *fiqh*, theology, philosophy and mysticism. More importantly there is required a knowledge of the political, economic and social developments in Shāṭibī's time as well. Without this background knowledge his views appear to be contradictory, vague or abstract, and hence difficult to follow.

The second reason has to do with a generally skeptical attitude of Islamicists towards studies of Islamic doctrines on the formal level. Gibb, for example, warns against formally studying Muslim theological doctrines arguing that since Islamic theology is always forced into extreme positions, it exhibits a predilection for words and form. Islamic doctrine thus presents an outer formulation rather than an inner function of reality. Hence Islamic doctrines, taken literally, are not of much help in understanding the inner religious attitudes of Muslims.[22]

Such warnings discouraged any study of Islamic doctrines *per se*, including legal theory. In his discussion of Islamic legal theory, S. Hurgronje dismissed a discussion of the question of whether all acts are forbidden by nature and that only those specified by the divine law may be allowed...saying that "these and similar questions may be of importance to the Imām al-Ḥaramayn, but they do not help us to a correct understanding of Islam".[23] Chehata maintains that *uṣūl al-fiqh* was born independently of *fiqh* and developed without influencing the science of law or being influenced by it.[24] Schacht concludes that the theory of *uṣūl al-fiqh* is of little direct importance for the positive doctrines of the school of law.[25] Why, if a study of *uṣūl al-fiqh* has no relevance to the understanding of *fiqh* and is merely a consideration of words and forms if studied *per se*, should it be studied at all? However, more recently Western scholars have been showing a growing interest in Islamic legal theory and at the same time a considerable number of studies on Shāṭibī have appeared in Arabic.[26]

The first printing of *al-Muwāfaqāt* in 1884, though diligently edited, did not contain any commentary or analysis of the work. In 1909, Mūsā Jārullāh published *Al-Muwāfaqāt* from Kazan, Russia. In his introduction to the book, Jārullāh described the book as "the only real work on the *uṣūl al-fiqh*" in Islamic literature. After a scathing criticism of Islamic literature on *tafsīr, ḥadīth, fiqh* and *uṣūl al-fiqh* for its indulgence in polemics and rhetorics and for neglecting the real issues of life and society, he observed that his contemporary movement for reform of Muslim institutions of learning would not achieve its goal unless books like *al-Muwāfaqāt* are included in the school curricula, in place of *al-Manār* and *al-Tawḍīh*. "Students need a book like *al-Muwāfaqāt* that presents the uṣūl al-fiqh in the real sense and introduces the students to freedom of thought, skill of legal reasoning (*ijtihād*) and spirit of independence".[27]

Mūsā Jārullāh wrote this introduction in Turkish language in order to address a wider range of readership. It was published along with a number of other Turkish texts on contemporary problems. Jārullāh explained that the previous edition of the book printed in Tunis, contained several errors that he had corrected in his edition. Besides these corrections he aimed to present a real model book on *uṣūl* to scholars and studetns of Islam in Russia. According to him,

> *Al-Muwāfaqāt* expounds the legislative objectives of the Qur'ān and Sunna more extensively and more clearly than any other book. It elaborates with minute details the basic human needs and secondary necessities of life. It explains the correspondence between human needs and legal texts in a very comprehensive manner. This book provides a liberal perspective on each issue for those who want to study them rationally with complete freedom.[28]

In 1913 some extracts from another of Shāṭibī's work, *al-I'tiṣām*, appeared in the Cairo journal *al-Manār*. These extracts stirred the interest of scholars in Shāṭibī. In 1916, Ignaz Goldziher, in his translation and critical study of Ghazālī's work *Faḍā'iḥ al-bāṭiniyya* made use of these extracts to compare Shāṭibī with Ghazālī. Although Goldziher's knowledge about Shāṭibī was limited (only the above-mentioned extracts and Turkish introduction were available to him), and although he confused *al-I'tiṣām* with *al-Muwāfaqāt* (as he insisted on identifying these extracts as part of *al-Muwāfaqāt*), yet he is the first European scholar who tried to place Shāṭibī's thought into a historical perspective. While comparing similarities in the treatment of the Bāṭinīs by Ghazālī and Shāṭibī, he found them identical. He, therefore, drew a general conclusion that "in many ways Shāṭibī is through and through penetrated with the ideas of Ghazālī".[29]

Rashīd Riḍā, himself a warrior against *bid'a*, was largely responsible for creating the image of Shāṭibī as a crusader against *bid'a*. After publishing the above-mentioned extracts from Shāṭibī on *bid'a* in *al-Manār,* he edited and published Shāṭibī's *al-I'tiṣām* in 1913/1914. This theme was further stressed by Rashīd Riḍā in the biography of Muḥammad 'Abduh which was published in 1931.[30]

Al-I'tiṣām was reviewed by D.S. Margoliouth in *The Journal of the Royal Asiatic Society* in 1916. In a very scanty review Margoliouth described the work as "occupied with juristic subtleties and distinctions which become more and more confused towards the end of the book".[31] Thus implicitly he dismissed the work as not worthy of further scholarly attention.

It was about the same time that, a notice on Shāṭibī was included in Brockelmann's Supplement. This notice was based entirely on the information provided by Goldziher. Some of the factual mistakes by Goldziher were also included by Brockelmann without correction.[32]

About the same time, Muḥammad Khuḍrī (d. 1927), a teacher at Gordon Law College in the Sudan at that time, published his book *Uṣūl al-fiqh*, for which, in many ways, he drew heavily upon Shāṭibī's *al-Muwāfaqāt*. He also disclosed in the preface that it was on the suggestion of Muḥammad 'Abduh that he had turned to *al-Muwāfaqāt* for understanding the nature of Islamic law (*asrār al-tashrī' al-Islāmī*).[33]

While Rashīd Riḍā's interpretation of Shāṭibī depended solely upon *al-I'tiṣām*, that of Khuḍrī was entirely shaped by *al-Muwāfaqāt*. In the former, Shāṭibī appears a crusader against *bid'a*, while in the latter as a philosopher-jurist. Khuḍrī argued that Shāṭibī's teachings presented the real spirit of Islamic law which had been forgotten by medieval jurists.

Muḥammad Ḥasan al-Ḥajwī (d. 1956), in his lectures on the history of Islamic Jurisprudence, given in 1918, did not differ greatly from Riḍā in presenting Shāṭibī's image as a reformer.[34] But believing in this image he misread Shāṭibī's concept of obedience (*ta'abbud*). Ḥajwī, in his lectures, maintained that the flexibility of Islamic law was lost in later Islamic history as the jurists extended *ta'abbud* even to those acts which fell under the category of *mu'āmalāt*. A certain correspondent, in order to refute Ḥajwī's argument, quoted Shāṭibī on the point that the consideration of *ta'abbud* is inevitable in *mu'āmalāt* as well. To reject this argument, Ḥajwī referred to 'Izz al-Dīn 'Abd al-Salām in his support and judged the quotation from Shāṭibī in this light as he said:

> This [statement of 'Izz al-Dīn] is opposed to your quotation from the author of *al-Muwāfaqāt* where he narrowed [the application of *maṣlaḥa*] by imposing *ta'abbud* on all categories of acts. But he (Shāṭibī) did not support his contention with any proof.[35]

We shall deal with Shāṭibī's concept of *ta'abbud* in chapter eight. It must, however, be pointed out at the moment that such an interpretation of Shāṭibī's view of *ta'abbud* is quite misleading. Shāṭibī certainly differentiated between two kinds of obligations, those which are absolute and not subject to change, consisting of *'ibādāt*, and those which are relative and subject to changes, consisting of *'ādāt* which include *mu'āmalāt*. The former are *ta'abbudī* and the latter *maṣlaḥī*. This distinction is maintained on the first level, i.e. that of *Shāri'*, though both may become *ta'abbudī* on the second level, i.e. that of *mukallaf*.

In 1941 López Ortiz published his invaluable detailed study of certain *fatāwā* (responsa) given by the Granadan jurists of the fourteenth century.[36] Among these Shāṭibī's *fatāwā* were also included. This study provides us with the actual historical context against which Shāṭibī's *al-Muwāfaqāt* can be studied. Although Ortiz's study is not concerned with the philosophical questions of a legal theory and thus does not include *al-Muwāfaqāt*, yet he confirms that in his *fatāwā*, Shāṭibī relied on the notions of *tashīl* (facilitation) and *istiṣlāḥ*. Shāṭibī defended custom against the rules of *fiqh*. It is also significant to note that Ortiz was impressed by the deep insight that Shāṭibī showed into the economic of the society.

Since Ortiz was concerned with Shāṭibī's *fatāwā* and not with his philosophy of law, one might be misled by his remarks to conclude that Shāṭibī's reference to *tashīl* and *istiṣlāḥ* was a measure of expediency. Such an understanding of Shāṭibī is incorrect because the principle of *maṣlaḥa* in Shāṭibī's legal philosophy is a basic concept; not an expedient method of legal reasoning. López Ortiz's remarks may, however, be best understood in reference to Shāṭibī's doctrine of the Ends of the law.

In 1951 'Abd al-Muta'āl al-Ṣa'īdī observed that in matters of dogma, Shāṭibī was rigid like other jurists such as Ibn Taymiyya and Ibn Qayyim. Ṣa'īdī refers to Shāṭibī's view on *ribāṭ* to uphold his point. He states that Shāṭibī declared that to dwell in a *ribāṭ* for the sake of *'ibāda* only, constituted *bid'a*.[37]

Fāḍil Ibn 'Āshūr and Ṣa'īdī, as we have already mentioned, credited Shāṭibī with providing an escape from the impasse that Islamic jurisprudence faced in the fourteenth century. Furthermore, according to Ibn 'Āshūr, Shāṭibī rejected the differentiation between theoretical and practical religion—a distinction which was maintained by a number of theologians and philosophers.[38] Shāṭibī insisted on the unity in the essence of religion. That is why he also opposed the practice of classification of *bid'a* into praise-worthy and condemnable.

Ibn 'Āshūr argues that Shāṭibī and Ibn Lubb had fundamental differences on the legally binding nature of certain acts. By binding nature Ibn 'Āshūr means the process of acts being or becoming *'ibādāt* or religious obligations. Ibn 'Āshūr concludes that Shāṭibī's concept of religion was more comprehensive than most other jurists' because he considered the payment of taxes to government to be a religious duty, thus regarding them as *'ibādāt*.

In a study of transactions in the *Sharī'a*, made in 1955, Ṣubḥī Maḥmaṣānī was struck by the modern subjective approach adopted by Shāṭibī in torts.[39] Shāṭibī maintained that if an act which is legal in itself is committed with the sole intent of inflicting injury upon others, it is legally prohibited and must be prevented. Maḥmaṣānī observed that this subjective approach is quite modern as it directs itself to the intent of the person exercising the right. This approach also stands in contrast to the traditional objective approach as formulated in the *Majalla*.

It was, perhaps, this finding that led Maḥmaṣānī to a further study of Shāṭibī. In his lectures in 1962 he admired him more enthusiastically. Maḥmaṣānī believes that the foundations of the modern renaissance in Islamic legal thought were laid in the fourteenth century by the Muslim jurists who wrote on the methodology and the ends of Islamic law. In these writings they were the precursors of western legal philosophers such as Montesquieu who taught that the evolution of law takes place conditioned by local, temporal and situational changes. Mahmaṣānī recalls Shihāb al-Dīn al-Qarāfī, 'Izz al-Dīn 'Abd al-Salām, Ibn Qayyim and Shāṭibī as such philosophers of law. Among them, however, he singles out Shāṭibī for the finest exposition of Islamic jurisprudence and philosophy of law.[40]

Since 1960 references to Shāṭibī's *al-Muwāfaqāt* have become so frequent in almost all works on Islamic law that a complete account of them is quite impossible. We will, however, take note of some of the more important recent studies.

In his *Islamic Methodology in History* published in 1965, Fazlur Rahman discusses Shāṭibī's views in detail to a far greater extent than earlier scholars. Rahman, in his *Islam,* considered *al-Muwāfaqāt* as a work on the philosophy of law and jurisprudence.[41] Rahman observed Shāṭibī's views on the following points: his concept of knowledge, his views about the role of human reason in acquiring knowledge, and his views on *ijtihād* and *taqlīd*. Since these points have been studied mainly in reference to Shāṭibī's epistemology, Rahman sees in Shāṭibī's thinking a "patent denial of faith in the intellectual and moral powers of man".[42]

Rahman, however, is reluctant to carry the above conclusion to Shāṭibī's legal thinking. He observes that although Shāṭibī "categorically denies that reason has any primary role in law-making or even in the formulation of the moral imperatives, yet he (Shāṭibī) himself has exercised a great deal of rational power in fixing the "goals of *sharī'a*".[43] He also finds an implicit confusion in Shāṭibī's statement about *ijtihād* that it "is the necessary duty of a Muslim" along with the stipulation that the *ijtihād* should not contradict the objectives of *Sharī'a*. Rahman finds this stipulation inconsistent because the objectives of the Lawgiver cannot be formulated without the operation of *ijtihād*.[44]

The above observations have significant implications for our study. Goldziher's suggestion of Ghazālī's thorough influence on Shāṭibī may mean Shāṭibī's acceptance of Ghazālī's view on *maṣlaḥa*. Ghazālī is known to have rejected *maṣlaḥa mursala*. His influence on Shāṭibī would thus amount to the rejection of the adaptability of Islamic legal theory to social changes. Shāṭibī's opposition of *bid'a* (innovation), as presented by Rashid Rida and others, signifies that he believed in the immutability of Islamic law. Ḥajwī, Ṣa'īdī and Rahman conclude that Shāṭibī was rigid, conservative and opposed to rational interpretation of legal matters. In other words, they are suggesting that Shāṭibī would oppose the accommodation of Islamic law to social changes.

On the other hand, Khuḍrī, Maḥmaṣānī and Lópes Ortiz have observed that his views in legal matters were flexible and that he preferred the consideration of human need to the hardship incurred in following the legal texts to the very letter. Ibn 'Āshūr's interpretation of Shāṭibī's concept of *dīn* (religion) and Ḥajwī's conclusion about Shāṭibī's conception of *ta'abbud* (obedience) have very serious implications for Shāṭibī's view of the adaptability of Islamic law. An all comprehensive concept of religion and an all-inclusive conception of obedience as held by Shāṭibī suggest that he viewed every legal and social change from the angle of "religion" and "obedience" which only imposes limits on adaptability of Islamic legal theory to social changes.

If the scholars are disagreed as to the assessment of Shāṭibī's *al-Muwāfaqāt*, their disagreement stems from their differences of understanding and interpretation of Shāṭibī's basic terms such as *bid'a*, *ta'abbud, dīn* etc. As is shown in the following chapters, the above terms are related to Shāṭibī's conception of *maṣlaḥa* which is the basis of his doctrine of *maqāṣid al-sharī'a*, and they cannot be properly understood in isolation from this conception.

For a proper appreciation of Shāṭibī's doctrine, one must study the doctrine as Shāṭibī himself presented it, in his own framework and structure. This we will do in the following chapters. Presently we would like to return to Shāṭibī's explanation of the title of the book in order to see how Shāṭibī himself placed the book in the history of Islamic legal theory.

As noted earlier, Shāṭibī explains that the book was called *al-Muwāfaqāt*, because it reconciled the schools of Ibn al-Qāsim and Abū Ḥanīfa. He does not elaborate specifically how and on what points he reconciled the two schools. However experts on Islamic legal principles note some points where Shāṭibī moved from Mālikī to the Ḥanafī position. For instance Abū Zuhra observes that Shāṭibī opted for the Ḥanafī position on the question of the indication of the meaning of general words (*'āmm*).[45] Without going into details we may add that Shāṭibī found the two schools agreeing with each other in principle, on the following points: *istiḥsān* (Ḥanafī) and *maṣlaḥa* (Mālikī)[46]; *'urf* and *'āda; dalāla* (denotation)[47] and *ḥiyal* (legal device).[48]On the last two points he clarified Mālikī and Ḥanafī positions, and found them in agreement in principle though differing in detail. He, however, defended Ḥanafī jurists saying that all their books were not available in al-Andalus and that these jurists were responsible and God-fearing persons, they could not support defiance of law.[49]

However, these three points are not enough to justify agreement between the two schools unless they are studied in the general context of the development of Islamic legal theory. We have earlier referred to 'Abd al-Muta'āl al-Ṣa'īdī's remarks crediting Shāṭibī for leading Islamic legal theory out of the impasse into which Shāfi'ī's *uṣūl* had led. This remark points to the proper context for the assessment of Shāṭibī's contribution. The remark is however, better understood in the light of Ibn Khaldūn's historiography of *uṣūl al-fiqh*.

Ibn Khaldūn[50] observed that there developed two trends or methodologies in the books on *uṣūl al-fiqh*. Firstly *ṭarīqat al-mutakallimīn* (juridical theology) that was epitomised by Shāfi'ī (d. 820) and then by Abū'l Ḥusayn al-Baṣrī (d. 1085), Imām al-Juwaynī (d. 1047) al-Ghazālī (d.1111), Sayf al-Dīn al-Āmidī (d. 1233) and others. Secondly *ṭarīqat al-Ḥanafiyyīn* (jurists method) developed by the Ḥanafī school as illustrated in the books on *Uṣūl* by al-Dabūsī (d. 1038) and al-Karakhī (d. 951) and later systematised by al-Bazdawī (d. 1089). The jurists' method concentrated on analysing and deriving general rules and principles from the doctrines of the school. In other words they found the regulating principles by an inductive analysis of the *furū'* (substantive law) in order to apply to new cases. Some examples of these principles are: "The general (*'āmm*) is as definite as the particular (*khāṣṣ*)", "No preference to a *ḥadīth* on account of multiple narrators", etc. The juridical theology, on the other hand, concerned itself more to theological questions like whether good and evil were known by human reason or by revelation. They laid more stress on the method of deduction from sources. The books in this school discussed the term *uṣūl* in the meaning of sources of law.

Shāṭibī used the Ḥanafī method of deriving rules and principles from the legal doctrines. He did not treat *uṣūl* as 'sources', the sense in which Shāfi'ī understood the term. In fact Shāṭibī deals only with the Qur'ān and Sunna in *al-Muwāfaqāt*, he does not discuss *ijmā'* and *qiyās* separately. While Ḥanafīs derived principles from the *fiqh* doctrines of the jurists of the school, Shāṭibī derived them from the Qur'ān and Sunna. That is why he calls his book *Al-Muwāfaqāt fī uṣūl al-Sharī'a* to distinguish it from *Uṣūl al-fiqh*. He uses inductive method to infer these principles and considers them exact, definite and certain contrary to Shāfi'ī jurists who regard *uṣūl al-fiqh* uncertain and opinionated.

Our explanation is supported also by Shāṭibī's reference to Ibn al-Qāsim as representative of Mālikī school. While Mālik collected and systematised the juristic practice in Madina, it was Ibn al-Qāsim who under the influence of the Ḥanafīs developed Mālikī doctrines by deriving regulating principles from them and extending their applications to new cases. He was therefore responsible for the systematic development of the Mālikī school.[51]

Using Ḥanafī method of generalisations Shāṭibī found that *maṣlaḥa* was the underlying principle in all *Sharī'a* laws. That is where Shāṭibī found the two schools coming close to each other. Shāṭibī observed that his contemporary methodologies in legal reasoning led to conflict and diversity in Islamic laws because in their analogies they treated *'illa* isolated from the total perspective of legal objectives. Shāṭibī developed a legal methodology which he called *maqāṣid al-sharī'a* that did not focus on *'illa* in a particular rule but related it with the intent of the Lawgiver. Usually jurists used the term *ḥikma* to denote general principles to distinguish it from the particular cause of a rule that was *'illa*.

In a recent study, Aḥmad al-Rīsūnī[52] has shed more light on the term *maqāṣid* as used by the jurists. According to him it is only in modern period that jurists have tried to define the term. Earlier, no such need was felt. The jurists used the term *ḥikma* more than *maqāsid*. While *'illa* was a particular cause *ḥikma* was a general cause or underlying reason. Frequently they were used interchangeably. Shāṭibī used *maqāṣid, ḥikma* and *ma'nā* as almost synonymous terms, *'illa* was all these things on a particular level. Al-Rīsūnī remarks that Shāṭibī often tends to revive ancient meanings of the terms. He therefore, used the term *'illa* in its original meaning.[53]

Thus according to Shāṭibī the proper method of Islamic legal reasoning was not to limit oneself to search for causes in a particular doctrine or case, but to review *Sharī'a* as a whole and discover the intent of the Lawgiver.

This methodology of Shāṭibī, however, touched upon some theological issues in which many Ash'arī theologians would disagree with him. Consequently, Shāṭibī clarified his position in a preamble to the exposition of *maqāṣid* doctrine. Shāṭibī argued that his doctrine was based on a generally agreed premise which is theological in its origin. The premise is that God instituted the *sharā'i'* (laws) for the *maṣāliḥ* (benefits, good) of the people, both immediate and future.[54] There exists, however, a difference of opinion among scholars concerning the details of this premise. For the purpose of our discussion the point needs to be explained briefly.

The *mutakallimūn* (theologians) accept the general and apparent meaning of the premise of *maṣāliḥ*, yet they differ if the *maṣāliḥ* are understood in terms of *'ilal* (pl. of *'illa*) meaning 'causes' or 'motives'. The Ash'arī theologians reject explicit as well as implicit causality in reference to God. For them, the premise implies that God is obliged by the consideration of *maṣāliḥ* to act in a certain way. Since such an obligation proposed limitation on God's omnipotence, the Ash'arīs rejected the idea that the *maṣāliḥ* are the *'ilal* of *sharā'i'*. They, however, accepted the premise by interpreting the *maṣāliḥ* to be the 'grace' of God, rather than the 'cause' of his acts. On the other hand, the Mu'tazila, even though they too believed in God's omnipotence, maintained that God is obliged to do good. Consequently they accepted the above premise, regarding *maṣāliḥ* as the *'illa* of *Sharī'a*.

The theological disagreement initially concerned God's acts, but it was extended to God's commands in the Qur'ān as they constitute His acts of speech. Thus the theological disagreement manifested itself in *uṣūl al-fiqh* as well. Theological arguments penetrated into *uṣūl* [*al-fiqh*] also because a number of writers on *uṣūl* were theologians.

Uṣūl al-fiqh, however, required a manner of thinking and a method of reasoning different from that of *kalām*. Legal thinking necessitated that the volition for voluntary human acts must be attributed to man himself if man is to be held legally responsible for his acts. Since obedience to Divine Commands thus depends on human volition, the Command must be shown to be motivated by the consideration of human interests. Consequently, the premise of *maṣāliḥ* must be accepted in *uṣūl* in terms of 'cause', 'motive' and 'purpose'. Some *uṣūliyyīn*, such as Ghazālī and others, in order to be consistent with their theological views, redefined the term *'illa* so as to rid it of the connotation of 'causality' and 'motivation' in which sense it was used and disputed in *kalām*. Passing from *kalām* to *Uṣūl*, the term *'illa* thus underwent a semantic change. For the explanation of the meaning it acquired in *Uṣūl*, we now turn to Shāṭibī.

Shāṭibī explains that Rāzī held that like His acts, God's commands also cannot be analyzed in terms of *'ilal* (causes) whereas the Mu'tazila believed that His Commands are caused (*mu'allala*) by the consideration of the *maṣāliḥ* of the people. The majority of the *fuqahā'* accepted the latter view in *fiqh*. Since it was inevitable that *'ilal* be established for *al-aḥkām al-shar'iyya* (the rules of *Sharī'a*), the *'illa* as used in connection with the *uṣūl* came to be interpreted as "the signs that make a rule known specifically".[55]

Shāṭibī argues that the premise of *maṣāliḥ* can be established in *Sharī'a* by method of induction, both as a general theme in *sharī'a* and in the description of the *'ilal* of various commands in detail. For instance, the Qur'ān explains the reasons for ablution, fasting and *jihād* as being cleanliness, piety and eradication of oppression, respectively.[56]

Shāṭibī's doctrine of *maqāṣid al-sharī'a* is an attempt to establish *maṣlaḥa* as an essential element of the ends of law. He treats the problem of the relativity of *maṣlaḥa*, the relationship of *maṣlaḥa* with *taklīf* and *ḥuẓūẓ* in sufficient detail. He tries to refute the implications of the theological determinism and the dilemma of the relativity of *maṣlaḥa* first by suggesting to study this problem on two levels. On the first level he discusses the *maqāṣid* of the Lawgiver and on the second level he deals with the *maqāṣid* of the *mukallaf* (obligee, subject of law). By proposing that *maṣlaḥa* is the objective of the Lawgiver on the first level, he suggests that it is the legislator who decides what is *maṣlaḥa*. Still, Shāṭibī stresses that since legislator's decision takes *mukallaf*'s interest into consideration, the identification of *maṣlaḥa* is not constant. The objective of the *mukallaf* (the subject of law) which also includes the legislator, if and in sofar as he is *mukallaf*, is obedience to the objectives of law.

A summary of the contents of *Al-Muwafaqāt* is given below:

CONTENTS OF THE BOOK

Al-Muwāfaqāt, presently published in four volumes, was organized by the author into five parts, first part consisting of premises and the other four parts consisting of four books i.e. *aḥkām* (rules), *maqāṣid* (objectives), *adilla* (sources) and *ijtihād* (legal reasoning).

1. **The book on Premises** discusses the definition, nature and scope of jurisprudence (*uṣūl al-fiqh*). It explains that the principles of jurisprudence are exact and certain and not related with abstract theories. This section also discusses the definition and scope of knowledge and reason, their inter-relationship, and the method of learning and education of legal principles.

2. **The book on *Aḥkām*** (rules) explains that there are two major divisions of rules: (i) *Taklīfī* (obligation-defining), (ii) *Waḍ'ī* (declaratory). The obligation-defining rules are valued on the scale of five categories: indifferent,

commendable, obligatory, reprehensible and prohibited. Shāṭibī analyses *mubāh* (indifferent) category in detail and explains its relationship with other categories, from the perspectives of part and whole, option, harm, and interest. He clarifies that the basic principle in this valuation is their conformity to the objectives of law. While the category of *mubāḥ* does not produce obligation or prohibition, it determines the trend, i.e. if it leads to good, its next higher categories would be commendable and obligatory, and the opposite would be reprehensible and prohibited.

The declaratory rules are valued on the basis of how a rule has been posited. There are three modes of construction: *sabab* (means) showing causal relation, *sharṭ* (condition) showing contingent relation and *māni'* (restrictive) showing restrictive relation. Shāṭibī explains that these three modes are not the objectives of law. He discusses the definition and qualifications of these three modes. In addition to these, Shāṭibī also discusses in the division the values of *ṣaḥīḥ* (valid) and *bāṭil* (void) and *'azīmat* (regular) and *rukhṣat* (allowance, exemption). He explains that the validity of an action depends on its conformity with the objectives of law. As to the legal concessions, he clarifies that rules of law are constructed on the level of general and minimal, taking convenience and physical feasibly of an action as a standard. Yet there may be people who opt for harder side. They are special people, and a common man is not obliged to follow that standard. However Shāṭibī makes it clear that hard and soft options are two ends of construction and are relative to a regular rule of law.

3. **The book on *Maqāṣid*** (objectives) is of central significance. We have analysed and discussed Shāṭibī's views on objectives in greater detail in our present book. The scheme of Shāṭibī's discussion of *maqāṣid* is as follows:

I. *Qaṣd* of the *Shāri'* (lawgiver/legislator's intent) has four aspects:

(i) First aspect: The primary intention of the Lawgiver in instituting law as such.

(ii) Second aspect: His intention in instituting it so as to be intelligible (*ifhām*).

(iii) Third aspect: His intention in instituting it to demand obligation (*taklīf*).

(iv) Fourth aspect: His intention in including the *mukallaf* under its command.

II. *Qaṣd* of the *mukallaf* (Obligee's intent)

The discussion in the first aspect deals with *maslaha,* its meanings, grades, characteristics and its relativity or absoluteness. The second aspect discusses the linguistic dimension of the problem of *taklīf* which was overlooked by other jurists. A command constituting *taklīf* (obligation) must be understandable by all of its subjects, not only in words and sentences but also in the linguistic and cultural meaning of understanding. Shāṭibī discusses this problem by explaining two terms: *al-dalāla al-aṣliyya* (essential meaning) and *ummiyya* (intelligible to commonality). The third aspect analyses the notion of *taklīf* in reference to *qudra* (power), *mashaqqa* (hardship) etc. The fourth exposes the aspect of *ḥuẓūẓ* in relation to *hawā* and *ta'abbud*. On the second level, i.e. that of *mukallaf*, Shāṭibī is largely concerned with the question of intention and acts.

4. **The book on the *Adilla*** (sources) deals with the sources on the whole as well as each of them separately. The general principles about sources explain that *maṣlaḥa* is the universal general principle which permeates in all injunctions. The universal principles are known by inductive analysis of the injunctions in the Qur'ān and Sunna. These principles are also not contradictory to each other. They complement each other, because the process of legal reasoning consists of two steps. Determining the cause of judgement, and pronouncing the judgement. In this process tradition and reason both are employed as essential components. As far as linguistic and semantic aspects of determining the cause are concerned, one must conform to the Arab usage. Also, in the process of legal reasoning distinction is maintained between rational proof and legal proof, the latter creates legal obligations. In this section Shāṭibī also deals with some additional aspects of the sources as they are legal texts. The following aspects are analysed in detail: *iḥkām/tashābuh* (clear and ambiguous), *awāmir/nawāhī* (modes of imperative and prohibitive injunctions), *'umūm/khuṣūṣ* (general and particular), *bayān / ijmāl* (exposition and concision).

Dealing with sources in particular, Shāṭibī explains why he limited himself to the discussion of *Kitāb* (Qur'ān) and *Sunna* only, and not dealt with the other two sources i.e. *ijmā'* (consensus) and *ra'y* (legal opinion). Speaking about the Qur'ān, Shāṭibī explains that the Qur'ān is the basic most source. In order to understand Qur'anic injunction some sciences are essentially required. They include knowledge of Arabic language, history and circumstances of revelation of particular verses, and abrogated verses. Other sciences, such as *'ilm al-kalām* (philosophical theology) that are not directly related to the deduction of laws from the Qur'ān, are not essential. Shāṭibī explains in detail how Ṣūfīs and others have introduced other sciences as essential requisite for understanding the Qur'ān. He clarifies that among the rules deducted from the Qur'ān, only those that conform to the Arab usage and to the Qur'ān and Sunna will be acceptable. He also stresses that Quranic injunctions must be understood from the historical perspective i.e. the verses revealed in Mecca are more in nature of general principles, and those in Madina are more detailed. While considering these two types of verses belonging to two different periods, both must be treated together as complementing to each other in their historical understanding.

Speaking on Sunna, Shāṭibī discusses its definition, semantic connotations and its validity. He clarifies that *Sunna* is also spoken for matters that are not *bid'a*. According to Shāṭibī Sunna means primarily the sayings, the actions and approvals of actions by the Prophet himself, but it also pertains to the practice of the Companions of the Prophet. The Sunna is next to the Qur'ān, and the Qur'ān is the source for the determination of the meaning of Sunna. The action and approval of the Prophet are higher in value than words of a ḥadīth when it is supported by the former two. Regardless of whether a Sunna has a legal value, all Sunan are valid.

5. **The book on *Ijtihād*** (Legal reasoning) deals with the definition, conditions and requirements for *ijtihād, mujtahid* (the expert jurist), the *fatwā* (legal opinion) and *iqtidā* (legal authority). Shāṭibī divides *ijtihād* into two types: one type relates to laws where no further legal reasoning may be required and the other type where such need continues. The first type pertains to the following process of legal reasoning: *tanqīḥ al-manāṭ* (distinguishing between various anchor points), *takhrīj al-manāṭ* (locating the anchor point) and *taḥqīq al-manāṭ* (identification of the anchor point on the general level).

This process is not applicable in each case. It is possible that in some cases it has already been sufficiently taken care of. The second type refers to the *taḥqīq al-manāṭ* (application of causes) to individual cases, and is a continuous process.

Shāṭibī discusses the requirements and qualifications for *ijtihād* as understanding of the objectives of law and the skill of legal reasoning and deduction of rules, and the sciences necessarily required for *ijtihād*. He stresses the principle of unity and uniformity in Islamic law and therefore discusses the problems of *khilāf* (disputation) and *ikhtilāf* (difference of opinion) in detail. In this regard he also analyses the following principles: *al-dharā'i'* (preventive measures), *ḥiyal* (legal devices), *murā'āt al-khilāf* (regard for conflicting laws), and *istiḥsān* (juristic preference). Discussing the causes of differences among the jurists, Shāṭibī stresses that in legal reasoning approach must be teleological, i.e. looking at the end and results of the action sanctioned in order to observe whether it serves the purpose of law. Shāṭibī treats *fatwā* as a product of *ijtihād*, a process of law making. Stressing on the importance of the role of a *muftī* (a jurist exercising *ijtihād*), he defines him as a successor to the Prophet. A *fatwā* can be expressed by oral or written statements, action and by approval. A *muftī*'s word and action must conform with each other. Whether a *fatwā* is binding and to what extent, Shāṭibī analyses the question of *fatwā*'s authority (*iqtidā*). He explains that a person who does not know about a religious matter must ask, but only from a reliable scholar. The authority of a *fatwā* arises from two sources (1) infallibility, either by revelation like Prophet or by consensus as in case of companions of the Prophet, and (2) official position. In the absence of a qualified *muftī*, the legal obligation does not obtain. Shāṭibī explains also the conditions and etiquettes of posing questions. The section is appended with a discussion of additional matters relating *ijtihād*: *ta'āruḍ* (conflict of sources), *tarjīḥ* (Preponderance) *'ilm al-jadal* (Disputation) and *istidlāl* (process of reasoning). He clarifies that legal reasoning does not necessarily conform to logical reasoning. In legal reasoning the first premise of the logical proposition is often not mentioned, because it is a primary rule.

The following chapters, therefore, analyse the concepts and terms that are components of Shāṭibī's doctrine of *maqāṣid al-sharī'a*.

NOTES AND REFERENCES

1. Abū Isḥāq al-Shāṭibī, *Al-Muwāfaqāt*, Vol. 1 (Beirut: Dār al-Ma'rifa, [1970]) Introduction: p. 24.
2. Abū'l Ajfān, *Fatāwā al-Imām al-Shāṭibī* (Tunis, 1987), p.47.
3. *Ibid.* pp. 47-48.
4. See Aḥmad Bābā, *Nayl al-ibtihāj* (Cairo, 1351 H.) p. 47.
5. See Abū'l Ajfān, *Fatāwā*, p. 59 and *Nayl*, p. 308.
6. *Ibid.*
7. Makhlūf, *Shajarat al-nūr al-zakiyya*. (Cairo: Al-Salafiyya, 1349 H.), p. 231.
8. 'Abdullah Dirāz, Introduction to *Al-Muwāfaqāt*, Vol. I. *op.cit.*, p. 6.
9. Abū Zuhra, *Al-Shāfi'ī* (Cairo: Dār al-Fikr al-'Arabī, 1978), p. 273.
10. Fāḍil Ibn 'Āshūr, *A'lām al-fikr al-Islāmī* vide Abū'l Ajfān, *Al-Ifādāt wa'l-inshādāt* (Beirut: Risāla, 1983), p. 31.
11. Malcolm H. Kerr, *Islamic Reform, The Political and Legal Theories of Muhammad 'Abduh and Rashīd Riḍā* (California: University of California, 1966), p. 55 ["The element in their jurisprudence which the modernists have particularly seized upon as the basis for dynamism and humanism is the notion of *maṣlaḥa* (welfare, benefit, utility".]
12. Muḥammad Khuḍrī, *Uṣūl al-fiqh* (Cairo: Maṭba' al-Istiqāma, 1938) p.11, relates that when he was appointed to teach Islamic law in Gordon Law College in Sudan, he planned to write a book on *uṣūl*. He discussed with 'Abduh, when the latter was visiting Sudan, who then recommended *al-Muwāfaqāt* to be used as a basis for the studies on the *asrār al-tashrī' al-Islāmī*.

    Also Muḥammad 'Abd Allāh Dirāz, in his introduction to *al-Muwāfaqāt*, Vol. I, (Maṭba' Tijāriya, n.d.) relates that "often we listened to the recommendation (*waṣiyya*) of the late (Shaykh 'Abduh) to the students to obtain this book, and I was ever anxious to execute his will." (pp. 12-13).
13. Abu'l A'lā Mawdūdī, *Islamic Law and Constitution* (Lahore: Islamic Publications, 1960), p. 113-114.
14. Mūsā Jār Allāh's (d. 1942) Kazan edition, in spite of patient search, is not available to us. However, Dr. Mehmed Erdoğan has reproduced an edited version of Mūsā Jārullah's introduction to Kazan edition in his Turkish translation of *Al-Muwāfaqāt*. See Erdoğan, *Şâtibî el-Muvâfakât, islâmî ilimler metodoligisi*, vol. 1 (Istanbul: iz Yayincilik, 1990). pp. xvii-xxiv.
15. Abū Zuhra, *Mālik* (Cairo: Maṭba' Aḥmad 'Alī, First edition published in 1946); Dawālībī, *al-Madkhal ilā 'ilm uṣūl al-Fiqh* (Beyrouth: Dār al-'ilmī l'il mala'īn, 1965), especially pp. 433-41; Iqbal, *Reconstruction of Religious Thought in Islam* (Lahore: Ashraf, 1965), pp. 169, 174; Yūsuf Mūsa, *al-Madkhal li dirāsāt al-fiqh al-Islāmī* (Cairo: 1961), pp. 196-202; Muṣṭafā Zaqrā, *al-Madkhal al-fiqhī al-'āmm*, Vol.1 (Dimashq: Maṭba' Jāmi'a Dimashq 1961), pp. 62ff., particularly p. 68, n. 1; Abū Sinna and others,

Madkhal al-fiqh al-Islāmī (Cairo: Jāmi'a Azhar, 1965), pp. 97-100, 119-131 and 163-165; 'Umar 'Abd Allah, *Sullam al-wuṣūl li 'ilm al-uṣūl* (Cairo: Dār al-Ma'ārif, 1956) pp. 73-76, 233-239.

16. Rashīd Riḍā, *Ta'rīkh al-ustādh al-Imām al-Shaykh Muḥammad 'Abduh,* Vol. I (Cairo: Dār al-Manār, 1350/1931), p. *jīm* and his introduction to *al-I'tiṣām*, (Cairo: Tijāriya, *circ.* 1332/1913) p. *jīm.*
17. Fāḍil ibn 'Āshūr, *A'lām al-fikr al-Islāmī fī tārīkh al-Maghrib al-'Arabī* (Tūnis: Maktabat al-Najāḥ, n.d.), pp. 71-72.
18. 'Abd al-Muta'āl al-Ṣa'īdī, *al-Mujaddidūn fi'l Islām* (Cairo: Maktabat al-Ādāb, n.d.), pp. 294-296, 309.
19. See George Makdisi, "The Juridical Theology of Shāfi'ī: Origins and Signifcance of Uṣūl al-fiqh", in *Religion, Law and Learning is Classical Islam* (Hampshire: Variorum, 1991) pp. 5-47.
20. 'Abd Allāh Dirāz, *op. cit.*, p. 11-12.
21. D.S. Margoliouth, "Recent Arabic Literature", in *Journal of Royal Asiatic Society* (London: 1916), pp. 397-98.
22. H.A.R. Gibb, *Studies on the Civilization of Islam* (Boston: Beacon, 1968), pp. 205-206.
23. Hurgronje, *Selected Works of C. Snouck Hurgronje,* (Ed.) G.H. Bousquet and J. Schacht, (Leiden: Brill, 1957), p. 287.
24. Chafique Chehata, "Logique Juridique et droit musulman", *Studia Islamica,* Vol. XXIII (1965), p. 16.
25. J. Schacht, "Fiḳh" in EI[2], Vol. II, p. 890.
26. For instance, see Muḥammad 'Abd Allah al-'Ajlān, "Adillat al-aḥkām al-shar'iyya fi uṣūl al-Shāṭibī", M.A. Thesis at Jāmi'at al-Imām Muḥammad bin Sa'ūd al-Islāmiyya, Riyāḍ, 1398 H; 'Umar Sulaymān al-Mīkhāl, "Aḥādīth al-I'tiṣām l'il Shāṭibī", M.A. Thesis, at the above University, 1405 H; Aḥmad al-Rīsūnī, *Naẓariyyat al-maqāṣid 'ind al-Imām al-Shāṭibī* (Riyāḍ: Al-dār al-'ilmiyya l'il-kitāb al-Islāmī, 1992).
27. See Urdu translation of Mūsā Jarullah's Introduction, Abd al-Hamid Birişik, "Al-Muwāfaqāt kī ishā'at ké muta'alliq chand bāten", *Fiḳr-o Naẓar*, October-December, 1993, p. 29.
28. *Ibid.* p. 28.
29. Ignaz Goldziher, *Streitschrift des Gazālī gegen die Baṭinijja-Sekte* (Leiden: 1916), pp. 32-34.
30. Riḍā, *Tārikh al-Ustādh...* (Cairo, 1931).
31. Margoliouth, *op. cit.*
32. Goldziher, *Op. cit.* p. 33. He says, "Meine Kenntnis von den Beziehungen dieses Satibi auf das Mustazhiri grunden sich auf Auszuge, die aus dem Kapitel (الاعتصام) der *Muwāfaqāt* in der arabischen Zeitschrift *al-Manār* unlangst".

    Goldziher called *Al-I'tisām* a chapter of *Al-Muwafaqāt* despite the fact that the title of the book in this issue was specifically mentioned as *"Kitāb al-I'tiṣām"* cf. *Al-Manār*, Vol. XVII (1913-14), pp. 54-63, 273-293.

    Elsewhere as well, on the basis of this conclusion, Goldziher, commenting on 'A. 'Alī al-Qārī's mention of a book on "al-Ḥawādith al-Bida'" by Shāṭibī, again suggested, "Es ist jedoch möglich, dass damit ein Kapitel der *al-Muwāfaqāt* gemeint sei." (op. cit., n. 1).

    This confusion was further carried on by Brockelmann, *Geschichte der arabischen Litteratur, S II*, p. 375, where he, probably basing his information on Goldziher's remarks, wrongly describes these excerpts in *Al-Manār* as "Auszuge" of *al-Muwafāqāt.*
33. Khuḍrī's *Uṣūl...* is available to us in its third edition, 1938 and second edition, 1933. The date of the first edition could not be known.
34. Muḥammad b. Ḥasan al-Ḥajwī, *al-Fikr al-sāmī fi tārīkh al-fiqh al-Islāmī* (Rabāṭ, 1345 A.H.), Vol. IV, p. 82.
35. *Ibid.*, p. 17.
36. López-Ortiz, J. "Fatwas granadinas de los siglos XIV y XV", *Al-Andalus*, Vol. VII (1941), pp. 73-127.

37. Ṣa'īdī, *op. cit.*, p. 311. Ṣa'īdī's views on Shāṭibī's rigidity are mostly unfounded. For instance his claim that Shāṭibī believed in only one saved sect, *Salaf Ahl al-Sunna*, and none else, is just opposite to what Shāṭibī maintained. cf. *Al-I'tiṣām,* Vol. II, pp. 217ff.
38. Ibn 'Āshūr, *op. cit.*, pp. 73-74.
39. Ṣubḥī Maḥmaṣānī, "Transactions in the Sharī'a", in *Law and the Middle East*, Vol. I, ed. M. Khadduri and H.J. Liebesny (Washington, 1955), p. 187.
40. Ṣubḥī Maḥmasānī, *Muqaddima fī iḥyā' 'ulūm al-sharī'a* (Bayrūt: Dār al-'ilm li'l mala'īn, 1962), pp. 22, 634, 65-67.
41. Rahman, *Islam* (London: Weidenfeld, 1966), p. 108.
42. Rahman, *Islamic Methodology in History*, (Karachi: Central Institute of Islamic Research, 1965), p. 154.
43. *Ibid.*, pp. 133-4.
44. *Ibid.*, p. 160.
45. Abū Zuhra, *Mālik, op. cit.* p. 267.
46. *Al-Muwāfaqāt*, Vol. 4, pp. 205-211; *Al-I'tisam*, Vol. 2, pp. 111-115.
47. *Al-Muwāfaqāt*, Vol. 2, p. 396. Shāṭibī here compares Ẓāhirī method with the Ḥanafī and favours Ḥanafī as closer to Mālikī.
48. *Ibid.*, Vol. 2, pp. 386-391.
49. *Ibid.*, p. 391.
50. Ibn Khaldūn, *Muqaddima* (Cairo: Bulāq, 1320 H.) p. 431.
51. See for details Abū Zuhra: *Mālik, op. cit.*p. 366.
52. Aḥmad al-Rīsūnī, *Naẓariyyat al-Maqāṣid 'ind al-Imām al-Shāṭibī* (Riyāḍ: Al-dār al-'ālamiyya li'l kitāb al-Islāmī, 1992).
53. *Ibid.*, p. 12.
54. *Al-Muwāfaqāt*, Vol. II (Cairo: Muṣṭafā Muḥammad, n. d.), p. 6.
55. *Ibid.*
56. *Ibid.*, p. 7.

CHAPTER FIVE

MAṢLAḤA

While reviewing the impact of Shāṭibī's *al-Muwāfaqāt* on modern Muslim thought in the preceding chapter, we noted that *maṣlaḥa* constitutes the core concept. This chapter studies *maṣlaḥa* more extensively. Since the concept gained more significance in the last two centuries, recent studies of the concept provide a more comprehensively comparative framework for the study of this concept. The chapter therefore begins with an overview of recent studies. Similarly since Shāṭibī's conception is informed by the exposition of the concept in the works of *Uṣūl al-fiqh* written by his predecessors, we have presented a summary of the jurists' analyses of the term. Thus the present chapter is divided into three parts: (1) Recent studies of *maṣlaḥa*, (2) *maṣlaḥa* in *Uṣūl al-fiqh*, and (3) Shāṭibī's analysis of *maṣlaḥa*.

Generally the utility of *maṣlaḥa* and its validity as a principle of legal reasoning is measured by Shāṭibī's predecessors as well as by most of the contemporary scholars with reference to the theory of four sources of Islamic law. It would be well in order if we begin this chapter with an explanation of this theory.

The theory of four sources of Islamic laws' (i.e. Qur'ān, Sunna, *ijmā'* and *qiyās*), developed originally by Imām Shāfi'ī and refined further by his followers like Ghazālī, Āmidī and Rāzī, was deeply influenced by the *ḥadīth* movement. The *ḥadīth* scholars insisted that *ḥadīth* was the science, the only exact science (*'ilm*). Not only was it sufficient to interpret the Qur'ān, but together with the Qur'ān it answered all the needs of the Muslim society. *Ḥadīth* and the Qur'ān provided the authoritative texts (*naṣṣ*, *nuṣūṣ*) to answer all questions. The influence of the *ḥadīth* movement on the four sources theory is evident in its insistence on Qur'ān and *ḥadīth* as primary and textual sources.

This theory of four sources of Islamic law was not accepted by all the Muslim jurists. Among the sunnī schools, the Ẓāhirīs rejected the authority of *ijmā'* and *qiyās*. Others, who accepted the authority of four sources, differed among themselves on the definitions of *ijmā'*, *qiyās* and *ḥadīth*. They also differed on the restriction of authoritative sources to these four only. Several other sources and principles such as *maṣlaḥa*, *istiḥsān*, *istidlāl*, *'urf*, *'āda*, *sadd al-dharī'a*, *'umūm al-balwā* etc. were recognized by other schools.

Gradually, however, the 'four sources theory' came to dominate and other theories adjustd themselves accordingly. The four sources came to be called primary and all others recognized by various schools were designated as secondary or supplementary. One significant consequence of the dominance of this theory was its focus on text as a touch stone. The validity of a source depended on its conformity with the texts (*nuṣūṣ*) i.e. the Qur'ān and *ḥadīth*. If a source was not supported by the text or was contrary to the tex, it was not authoritative.

This criterion was applied even to *qiyās* and *ijmā'*, which are primary sources. For a *qiyās* to be valid it was necessary that its analogy be based on a text of the Qur'ān or *ḥadīth*. The theory further insisted that it was the text that determined explictly the basis of analogy. If this basis (*'illa*) was not specifically and explicitly given in the text, it was not valid. This view was not acceptable to all the jurists, because first, this method limited legal reasoning to deduction from a particular and individual text. It discouraged inductive reasoning from collective textual evidence in a case. Secondly, this method was also not free from arbitrariness, as the selection of a particular text among several other relevant textual evidence depended on the arbitrary choice of the jurist.

Similar to *qiyās*, the 'four sources' theory applied this criterion to other sources as well. Some sources/principles such as *istiḥsān* (juristic preference) and *istiṣlāḥ* (consideration of *maṣlaḥa)* were condemned as mere persuit of pleasure. Other principles were also subjected to the same treatment and were categorised accordingly. They were acceptable (*mu'tabar*) if they were endorsed by the textural evidence, rejected (*mulghā*) if they were not endorsed, or were contrary or the text was silent.

Maṣlaḥa was thus categorised by the Shāfi'ī jurists into *maṣlaḥa mu'tabara* (authoritative, if it was endorsed by the text), *maṣlaḥa mulghā* (rejected, if it was not supported by the text) and *maṣlaḥa mursala* (neither supported nor rejected by the text). It was in this perspective that *maṣlaḥa* was not regarded an independent source or principle. Consequently since there was apparently no disagreement on the first two categories of *maṣlaḥa*, *maṣlaḥa mursala* came to represent *maṣlaḥa*.

Looking at the development of Islamic legal tradition, one finds law courts relying on *'urf* and *'āda* (custom), local traditions of the understanding of the Qur'ān, Sunna, and *ra'y* (considered opinion growing out of the above sources). The Ḥanafī principle of *istiḥsān* which preferred analogical reasoning based on an implicit meaning of the text where explicit analogy was contrary to the purpose of law, was a method of *ra'y* and was closer to the Mālikī principle of *istiṣlāḥ*. Similarly, the principles of *sadd al dharā'i'* (preventive measures), *'umūm al-balwā* (general necessity) were not endorseable by an explicit text, but was supported by an inductive analysis of the texts. Further, *maṣlaḥa* is an underlying principle of all the rulings in the Qur'ān and *ḥadīth*. It may be sometimes supported not by an explicit text, but by the overall support of the textual sources. It is thus a more universal and reliable principle than a principle of deductive reasoning. Yet *maṣlaḥa* was subjected to the same criticism.

It is therefore necessary to study *maṣlaḥa* independently, without restricting it to the four sources theory. Unfortunately most studies of *maṣlaḥa*, even in modern times, look at it from the perspective of four sources theory and therefore focus on *al-maṣlaḥa al-mursala* rather than on *maṣlaḥa* itself.

1. RECENT STUDIES OF *MAṢLAḤA*

Recent studies on *maṣlaḥa* can be generally divided into two groups. First, there are studies dealing with *al-maṣlaḥa al-mursala* and, second, those dealing with *maṣlaḥa* as such. The focus in the first group of studies is not on *maṣlaḥa* proper but on *al-maṣlaḥa al-mursala*, for them *istiṣlāḥ* is in no way different from *al-maṣlaḥa al-mursala*.

Ignaz Goldziher compared *istiṣlāḥ* with *istiḥsān* saying that the latter is a Ḥanafī principle according to which a decision reached by analogy can be dismissed when the legislator finds that this decision opposes a certain matter which he believes is useful. That is to say that *istiḥsān* removes the rigidity of law depending upon the discretion of an individual jurist. *Istiṣlāḥ*, on the other hand, depends upon a rather objective method; it removes the rigidity of law in consideration of general human 'interest' (*maṣlaḥa*) which is sufficiently defined. He also suggests that *istiṣlāḥ* partially resembles the Roman legal principle of *utilitum publicum* as well as Rabbinic law.[1]

N.P. Aghnides and G.H. Bousquet also refer to *istiṣlāḥ* in the same sense. Aghnides defines it as a principle that consists in recommending a thing because it serves a useful purpose, although there is no express evidence in the revealed sources to support such action.[2] Bousquet's definition is as follows: "*Istiṣlāḥ* consists of discarding by exceptional disposition the rules deduced by *qiyās* in cases where the application of general rules would lead to illogical, unjust and undesirable results''.[3]

J. Schacht's treatment of *maṣlaḥa* differs from that of the above scholars. Yet he describes *istiṣlāḥ* as a special form of analogy, or rather a type of *istiḥsān* used by early Mālikī scholars and which later came to be called *istiṣlāḥ*.[4] Schacht re-emphasises that *istiṣlāḥ* is identical with the Roman legal principles of *utilitas publica* which characterises *jus honourarium*.[5]

R. Paret also finds *istiṣlāḥ* to be connected with *istiḥsān*, but the former is more limited and definite as it replaces a general principle such as "finding good", by a rather specific principle, such as "according to the demand of human welfare (*maṣlaḥa*)". *Maṣlaḥa* thus is the material principle underlying *istiṣlāḥ* which is a method of reasoning. In actual details where Paret traces the history of *istiṣlāḥ*, he specifically refers to *al-maṣlaḥa al-mursala,* rather than to *maṣlaḥa* as such. This is why he finds nothing of much importance after Ghazālī had theorized about *istiṣlāḥ*. Paret's references to *uṣūl* are confined to the discussions of *al-maṣlaḥa al-mursala*.[6]

Analyzing the treatment of *maṣlaḥa* by modern Muslim scholars such as 'Abduh and others, A. Hourani criticised their use of *maṣlaḥa* in a utilitarian sense. He argued that such an interpretation of *maṣlaḥa* was not justified; "for the traditional thought, *maṣlaḥa* had been a subordinate principle, a guide in the process of reasoning by analogy rather than a substitute for it".[7]

Von Grunebaum, in his study of the concept of reason in Muslim ethics, concluded that *istiṣlāḥ* (the public interest) is unmistakably one point at which human "reason" is permitted to impinge on traditional or systematic considerations that would normally be viewed as the determining factors of *shar'ī* developments.[8]

Although all of the above opinions agree in regarding *maṣlaḥa* as a principle that removes rigidity and that suggests adaptability to changes based on human needs, yet according to them its function is restricted to exceptional cases or to the use of a special form of analogy. The reason for such a limited view of *maṣlaḥa* in these studies is either that they have studied only *al-maṣlaḥa al-mursala* to the exclusion of other aspects of *maṣlaḥa* or that they have equated *al-maṣlaḥa al-mursala* with *maṣlaḥa*.

There are, however, a few studies which evince an integral approach to the problem of *maṣlaḥa* and study the concept of *maṣlaḥa* independently. Among such studies, the following five are relevant to our point. G.F. Hourani has examined *maṣlaḥa* as an ethical concept. M.H. Kerr, Sa'īd Ramaḍān al-Būṭī, and Ḥusayn Ḥāmid Ḥassān have analyzed it in particular reference to legal theory. É. Tyan has studied it as a principle of methodology.

Tyan describes *maṣlaḥa* as 'general interest', 'social utility' and 'good' and has defined *istiṣlāḥ* as "to recognize a rule as useful"[9] He distinguishes two conceptions of *istiṣlāḥ*. In the original conception of *istiṣlāḥ*, the interests (*maṣāliḥ*) were divided into three categories according to its recognition by the law, the last category being *al-maṣāliḥ al-mursala*. The directing principles in this kind of research consisted essentially in considering the elements of social utility (*maṣlaḥa*) and of affinity (*munāsaba*). The speculation according to this conception of *istiṣlāḥ* remains within the limits of law.

The other conception of *istiṣlāḥ* is more extensive.[10] According to this conception, *istiṣlāḥ* "may be employed not only in relation to matters which are not regulated by the precise texts of law, but also in those matters which have been subjected to such regulations, so much so that it is legitimate to make it prevail over precise rules or over conflicting or contradicting regulations, provided that, in the final analysis, they (the rules derived from this method of reasoning) remain in conformity with the objectives of law, i.e. they accord with the five major interests (religion, physical integrity, descendance, patrimony and mental faculty)".[11] Tyan, thus, concluded that *istiṣlāḥ* "is a method of interpreting already existing rules by disengaging the spirit of these rules from the letter; exceptions and extensions are reached which command practical utility and correspond to the fundamental goals of the law".[12]

G.F. Hourani studied *maṣlaḥa* as an ethical concept in medieval Islam.[13] He observes that there were two theories of value in medieval Islam: one, that of objectivism, i.e. that the value has real existence; the second theory of value was that of theistic subjectivism, that the values are determined by the will of God. The theory of objectivism was expounded by the *Mu'tazila*. The idea of rational good was called by them *ḥasan* or *maṣlaḥa*. The theory of theistic subjectivism was maintained by the Ash'arīs. The opposition of these two theories manifested itself in the field of *fiqh* also. Jurists in the early period used certain methods which did not correspond with 'theistic subjectivism'. Principles such as *istiḥsān* and *istiṣlāḥ* tended rather towards 'objectivism'. The ethical basis of these principles, however, remained unarticulated. The Mu'tazilī theory of rational good [that there is an objective good including a real public interest (*maṣlaḥa*) and a real justice (*'adl*), and that they could be recognized by human reason] could have provided a basis to support the above principles. But the theory of objectivism was superseded by theistic subjectivism. Why? Hourani suggests that, apart from religious and political factors that prevented objectivism from being adopted by the lawyers, the Mu'tazilī theory of objectivism had its own deficiencies. First it could not show how moral judgement operates. Second, it could not fill up the theoretical gap between means (moral and legal acts) and the end (the eternal happiness in the world hereafter for Muslims).

On the other hand, the theory of theistic subjectivism corresponded with Shāfi'ī and Ẓāhirī views on legal reasoning, which opposed the use of *ra'y* and any judgement independent of the revelation. Shāfi'īs denied the objective value of idle fancy, *ẓann* and *hawā*. Theologically also the theory of objectivism appeared to curtail the omnipotence and omniscience of God, which the theory of theistic subjectivism promoted.

Hourani's study of *maṣlaḥa*, chronologically, is confined to the early period of Islamic tradition. Because of this limitation he could not take into consideration the development in the treatment of *maṣlaḥa* by later *uṣūliyyīn* such as Shāṭibī. In fact, Hourani's criticism of objectivism is mainly ethical. The three deficiencies that he ascribed to *maṣlaḥa* as an objective value are not found in Shāṭibī's conception of *maṣlaḥa* as a legal value.

Muḥammad Sa'īd Ramaḍān al-Būṭī presented his doctoral dissertation, *Ḍawābiṭ al-maṣlaḥa fi'l-sharī'at al-islāmiyya*, at Azhar University in 1965. In his introduction to the published edition of this dissertation Būṭī explains that the Orientalists, whom he regards as new crusaders against Islam, have adopted a new measure to destroy Islam. They are urging Muslims to open the gate of *ijtihād,* and in order to accomplish this end they refer to the concept of *maṣlaḥa* as the fundamental principle of *Sharī'a*. He is, however, convinced that the real motive behind this proposal for *ijtihād* is the destruction of Islam. He admits that the gate of *Ijtihād* has never been closed and that the Lawgiver has given full consideration to the principle of *maṣlaḥa*, but this principle has always been restricted with a number of qualifications.[14] After detailed analysis of the etymology and concept of *maṣlaḥa*, he deduces the qualifications which the traditional jurists had suggested in application of this principle. He also compares this concept with the concept of 'utility' and 'pleasure' in the philosophies of Stuart Mill and J. Bentham.

Būṭī concludes that *maṣlaḥa* in its unqualified sense is identical with the above concepts which he considers as purely hedonistic. The qualified concept of *maṣlaḥa*, however, contradistinguishes itself from utility and pleasure as it takes into consideration the following three characteristics. First it is not limited to this world only but equally includes the hereafter. Second, the Islamic value of good is not material. Third, the consideration of religion dominates other considerations.[15] He has thus concluded that if these and other qualifications are disregarded "and the term *maṣlaḥa* alone is held up as a light post and a criterion, then upon my life! an *ijtihād* such as that will descend upon Muslims from all sides. [To prove such terrifying results after opening the gate of *ijtihād*] it suffices to observe the evil that brings the laws of *Sharī'a* out of the fortress of texts into the open, exposed to desires and arbitrary opinions that deceive (us) behind the name of *maṣlaḥa* and *manfa'a*."[16]

If Būṭī's expositions of *maṣlaḥa* and its qualifications are accepted, *maṣlaḥa*, as a matter of fact, becomes superfluous as a legal concept. The consideration of *maṣlaḥa* by the *Shāri'*, then is limited to the *Shāri'*'s commands only. In other words, *maṣlaḥa* has no independent value. This is the logical conclusion from Būṭī's view of Islamic law according to which he rejects a distinction between this world and the hereafter. He does not separate *mu'āmalāt* from *'ibādāt* but rather considers the former a part of the latter. He does not distinguish between *ḥuqūq Allāh* and *ḥuqūq al-'ibād*. In fact, his conception of Islamic law is that of *ta'abbud* (mere obedience). On all these points he is in disagreement even with the jurists who imply the concept of *maṣlaḥa* in reference to human needs. His disagreement becomes particularly evident if his conclusions are compared with Shāṭibī's conception of *maṣlaḥa*.

Būṭī frequently refers to Shāṭibī in his dissertation, but these references are selective and often out of the context. Būṭī's study fails to bring out the real significance of the concept of *maṣlaḥa* mainly because he has not given full consideration to the proponents of this concept such as Shāṭibī.

The same deficiency is found in M. Kerr's study of *maṣlaḥa*, which also offers a detailed analysis of the concept. Examining Rashīd Riḍā's legal doctrines, Kerr observed that the logical conclusion of Riḍā's arguments for the use of *maṣlaḥa* would be that it is something equal to natural law and that *istiṣlāḥ* does not depend on the texts and *qiyās*. Such conclusions, however, are not spelled out by Riḍā himself.[17] Why? According to Kerr, the failure to spell out the full implications of the argument has to do with the theological nature of Islamic law which influences even *maṣlaḥa*, theoretically the most liberal principle of legal interpretation in Islamic jurisprudence. The theological foundations of Islamic law insist on minimizing the role of human reason in the formulation of law.[18]

Before he goes into a detailed analysis of the concept of *maṣlaḥa* in traditional jurisprudence, Kerr clarifies two general aspects of Islamic law which, in turn, affect the function of *maṣlaḥa*. Firstly, Islamic law has its basis in revelation and thus is an expression of the will of God. Kerr refers to the theological differences between Ash'arīs and Mu'tazilīs about the will of God. In contrast to the Mu'tazila, Ash'arīs denied freedom in man's acts. Consequently, the intellectual spirit and methods of Islamic jurisprudence "could not entirely escape the influence of the law's theological underpinnings, which proclaimed that reason is essentially irrelevant to the substance, determination and obligatory character of moral principles."[19]

The second aspect that affected *maṣlaḥa* was the emphasis on *qiyās*. According to Kerr, the method of *qiyās* itself is a means of protecting the authority of revelation.[20] In fact, the term *'illa* in jurisprudence is not applied in the usual sense of cause and effect. *'Illa* is not a value judgement, but only the attribute or the characteristics of the matter under consideration that gives rise to the judgment.[21] Further, the limitations of the means to identify *'illa* are also confined to the use of indication within the text. *Munāsaba* (suitability, affinity) is the only means that goes beyond the indication of the texts. Kerr finds even *munāsaba* to be a conservative, circumscribed and timid acknowledgement of the place of social utility (*maṣlaḥa*) in God's commands. In fact, he concludes, in final analysis even *munāsaba* is subordinate to the indications of the text.[22]

Kerr, thus treats *maṣlaḥa* as one of the aspects of *munāsaba*. He also divided *maṣlaḥa* on the basis of conformity to the sources, and thus *al-maṣāliḥ al-mursala* is only a form of *qiyās*, because whereas *qiyās* looks for the *'illa, al-maṣāliḥ al-mursala* seeks *ḥikma,* a more general term than *'illa*. Kerr concludes that because it is not based on a specific *'illa, istiṣlāḥ* has been a subsidiary and occasional technique of disputed validity.[23]

In final analysis Kerr comes to equate *maṣlaḥa* with *al-maṣāliḥ al-mursala*.

> The *maṣlaḥa* is therefore a more specific term for *ḥikma* and since it is known in each case not by direct indication in the textual source but by the jurist's own judgement, it is a *maṣlaḥa mursala.*[24]

Kerr also confines *maṣlaḥa* to its correspondence with the textual sources. It is noteworthy that Kerr, in his discussion, refers to such jurists as Ghazālī and Qarāfī who viewed *maṣlaḥa* in the above terms. He also discusses the views of Ibn Taymiyya, Ibn Qayyim and Ṭūfī whom he chose as proponents of the validity of *maṣlaḥa* as a principle of legal interpretation. But these jurists, too, regarded *maṣlaḥa* as subordinate to the textual sources and *qiyās*. The consideration of *maṣlaḥa*, according to them, would prevail over the texts and *qiyās* only when the latter are harmful to obey.

Kerr has not taken into account jurists such as Shāṭibī, who favour *maṣlaḥa* as an independent legal principle. The significance of studying Shāṭibī's views is evident from Tyan's analysis of *istiṣlāḥ* which gives a more integral picture of *maṣlaḥa*. The absence of Shāṭibī from Kerr's analysis of *maṣlaḥa* is regrettable. According to Kerr, Rashīd Riḍā, whose views led Kerr to study the concept of *maṣlaḥa* in detail, characterises Shāṭibī "as exceptionally outspoken in his defence of *istiṣlāḥ*.[25] Yet Kerr did not include Shāṭibī in his list. It comes as a further surprise that Shāṭibī was not only disregarded but also suffered a sort of indifference when Kerr, probably following Paret,[26] confused him with Abū'l Qāsim al-Shāṭibī.[27]

Another recent significant study of *maṣlaḥa* by Ḥusayn Ḥāmid Ḥassān, *Naẓariyyat al-maṣlaḥa fī'l-fiqh al-Islāmī*[28] is a very detailed study of the concept *maṣlaḥa* in thoery and practice of the four schools. He notes that in *Uṣūl al-fiqh, maṣlaḥa* is discussed at two points: first as a criterion for determining a *munāsib* (affinitive) whether a certain evidence is acceptable in Islamic law, and secondly as an independent legal evidence. Analysing definitions of *maṣlaḥa* by Ghazālī, Ṭūfī and Khawārizmī, Ḥassān adopts Ghazālī's framework to analyse the concept in the four schools: "*maṣlaḥa* is synonymous with the concept of *munāsib* or *mukhīl* (uncertain idea) belonging to *qiyās*".[29] Again, summarising discussion of *maṣlaḥa* in Islamic legal theory, Ḥassān enumerates four systems of categorisation of *maṣlaḥa*: (1) on the basis of whether it conforms to the textual evidence, (2) on the basis of the nature of the evidence of *maṣlaḥa,* (3) on the basis of the scope of *maṣlaḥa,* and (4) on the basis of change and continuity. He concludes this discussion in favour of Ghazālī's definition and categorisation.[30] Naturally, therefore, he focusses on Shāṭibī's analysis of *al-maṣlaḥa al-mursala* and *al-istidlāl al-mursal* to explain Mālikī concept of *maṣlaḥa*. He treats Shāṭibī's discussion of *maṣlaḥa* in the framework of *al-maṣlaḥa al-mursala.*[31]

To sum up, present studies on *maṣlaḥa* generally present an unbalanced analysis of this concept. They have failed to see the real significance of this principle as it was conceived and employed by those jurists who viewed it as an independent principle. A study of Shāṭibī's concept of *maṣlaḥa* as already indicated by Tyan, can fill this gap.

2. *MAṢLAḤA* IN *UṢŪL AL-FIQH*

Shāṭibī's philosophy of Islamic law is, in fact, a continuation of the discussion of the concept of *maṣlaḥa* that had appeared in major works of *Uṣūl al-fiqh* prior to Shāṭibī, particularly as it developed in Mālikī school from Mālik's conception of common good. Although Mālik did not use the term *maṣlaḥa* specifically but due to his consideration of such principles as *istidlāl* in his legal reasoning *istiṣlāḥ* or application of the principle of *maṣlaḥa* became particularly associated with Mālikī school. The following is a historical and systematic analysis of this concept in the texts of *Uṣūl al-fiqh.*

ETYMOLOGY

Etymologically the word *maṣlaḥa* is an infinitive noun of the root *ṣ-l-ḥ*. The verb *ṣaluḥa* is used to indicate when a thing or a man becomes good, uncorrupted, right , just, virtuous, honest. Or it is alternatively employed to indicate the state of possessing these virtues. When used with the preposition *li* it gives the meaning of suitability. *Maṣlaḥa* in its relational sense means a cause, a means, an occasion, or a goal which is good. It is also said of a thing, an affair or a piece of business which is conducive to good or that aims at good. Its plural form is *maṣāliḥ*. *Mafsada* is its exact antonym. In Arab usage, it is said: *naẓara fī maṣāliḥ al-nās,* which means: "He considered the things that were for the good of the people." The sentence *fī'l-amr maṣlaḥa* is used to say: "In the affair there is that which is good [or the cause of good]."[32] *Istiṣlāḥ*, the tenth form, means to seek *maṣlaḥa*.

QUR'ĀN

In the Qur'ān various derivatives of the root *ṣ-l-ḥ* are used, the word *maṣlaḥa*, however, does not appear there. The Qur'ān uses *ẓalama* ('He did wrong'.) [V:9] and *fasada* ('He/it got corrupted'.) [XXXVI:125; XXVII: 142, II:220] as opposite terms to *ṣaluḥa*. *Ṣāliḥ,* the active participle of *ṣ-l-ḥ*, occurs very frequently in the Qur'ān. On one occasion the meaning of this term is elaborated textually as follows:

> They believe in God and in the last day and enjoin goodness and forbid evil and hasten to do good deeds, and these are the *righteous ones (ṣāliḥīn)*.[33]

Whereas it is clear that its use in the early period and in the Qur'ān was essentially related to the meanings of good and utility, there can be no doubt that the word had not become yet a technical term.

It is quite often claimed that *maṣlaḥa* as a principle of legal reasoning—broadly speaking, to argue that 'good' is 'lawful' and that 'lawful' must be good—came to be used at a very early period in the development of *fiqh*. The use of this principle is attributed, for instance, to the early jurists of the 'Ancient schools of law' or even to the companions of the Prophet. Among the founders of the schools of law, it is associated with Mālik b. Anas. There seems, however, to be a confusion in these statements in equating the use of *maṣlaḥa* as a general term with its use as a technical term. The early use of *maṣlaḥa* in a general sense is similar to other terms such as *ra'y*. Rudi Paret has observed that the word *maṣlaḥa* as a technical term is not used by Mālik or Shāfi'ī; hence this concept must have developed in the post-Shāfi'ī period.[34]

Paret's observation, however, does not refute the possibility that considerations similar to *maṣlaḥa* were employed by pre-Shāfi'ī jurists. Such considerations do not seem to have been formulated in technical legal terms. The proponents of the use of *maṣlaḥa* in the early period have, apparently, referred to early jurists using considerations similar to *maṣlaḥa*. 'Umar Abdullāh, for instance, has argued that concept of *maṣlaḥa* should not be identified with the 'word' or 'term' *maṣlaḥa* in order to conclude that absence of the 'use' of the term in early legal texts would amount to the inexistence of the concept of *maṣlaḥa*.[35] It is, therefore, not incorrect to say that the post-Shāfi'ī development of the concept of *maṣlaḥa* was a continuation of such early methods of reasoning as were not yet formally defined. Later, when Shāfi'ī's definition of the method of reasoning in terms of 'sources' and his insistence that the reasoning be linked with the revealed texts through *qiyās*, prevailed over other methods, the concept and method of *maṣlaḥa* was also analysed, and refuted especially by Shāfi'ī jurists in terms of 'sources'.

JUWAYNĪ (d. 1047)

From Imām al-Ḥaramayn al-Juwaynī's (438/1047) *al-Burhān,* it appears that by his time the validity of reasoning on the basis of *maṣlaḥa*, for which he uses the term *istiṣlāḥ*, had become a problem controversial enough to bring forth three schools of thought in this respect. Qāḍī Abū al-Ṭayyib al-Ṭabarī and a number of *Mutakallimūn* maintained that the acceptable *maṣlaḥa* is only that which has a specific textual basis (*aṣl*). They, therefore, disallow *istidlāl* or *istiṣlāḥ*. The *mursala* (a *maṣlaḥa* not based on such an *aṣl*) and such as are contradictory to the textual evidence (*dalīl*) are not valid. The second school is attributed to Mālik who held that a *maṣlaḥa* was abided by without any consideration of the condition of similarity or whether it corresponded with the texts or not. The third school of thought is attributed to Shāfi'ī and to the majority of Ḥanafīs in general. They believe that *maṣlaḥa,* even if it is not supported by a specific text, can still be used, provided that it is similar to those *maṣāliḥ* which are unanimously accepted or which are textually established.[36]

This comment by Juwaynī does not help us in determining the chronology of the use of *maṣlaḥa* but it is very significant to note what divides these schools on *maṣlaḥa*. First, the comment shows that the method of reasoning on the basis of *maṣlaḥa* was different from other methods of reasoning that sought basis in the revealed texts. Second, if we accept the attribution of *maṣlaḥa* to the names of the jurists given in this comment, it also shows that the method of *maṣlaḥa* in its early formulation by Mālik and his followers was independent of the consideration of 'sources' or 'bases', and further that *maṣlaḥa* was accepted by others if it conformed to 'sources'—to the text in the case of the first group and to *ijmā'* in the case of the second group. They rejected only *al-maṣlaḥa al-mursala* because it did not conform with the sources. This explains why the concept of *maṣlaḥa* which originally was not necessarily conceived and confined within the framework of 'sources', came to be seen, particularly by later Shāfi'īs, in reference to 'sources'. This confused the discussion of the concept of *maṣlaḥa* as we shall see at a later moment. One indication of this confusion that may be noticed in the following analysis, is the tendency to discuss *maṣlaḥa* at two levels, i.e. first with reference to need and effectiveness, and second in reference to sources. In regards to their validity these two levels are not distinguished.

Juwaynī considered *istiṣlāḥ* in his scheme of *'illa* and divided it into five categories. First is the category where its *ma'nā* (concept) is rationally understandable affirming the end of *al-iyālat al-kulliya* (Common good) and *al-siyāsiyyat al-'āmmiyya* (public interest). It is related to certain essential necessities (*ḍarūra*) which are inevitable. The second category concerns what is a general need (*al-ḥājat al-'āmma*), but below the level of *ḍarūrī*. Third is the category which belongs to neither of the above, but rather concerns something which is noble (*mukarrama*) e.g. cleanliness. The fourth category is similar to the third in terms of need, yet, in terms of priorities, the fourth comes later as it is only a means to a commendable matter, for example *kitāba* (writing contract) is a cause for a commendable matter, namely manumission of slave. The fifth category concerns those *uṣūl* whose *ma'nā* (idea) is not obvious, and is not demanded by *ḍarūra* nor by *ḥāja*; nor is it required as a *mukarrama*. Examples of this category are the purely physical *'ibādāt*.[37]

Juwaynī remarks that need (*ḥāja*) and *istiṣlāḥ* are considered specific reasons in judging a particular case with regard to universal rules. He illustrates it by the example of the contract of hire. *Qiyās* rejects it because it requires that only an existing commodity be exchanged with an existing commodity but *Istiṣlāḥ* allows it as a special case. He refutes the objection that if something is not allowed by *qiyās* it cannot be allowed by *istiṣlāḥ* as well, because *istiṣlāḥ* is in fact a specific or partial *qiyās*. Juwaynī clarifies that *ḥāja* is the root (*aṣl*) and *istiṣlāḥ* is a branch (*far'*).[38] As we shall see later Shāṭibī argued that *maṣlaḥa* was the basic principle for the various categories of need. Thus he was able to clarify the ambiguity that was found in Juwaynī's treatment.

Maṣlaḥa as a technical term is not used in the Ẓāhirī jurist Ibn Ḥazm's (456/1065) *al-Iḥkām fī uṣūl al-aḥkām*, or in Ḥanafī jurist, al-Bazdawī's (d. 482/1089) *Uṣūl*.

BAṢRĪ (d.1085)

The term *maṣlaḥa* and its plural *maṣāliḥ* are used by the Mu'tazilī Abū'l Ḥusayn al-Baṣrī (d. 478/1085) in a general sense as well as a technical term. To him *maṣāliḥ* are good things, and *maṣlaḥa* means goodness. Baṣrī discusses *maṣlaḥa* in reference to *istiṣlāḥ* (reasoning) and *'illa* (reason), and in arguments against his opponents who maintain that *maṣāliḥ* cannot be known through reasoning at all. At one point he defines *al-maṣāliḥ al-shar'iyya* as those acts which we are obliged by the *Shāri'* to perform such as the *'ibādāt*.[39] Related to these acts are means to achieving the *shar'ī* commands; these means are also connected with *maṣāliḥ*. These means are *dalīl, amāra, sabab, 'illa,* and *sharṭ* whose illustrations are given respectively as follows: the validity of consensus, analogy, measurability for *ribā*, and the conditions in contracts of sale. All of these means are connected with *maṣlaḥa*.[40] For instance, the connection between *amāra* and *'illa* is explained as follows:

> When a correct sign (*amāra*) indicates (*dallat*) a quality (*wasf*) being reason (*'illa*) we decide that it is the basis of *maṣlaḥa*... It indicates that the basis of *maṣlaḥa* is to be found wherever an *'illa* is found.[41]

For Baṣrī, then, *maṣlaḥa* is an end for which *'illa* and other related terms are means. Baṣrī, however, does not elaborate what these *maṣāliḥ* are and what the connection is between *al-maṣāliḥ al-shar'iyya* which he mentions, and the other *maṣāliḥ* which he does not mention.

In the following centuries, however, the concept of *maṣlaḥa* advanced quite significantly. There are two main stages in the development of this concept before Shāṭibī. One is represented by Ghazālī in the early twelfth century, the other by Rāzī in the early thirteenth century.

GHAZĀLI (d. 1111)

In Ghazālī's *al-Mustasfā*, the problem of *maṣlaḥa* is discussed more clearly and fully than by Baṣrī or Juwaynī. Ghazālī defines *maṣlaḥa* as follows:

> In its essential meaning (*aṣlan*) it [*maṣlaḥa*] is an expression for seeking something useful (*manfa'a*) or removing something harmful (*maḍarra*). But this is not what we mean, because seeking utility and removing harm are the purposes (*maqāṣid*) at which the creation (*khalq*) aims and the goodness (*ṣalāḥ*) of creation [mankind] consists in realizing their goals (*maqāṣid*). What we mean by *maṣlaḥa* is the preservation of the *maqṣūd* (objective) of the law (*shar'*) which consists of five things: preservation of religion, of life, of reason, of descendents and of property. What assures the preservation of these five principles (*uṣūl*) is *maṣlaḥa* and whatever fails to preserve them is *mafasda* and its removal is *maṣlaḥa*.[42]

Maṣlaḥa as understood in the above definition is then divided into the following three categories. First, the type of *maṣlaḥa* which has a textual evidence in favour of its consideration. Second is the type which is rejected by a textual evidence. The third is the type where there is neither a textual evidence in favour, nor against it. The first category is valid and can be the basis for *qiyās*.[43] The second is obviously forbidden. It is the third category which needs further consideration. Accordingly, the element of *maṣlaḥa* contained in the third category is further examined from the viewpoint of is effectiveness (*quwwa*). From this angle there are three grades of *maṣlaḥa*: *ḍarūrāt, ḥājāt, taḥsīnāt* or *tazyīnāt*. The preservation of the above-mentioned five principles is covered in the grade of *ḍarūrāt*. This is the strongest kind of *maṣlaḥa*. The second grade consists of those *maṣāliḥ* and *munāsabāt* which are not essential in themselves but are necessary to realize the *maṣāliḥ* in general. The third grade is neither of the above but exists only for the refinement of things.[44]

Keeping this classification in mind, only such *al-maṣlaḥa al-mursala* i.e. not supported by textual evidence, will be accepted as has three qualities: *ḍarūra, qaṭ'iyya, kulliyya*. Ghazālī illustrates the point with an example:

> If unbelievers shield themselves with a group of Muslim captives, to attack this shield means killing innocent Muslims—a case which is not supported by textual evidence. If Muslim attack is withheld, the unbelievers will advance and conquer the territory of Islam. In this case it is permissible to argue that even if Muslims do not attack, the lives of the Muslim captives are not safe. The unbelievers, once they

conquer the territory, will rout out all Muslims. If such is the case, then it is necessary to save the whole of the Muslim Community rather than to save a part of it. This would be the reasoning which is acceptable, as it refers to the above three qualifications. It is *ḍarūrī* because it consists of preserving one of the five principles, i.e. protection of life. It is *qaṭ'ī* because it is definitely known that this way the lives of the Muslims will be saved. It is *kullī*, because it takes into consideration the whole of the community, not a part of it.[45]

The other two grades of *maṣāliḥ* (i.e. *al-maṣāliḥ al-mursala* that are *ḥājāt* or *taḥsīnāt*), however, are not admissible if they are not supported by a specific textual evidence. If these are supported by the text, the reasoning is then called *qiyās*, otherwise, it is called *istiṣlāḥ* which is similar to *istiḥsān*, and, hence invalid.[46]

Ghazālī counts *istiṣlāḥ* along with *istiḥsān* among the methods of reasoning which do not have the same validity that *qiyās* has. He calls such methods '*uṣūl mawhūma*' - those principles in which the *mujtahid* relies on conjucture or on his discretion rather than on the tradition.[47]

The above definition and classification of *maṣlaḥa* have a particular place in Ghazālī's structure of the discussion of *uṣūl al-fiqh*. A brief analysis of this structure will reveal the place that Ghazālī gave to the concept of *maṣlaḥa*. Ghazālī divides the discussion of *uṣūl* in *al-Mustaṣfā* into six parts. Apart from the first two parts which deal with introductory matters such as definition of *uṣūl* and an introduction to methods of logic, the remainder of the four parts discusses the following subject matters of *uṣūl: ḥukm* (command); *adilla arba'a,* the four sources i.e. Qur'ān, Sunna, *ijmā'* and *'aql;* method of reasoning (*istithmār*), i.e. interpretation and analogy; and *taqlīd* and *ijtihād*. The above treatment of *maṣlaḥa* appears as an annex to the discussion of the four sources, where he argues that *maṣlaḥa* is not one of the four reliable sources.[48] Also it is significant that it is not discussed in the part dealing with methods of interpretation and analogy, although its connection is implied.

References to *maṣlaḥa*, however, appear in other parts also. In the part on *ḥukm,* where Ghazālī discusses its essential meaning (*ḥaqīqa*) and its four components, *maṣlaḥa* is mentioned occasionally. The four components of *ḥukm*, according to Ghazālī are the following: (1) *ḥākim* (the one who gives judgement; the legislator, sovereign); (2) *ḥukm* (the judgement); (3) *maḥkūm 'alayh* (subject of command, i.e. *mukallaf*); (4) *maḥkūm fīh* (the object of command, i.e. the act [of *mukallaf*]).

Discussing the meaning of *ḥukm*, he deals with the question of whether the goodness or badness of acts (both human and divine) is known objectively or through *shar'*. His description of *ḥasan* is similar to his above definition of *maṣlaḥa* in its essential meaning.[49] At one point he even uses the term *maṣāliḥ* in place of *ḥasan*.[50] He frequently refers to *mafsada* in the course of his analysis of *maḥkūm fīh,* in dealing with the question whether only voluntary acts are objects of command or not. He regards it a *mafsada* if involuntary acts are also considered as objects of command.[51]

Reference to *maṣlaḥa* is made again in the part on methods of reasoning. Dealing with the method of *qiyās* (analogy), he explains that *qiyās* has four components: (1) *aṣl,* the root to which analogy is made; (2) *far'* the branch for which analogy is sought; (3) *'illa*, the reason on the basis of which analogy is made; (4) *ḥukm*, the judgement to which the analogy leads. Ghazālī clarifies that *qiyās* in *Uṣul al-fiqh* differs from *qiyās* in philosophy, not only in the form of reasoning but also in the conception of *'illa* itself. The *'illa* in *fiqh* is not 'cause' but merely a 'sign'.[52] Naturally then the methods of finding the *'illa* are also different. In *Uṣul al-fiqh, 'illa* is sought in a *naqlī* (traditional) evidence, i.e. the Qur'ān, Sunna and *ijmā'*. This *'illa* may be explicit (*ṣarīḥ*), or implicit (*īmā*). It may be known from the sequence and order of the command (*sabab* and *tartīb*) or by *instinbāṭ* (inference). The only valid methods of *istinbāṭ* are two: (1) *al-sabr wa'l-taqsīm* (observation and classification; method of exclusion), and (2) *munāsaba* (affinity).[53] It is in reference to *munāsaba* that *maṣlaḥa* as a main element of affinity with *shar'* is frequently discussed.

Ghazālī defines *munāsib* as "that which, like *maṣāliḥ*, becomes regulated [is achieved rationally: *intaẓama*] as soon as it is connected with the command (*ḥukm*).[54] For a discussion of the meaning, classification and grades of *munāsib*, Ghazālī refers to the annex in his book which is significantly enough the discussion of *maṣlaḥa* and its grades.

Munāsaba and *maṣlaḥa* are, however, not identical. Although Ghazālī's analysis of *munāsib* in terms of effectiveness and validity resembles his discussion of *maṣlaḥa*, yet the details vary. Among the various classifications of *munāsib*, one is of particular significance for us. It explains the relationship between *munāsib* and *maṣlaḥa,* as well as the difference between *istiḥsān* and *istiṣlāḥ* in the eyes of Ghazālī. *Munāsib* is divided into four categories: first, a *munāsib* which is suitable to and is supported by a specific textual evidence. Second a *munāsib* which is neither suitable to nor is supported by a textual evidence. Third, a *munāsib* which is not suitable to but is supported by a textual evidence. Fourth, a *munāsib* which is suitable to but not supported by a textual evidence.[55] Ghazālī adds that in the above classification the first category is acceptable to all jurists. The second category is called *istiḥsān* which clearly means to make laws according to personal discretion. The fourth is called *istiṣlāḥ* or *al-istidlāl al-mursal*. It is clear from this classification that *maṣlaḥa* is the basic consideration for deciding the suitability or *munāsaba* of something which *istiḥsān* lacks. But again the *munāsaba* of *maṣlaḥa* further depends on its suitability or conformity to the text in general; otherwise it will fall into the category of *istiḥsān*.

From Ghazālī's treatment of *maṣlaḥa*, it can be concluded in general, that his predilection for theologization of *fiqh*[56] and for *qiyās* as a method reasoning, led him to examine the concept of *maṣlaḥa* with reservations. From the point of view of theology, he rejected the conception of *maṣlaḥa* in terms of human utility; furthermore, he subjected it to scrutiny on the basis of revealed texts. Secondly, he made the method of reasoning by *maṣlaḥa* subordinate to *qiyās*. He did not reject *maṣlaḥa* altogether, as he did *istiḥsān*, but the qualification he provided for the acceptance of *maṣlaḥa*, did not allow it to remain an independent principle of reasoning.

Furthermore, with the above limitations on the concept of *maṣlaḥa*, he could not bring into focus the other elements which are in his discussion quite relevant to *maṣlaḥa*, such as *taklīf, ḥaqīqat al-ḥukm, fahm al-khiṭāb, niyya, ta'abbud,* etc. The discussions of these elements are scattered through various chapters in his *al-Mustasfā*. Also, he did not see the necessary relationship between different categories of *maṣlaḥa*. Some of the above points were taken into consideration by jurists after Ghazālī, but more systematic consideration was given them by Shāṭibī, as we shall see later.

Ghazālī's classification and definition was followed by a number of jurists. At least according to the channel of the *uṣūl* works that is mostly known to us, Ghazālī's influence, particularly in reference to *maṣlaḥa*, is very strong. As Ibn Khaldūn noticed, Baṣrī's book *al-Mu'tamad* and Ghazālī's *al-Mustasfā* remained a major source of influence for later writers on *uṣūl,* until the appearance of Rāzī's monumental work *at-Maḥṣūl.*[57]

RĀZĪ (d. 1209)

Al-Maḥṣūl combined the above two works by Baṣrī and Ghazālī and reformulated a number of concepts. Rāzī's *Maḥṣūl* then in turn became a source of considerable influence for later *uṣūl* works. This influence is evident from the number of commentaries and abridgements on *al-Maḥṣūl* that were written in later periods. This work influenced even Mālikī and Ḥanafī *uṣūl* which had so far taken exception to Shāfi'ī influence. We need not go into details, but it must be mentioned that Qarāfī (684/1285), Ibn Ḥājib (646/1249) and Ibn 'Abd al-Salām, with whom Shāṭibī was familiar and in general opposed, were largely under the influence of Fakhr al-Dīn al-Rāzī's (606/1209) *al-Maḥṣūl*.

Rāzī's *al-Maḥṣūl*[58] is structured more on the pattern of Baṣrī's *al-Mu'tamad* than on Ghazālī's *al-Mustasfā*. Rāzī deals with the definitions of the basic terms in the introduction. Significantly enough, the discussion about the meaning and classification of *ḥukm* and the question of the goodness of acts constitute more than half of this chapter. The scheme of the rest of the chapters is exactly the same as that of Baṣrī. References to *maṣlaḥa* are made, therefore, at three places: in the introduction where the question of the goodness of acts is discussed, in the chapter concerning *qiyās* where the question of *munāsaba* as a manner of finding *'illa* is dealt with, and in the last chapter where *al-maṣāliḥ al-mursala* are discussed as one of the ways of knowing the commands of the *sharī'a* in addition to *qiyās*.

Rāzī does not define *maṣlaḥa* but it seems that in his thinking *munāsib* and *maṣlaḥa* are quite closely associated with each other. He gives two definitions of *munāsib*. First, *munāsib* is defined as "what leads man to what is agreeable (*yuwāfiq*) to him both in 'acquisition' (*taḥṣīl*) and 'preservation' (*ibqā'*).[59] He explains that *taḥṣīl* means to seek "utility" (*manfa'a*), and *manfa'a* is pleasure (*ladhdha*) or its means. *Ladhdha* is to achieve what is suited (*mulā'im*). *Ibqā'* is explained similarly as removing harm (*maḍarra*), which is *alam* (pain) or its means. Both *ladhdha* and *alam* are evident and cannot be defined. Thus *munāsib* in its final analysis is related to *ladhdha* in the positive sense and to *alam* in the negative sense. The second definition of *munāsib* is given as that which is usually (*fi'l 'āda*) suited to the actions of the wise.[60]

Rāzī then clarifies that the first definition is accepted by those who attribute *ḥikam* and *maṣāliḥ* as causes or motives to God's commands. The second definition is employed by those who do not accept the above causality.[61] This explanation takes us back to Rāzī's own view on the problem of causality and God's commands. This question is first dealt with in the course of discussion whether the goodness or badness of things is rational or established by *shar'*. He argues that in as much as the definition and understanding of good as something "suited to nature (of man)", or as "a quality of perfection" is concerned, undoubtedly good and bad are rational. The point in question is however, whether good and bad can be defined in reference to praise or blame as the Mu'tazila have done.[62] Rāzī, after detailed analysis, concludes that, if defined in the latter sense, good and bad can be established only by *shar'*.[63] The question then is whether what is praised in God's commands corresponds with the rational good or not. If it corresponds, can this correspondence be understood as cause or motive?

Rāzī answers this question in detail in his discussion of *munāsaba* as a manner of *'illa*. He argues that to prove that *manāsaba* can be *'illa*, there are three premises to be established: first, that God issued the commands for the *maṣāliḥ* of the people; second, that the case in question consists of a *maṣlaḥa*, and third, that it can be shown that the probable reason for God's issuing this particular command is this particular *maṣlaḥa*.[64] Giving six proofs, he establishes the first premise that the commands are issued because of *maṣāliḥ*. He explains, however, that in contradiction to the Mu'tazila, the *fuqahā'* do not regard *maṣlaḥa* as *gharaḍ* (personal motive); they rather view it in terms of *ma'nā* (significance) or *ḥikma* (rationale). In fact, here is not much difference between the two positions. The difference is as follows: whereas the Mu'tazila believe that God is obliged to consider *maṣlaḥa*, the *fuqahā'* stress that He is not obliged to do so. God has done so because of His grace.[65] The second premise needs no explanation. The third premise, that this particular command attributes a specific motive to God's acts and Commands, is a position which Rāzī does not accept.[66] Rāzī resolves this problem by explaining it in the following terms:

> Muslims believe that the revolving of the heavens, the rising and the setting of the stars, the continuity of their forms and the lights are not obligatory, yet it has been God's custom to continue them in one state. Inevitably it provides the probability that this [i.e. what happens today] will continue tomorrow and after tomorrow with the same qualities... To sum up, if a certain thing occurs repeatedly many times, it gives the probability that when it happens [next] it will happen the same way... Now, when we observe *sharā'ī'*, we find that the commands and *maṣāliḥ* occur together, without being separated from each other, this is known inductively...[67]

To sum up, Rāzī stresses that no motive or cause can be attributed to God's acts or commands; yet he admits that God's commands coincide with *maṣlaḥa* of the people, and this *maṣlaḥa* or *munāsaba* can be considered *'illa* for that command. The paradox in his position is resolved by two explanations; first, that these *maṣāliḥ* are coincidental with God's acts, only accidentally, not in terms of cause and effect and, secondly, that it has happened this way not as a necessary correlation between *maṣlaḥa* and command, because God is not obliged to act this way. Rather, God has acted as He has as a Grace, so that a sign may be established to make His Command known.

Rāzī has offered these explanations in view of the possible objections against his admission of *ta'līl af'āl Allāh*, (to attribute causes to God's acts). It is significant to note that Rāzī recounts the possible criticism of his position in lengthy detail while his own defense is very short and quite unsatisfactory. The criticism consists of more than ten objections.[68] Rāzī's answer to this criticism is very brief. Two main points in his answer are as follows:

> We have explained that God's commands are issued (*mashrū'a*) because of the *maṣāliḥ*. As to the rational arguments that you have enumerated, they are not applicable here (*ghayr masmū'a*). Because if they are established they would infringe upon the legal obligation (*taklīf*), whereas the controversy over analogy (*qiyās*), whether in favour or in opposition, is based on the acceptance of the obligation. This well-considered answer rebuts all what you have mentioned.[69]
>
> Secondly, your criticism applies to those "who maintain that to attribute *maṣāliḥ* as *'illa* to God's commands is rationally necessary. It is not

applicable to the one who holds that it is not obligatory for God but He has done so because of His Grace.[70]

Thus Rāzī could maintain that *munāsaba* or *maṣlaḥa* was evidence for *'illa*, and could still insist that God's commands had no motives. It is with this reservation that Rāzī apparently accepted the first definition of *munāsib*. This is also the reason why he divides *munāsib* into two categories: *ḥaqīqī* (true) and *iqnā'ī* (apparent). *Ḥaqīqī* is that *munāsib* which consists of either a *maṣlaḥa* in this world or one in the hereafter. *Iqnā'ī* only appears to be a *munāsib*; but in fact it is not.[71]

Like Ghazālī, Rāzī also divides *maṣlaḥa* into *ḍarūrī, ḥājī* and *taḥsīnī*. He divides *munāsib* according to *ta'thīr* (effectiveness) and *shahādat al-shar'* (textual evidence), and *mulā'ama* (suitability).[72] With the exception of certain differences of detail, he is generally in agreement with Ghazālī.

In general, the attempt at theologizing the concept of *maṣlaḥa* by Ghazālī was completed by Rāzī with much more emphasis. Ghazālī objected that a conception of *maṣlaḥa* in reference to human utility alone and independent of God's determination, is not theologically possible. Rāzī gave this general objection a specific theological content. He made it clear that even to attribute the consideration of *maṣlaḥa* in terms of human utility to God's commands, is to attribute causality to His acts and hence theologically impossible. Both of these positions led to a kind of *ijbār* (determinism).[73] Both implied that God's commands demand obedience in their own right, not because of *maṣlaḥa*. If there existed the content of *maṣlaḥa* in *sharī'a*, it was to be explained by the grace of God or by accident, as Rāzī held. These positions rendered the question of moral and legal responsibility meaningless. Rāzī admitted such implications of his position for the question of *taklīf* as well as for the problem of reasoning by analogy, but he did not elaborate it further.

Briefly, the concept of *maṣlaḥa* which was originally a general method of reasoning for jurists and as such a free principle, came to be limited by its opponents on two considerations: first, theological determinism which tended to define *maṣlaḥa* as whatever God commands. Second, methodological determinism which, aiming to avoid the apparent arbitrariness in legal reasoning, tried to subject *maṣlaḥa* to *qiyās* so as to link it with some more definite basis. Both considerations were inadequate. First, in order to decide that something is *maslaha*, even to say that God's command are based on *maṣlaḥa*, some criterion outside these commands has inevitably to be accepted. This was precisely what theological determinism denied. Second, to proceed by *qiyās*, one must seek an *'illa*, which was either denied because of theological reasons or was interpreted so as to mean 'sign'. The implications of this position are obvious. On the one hand, it insisted that further extension of rules must be in units; every new deduction must have a specific link in *Sharī'a*. It denied the extension of law as a whole. On the other hand, it refused to take social needs into consideration, because it insisted upon deducting laws from specific rulings of *Sharī'a*, not even from the general intent of the law.

FIVE TRENDS

If we look at the major works on *uṣūl al-fiqh* during the period between Rāzī and Shāṭibī, we find five trends. First, there are jurists whose conception of *maṣlaḥa* is either dominantly similar to that of Rāzī or who have simply juxtaposed Ghazālī's and Rāzī's definitions of *munāsib* and *maṣlaḥa*. Among Mālikī jurists Shihāb al-Dīn al-Qarāfī (684/1285),[74] and among Ḥanafīs Ṣadr al-Sharī'a al-Maḥbūbī (747/1346),[75] stay closer to Rāzī. Accepting Rāzī's criticism of *maṣlaḥa*, Qarāfī even goes further. He raises serious doubts whether *maṣlaḥa* can ever be defined and justified in clear terms. Jamāl al-Dīn al-Isnawī (771/1370)[76] and Tāj al-Dīn al-Subkī (771/1369)[77] combine Ghazālī and Rāzī. Sa'd al-Dīn al-Taftāzānī (792/1290)[78] interprets the Ḥanafī position, mainly that of Bazdawī (482/1089), in Rāzī's framework.

The second trend is reflected by those jurists who reject *al-maṣlaḥa al-mursala* as a valid basis of reasoning. In this category falls the Shāfi'ī jurist Sayf al-Dīn al-Āmidī (631/1234)[79] and the Mālikī Ibn Ḥājib (646/1249).[80] In their arguments against *al-maṣāliḥ al-mursala* both follow Ghazālī rather than Rāzī. To them a *maṣlaḥa* is acceptable only if it is textually supported.

IBN 'ABD AL-SALĀM

The third trend is illustrated by the Shāfi'ī jurist, 'Izz al-Dīn Ibn 'Abd al-Salām (660/1263). He was inclined towards *taṣawwuf*[81] in his treatment of the concept of *maṣlaḥa*. This needs a detailed observation.

To Ibn 'Abd al-Salām *maṣlaḥa* means *ladhdha* (pleasure) and *faraḥ* (happiness) and the means leading to it.[82] The *maṣāliḥ* are then divided into two kinds, *maṣāliḥ* of this world and the *maṣāliḥ* of the hereafter. The former can be known by reason, while the latter can only be known by *naql* (tradition, revelation).[83] In view of the people's knowledge, however, the conception of *maṣāliḥ* differs according to the level of the approach of the people. The lowest level is that which is common to all men. Higher than this is the level on which the *adhkiyā'* (the wise people) conceive the *maṣāliḥ*. The highest level is peculiar to the *awliyā' Allāh* (friends of God, Ṣūfīs) alone. The *awliyā'* and *aṣfiyā* prefer the *maṣāliḥ* of the hereafter to those of this world. "The reason is that the *awliyā'* are anxious to know His commands and law [in their reality], hence their investigation and reasoning (*ijtihād*) are the most complete one".[84]

Elsewhere, Ibn 'Abd al-Salām divides *maṣāliḥ* as 'rights' into two major divisions. First are the rights of God, and second, the rights of men. The rights of God fall into three categories: rights which belong purely to God such as *ma'ārif* (perceptions) and *aḥwāl* (mystic states); second, rights which combine rights of God and those of men such as *zakāt*; and third, those which combine rights of God, and of His Prophet, and of the poeple in general. The rights of men are also of three categories; rights of *nafs* (self), rights of men toward each other, and rights of animals toward men.[85]

The above references which are recurrent themes in his *Qawā'id al-aḥkām,* indicate that Ibn 'Abd al-Salām's legal thinking was deeply influenced by mysticism. For instance, he did not reject *ḥuqūq al-nafs,* but a *maṣlaḥa* aiming at the realization of such rights was lower in rank than one which aimed at *ma'rifa* and *aḥwāl*. In fact, Ibn 'Abd al-Salām represents the stage where the Ṣūfī conception of *maṣāliḥ* came to permeate *uṣūl al-fiqh*. It is not possible at this point to go into details of the Ṣūfī conception of human *maṣāliḥ* and its history. It must, however, be pointed out that at a very early stage in Ṣūfism, rejection of *ḥuẓūẓ al-nafs* (pleasures of the animal soul) became significant as a means of controlling the *nafs*. In Sarrāj's (378/987) *al-Luma', ḥuẓūẓ al-nafs* are frequently opposed to *ḥuqūq al-nafs*.[86] *Zuhd* is defined as abandoning the *ḥuẓūẓ*.[87] The *ḥuqūq* are defined as *aḥwāl, maqāmāt, ma'ārif,* etc.[88]

Ḥuẓūẓ had an apparent connection with *maṣāliḥ,* and more particularly, with the question of *rukhṣa* (legal allowance) in case of hardship. The Ṣūfī stress on *zuhd, war'* and *ikhlāṣ* required abandoning of *ḥuẓūẓ*. An obvious example of this influence of *taṣawwuf* on *fiqh* and *uṣūl al-fiqh* may be seen in Qushayrī's *waṣiyya* (will) to his disciples where he advised them against opting for such allowances because "when a *faqīr* falls down from the level of *ḥaqīqa* to that of *rukhṣa* of *Sharī'a,* he dissolves his covenant with God and violates the mutual bond between him and God."[89]

Closer to the period of Shāṭibī, the opposition to *ḥuẓūẓ* appears still stronger. Abū'l-Ḥasan al-Shādhilī (656/1259) with whom Ibn 'Abd al-Salām's connections are claimed,[90] used to define *tawḥīd* (unification) in terms of abandoning the *ḥuẓūẓ al-nafs*.[91] He also explained it as a curse from God when someone is found indulging in the *ḥuẓūẓ* so to be barred from *'ubūdiyya* (servitude).[92]

Ibn 'Abbād al-Rundī (792/1390), the famous Shādhilī, with whom Shāṭibī was in correspondence on matters relating to *taṣawwuf* and *fiqh*, also stressed the rejection of *ḥuẓūẓ*. Commenting on the ḥikam of Ibn 'Aṭā Allāh, Ibn 'Abbād said that "the *nafs* always seeks *ḥuẓūẓ* and runs away form *ḥuqūq*; hence if you are confused in two matters, always choose what is harder for the *nafs*".[93] Elsewhere, commenting on the *ḥikma:* "The coming of *fāqāt* (trial by wants and needs) is a happy occasion for the disciples", Ibn 'Abbād explained that the Ṣūfī, contrary to an ordinary Muslim, finds pleasure by losing his *ḥuẓūẓ*. Situations of neediness provide a disciple with purity of heart, which is not achieved by *ṣawm* (fasting) or *ṣalāt* (praying), because in *ṣawm* and *ṣalāt* there is a possibility of *hawā* (desire) and *shahwa* (lust).[94]

The Ṣūfī view of obligation to God, thus, had serious implications for *maṣlaḥa* in terms of human utility. It not only denied human interest as a basis of consideration, but also insisted on abandoning human interests to purify the obligations as "complete obedience to God". These implications were not generally recognized by the jurists. Ibn 'Abd al-Salām accepted the Ṣūfī view, but in his attempt at synthesis between the two he was led either to deny the *maṣāliḥ* of this world altogether, or to accept the two on separate grounds.

IBN TAYMIYYA (d. 1328)

The fourth trend is represented by Ibn Taymiyya (728/1328) and Ibn Qayyim al-Jawziyya (751/1350). Ibn Taymiyya tried to find a middle way between the two extremes of total rejection and total acceptance of *maṣlaḥa*. He considered *al-maṣāliḥ al-mursala* similar to the methods of *ra'y, istiḥsān, kashf* (mystic revelation) and *dhawq* (mystic taste) of whose validity he was suspicious,[95] and hence rejected them. On the other hand, he refuted the moral implications of the denial of *maṣlaḥa* to the commands of God.

Ibn Taymiyya also counts *al-maṣāliḥ al-mursala* as one of the seven ways of knowing the commands of God, along with the traditional sources of law. He defines *al-maṣāliḥ al-mursala* as follows:

> [It is a decision] when a *mujtahid* considers that a particular act seeks a utility which is preferable, and there is nothing in *shar'* that opposes this [consideration].[96]

Ibn Taymiyya, however, concludes that to argue on the basis of *al-maṣāliḥ al-mursala* is to legislate in matters of religion, and God has not permitted this. To do so is similar to *istiḥsān* and *taḥsīn 'aqlī.*[97] He admits that *Sharī'a* is not opposed to *maṣlaḥa*, but when human reason finds *maṣlaḥa* in a certain case where there is no supporting citation in the text to be found, only two things are meant. Either there definitely is a text which the observer does not know or one is not dealing with a *maṣlaḥa* at all.[98] The obvious assumption in Ibn Taymiyya's arguments is that all the possible *maṣāliḥ* are already given in the Text. The other assumption is, of course, that all of God's commands are based on *maṣlaḥa*. The latter assumption is of particular significance to Ibn Taymiyya, as it has to do with the moral responsibility of man, a matter which he stressed very much. He condemned both the Mu'tazila and the Jabriyya in reference to the question of *maṣlaḥa*. The Mu'tazila argued that God is obliged to command only what is good for man. They conceived God's actions as analogous to man's actions. They assumed that whatever is morally obligatory for man must be obligatory for God. Ibn Taymiyya refuted this. But he also refuted the Jabriyya position that God's commands are not based on *maṣlaḥa*. He questioned their assumption that the intention of *maṣlaḥa* is a limitation upon God's acts. The Jabriyya argued that a command does not necessitate will (*irāda*). Ibn Taymiyya saw in this argument a theological advantage, but morally such a doctrine was harmful. Ibn Taymiyya, therefore, set out to analyse this generally accepted doctrine. He clarified that in reference to God there are two kinds of wills (*irāda*): *al-irāda al-shar'iyya al-dīniyya* (the legal and the religious will) and *al-irāda al-qadriyya al-kawniyya* (the potentive creative will). The laws of God are the expression of His first will.[99]

The consideration of *maṣlaḥa*, or as Ibn al-Qayyim, following al-Juwaynī and Ibn Taymiyya, often calls it *siyāsa,* plays an important part in explaining legal obligations, legal reasoning and legal change in Ibn al-Qayyim's *I'lām al-muwaqqi'īn*. He expounds the principles of Ḥanbalī *fiqh*, and enumerates the following five as sources and principles: (1) *nuṣūṣ,* (2) the *fatāwā* of the companions of the Prophet, (3) selection from the opinions of the companions, (4) *al-ḥadīth al-mursal* (a report of a saying of the Prophet which lacks a link in the chain going back to the Prophet), (5) *qiyās l'il-ḍarūra.*[100] Thus it is in reference to the three sources that the consideration of *maṣlaḥa* is expounded. Ibn al-Qayyim explains that it is valid to attribute *'illa* to the commands of God, because the Qur'ān and the *Sunna* of the Prophet are replete with examples where reasons are given to explain the command.[101] The larger part of the *I'lām* is devoted to illustrating how various commands are based on certain reasons which he calls *ḥikma* or *maṣlaḥa*.

The following passage contains a clear statement of his views on *maṣlaḥa*. In a chapter where he explains how "*fatāwā* may change according to the change in time and place, etc...", Ibn al-Qayyim says:

> This chapter is of great significance. Due to the ignorance of the matters [to be discussed in this chapter] grave errors have been committed in reference to *Sharī'a.* As a result hardship and severity have been brought forth [upon people]. Such obligations have been imposed as are not required, if one judges by the magnificent *Sharī'a* which keeps the highest level of *maṣālih*. The foundations of *Sharī'a* are laid on the *ḥikma* and *maṣāliḥ al-'ibād,* in this world of living (*ma'āsh*) and in the world of return (*ma'ād*). The *Sharī'a* is all justice, kindness, *maṣāliḥ* and *ḥikma*. Hence any rule which departs from justice to injustice... from *maṣlaḥa* to *mafsada*... is not part of *Sharī'a* even though it is arrived at by *ta'wīl* (literal interpretation).[102]

ṬŪFĪ (d. 1316)

The fifth trend is illustrated by Najm al-Dīn al-Ṭūfī (716/1316). He justified the use of *maṣlaḥa* even to the extent of setting aside the text. He stressed *maṣlaḥa* as the basic and overriding principle of *Sharī'a*. *Maṣlaḥa*, therefore, prevails over all other methods such as *ijmā'*.[103] Ṭūfī regards *maṣlaḥa* as a fundamental principle.

Ṭūfī's preference of *maṣlaḥa* over against texts and *ijmā'* was also prompted by his belief that textual sources as well as the opinions on which *ijmā'* is claimed were diverse, inconsistent and often self-contradictory. The principle of *maṣlaḥa* provided a consistent method of decision.[104] Ṭūfī, however, did not elaborate any concrete criterion of *maṣāliḥ,* how they are to be decided, especially in a case where there is a question of choosing among more than one *maṣlaḥa*. He goes on to the extreme of suggesting a decision by drawing of lots.[105]

Ṭūfī's weakness in developing the concept of *maṣlaḥa* as a fundamental principle of reasoning lies in the fact that in final analysis he too regarded *maṣlaḥa* in the perspective of 'four traditional sources'. For him recourse to *maṣlaḥa* was necessary only after the traditional sources had failed.

From the above survey we may conclude that the concept of *maṣlaḥa* with its simple beginnings unfolded its various aspects as it came into contact with theology, *taṣawwuf,* logical analysis and, most significantly, with social and legal changes. Theological determinism introduced by Ash'arī jurists appeared largely in the discussion of *taklīf.* To Ash'arīs, obligation is created by divine command. The Mu'tazila refuted this sense of theological determinism. They differentiated between two senses of obligation: *taklīf* and *wujūb,* the latter was rational and ethical, while the former was theological.[106] In other words, mere command does not oblige a man to act; it only informs him. What obliges man is the knowledge of good and bad, or of useful and harmful. Commenting on this position, G.F. Hourani concludes that this interpretation should have been acceptable to the legal concept of obligation. Yet there were certain complexities. First, if legal obligation is based on one's knowledge of utility, it may lead to arbitrariness, and furthermore this criterion in its absolute sense is not universally applicable. All the things which are apparently useful also have certain elements which are harmful either to the person concerned or to others. Second, all the rules of *Sharī'a* do not conform to the rule of utility; there are obvious hardships and disadvantages in obeying them. Third, to preserve an order and a system the decision of utility cannot be left to the individual. Who should then decide?

Still another aspect of the relationship of *maṣlaḥa* and *taklīf* was brought forth by the Ṣūfīs. The consideration of seeking utility and avoiding harm leads one to view obligation in a formal sense. Whenever there is a choice between hard and soft, a *maṣlaḥa*-oriented person chooses the latter. Not only that, to avoid harm to himself, one seeks devices which are legal; and since he is a utility seeker, he feels satisfied by escaping the full implications of legal obligation. To Ṣūfīs, this attitude, even in its lawful aspects, was quite opposite to the meaning of obligation towards God. They opposed this attitude as *ḥuẓūẓ* of *nafs* (lower soul) who is one of the enemies of the traveller on the path of God.

Shāṭibī tried to find an answer to the above theological, moral and Ṣūfī questions. He concentrated on the concept of *maṣlaḥa* itself, in contrast to other jurists who focused on *al-maṣāliḥ al-mursala*. At a point where Shāṭibī rejects the connection of the method of reasoning by *maṣlaḥa* with *bid'a* we find an elaborate discussion of why and how he did not agree with the general understanding of the term *al-maṣāliḥ al-mursala* by other jurists.[107] Now we turn to Shāṭibī's analysis of *maṣlaḥa*.

3. SHĀṬIBĪ'S ANALYSIS

According to Shāṭibī, the primary objective of the Lawgiver is the *maṣlaḥa* of the people. The obligations in *Sharī'a* concern the protection of the *maqāṣid* of the *Sharī'a* which in its turn aims to protect the *maṣāliḥ* of the people. Thus *maqāṣid* and *maṣlaḥa* become interchangeable terms in reference to obligation in Shāṭibī's discussion of *maṣlaḥa*.

Shāṭibī defines *maṣlaḥa* as follows:

> I mean by *maṣlaḥa* that which concerns the subsistence of human life, the completion of man's livelihood, and the acquisition of what his emotional and intellectual qualities require of him, in an absolute sense (2:25).[108]

This is the definition of *maṣlaḥa* in its absolute sense. Shāṭibī, however, takes into account various other senses in which *maṣlaḥa* can be studied. The *maṣāliḥ* belong either to this world or to the world hereafter. Further, these *maṣāliḥ* can be seen as a system; belonging to different grades and with a definable relationship with each other.

A significant element in the meaning of *maṣlaḥa* is the sense of 'protection of interests'. Shāṭibī explains that *Sharī'a* deals with the protection of *maṣāliḥ* either in a positive manner as when to preserve the existence of *maṣāliḥ*, *Sharī'a* adopts measures to support their bases. Or in a preventive manner; to prevent the extinction of *maṣāliḥ* it adopts measures to remove any elements which are actually or potentially disruptive of *maṣāliḥ* (2:8).

Shāṭibī divides the *maqāṣid* or *maṣāliḥ* into *ḍarūrī* (necessary), *ḥājī* (needed) and *taḥsīnī* (commendable). The *ḍarūrī maqāṣid* are called necessary because they are indispensable in sustaining the *maṣāliḥ* of *dīn* (religion and the hereafter) and *dunyā,* in the sense that if they are disrupted the stability of the *maṣāliḥ* of the world is disrupted. Their disruption results in the termination of life in the world, and in the hereafter it results in losing salvation and blessings (2:8). The *ḍarūrī* category consists of the following five: *Dīn* (religion), *Nafs* (self), *Nasl* (family), *Māl* (property) and *'Aql* (intellect) (2:10).

Scholars, says Shāṭibī, have observed that these five principles are universally accepted. Analysing the aims of the *shar'ī* obligations, we find that *Sharī'a* also considers them necessary. The *shar'ī* obligations can be divided from the viewpoint of positive and preventive manners of protection into two groups. Falling into the positive group are *'ibādāt* (rituals, worship), *'ādāt* (habits, customs) and *mu'āmalāt* (transactions), and falling into the preventive group are *jināyāt* (penalties).

'Ibādāt aim at the protection of *dīn* (religion). Examples of *'ibādāt* are belief and the declaration of faith (the Unity of God, the Prophethood of Muḥammad), *ṣalāt, zakāt, ṣiyām* and *ḥajj. 'Ādāt* aim at the protection of *nafs* (self) and *'aql* (intellect). Seeking food, drink, clothing and shelter are examples of *'ādāt. Mu'āmālāt* also protect the *nafs* and *'aql* but through *'ādāt.* Shāṭibī defines *jināyāt* as those which concern the above five *maṣāliḥ* in a preventive manner; they prescribe the removal of what hinders the realization of these interests. To illustrate *jināyāt,* he gives examples of *qiṣāṣ* (retaliation) and *diyat* (blood money) for *nafs,* and *ḥadd* (punishment for drinking intoxicants) for the protection of *'aql* (2:8-10).

The *ḥājiyāt* are so called because they are needed in order to expand (*tawassu'*) the purpose of the *maqāṣid* and to remove the strictness of literal sense the application of which may lead to impediments and hardships and eventually to the disruption of the *maqāṣid* (objectives). Thus if the *ḥājiyāt* are not taken into consideration along with the *ḍarūriyāt* the people on the whole face hardship. The disruption of *ḥājiyāt* is, however, not disruptive of the whole of *maṣāliḥ,* as is the case with the *ḍarūriyāt.* The following are the examples of *ḥājiyāt*: in *'ibādāt,* concessions in *ṣalāt* and *ṣawm* on account of sickness or journey which otherwise may cause hardship in prayers, fasting, etc.; in *'ādāt,* the lawfulness of hunting; in *mu'āmalāt,* permission for *qirāḍ* (money lending or commenda), *musāqāt* (agrarian association) and in *jināyāt,* allowances for weak and insufficient evidence in decisions affecting public interest (2:10-11).

Taḥsīniyāt means to adopt what conforms to the best of customs (*'ādāt*) and to avoid those manners which are disliked by wiser people. This type of *maṣlaḥa* covers noble habits (ethics, morality). Examples of this type are as follows: in *'ibādāt,* cleanliness (*ṭahāra*) or decency in covering the privy parts of the body (*satr*) in prayer: in *'ādāt*, etiquette, table manners, etc.; in *mu'āmalāt,* prohibition of the sale of unclean (*najis*) articles or the sale of surplus food and water, and depriving a slave of the position of witness and leadership, etc.; for *jināyāt,* the prohibition of killing a free man in place of a slave, etc. (2:11-12).

Shāṭibī regards the above division of *maṣāliḥ* as a systematic structure consisting of three grades, connected to one another. His detailed analysis reveals two aspects of their relationships with one another. First, every grade separately requires annexion of certain elements which supplement and complement this grade. Second every grade is related to the others (2:12).

Every one of the three grades requires certain elements to achieve the fuller realization of its objectives. For instance, *qiṣāṣ* (retaliation) cannot be realized without a condition of *tamāthul* (parallel evaluation). This position, however, calls for two clarifications: first, a lack of these complementary elements does not amount to a negation of the essential objectives; second, the consideration and realization of the complementaries must not bring about a negation of the original objectives—that is to say, if the consideration of a complementary results in the annulment of the original objective, its consideration will not be valid. First, because the complementary element is like a quality (*ṣifa*). If the consideration of a quality results in the negation of the qualified object (*mawṣūf*), the qualification is negated as well. Second, even if it is supposed that the consideration of the complementary results in the realization of its interests at the cost of the original objective, it is stressed that the realization of the original be preferred (2:14).

The above situation is illustrated by the following example. The eating of carrion is allowed in *Sharī'a* to save life. The reason is that the preservation of life is of utmost importance, and preservation of *murū'a* (manliness, honour) is only complementary (*takmīlī*) to the protection of life. Impure and polluted things are prohibited in order to preserve honour and to encourage morality. But if the preservation of the complementary, i.e. to preserve honour by avoiding eating unclean things, leads to the negation of the original interest, i.e. the preservation of life, the consideration of the complementary is forsaken.

Another example may be seen in the act of sale which is a *ḍarūrī maṣlaḥa* while the prohibition of risk and ignorance in sale transactions is complementary. If complete negation of risk is stipulated, the result will be complete negation of the act of sale.

The relationship of the above three grades of *maṣāliḥ* with one another is the same as that of the complementary *maṣāliḥ* to the original objective of the law. The *taḥsīniyāt* are thus complementary to the *ḥājiyāt* which are complementary to the *ḍarūriyāt*. The *ḍarūriyāt* are the fundamentals of *maṣāliḥ*.

In view of the above explanation, Shāṭibī deduces the following five rules in this relationship:

1. *Ḍarūra* is the basis of all *maṣāliḥ*.
2. The disruption (*ikhtilāl*) of a *ḍarūrī* necessitates the disruption of other *maṣāliḥ* absolutely.
3. The disruption of a *ḥājī* or a *taḥsīnī* does not necessitate the disruption of the *ḍarūrī* itself.
4. In a certain sense, however, an absolute disruption of *taḥsīnī* or *ḥājī* necessitates the disruption of a *ḍarūrī*.
5. The preservation (*muḥāfaẓa*) of *ḥājī* and *taḥsīnī* is necessary for the sake of *ḍarūrī* (2:16-17).

These rules may be illustrated by *qiṣāṣ* (lex talionis). *Qiṣāṣ* is *ḍarūrī*, and *tamāthul* (parallel evaluation, consideration of equality) in *qiṣāṣ* is *taḥsīnī* and *takmīlī*. To illustrate the first rule, *tamāthul* (*taḥsīnī*) is complementary and exists only because of *qiṣāṣ* (*ḍarūrī*). Thus a *ḍarūrī* (*qiṣāṣ*) is the basis of a *taḥsīnī (tamāthul*). The parallel evaluation by itself is meaningless.

To illustrate the second rule, if there is no *qiṣāṣ*, there is no consideration of *tamāthul*. In other words, the disruption of the *ḍarūrī* means the same for the other grades of *maṣāliḥ* necessarily. If the principle of equality is disregarded, it will affect other principles of public interest.

To illustrate the third rule, the disruption of *tamāthul* does not require disruption of *qiṣāṣ*. In other words, if at times parallel evaluation is not followed, it should not mean that the rule of *qiṣāṣ* is obsolete.

The fourth and fifth rules can be appreciated if one grasps the sense in which *ḍarūrī* is affected by the disruption of other *maṣāliḥ*. Shāṭibī explains the effect of other *maṣāliḥ* on *ḍarūrī maṣāliḥ* with the following four similes:

1. The relationship of other *maṣāliḥ* to *ḍarūrī (maṣāliḥ)* is like that of protective zones (*ḥimā*). The interruption (*ikhlāl*) of one protective zone amounts to the interruption of the next zone and eventually to the disruption of the *ḍarūrī (maṣāliḥ)* which are at the centre of these zones.
2. This relation may also be understood as that of the part and the whole; other *maṣāliḥ* together with the *ḍarūrī (maṣāliḥ)* make one whole. The disruption of the parts obviously means the disruption of the whole.

3. The *ḥājiyāt* and *taḥsīniyāt* can be understood as individuals in relation to the universal, i.e. *ḍarūriyāt*.

4. The *ḥājiyāt* and *taḥsīniyāt* serve the *ḍarūrī (maṣāliḥ)* as a prerequisite (*muqaddima*), or as interrelated (*muqārin*) (2: 16-24).

As mentioned above, the *maṣāliḥ* are also divided into those belonging to this world and those which concern the Hereafter. First are the *maṣāliḥ* of this world. There are two angles from which the *maṣāliḥ* of this world can be observed. The first angle is to observe them as they actually exist, and the second is to observe them on the basis of *shar'ī* proclamation.

Examining *maṣāliḥ* as they exist in this world, we see that they are not found as absolutely pure *maṣāliḥ*. Rather, they are mixed with discomfort and hardship, however big or small, and which may precede, accompany or follow the *maṣālih*. Similar are the *mafāsid* (opposite of *maṣāliḥ*) which also are not pure but are found to be mixed with a certain amount of comfort and enjoyment. The entire phenomenon in this world points to the fact that this world is created from a combination of opposites and that it is impossible to abstract (*istikhlāṣ*) only one side. It is for this reason that the *maṣāliḥ* and *mafāsid* in this world are known only on the basis of the pre-dominant side; if the side of *maṣlaḥa* dominates, the matter at issue is considered, customarily, a *maṣlaḥa*, otherwise a *mafsada*. In these matters thus, the determining factor is the prevalent custom (*'āda*) (2:26).

It must be noticed here that this principle is applicable only to acts relating to *'āda,* and only to the determination of *maṣlaḥa* or *mafsada* in this world through knowing them as they exist. Acts which are not *'ādāt* are not governed by this principle (2:26).

The second approach to considering the *maṣāliḥ* of this world is to observe them in reference to their connection with *shar'ī* proclamation (*khiṭāb*). The basic rule in this approach is that the *maṣāliḥ* or *mafāsid* as taken into consideration by the *Shāri'* are pure. If they are supposed to be mixed (*mashūba*), they are not so in the reality of *shar'* (2:27). As explained above, *maṣlaḥa* or *mafsada,* in this world, is determined by the predominant side (*al-jihat al-ghāliba*) of a matter. It is the predominant part which is the object of *shar'ī* proclamation. The dominated (*al-maghlūba*) part, whether *maṣlaḥa* or *mafsada* is not the objective of the *Shāri'*.

Why is it then that the dominated elements, even though they may be *maṣlaḥa*, are not the objective of *Sharī'a*? On the other hand, how can they, when they are not the objectives of *Sharī'a,* still be *maṣlaḥa*? Shāṭibī solves this apparent contradiction with the following explanation. He argues that *al-maṣlaḥa al-maghlūba* is that which is considered as such according to the acquired habitude (*al-i'tiyād al-kasbī*) alone, i.e. without adding the *shar'ī* requirements of *maṣlaḥa*. Customarily such a *maṣlaḥa* is not considered worth seeking. This is the part of *maṣlaḥa* which is also not the objective of the Lawgiver insofar as the *shar'iyya* (legality) of rules (*aḥkām*) as a whole is concerend.

Further, if the dominated part were also taken into account by the *Shāri'*, no act could have been the subject of command or of prohibition. Obviously such is not the case. If it is supposed that the dominated part in a mixed *maṣlaḥa* is the object of prohibition and the dominating part that of command, then one and the same act becomes the object of command and prohibition at one and the same time, which would have been a *taklīf mā lā yuṭāq* (impossible obligation) as well as an absurd situation (2:28).

The above explanation, however, does not clarify the existence or occurrence of *mafsada* despite the *Shāri'*'s intention to the contrary. Shāṭibī elaborates the matter by saying that the above position may appear to be that of the philosophers and of the Mu'tazila on the existence and occurrence of evil. According to the philosophers, God created a world in which good is mixed with evil. It is good, however, which is the purpsoe of creation. He did not create the world for evil, even though evil may occur along with good. The Mu'tazila believed that evils are not intended to occur, their occurence is against God's will (*irāda*).

Shāṭibī first denies the apparent similarity between his and the above positions. He argues on the basis of a distinction between two intentions (*qaṣd*) of God. First there is the intention of creation (*al-qaṣd al-khalqī al-takwīnī*) and second the intention of legislation (*al-qaṣd al-tashrī'ī*). The positions of the philosophers and the Mu'tazila concern the former and Shāṭibī's the latter. As he argues, the occurence of *mafsada*, despite God's will and intention for *maṣlaḥa*, is justifiable in the case of *al-qaṣd al-tashrī'ī*, because a man is held free (*mukhtār*) so as to be legally responsible for his acts. This position is not justified in the case of *al-irāda al-takwīniyya*, as this would imply imperfection in God's powers (2:30).

In the above discussion *maṣlaḥa* was related with the cases where it could be determined on the basis of habits and practice. There are cases where habitude is not so definitive. For instance, eating carrion in case of dire need and killing a murderer for the prevention of crimes. These acts are considered *maṣlaḥa* despite the fact that in essence they are not so. In other words, unlike the cases in the above discussion where the acts, despite their consisting of certain aspects of *mafsada,* are regarded as *maṣlaḥa* in themselves on the whole, the acts in the above examples, though *mafsada* in themselves, become *maṣlaḥa* because of certain external considerations. The supposition in this case is that the external consideration can dominate internal consideration. How this domination is decided needs elaboration.

In view of the above situation, logically, there are two positions; either both considerations are equal in such a manner that one cannot be preferred to the other, or one of them can be preferred. The former position probably does not exist in *Sharī'a*, because that would mean that *Sharī'a* intended prohibition and permission simultaneously. Furthermore, if one side is preferrable, it is still possible that the *Shāri'* intended the other side. Both sides will always be weighed by a *mujtahid*. We are obliged only to do what, after weighing both sides, appears to us (*yanqadiḥu*) the intention of the *Shāri'*, not what is intended by the *Shāri'* in reality (in His mind) (2:31). In this way, after the decision of a *mujtahid*, the possibility that the other side might be intended has to be disregarded insofar as fulfilling an obligation is concerned. The possibility is, however, not finally disregarded insofar as *naẓar* (examination, investigation) is concerned.

A group of scholars who believed the above possibility to be applicable in the case of obligations as well, maintained the principle of *murā'at al-khilāf*. We shall explain this principle later. At the moment it may be noted that this principle, to Shāṭibī, meant an impossible and hence void obligation.

Shāṭibī sums up the above discussion by saying that *al-jihat al-marjūḥa* (the dominated aspect), when it is found mixed with *al-jihat al-rājiḥa* (the dominating aspect), is not the objective of a legal obligation. This principle governs all problems which are subject to *ijtihād* (legal reasoning) irrespective of whether one believes a *mujtahid* to be always correct or not. Hence reasoning by analogy must go on (*al-qiyās mustamirrun*) and the demonstrative proof must remain free and unqualified (*al-burhān muṭlaqun*)(2:32).

So far the discussion has been concerned with the *maṣāliḥ* of this world. The *maṣāliḥ* of the hereafter are also pure (such as the blessings of paradise) as well as mixed (*mumtazija*) such as the punishment of hell sometimes meted out even to those who believe in the unity of God. The basic rule in such *maṣāliḥ* and *mafāsid* is that they are all determined according to *Sharī'a*, because the reason has no place in matters relating to the hereafter.

Sometimes a confusion may arise because of considering pure *maṣāliḥ* or *mafāsid* as mixed. For instance the blessings bestowed upon the prophets in paradise differ from those given to others. Those in lower ranks may be regarded as being punished by the absence of the blessings given to those in higher ranks. According to Shāṭibī, this confusion arises because a distinction is not maintained between species and their individual examples. The individuals may differ in special characteristics, but they do not differ in relation to their species; they are all equal members of the species. This membership is the fact that determines their *wasf* (quality) (2:36).

From the above discussion, Shāṭibī deduces the following rules as characteristics of *maṣlaḥa*:

1. The purpose of divine law (*tashrī'*) is to establish (*iqāma*) *maṣāliḥ* in this world and in the hereafter, but in a way that they do not disrupt (*yakhtall*) the system of *shar'*.
2. The *Shāri'* intends the *maṣāliḥ* to be absolute.
3. The reason for the above two considerations is that *Sharī'a* has been instituted to be *abadī* (eternal, continuous), *kullī* (universal) and *'āmm* (general) in relation to all kinds of obligations (*takālīf*), *mukallafīn* (subjects of law) and *aḥwāl* (conditions, states) (2:37).

The above three characteristics thus require *maṣlaḥa* to be both *muṭlaq* (absolute) and *kullī* (universal). The absoluteness means that *maṣāliḥ* should not be relative and subjective. Relativity is usually based on equating a *maṣlaḥa* with one of the following: *ahwā' al-nufūs* (personal likings), *manāfi'* (personal advantages), *nayl al-shahawāt* (fulfilment of passionate desires) and *aghrāḍ* (individual interests). According to Shāṭibī all of the above considerations render the concept of *maṣlaḥa* relative and subjective, which is not the consideration of *Shāri'* in *maṣlaḥa*, though it may be so in *'āda*.

He argues on the following grounds: First, the objective of *Sharī'a* is to bring the *mukallafīn* out of the dictates of their desires so as to make them servants of God. This objective rejects the consideration of personal liking as an element in the consideration of *maṣlaḥa*. Second, the *maṣāliḥ* cannot be considered as mere *manāfi'* becuase in *'āda* as well as in *shar'* they are mixed with disadvantages. The point of emphasis here is that *naf'* is not essential in the consideration of *maṣāliḥ* in *'āda* nor is it in *shar'*. In *'āda* some higher goal like the subsistence of life constitutes the basic consideration in determining *maṣlaḥa*. In *shar'* the consideration must still be higher, and that is the consideration of the hereafter.

Third, the consideration of the fulfilment of personal desires also renders the concept of *maṣlaḥa* highly relative. The consideration of personal desire varies from state to state, person to person, and time to time. It is so relative that it cannot be a criterion for determining *maṣlaḥa*. Fourth, consideration of individual interests leads not only to a divergence but, more significantly, also to a conflict with others and to the deprivation of others' interests.

Consequently, relativity and subjectivity are excluded from the *shar'ī* consideration of *maṣlaḥa*, it must, therefore, be absolute. In *Sharī'a* this absoluteness is provided by the stipulation that *maṣlaḥa* must aim at the subsistence of life in this world commensurately with the life in the next world.

The second characteristic of *maṣlaḥa* is its universality (*kullī*). This universality is not affected by the *takhalluf* (falling short) of its particulars. For instance the penalties are imposed on the basis of the universal rule that they generally restrain people from committing crimes. Yet, there are people who, despite being punished, do not abstain from committing a crime. Nevertheless, such exceptions do not affect the validity of the general rule about the penalty (2:52). In *Sharī'a* it is *al-ghālib al-aktharī* (the major dominant) which is the general-definitive element (*al-'āmm al-qaṭ'ī*) in the consideration of a *maṣlaḥa*. This is the characteristic (*sha'n*) of inductive universals (*al-kulliyāt al-istiqrā'iyya*). An illustration of this universal may be found in the universal rules of a language. The universals of a language are closer to those of *Sharī'a*, because both are *waḍ'ī* (instituted, conventional) not *'aqlī* (speculative). The inductive universals (in Arabic grammer, for instance) remain valid even if some of their particulars do not conform to them (2:52-53).

In reference to the characteristics of *maṣlaḥa*, Shāṭibī takes into consideration the criticism of this concept by other jurists. Among them he specifically refers to Fakhr al-Dīn al-Rāẓī, Shihāb al-Dīn al-Qarāfī and Ibn 'Abd al-Salām, and answers their criticism. We have summarised the views of the three jurists in the preceding pages. As this criticism and answers are quite relevant to the discussion of *maṣlaḥa*, a brief summary of this debate is given below.

Analysing the position of those who favour *maṣlaḥa*, Rāzī refers to their argument that the basic rule in *manāfi'* (useful things) is *idhn* (permission, lawfulness) and in *maḍārr* (harmful things) is *man'* (abstention) (2:40). Shāṭibī rejects this analysis as an unfaithful representation of the *maṣlaḥa* view. It is not possible to speak about *manāfi'* and *maḍārr* only in absolute terms because they do not exist as absolute in reality; actually they are largely relative. Second, since the *maṣāliḥ* refer to *shar'ī* proclamations which take into consideration the differences among persons, times and states, it is inadequate to talk in absolute terms. Third, since no *manāfi'* are to be found that are not mixed with *maḍārr*, if we accept Rāzī's principle, we will have also to accept that *'idhn* and *nahy* (prohibition) can apply to one and the same thing -- which is absurd.

Shihāb al-Dīn al-Qarāfī, the commentator on Rāzī's *al-Maḥṣūl,* had some doubts about the principle that *maṣlaḥa* constituted the basis of legal obligations. He argued that *maṣlaḥa* cannot be the basis of *ibāḥa*, becuase *maṣlaḥa* cannot be realized and hence defined in simple and absolute terms, as no *maṣlaḥa* can be gained without *alam* (pain) and *mafāsid* (evils). Thus to maintain that every *mubāḥ* must be based on *maṣlaḥa* amounts to a complete negation of *mubāḥ*. Second, in order to argue that *maṣlaḥa* is the basis of obligation, *maṣlaḥa* must be defined in absolute terms and not in reference to certain specific factors, because this process of preference of one specific consideration to another is never-ending and because it does not provide a universally accepted basis of definition. Furthermore, this position cannot be supported on the ground that *maṣlaḥa* is that whose violator is punished by God. This definition is not acceptable because it is based either on the assumption that God punishes only evil and this manner of argument is *dawr* (arguing in circle) or on the assumption that every obligation from God is a *maṣlaḥa*, simply because it is an obligation.

Qarāfī adds that the *maṣlaḥa* view is difficult to maintain for our people (*aṣḥābunā* [*Ash'arīs?*]), as well. They cannot say that God takes *maṣlaḥa* into consideration over against *mafsada*, because there are many *mubāḥāt* in which this consideration is lacking. The only proof they have is an argument on the basis of the induction of the obligations, and this also is based on a claim to know the *asrār* (secrets, rational explanation) of *fiqh*. They are thus necessarily led to the position that God's actions, commands and considerations are entirely dependent on His will and nothing else. The Mu'tazila were also led to the same conclusion (2:42).

To answer Qarāfī, Shāṭibī refers to his own discussion of the relativity of *maṣlaḥa* to explain how the *ibāḥa* (permissibility) of a *maṣlaḥa* is determined. Second, he explains that a survey of the rules of *Sharī'a* by the method of induction proves that *Sharī'a* has taken into consideration what is regarded as *maṣlaḥa* in customary practice as well. He argues that such a survey provides the *ḍawābiṭ* (determining factors) of *maṣlaḥa*. An inductive examination of events where *al-takālīf al-shar'iyya* (legal obligations) have been realized in practice shows that these *takālīf* and *mubāḥāt* did not harm human interests (or *maṣāliḥ*) but have confirmed them and established them, thus *ibāḥa* and *maṣlaḥa* are compatable with each other.

Ibn 'Abd al-Salām distinguished between *maṣāliḥ al-dār al-ākhira* and *al-maṣāliḥ al-dunyawiyya* on the basis that the former can be known only by *Shar'* while the latter are known by needs, experience, custom and by considerations of probability. He even says that when one wants to know a *maṣlaḥa*, he may simply find it rationally, supposing that the *Shāri'* has given no indication. Judgement is reached rationally in this manner except in the case of *ta'abbudāt* where *maṣāliḥ* or *mafāsid* are not given.

Shāṭibī, quoting Ibn 'Abd al-Salām here, probably to indicate his disagreement, refers to him not by name but by terms such as *ba'ḍ al-nās* (some person) and *hādha al-qā'il* (this speaker). However, since the extracts cited by Shāṭibī are traceable in Ibn 'Abd al-Salam's *Qawā'id*, there is no doubt that Shāṭibī is referring to Ibn 'Abd al-Salām here. To Shāṭibī *maṣāliḥ* in the hereafter are not independent of the *maṣāliḥ* of this world. Hence not only *al-maṣāliḥ al-ukhrawiyya* but also the *dunyawiyya*, as long as they are obligations, are known by *Shar'* alone. If the distinction between the two *maṣāliḥ* were absolute, the *Shar'* would have been concerned only with *al-maṣāliḥ al-ukhrawiyya*. In fact, to realize the *ukhrawiyya,* the establishment of the *dunyawiyya* is inevitable. Shāṭibī refutes the implication in Ibn 'Abd al-Salām's statement that the *dunyawiyya* are rational and hence the consideration of *Shar'* is only supplementary (2:48).

Shāṭibī uses the terms *istiṣlāḥ, istidlāl* and *al-maṣlaḥa al-mursala, al-istidlāl al-mursal* and *istiḥsān* as synonyms of *maṣlaḥa* because they all belong to this concpet. As we have mentioned earlier the validity of *maṣlaḥa* as a legal evidence has been the most debated question in Islamic legal theory. Usually *maṣlaḥa* is considered an evidence external to four sources i.e. the Qur'ān, Sunna, *ijmā'* and *qiyās*. *Maṣlaḥa* is therefore often *al-maṣlaḥa al-mursala* because it is not supported explicitly by a specific source.

Shāṭibī does not treat *maṣlaḥa* in the framework of the four sources. Firstly, his conception of the sources of law is limited to the Qur'ān and Sunna. He does mention *al-Kitāb*, *Sunna*, *ijmā'* and *qiyās* as four sources of Islamic law at one place (3:5) and he substitutes *ra'y* for *qiyās* (3:345), yet he explains that "since *Kitāb* and *Sunna* are the bases for other evidence, we have limited our examination (of evidence) to these two only (3:345). Secondly he clarifies that reference to sources is made only to ascertain whether the authority of an evidence is definitive or conjectural.

The criterion for this judgement are the texts of the Qur'ān and Sunna, if an evidence is supported by these texts it is definitive, otherwise it is conjectural. In case an evidence is contrary to these texts it must be rejected. Some jurists have allowed such evidence, calling it *al-munāsib al-gharīb*, and relating it to the concept of *maṣlaḥa*. Shāṭibi stresses that such evidence, even a *khabr al-wāḥid*, if it is definitely contrary to texts, it must be rejected. He explains that its relevance to *munāsib* or *maṣlaḥa* obtains only when its contrariness is conjectural, not definite. In that case it is open to *ijtihād* (3:18). Shāṭibī defined *al-munāsib al-gharīb* as an evidence which is not endorsed by a specific text, yet it is not definitely contrary to it (3:25).

Shāṭibī explains that an evidence not deduced from a specific text falls in the category of rationally derived evidence for which methods like *qiyās* are employed. *Al-munāsib al-gharīb* also belongs to this cateogry as its cause is not derived from text, but by the method of analogy. According to Shāṭibi *istiḥsān, istiṣlāḥ* and *istidlāl* are also such methods which do not derive rules from specific texts but apply reason to infer rules (3:41).

Shāṭibī develops this point further in his book *al-I'tiṣām* where he refutes the claim that *bid'a* is analogous to *al-maṣlaḥa al-mursala*. We have summarised Shāṭibī's discussion of *al-maṣlaḥa al-mursala* in chapter ten where it is more relevant to the discussion of *bid'a*. Here we are referring only to those points of his discussion which are pertinent to the question of sources.

Illustrating with ten examples from the opinions of the companions of the Prophet, he argues that when a rule is based on the idea of affinity with the revealed law, there is either an explicit legal evidence to endorse it, or it is rejected specifically by it. The legal position of that idea in both cases is evident, acceptable in the former and rejected in the latter. It is debatable only when there is no specific evidence to endorse it or reject it. In such a case, if one finds one specific text that endorses that idea implicitly, but that consideration is absent in other acts of law, and it cannot be regarded as a reliable genus for further extension, this idea cannot be accepted as a legal cause. It is rejected despite its being endorsed implictly by a text. Therefore *istidlāl* and *maṣlaḥa* do not belong to this category.

Istidlāl, maṣlaḥa, istiṣlāḥ, al-maṣlaḥa al-mursala belong, on the other hand, to an idea which conforms to the acts of law in general, and as a whole. It is neither endorsed or rejected by a specific legal text, but it has affinity to a large number of laws to the extant that one may regard it as a genus on which the Lawgiver relies as a whole, though not as a specific evidence.[109] Shāṭibī, thus, concludes that *al-maṣlaḥa al-mursala* finally aims at the protection of an essential need and removal of hardship, and thus closely related to *maṣlaḥa*.[110]

MODERN DEVELOPMENTS

It seems that Shāṭibī's method of treatment of sources as a whole, and defining *maṣlaḥa* beyond the confinement of specific textual support was not developed further after him. Usually *maṣlaḥa* was treated as *al-maṣlaḥa al-mursala* as an extra principle to the four sources. It was in the nineteenth century that the concept of *maṣlaḥa* as an independent principle re-emerged. In the beginning the idea appeared without reference to Shāṭibī, but gradually as we have seen in the preceding chapter, the jurists began to refer more and more to Shāṭibī.

With the expansion of the magnitude of social change affecting all departments of life utilitarian philosophies became popular. The movement of modernism in Islam searched in Islamic tradition for a principle that would help them grapple with the changing conditions. They found in *maṣlaḥa* such a concept. Naturally therefore more attention was paid to the study of this concept in modern times than even before.

In 1857 the *'Ahd al-Amān,* a document of reforms, was issued in Tunisia. This document later became the fundamental legal instrument in the 1860 Constitution—"the first Constitution to be issued in any Muslim country in modern times".[111] In its preamble, *maṣlaḥa* was referred to as the principle of interpretation of law: "God... who has given justice as a guarantee of the preservation of order in this world, and has given the revelation of law in accordance with human interests [*maṣāliḥ*][112]". The document then expounded the following three principles as the components of the concept of *maṣlaḥa*: "Liberty, security, equality".[113]

In 1867 Khayr al-Dīn Pasha, in his *Aqwam al-masālik*, reaffirmed that the principle of *maṣlaḥa* must be the supreme guide of the government.[114] He found this principle extremely significant as it could be used to justify a change of institutions in the interest of the public as well as to condemn a change when it opposed public interest.[115]

In 1899, in his speech on the reforms in the court systems in Egypt and the Sudan, Muḥammad 'Abduh also stressed the use of *maṣlaḥa* as a guiding principle in law making.[116] J. Schacht has argued that the principle of *maṣlaḥa*, according to 'Abduh, was preferable to the literal application of Islamic law.[117] Henry Laoust has also observed that the principle of *maṣlaḥa* was one of the two ideas on the basis of which 'Abduh considered Islam to be superior to Christianity. It is because of this principle that Islam has a sense of reality more developed than Christianity.[118]

It is to be noted that Khayr al-Dīn and 'Abduh both referred to *maṣlaḥa* as a principle of interpretation of law—and as such a principle of change, dynamism and adaptability. The same theme, in varying versions, has been repeated by a large number of modern Muslim scholars of Islamic law. Among them the following are notable illustrations: Rashīd Riḍā, Ṣubḥī Maḥmaṣānī, 'Abd al-Razzāq al-Ṣanhūrī, Ma'rūf al-Dawālībī, Muṣṭafā al-Shalabī, 'Abd al-Wahhāb Khallāf, Muḥammad al-Khuḍrī and Muṣṭafā Abū Zayd.[119]

While Muslim modernists viewed *maṣlaḥa* as a principle of change and adaptability, the conservative Muslim scholars were critical of such interpretations. We cannot go into a detailed analysis of the conservative view. Only to illustrate it we refer here to Zāhid al-Kawtharī's views. In 1906, *al-Manār* published Najm al-Dīn al-Ṭūfī's treatise on *maṣāliḥ*. We have already referred to Ṭūfī as a representative of radical views on *maṣlaḥa*. For example, he held that the principle of *maṣlaḥa* could even restrict (*takhṣīṣ*) the application of *ijmā'* as well as that of the Qur'ān and *Sunna* if the latter were harmful to human interests. This publication raised a strong reaction among the conservative group of scholars in Egypt. Consequently Ṭūfī as well as the concept of *maṣlaḥa* was bitterly opposed. Only to illustrate this opposition, we quote Zāhid al-Kawtharī's criticism of Ṭūfī as follows:

> One of their spurious methods in attempting to change the *Shar'* in accordance with their desires is to state that 'the basic principle of

> legislation in such matters as relating to transactions among men is the principle of *maṣlaḥa*; if the text (*naṣṣ*) opposes this *maṣlaḥa*, the text should be abandoned and *maṣlaḥa* should be followed'. What an evil to utter such statements, and to make it a basis for the construction of a new *Shar'*!
>
> This is nothing but an attempt to violate divine law (*al-Shar' al-Ilāhī*) in order to permit in the name of *maṣlaḥa* what the *Shar'* has forbiddin. Ask this libertine (*al-fājir*) what is this *maṣlaḥa* on which you want to construct your law?... The first person to open this gate of evil ... was Najm al-Ṭūfī al-Ḥanbalī ... No Muslim has ever uttered such a statement ... This is a naked heresy. Whoever listens to such talk, he partakes of nothing of knowledge or religion.[120]

Kawtharī did not deny the fact that the *Shar'* took into consideration the interests and good of the people, but he insisted on the fact that what is good and what is bad can only be known through revelation. *Maṣlaḥa* as an independent principle of the interpretation of law has, therefore, no validity whatsoever.

Kawtharī's criticism of *maṣlaḥa* is typical of the traditional view of the concept. To him *maṣlaḥa* is arbitrary and merely personal. In fact this fear of arbitrariness concerning the reasoning on the basis of regard for human interests, and hence considered to be the violation of Divine law is a familiar feature in the history of the Islamic legal theory. *Maṣlaḥa* and similar legal principles which were employed in favour of the adaptability of Islamic law, were opposed on the same grounds. We have seen in this chapter that Shāṭibī treated *maṣlaḥa* as a core concept of his doctrine of *maqāṣid al-Sharī'a* in order to refute as well as pre such criticism. The other essential terms and concepts of this doctrine are analysed in the subsequent chapters.

NOTES AND REFERENCES

1. Goldziher, "Das Prinzip des Istiṣḥâb in der Muhammedanischen Gesetzwissenschaft", *Wiener Zeitschrift für die Kunde des Morgenlandes*. Vol. I (1887), pp. 128-236; *vide* Summary in French by G.H. Bousquet, in *Arabica* VII (1960), pp. 12-15. The points of resemblance with Roman and Rabbinic law are not elaborated but most probably Goldziher means certain areas of flexibility in contrast to the strict application of law.
2. N.P. Aghnides, *Mohammedan Theories of Finance* (London: Longman, 1916), p. 102.
3. G.H. Bousquet, *Précis de droit musulman* (Alger: Maison des Livres, 1947), p.37.
4. J. Schacht, *The Origins of Muhammadan Jurisprudence* (Oxford: Clarendon, 1959), p. 111, n. 1.
5. *Ibid.*, "Classicisme, traditionalisme et ankylose dans la loi religieuse de l'Islam", Brunschvig et als (ed.), *Classicisme et déclin culturel dans l'histoire de l'Islam*, (Paris, 1957), p. 158, note no. 4.

6. Rudi Paret, "*Istiḥsān and Istiṣlāḥ*", *Encyclopaedia of Islam,* Vol. IV (Leiden: Brill, 1978). pp. 255-259.
7. Albert Hourani, *Arabic Thought in the Liberal Age, 1798-1939* (London: Oxford University Press, 1962), p. 234.
8. G.E. Von Grunebaum, "Concept and Function of Reason in Islamic Ethics", *Oriens,* Vol. 15(1962), p.15.
9. É. Tyan, "Méthodologie et sources du droit en Islam", *Studia Islamica*, Vol. X (1959), p. 97.
10. *Ibid.*
11. *Ibid.*
12. *Ibid.*, p. 98.
13. G.F. Hourani, "Two Theories of Value in Medieval Islam", *Muslim World,* Vol. L (1960), pp. 269-278.
14. Sa'īd Ramaḍān al-Būṭī, *Ḍawābiṭ al-maṣlaḥa fī al-sharī'at al-Islāmiyya,* (Dimashq: Umawiya, 1966-67), pp. 12-14.
15. *Ibid.*, pp. 23-60.
16. *Ibid.*, p. 414.
17. M. Kerr, "Rashīd Riḍā and Legal Reform", *Muslim World*, 1960, p. 108.
18. *Islamic Reform* (California, 1966), p. 56.
19. *Ibid.*, p. 60.
20. *Ibid.*, p. 77.
21. *Ibid.*, p. 67.
22. *Ibid.*, p. 73.
23. *Ibid.*, p. 76.
24. *Ibid.*, p. 81.
25. *Ibid.*, *Muslim World, op. cit.*, p. 107.
26. R. Paret ("Istiḥsān and Istiṣlāḥ"), *Shorter Encyclopedia of Islam,* Leiden: Brill, 1961, p. 185, and again in E.I^2, vol. IV, p. 258) mentioned 1194 as the year of Shāṭibī's (d. 1390) death, which is in fact the year in which Abū'l Qāsim Muḥammad b. Fīra al-Shāṭibī died. See Brockelmann, *G.A.L.* (Brill, 1943), p. 520, and F. Krenkow, "Shāṭibī", in *E.I.*^{1}, Vol. IV, p. 337-338. Unfortunately, the same error is repeated in the heavily edited and revised version of Paret's article in the Urdu Encyclopaedia of Islam, *Urdu dā'ira ma'ārif Islāmiyya* (Lahore: Dānishgāh Panjab), Vol. II, (pp. 586-591), p. 589.
27. Kerr, *op. cit.*, p. 194, referring to Riḍā's mention of Shāṭibī, he rightly quotes his year of death, but in his index on p. 247 identifies him as Abū'l Qāsim b. Firra ash-Shāṭibī.
28. Ḥusayn Ḥāmid Ḥassān, *Naẓariyyat al-maṣlaḥa fī'l-fiqh al-Islāmī* (Cairo: Maktabat al-Mutanabbī, 1981), originally a doctoral dissertation submitted at Jāmi'at al-Azhar.
29. *Ibid.* p.8.
30. *Ibid.* p. 42.
31. *Ibid.* pp. 51-68.
32. See Lane, *An Arabic-English Lexicon,* Book IV (London: Williams Norgate, 1863-93), pp. 1714-1715.
33. The Qur'ān: 3: 114, Rāghib al-Iṣfahānī, *Al-Mufradāt fī gharīb al-Qur'ān* (Karachi: Tijārat Kutub, 1961), p. 286, also confirms that in the Qur'ān *Ṣalāḥ* is often opposed to *fasād* and *sayyi'a.*
34. R. Paret, *op. cit.*
35. 'Umar 'Abdullah, "Mālik's Concept of *'Amal* in the Light of Mālikī Legal Theory", Ph.D., Dissertation (Chicago, 1978), vol. I, p. 14ff., 18.
36. Al-Juwaynī, *al-Burhān fī uṣūl al-fiqh,* Edited by 'Abd al-'Aẓīm al-Dīb (Qaṭar 1399 H) Vol.2, p.1113. [MS. III Ahmet 1321, Photo I.R.I. no:219, fol. 135a]. See also Muṣṭafā al-Shalabī, *Ta'līl al-aḥkām* (Cairo: Azhar, 1949), pp. 292ff.
37. *Al-Burhān* [MS fols. 108ff.], vol. 2, pp. 923 ff.
38. *Ibid.* p. 932.
39. Abū'l Ḥusayn al-Baṣrī, *al-Mu'tamad fī uṣūl al-fiqh,* Vol. II (Dimashq: al-Ma'had al-'Ilmī al-Firansī, 1964), p. 888.

40. *Ibid.*
41. *Ibid.* p. 805.
42. Ghazālī, *al-Mustasfā min 'ilm al-uṣūl.* Vol. I (Baghdad: Muthannā, 1970), pp. 286-87.
43. *Ibid.*, p. 284.
44. *Ibid.*, p. 290.
45. *Ibid.*, pp. 294-295.
46. *Ibid.*, Vol. II, p. 306.
47. *Ibid.*, Vol. I, pp. 274, 284. Following Shāfi'ī, Ghazālī says on p. 315:

من استصلح فقد شرع كما ان من استحسن فقد شرع

48. *Ibid.*, Vol. I, pp. 284-315.
49. *Ibid.*, pp. 56-57.
50. *Ibid.*, p. 60.
51. *Ibid.*, p. 87.
52. *Ibid.*, Vol. II, p. 230.
53. *Ibid.*, Vol. II, pp. 295ff.
54. *Ibid.*, p. 297.
55. *Ibid.*, Vol. II, p. 306.
56. *Ibid.*, Vol. I, pp. 5-7, Ghazālī complains that the Transoxian jurists, such as Abū Zayd have tried to bring too much *fiqh* into *Uṣūl al-fiqh* (p. 10).
57. Ibn Khaldūn, *Muqaddima* (Cairo: Būlāq, 1320 A.H.), p. 431.
58. Fakhr al-Dīn al-Rāzī, *"al-Maḥṣūl fī uṣūl al-fiqh"*, MS. Yale University, Nemoy, A-1039 (L-643); *Al-Maḥṣūl fī 'ilm uṣūl al-fiqh*, edited by Ṭāhā Jābir Fayyāḍ al-'Alwānī, (Riyāḍ: Jāmi'at al-Imām Muḥammad b. Sa'ūd, 1980).
59. *Ibid.*, vol. 2, part 2, p. 218 [MS. Pt.2, f. 87a)
60. *Ibid.*
61. *Ibid.*
62. *Ibid.*, vol. I, p. 159 [Ms. part 1, f. 9a].
63. *Ibid.*, p. 181 [Ms. f. 13a].
64. *Ibid.*, vol. 2, Pt.2. p. 242 [Ms. part 2, f. 90b].
65. *Ibid.*
66. *Ibid.*,p. 243 [Ms. f. 92a].
67. *Ibid.*, p. 246, [Ms. f. 92b].
68. *Ibid.*, pp. 251-273, [Ms. ff. 92-97].
69. *Ibid.*, p. 270, [Ms.f. 97b].
70. *Ibid.*
71. *Ibid.*, p. 225, [Ms.f. 88b].
72. *Ibid.*, p. 220 ff., [Ms.ff. 87-90].
73. Most probably this is the *ijbār* to which Shāṭibī refers in *al-Muwāfaqāt* when he says: "We walked devotedly and assumed we were going on the right path, until we faced sheer determinsim (*ijbār*) instead of choice", Vol. I, *op. cit.* p. 19.
74. Qarāfī, *Tanqīḥ al-fuṣūl fī 'ilm al-uṣūl,* in *al-Dhakhīra* (Cairo: Maṭba' Kulliya al-Sharī'a, 1961), pp. 144-46.
75. Ṣadr al-Sharī'a al-Maḥbūbī, *al-Tawḍīḥ wa'l-tanqīḥ,* Vol. II (Cairo: Maṭba' Bōsanawī, 1304 A.H.), pp. 536-540.
76. Jamāl al-Dīn al-Isnawī, *Nihāyat al-su'l,* commentary on Bayḍāwī's *Minhāj al-wuṣūl,* on the margin of Ibn Amīr al-Ḥājj, *al-Taqrīr wa'l-taḥbīr* (Cairo: Būlāq, 1317 A.H.), Vol. III, pp. 134-140.
77. Tāj al-Dīn al-Subkī, *Jam' al-jawāmi',* in 'Abd al-Raḥmān al-Bannānī, *Ḥāshiya ... 'alā matn jam' al-jawāmi',* Vol.II, (Cairo: Muṣṭafā Bābī, 1937), pp. 270-285.
78. Sa'd al-Dīn al-Taftāzānī, *Sharḥ al-tawḍīḥ wa'l-tanqīḥ* (Cairo: Bōsanawī, 1304 A.H.), Vol. II, pp. 548-683.
79. Sayf al-Dīn al-Āmidī, *al-Iḥkām fī uṣūl al-aḥkām,* Vol. IV (Cairo: Maṭba' Ma'ārif, 1914), p. 215-217.

80. Ibn Ḥājib, *Mukhtaṣar muntahā al-uṣūlī,* Vol. II (Cairo: Būlāq, 1317 A.H.), p. 289.
81. Ibn 'Abd al-Salām was initiated into the Suhrawardiya Ṭarīqa. He is also claimed to have joined the Shādhiliyya. His relationship with Ibn 'Arabī has, however, been a subject of dispute. For details see Riḍwān 'Alī Nadwī, *Al-'Izz b. 'Abd al-Salām* (Damascus: Dār al-fikr, 1960), pp. 103-110.
82. Ibn 'Abd al-Salām, *Qawā'id al-aḥkām fī maṣāliḥ al-anām,* Vol. I (Cairo: Istiqāma, n.d.) p. 10.
83. *Ibid.*, p. 6.
84. *Ibid.*, p. 24.
85. *Ibid.*, p. 129.
86. R.A. Nicholson (Ed. Comm.), Abū Naṣr al-Sarrāj, *Kitāb al-luma' fi 'l-taṣawwuf* (London: Luzac, 1914), p. 134.
For this opposition of terms cf.
Abū Bakr al-Kalābādhī, *al-Ta'arruf li madhhab ahl al-taṣawwuf* (Cairo: 'Isā al-Bābī, 1960), p. 23.
Najm al-Dīn Kubrā, *Fawā'iḥ al-jamāl,* ed. Fritz Meier, (Wiesbaden: Steiner, 1957), p. 71 (Introduction), pp. 5-6 (Text).
87. Sarrāj, *op. cit.*, p.47. (quoting a Ṣūfī Ruwaym b. Aḥmad).
88. *Ibid.*, p. 336.
89. Abū'l Qāsim al-Qushayrī, *al-Risāla fī 'ilm al-taṣawwuf* (Cairo: Muḥammad 'Alī, 1948), p. 181.
90. See above, n. 81.
91. 'Abd al-Ḥalīm Maḥmūd, *al-Madrasa al-shādhiliyya wa imāmuhā Abū'l Ḥasan al-Shādhilī* (Cairo: Dār al-Kutub al-Ḥadītha, 1387 A.H.). p. 130.
92. *Ibid.*, p. 137.
93. Ibn 'Abbād al-Rundī, *Sharḥ al-ḥikam l'il-Imām Abī'l-Faḍl Aḥmad b. Aṭā' Allāh al-Iskandarī* (Cairo: Muṣṭafā Āfandi, 1320 A.H.), p. 99.
94. *Ibid.*, p. 106.
95. Ibn Taymiyya, *Qā'ida fī'l mu'jizāt wa'l karāmāt wa anwā' khawāriq al-'ādāt* in *Majmū'at al-rasā'il wa'l masā'il,* Vol. V (Cairo: Maṭba' Manār, 1349 A.H.), p. 22.
96. *Ibid.*
97. *Ibid.*, p. 23.
98. *Ibid.*
99. *Ibid.*, p. 30.
100. Ibn Qayyim, *I'lām al-muwaqqi'īn,* Vol. I (Cairo: Sa'āda, 1955), pp. 29-32.
101. *Ibid.*, pp. 197ff.
102. *Ibid.*, Vol. III, p. 14.
103. Najm al-Dīn al-Ṭūfī, *Sharḥ al-arba'īn,* included as appendix to Muṣṭafā Zayd, *al-Maṣlaḥa fī'l-tashrī' al-islāmī wa Najm al-Dīn al-Ṭūfī* (Cairo: Dār al-fikr al-'Arabī, 1954), p. 18.
104. *Ibid.*, pp. 35-37.
105. *Ibid.*, p. 47.
106. G.f. Hourani, *Islamic Rationalism, The Ethics of 'Abd al-Jabbār* (Oxford: Clarendon, 1971), pp. 57, 115, 118.
107. Shāṭibī, *al-I'tiṣām* (Cairo, 1332 A.H.), Vol. II, pp. 95-140.
108. The numbers in the parenthesis in the text of this chapter refer to the volume number and pages of *al-Muwāfaqāt* (Cairo: Muṣṭafā Muḥammad, n.d.). For instance 2:25 means Vol. 2, p. 25.
109. *Al-I'tiṣām, op. cit.* pp. 111-115.
110. *Ibid.* p. 133.
111. Hourani, *op. cit.* p. 65.
112. Muhammad Bayrām, *Ṣafwat al-i'tibār*, Vol. II, p. 11, vide Hourani, *op. cit.*, p. 64.
113. *Ibid.*, p. 93.
114. *Ibid.*, p. 92.
115. *Ibid.*, p. 93.

116. Muftī Muḥammad 'Abduh, "*Taqrīr muftī al-diyār al-Miṣriyya fī iṣlāh al-maḥākim al-shar'iyya*", *al-Manār*, Vol. II (1899) p. 761.

117. Schacht, "Muḥammad 'Abduh", *Shorter Encyclopaedia of Islam* (Leiden: Brill, 1961), p. 406.

118. Henry Laoust, *Le Califat dans la doctrine de Rasid Rida* (Beyrouth, 1938), p. 273, n. 61.

119. The following works stress the dynamism of *maṣlaḥa* as a principle of interpretation of Islamic law: Rashīd Riḍā, *Yusr al-Islām* (Cairo: Nahḍa, 1956), pp. 72-75; Ṣubḥī Maḥmaṣānī, *Falsafat al-tashrī' fi al-Islām*, transl. by F.J. Ziyadah (Leiden: Brill, 1961). (Arabic Ed. Bayrut, 1952), pp. 130-133, 205f; 'Abd al-Razzāq al-Ṣanhūrī, "Wujūb tanqīḥ al-qānūn al-madanī al-Miṣrī", in *Majallat al-Qānūn wa'l Iqtiṣād,* Vol. 6(1963) 3-144. *vide* Kerr, *op. cit;* Ma'rūf Dawālībī, *al-Madkhal ilā 'ilm uṣūl al-fiqh* (Bayrūt: Dār al-'ilm l'il-mala'īn, 1965), pp. 442-450; Muṣṭafā al-Shalabī, *Ta'līl al-aḥkām, 'arḍ wa taḥlīl li ṭarīqat al-ta'līl wa tatawwurātihā fī 'uṣūr al-ijtihād wa'l-taqlīd* (Cairo: Azhar, 1949), pp. 278-384; 'Abd al-Wahhāb Khallāf, *Maṣādir al-tashrī' al-islāmī fī mā lā naṣṣa fīhī,* (Cairo: Dār al-Kutub al-'Arabī, 1955), pp. 70-122; Muṣṭafā Zayd, *al-Maṣlaḥa fī al-tashrī' al-islāmī wa Najm al-Dīn al-Ṭūfī* (Cairo: Dār al-Fikr al-'Arabī, 1954); Muḥammad Khuḍrī, *Uṣūl al-fiqh* (Cairo: Muṣṭafā Muḥammad, 1933).

120. Zāhid al-Kawtharī, *Maqālāt al-Kawtharī*, posthumous publication in 1372 A.H., as quoted by Muṣṭafā Zayd, *op. cit.*, pp. 164-66.

CHAPTER SIX

DALĀLA: LANGUAGE AND LAW

In Shāṭibī's philosophy of law, the following four principles constitute the objectives of law:

1. Welfare of mankind (*maṣlaḥa*)
2. Universal intelligibility
3. Accordance of legal duties with human natural ability, and
4. Conformity with reasonable customs.

The preceding chapter discussed Shāṭibī's views on *maṣlaha* as being the primary objective of law. The present chapter explains Shāṭibī's view of the second *maqṣid* of *Sharī'a*: intelligibility. *Sharī'a* was revealed in such a manner that it was to be intelligible for every *mukallaf*. Although Shāṭibī does not say so explicitly, his analysis of *dalāla* develops an argument against the Ẓāhirīs and the Ḥadīth-group who discouraged any interpretation of *sharī'a* on the rational basis. The Ẓāhirīs attach more significance to the letter of the law (*lafẓ*: words) than to the spirit of the law (*ma'nā*: meaning). Shāṭibī, on the contrary contends that it is the meaning which is important, and not the word alone. Thus, he indirectly leads to the conclusion that interpretation of *Sharī'a* by *maṣlaḥa* serves to fulfil the objectives of *Sharī'a*, because *maṣlaḥa* provides basic meanings to the words of law. Shāṭibī's discussion of intelligibility has therefore two parts: (1) theory of language and meaning (*dalāla*) and (2) universal intelligibility (*ummiyya*).

1. SHĀṬIBĪ'S THEORY OF LANGUAGE AND MEANING

Traditionally, the structure of any science or a body of knowledge consists of three parts: (1) *mawḍū'*: the subject-matter of that particular science. It is the central point of all the discussions in that science. (2) *mabādī*: the accepted bases or assumptions which are established elsewhere and are taken as granted in this science. (3) *masā'il*: the various propositions discussed in that science with specific reference to the subject-matter of the science. The scholars varied among themselves on treating linguistic problems in *Uṣūl al-fiqh* as *mabādī*, or *masā'il*. For instance, in their respective books on *Uṣūl al-fiqh* Āmidī deals with them as *mabādī*, while Ghazālī treated them as *masā'il*.[1]

The science of *Uṣūl* has been perennially concerned with the theories of meaning. These theories were discussed as principles (*mabādī*) or the problems (*masā'il*) of *Uṣūl al-fiqh*. Among a considerable number of such problems, the issues most commonly discussed by *uṣūliyūn* were: the problem of the foreign vocabulary of the Qur'ān, the problem of *ishtirāk* and the problem of *asmā' shar'iyya*. In other words, we may say that a Muslim jurist encounters the problem of language in his sources (the Qur'ān and the *Ḥadīth*), in his methodology (*qiyās*, logic), and in his terminology. We will return later to the legal aspect of these problems. Let us first discuss their linguistic aspect.

FOREIGN VOCABULARY IN THE QUR'ĀN

The Qur'ān in several places claims to be revealed in plain Arabic,[2] yet it includes a number of non-Arabic words. This situation confused many a scholar. Suyūṭī[3] found disagreement among scholars on this problem to such an extent that he divided scholars into two groups. The first group denied any occurrence of foreign words in the Qur'ān. The second group did not deny their foreign origin but did not find it contradictory to the Qur'anic claim because these words were understood by the Arabs after all. Suyūṭī counted Shāfi'ī in the first group. But, as Shāṭibī pointed out, it was an obvious error. This misunderstanding was, however, widespread among scholars even as late as in the time of Āmidī.[4]

Shāṭibī maintains that when the Qur'ān claims clarity, it is not the problem of the vocabulary that is involved, but rather that of "indication" and "understanding" (2:45).[5] Shāṭibī also says that Shāfi'ī[6] was the first to point out this distinction but even his statement was taken in reference to the vocabulary of the Qur'ān (2:46). Shāṭibī explains it as follows:

> When we say that the Qur'ān was revealed in the language of the Arabs and that it is simple and pure Arabic, and there is nothing foreign in it, we mean that God revealed it in the language of the Arabs as they understood it within its particular vocabulary, styles of expression, and according to the usage of the Arabs. It expresses sometimes an idea in "general" terms and refers to its obvious external meanings. The Arabs express themselves sometimes in a language which has no words, only meaning, as, for instance, the language of gestures.... A particular thing may have several names in Arabic and several things may have only one name. All of these usages were well-known among the Arabs and this usage created no ambiguity or doubt. The Qur'ān must, therefore, conform to this usage so that it could be understood on the

basis of Arab usage. Arabic usage cannot be explained in terms of the usage of foreign language (2:45-56).

Both Shāfi'ī and Shāṭibī seem to be pointing out a concept of language which is absent in the treatment of the other participants in the controversy. To Shāfi'ī and Shāṭibī, the language is not only a collection of words but a system with a relationship structure consisting of things and names. This is why when a foreign (loan) word enters into the system, it acquires a new meaning and a new function. It neither functions in its original meaning nor does it convey the meaning expressed by words already existing in the recipient language. This can, therefore, be understood only as it functions in the new system.

ORIGIN OF LANGUAGE

Scholars had different theories on the origin of language. Āmidī sums up the views of the scholars by dividing them into four groups:[7]

(a) Ashā'ira, Ẓāhiriyya and a number of *fuqahā'* hold that the originator (*wāḍi'*) of languages is God. Language was made known to man through *waḥy* (revelation) and *tawqīf* (periodical Divine instruction).

(b) Bahshamiyyah and a number of *mutakallimūn* maintained that the originator of language are its speakers. The manner of knowing language is *iṣṭilāḥ* (convention) proposed by one individual or a group.

(c) Abū Isḥāq Isfarā'īnī took a middle stand. He believed that the origin of that part of language on which agreement is actual and necessary, is *tawqīf* and the rest is by both *tawqīf* and *iṣṭilāḥ*.

(d) Āmidī, quoting Bāqillānī in his support, admits the possibility of all of the above three views. He, however, maintains that if one is seeking a certain and definite conclusion, then none of the above positions can be rejected: that is, not one of them can be singly rejected. If one is seeking the proximate truth (*ẓann*), then Ash'arī's position is closer to truth.

Shāṭibī dismissed these discussions as being outside the subject-matter of *uṣūl* (1:17). The problem relevant to *uṣūl* concerns the manner in which words or sentences express the meaning. Thus the problems like *ishtirāk, asmā' shar'iyya* and *ibtidā' al-waḍ'* are not relevant as such but only if they are the problems of indication.

WORD AND MEANING

Shāṭibī regarded the indication (*dalāla*) as the most essential aspect of language. Contrary to traditional treatment of this aspect he gives up the *lafẓ-ma'nā* relationship view of the indication. Analysing the aspect of indication in Arabic language he discovered that this aspect can be viewed on two levels (2:46). On the first level it consists of absolute/simple (*muṭlaq*) utterances of words (*alfāẓ*) and expressions (*'ibārāt*) which indicate the absolute/simple (*muṭlaq*) meaning. He also calls them *ma'ānī aṣliyya*, (2:47) *ma'ānī mabthūtha* (2:60) *ma'ānī mujarrada*, (4:105) and *ma'nā tarkībī* (2:60). This level of indication is that of fundamental indication (*dalāla aṣliyya*).

On the second level it consists of conditional (*muqayyida*) words and expressions which indicate the subservient (*khādima*) meaning. This indication is called subsidiary indication (*dalāla tābi'a*).

It is on the first level that all languages share with each other because without any exception this is the ultimate aim of any speaker (2:46). Let us illustrate the above with an example.

A certain person has performed an act, say standing up. Now a speaker of any language, if he wants to report this event, can do so without difficulty. In other words, any person speaking any language can talk about the same thing and say the same thing without depending on one language. This is how one quotes the statements of others from a different language into his own or within one language in his own words (2:46,48).[8] One may also say that at that level it is an idea, a sense, a meaning which can be expressed in any language.

The second level is restricted to the particularities of a certain language. This level of indication deals with sentences and words. It is conditioned by the grammatical rules and styles of expression in this particular language. The above example ("Zayd stood up") in Arabic may be expressed in the following sentences:

1. *Qāma Zaydun* [stress on the predicate].
2. *Zaydun qāma* [stress on the subject].
3. *Inna Zaydan qāma* [to remove the doubt about the event].
4. *Wallāhi inna Zaydan qāma* [to refute the disputation about the event].
5. *Qad qāma Zaydun* [to announce the occurence of an expected event].
6. *Innamā qāma Zaydun* [to deride someone who denies the event].

These sentences can be multiplied with the rules of grammar and stylistic devices, but all of them rotate around the notion of Zayd's standing up (2:47). These devices add meanings to the statement but they are not the ultimate aim of the speaker, rather they are complementary and supplementary.

It is, therefore, at the second level that the idea is bound in the usage of a particular language. The nuances and the various shades of meaning of the expression at the second level can be understood only with reference to the particular usage.

The first level, in fact, is deemed independent of language. The indication is not limited by the particularities of the language on the first level while it is so on the second level. Shāṭibī, thus, concluded that the translation of the Qur'ān into any other language is impossible on the second level but is possible on the first (2:47), because the usage of one language differs from that of the other language. One can probably argue further on the same line by saying that, for Shāṭibī, this universal element in language makes the communication possible among speakers of different languages. It is on the basis of this principle that he claimed that all differences about the details of a rule can be removed by reducing it to the essentials of the rule.

This universality exists not only in *ikhbār* (proposition) but also in words/meanings. We may use different words and still mean the same thing. The reason is that all such words consist of one part of the meaning that they indicate as a whole in a more general word. Shāṭibī referred to this principle to explain the causes of *khilāf* (disagreement) in law.

> Something is reported from the Prophet... by way of explanation [of certain Qur'anic word]. This reported meaning is explained as a part of the contents of that word. Then there are also reported other meanings which are also contained in that word. The commentators have fixed each of these meanings in the text, on the basis of these reports. The existence of these differing meanings is explained as *khilāf* (conflict of law). For instance, in the explanation of the Qur'anic term *mann*, various meanings have been reported. All of them are included in the indication of the word *mann*; *mann* as a whole includes all the blessings which are individually mentioned by the scholars (4:140).

In this example, after examining the various meanings of the word *mann,* Shāṭibī concluded that "all of them referred to various kinds of food and comforts. The common and shared meaning of all of them was blessing of Allah." Thus by transferring the meaning from the second to the first level he resolved the conflict.

In fact we see a process in which "referents" are mentioned for a word, and Shāṭibī reduces these referents to their most common "idea" which is the "essential meaning". From another point of view Shāṭibī calls this *ma'nā tarkībī*.

> The word is only a means to achieve the intended meaning. The meaning is the goal. But neither of the meanings individually is the

goal. Often no importance is attached to the solitary (*ifrādī*) meaning when the compound meaning (*tarkībī*) conveys a different sense (2:60).

Shāṭibī uses the terms *ma'nā tarkībī, ma'ānī mabthūtha, ma'ānī mujarrada, ma'ānī muṭlaqa,* and *ma'ānī aṣliyya* for the indication on the first level. *Ma'nā tarkībī* is probably restricted to 'concepts' while other terms belong to 'proposition'. Shāṭibī did not, and most probably would not, like to use the terms 'concept' and 'proposition'. We are using them to simplify this point.

One can probably easily see that the indication on the second level proceeds from *alfāẓ* and *'ibārāt* to *ma'ānī* and on the first level from *ma'ānī* to *ma'ānī* without depending on words. Concluding his arguments about the possibility of translation of one language to the other only on the first level, because no two languages can be equal to each other on the second level, Shāṭibī realized this implication as he remarked:

> Sometimes the ancient logicians and their followers among the moderns point out to something like that. But what they say is insufficient and inconclusive (2:40).

Here Shāṭibī does not deny the common ground with logic, but what he deprecates is the logicians' claim that 'definition' stands for the search for the reality of things, because their methods were insufficient and their findings inconclusive. First of all, methods enunciated by the logicians necessitated this impossibility. Their search for essence through genus and differentia is like shooting in the dark (1:26).[9] His argument can be summarised as follows: The essences (*jawāhir*) entail several differentia (*fuṣūl*) which [are likely to] remain unknown.Further, the essence is defined by negative matters (*umūr salbiyya*) as well. Logically, the particular essential (*al-dhātī al-khāṣṣ*), if it is known by other than this particular quiddity (*māhiyya*), will not be a particular. If it is not known (by other than this quiddity) it will not be evident (*ẓāhir*) to the sense and thus un-knowable (*majhūl*). If this particular is defined by other than its particularity it will not be a proper definition. The fact that makes it particular is the essential particular in the first place. Consequently, one has to refer necessarily to the sensible or external factors in one way or another. In any case, it does not lead to the definition of the quiddities (1:26). Shāṭibī, therefore, concludes that:

> The reality (*ḥaqīqa*) can be known only when all of its essentials are known. Since there is a possibility that some essentials may remain unknown, the knowledge of the quiddity remains doubtful.... It is, therefore, obvious that the definitions are impossible on the conditions laid down by the proponents of definitions (*arbāb al-ḥudūd*).... Much more so in *shar'ī* sciences.... The quiddities of the things in their reality are known only to their Originator (*Bāri'*).... (2:26,27)

His skepticism about logic was probably the main reason why Shāṭibī did not entertain the idea of the need of an artificial universal language. To Shāṭibī, the knowledge of things was possible through language and not through logic (2:37). Consequently he confined himself to language. Viewing Shāṭibī's discussion of the problem one may ask: was he thinking of a "universal language"?

One may also find certain similarities in Shāṭibī with Leibniz. For instance, Leibniz's method of reducing several cases to a single formula as a method of universal[10] is comparable with Shāṭibī's view of reducing *khilāf* to *qawl wāḥid* (4:74). Nevertheless, Leibniz and other philosophers of universal language have quite a different approach to the universality of the language. Their aim was to create a universal language --- calculus of human thought --- to avoid the ambiguities of ordinary language.[11] A small number of simple ideas which form the alphabet of human thought would be denoted by "universal/real characteristics".[12] Thus reasoning would no more be affected by the limitations of the ordinary language.

It is quite obvious that Shāṭibī observed the universal element in the language, yet he did not think of the need of creating any artificial language. Nor did he think of discarding the ordinary language for lack of exactness. He believed that the fault lay with the method of logic rather than with language.[13]

On the whole, Shāṭibī's theory of language can be compared more appropriately with the 'ordinary language theories'.[14] The rejection of 'referential' theories of indication[15] in favour of 'total situation'[16] and 'game context'[17] theories of indication in 'ordinary language' philosophy are comparable to Shāṭibī's stipulation of *ummiyya* for understanding Arabic indication in the Qur'ān.

Ordinary language philosophers hold that a 'word' or a 'sentence' is understood only in a 'context' and by the 'usage'. The speech is not only a means but an act as well.

Shāṭibī observes this 'total situation' on the second level. It consists of grammar, style, intellectual make-up (world-view?) and intellectual capacity. In concluding his discussion on language he went even further. According to him the action of the speaker (sometimes even without words) also plays a significant role in this total situation. Shāṭibī finishes his discussion with the following remarks:

> ... "The judgement (*ḥukm*) is not derived on the basis of what meanings are posited (*waḍ'*) for the words but on some other basis, that is the aspect of following the action (*iqtidā' bi'l af'āl*)" (2:75).

2. UNIVERSAL INTELLIGIBILITY

The universality within a language system should better be termed as 'generality'. In case of Arabic language, Shāṭibī adopted the term *ummiyya* (2:48). The choice of this term is essentially motivated by his doctrine of the universality of law. The implied question in his search was related to the understanding of the Qur'ān . The *ummiyya* in this context refers to the simple intellectual state of the initial addressees of the Qur'ān (2:49).

To start with, Shāṭibī identified the Arabs of the Qur'anic period as *ummiyyūn* and further defined it as 'ignorance of the sciences of the ancients' (2:49). From Shāṭibī's analysis of the *ummiyya* of Arabs, it emerges that the generality of indication in a particular language is reached by the following principles (2:48-66).[18]

(1) By adherence to the general knowledge (*ma'hūd*) of the speakers of the language (2:50-52).[19] The understanding is conditioned by the facts and the data well-known to its speakers. These data refer to the following:

a) The sciences commonly known to its speakers.

b) The social and ethical values.

c) The nature and character of the speakers.

(2) By adherence to the established conventions in a language and its rules (2:56-61). This refers to the following:

a) The attitude and practice of the speakers to word - meaning relationship. Which one is considered more essential, word or meaning?

b) Their attitude and practice in grammar rules.

c) Their attitude to the styles of expression.

Shāṭibī observed that the Arab attitude to these rules was conventionally flexible (2:56-61).[20]

(3) The generality of intelligibility. The statement of rules must be intelligible for all the addressees as a whole (2:59). This refers to the capability of understanding. Since the people are not equal or mutually close to each other in understanding things, the generality of comprehension implies only those matters which are liable to be commonly understood. Human beings do come to a general understanding in most of their worldly matters (2:59).

The idea of *Sharī'a* being universally intelligible was accepted generally, but the scholars conceived intelligibility in terms of language. According to them the Qur'ān was understandable because it was in Arabic language.

To satisfy the requirements of universality and certainty in the intelligibility of *Sharī'a*, it is necessary not only to confine the intelligibility to the essential meaning as evident from the context, but also to the fact that the meanings so found must accord to Arab usage. For this the following two aspects may be considered as determining factors: first the Arab usage in word-meaning relationship, and second, the Arab intellectual milieu. The consideration of Arab usage is so essential that "if the Arabs have an incessant custom in their language, it cannot be validly disregarded in the comprehensibility of the *Sharī'a*, and if there is no such custom even then it is not valid to adopt for its comprehension something which is not well known to them (Arabs)" (2:82).

The Arab usage in this regard is that the words are not followed slavishly in their indication of meaning. The Arabs do not confine themselves to one and the same word, and the replacement of words does not seem to affect their statements. The above fact can be illustrated by the following examples. The Arabs often disregard the general rules of language. For instance, they frequently employ the styles of poetry in prose, even though such a style is not required and despite the fact that it is contrary to prose styles. What is significant to note, however, is that customarily such a deviation does not seem to affect the speech (2:83).

Second, one of the characteristics of Arab usage is that they frequently replace original words with their synonyms, and this practice is not considered to imply contradiction or confusion in speech as long as the intended idea (*al-ma'nā al-maqṣūd*) subsists. The seven readings of the Qur'ān are examples to this effect. Further, a number of examples are found in the transmission of verses. For instance, Ibn al-A'rābī (d. 848), the famous linguist, once recited:

> *Wa mawḍi'in zīrin la urīdu mabītah*
> *ka'annī bihī min shidda(t) al-raw'i anīsu*
>
> [I do not want to spend night in a place of *zīr* (like a conical jar), as if, because of intensive fright, I am familiar with it].

One of his listeners corrected, reminding him that on another occasion he had recited *'wa mawḍi'in ḍīqin'* (a narrow place) instead of *'wa mawḍi'in zīrin'*. Ibn al-A'rābi replied regretting that the enquirer had been with him for such a long time and yet did not know that *'zīr'* and *'ḍīq'* are one and the same (2:84).

Arabic poetry has been transmitted by varying reports and with a diversity of words. On the whole, one learns that the Arabs do not strictly adhere to a particular word specifically so as to regard synonymous words as weaker and defective. The few exceptions from this usage belong to peculiar cases where only one meaning is possible (2:84).

The Arabs often disregard part of the grammatical rules of a word, although never as a whole. An example of such disregard are the subtle rules (*al-aḥkām al-laṭīfa*) which the words demand according to theoretical analogy (*al-qiyās al-naẓarī*) but which are, nevertheless disregarded. To illustrate, Shāṭibī says that the words *'amūd*, *ya'ūd*, and *ṣa'īd*, strictly speaking, do not rhyme, yet they are often used to rhyme in Arabic poetry. The reason is that the Arabs' aim for the refinement of their language does not confine them to a pedantic concern (*ta'ammuq*) for these rules (2:84). The best appreciated piece of literature, according to the Arabs, is that which avoids unnecessary artificiality. When a poet is found pedantically indulging in refinement of his diction he is no more regarded as worthy to be followed (2:84).

To sum up, the Arab usage pays more attention to meaning than to words, because "the word is only a means to reach the desired meaning, whereas the meaning is the goal" (87).

Shāṭibī's discussion of the universality of the intelligibility of *Sharī'a* does not seem to solve directly the contradiction which emerges in case of those who know no Arabic. We may, however, infer from the general trend of his argument two levels of the universality of intelligibility which may serve as an indirect answer to the question. On the first level the universality of intelligibility is confined to the Arabs. Shāṭibī maintains that the *Sharī'a* is cast in a language which is understood by all Arabs and it is in this sense that it is Arabic. On the second level the *Sharī'a* is universally intelligible, even by the non-Arabs. Here, intelligibility refers to a more special sense of 'meaning'; it does not refer to the indication by words, syntax or grammar. This is the special sense of 'meaning' in which the meaning is separated from words, syntax, grammar, etc., and thus, actually goes beyond any language. In this state of abstraction they are ready to be understood by speakers of all languages. These meanings are ready to be translated into other languages. This 'meaning', nevertheless, initially comes from the first level of intelligibility which is achieved from the context of a speech in a particular language.

Shāṭibī calls the process, which indicates this special 'meaning', *al-dalāla al-aṣliyya* the basic indication which may explain how Shāṭibī proposes that *Sharī'a* can be understood even by those who do not know Arabic.

It follows from the above discussion that it is the collective meaning which is the objective of the Lawgiver. It is intelligible to speakers of that language at all levels of understanding. It is translatable into all languages and thus universally understandable. It also follows that such methods of legal reasoning that restrict themselves to a single meaning in an individual textual expression fail to achieve this objective. It is therefore only the method of induction that provides collective meaning and assures universal intelligibility. The method of *qiyās*, if it applies the method of deduction of inferring rules from an individual textual statement, is weaker against the method of *maqāṣid al-sharī'ah*. The latter is universally understood as it applies the inductive method of inference.

The second consideration for universal intelligibility is the consideration of the intellectual level of the addressees of a speech. Obligation depends on comprehension in the sense that one cannot be held responsible for more than he can understand. Comprehension, however, does not depend simply on the familiarity of words and meaning, but also on many other things. The degree of comprehensibility may differ from person to person in specific matters because men are not equal in their individual mental make-ups. They, however, come to agree with one another in general matters, and this is the condition according to which *maṣāliḥ* function in this world (2:85).

Shāṭibī calls this level *ummiyya* and characterises *Sharī'a*, the Divine Law, by that term. This term has been used in the Qur'ān with reference to the Prophet (7:156, 157), Arabs (3:20, 75, 62:2) and some groups among the people of the Book (2:78). Muslim scholarship has generally defined the term *ummī* as unlettered, derived from *umm* (mother) indicating that the person was in the same state as his/her mother had borne him/her. The illiteracy of the Prophet was used as a theological argument for the truthfulness of the Prophet and the miraculous nature of the Qur'ān.

Non-Muslim scholarship has not generally accepted this definition. There is almost a consensus among them that the term is derived from a Hebrew phrase meaning "the people of the world in general". This phrase has been further defined to mean people other than ethnic Jews. Thus *ummī*, according to these scholars, means 'gentile or native'. This ethnic definition was rejected by A. Sprenger who asserted affinity between the terms *ummī* and *umma*, *ummī* meaning belonging to *umma*, nation. Analyzing all these various definitions, and rejecting them as failing to explain its usage in the Qur'ān and Muslim tradition, K. 'Athamina defines it as a group of people who considered the Holy Book to be merely tales and fable.[21] This definition may explain the term as it is used in the Qur'ān with reference to the Arabs and the People of the Book, but it cannot be meaningfully applied to the Prophet as an epithet.

Shāṭibī explains that the term *ummiyya* was used for Arabs in general because they did not possess the sciences of the Ancient people, i.e. the Greeks and others. They were not literate in the sense that their culture and civilization did not depend on literacy and written word. Theirs was an oral culture that relied on memory for record rather than on writing. It does not mean that writing did not exist in this culture or that it was not valued. It only means that word of the mouth was more reliable in this culture than the written word. Since it was an oral culture, very little of the other literate cultures had been transmitted to the Arabs.

To call the Arabs *ummiyyīn*, however, does not mean that they were completely ignorant and uncultured. On the contrary they did possess certain branches of knowledge such as astronomy, knowledge of weather, history and medicine, etc. Shāṭibī takes several pages only to enumerate the various sciences (2:71-79) that were known to pre-Islamic Arabs.

In view of the above discussion, *ummiyya* would be understood as the level of understanding of a common man, as the Arabs were in general at the time of the revelation of the Qur'ān. This consideration implies that in understanding the *Sharī'a*, one should not demand more than what an *ummī* can generally understand. Particularly as, in the case of exegesis of the Qur'ān, scholars have introduced matters which were not intelligible for the common people. This consideration would also require that the obligation whether pertaining to beliefs (*i'tiqādiyāt*) or to actions (*'amaliyāt*) must be within the intellectual capacity of an *ummī*. Otherwise, obligations would concern only the elite and not people in general. If an obligation surpassing this intellectual capacity were made to apply to people in general, it would constitute an impossible obligation. This conclusion is strongly supported by the attitude of the companions of the Prophet who did not indulge in speculative discussions. Also in practical matters the *Sharī'a* uses commonly observable facts rather than complicated speculations as criteria, as for instance, the rising or setting of the sun rather than an astronomically defined schedule for times of prayers (2:90).

It must, however, be made clear that by insisting on the comprehensibility of the *Sharī'a* to *ummiyyīn*, Shāṭibī neither claims that every thing in the Qur'ān or *Sharī'a* is and must be understood by an *ummī*, nor does he discourage any thinking or action beyond the comprehensibility of an *ummī*. Rather what he stresses is the rational and universal comprehensibility of obligation without which the sense of obligation is not complete. Additional considerations may supplement or refine the knowledge of an obligation but the absence of such considerations does not make it any the less obligatory. The question of comprehension is restricted, furthermore, to those matters which are relevant to the fundamentals (*qawā'id*) of *Sharī'a* and has no meaning for theological matters (*umūr ilāhiyya*). The latter are additional matters which are not primarily obligatory (2:91).

The function of the jurist is to understand a particular statement at the second level (e.g. in Arabic) and to transform it to the first level (universal) for better communication. This distinction of two levels is very essential principle in Shāṭibī's treatment of *uṣūl*. On the basis of this principle he explains the unity in the *Sharī'a* (4:58,74).

He dismisses the existence of conflict, contradiction and difference in divine laws, arguing that at the fundamental level there is unity, variety and disagreements, apparent at the second level, are not the intention and objective of law.

According to Shāṭibī, therefore, a jurist does not aim at the reality of things as such, but at the essential meanings of statements as can be understood from the text. The reality to which the logicians refer as essence was, according to Shāṭibī, the meaning of words at the first level.

Shāṭibī's discussion of *ummiyya* as a characteristic of law should also be understood with reference to legislation and interpretation. The language used in framing laws should be such as is universally understood.

NOTES AND REFERENCES

1. See Āmidī, *al-Ihkām fī uṣūl al-aḥkām*, vol. I (Cairo: Ma'ārif, 1914), pp. 16ff; Ghazālī, *al-Mustaṣfā min 'ilm al-uṣūl,* vol. I (Baghdad: Muthannā, 1970), pp. 317ff.
2. The Qur'ān, 26:195; 12:2; 39:28; 43:3; 16:103.
3. Suyūṭī, *al-Itiqān fī 'ulūm al-Qur'ān*, vol. I (Cairo: Muṣṭafā Muḥammad, 1368 H), pp. 136-138. Also see Arthur Jeffery, *The Foreign Vocabulary of the Qur'ān* (Baroda, 1938), Intro. pp. 2-11.
4. Āmidī, *al-Iḥkām.*, pp. 49ff.
5. Numbers in parenthesis refer to Shāṭibī, *al-Muwāfaqāt,* ed. 'Abd al-Ḥamīd (Cairo: Maktaba Muḥammad 'Alī, 1969).
6. See Shāfi'ī, *al-Risāla*, ed. Aḥmad Muḥammad Shākir (Cairo: Muṣṭafā al-Bābī, 1940), p. 52.
7. Āmidī, *al-Ihkām,* p. 104ff.
8. Compare this view of Shāṭibī with Mattā (d. circa 940). He asserted that translation preserved the meanings and rendered superfluous the original language in which they were expressed. This means that the meaning of the utterance can be separated from the utterance. The art that deals with meaning (logic) enables one to know everything that is meaningful in all the utterances in whatever the language without being expert in that langauge (Muhsin Mehdi, "Language and Logic in Classical Islam", in G.E. Von Grunebaum (ed.), *Logic in Classical Islamic Culure* (Wiesbaden, 1970), p. 71.
9. Shāṭibī regarded such search as unnecessary, especially in case of the Qur'anic exegesis (p. 23). It seems that the absoluteness of the Aristotalian search for reality through definition still haunts Islamicists. To them any rejection of the method of definition is so puzzling that it has to be explained with reference to the theological motives of the Muslim scholars. Shāṭibī's rejection of the method of definition is interpreted by F. Rahman as "a patent denial of faith in the intellectual and moral power of man" (*Islamic Methodology in History,* Karachi, 1965, p. 154). Van Ess explains the contentedness of scholars on simple description with reference to the ontology of the *mutakallimūn*: "They comprehended things as conglemoration of accidents, without any substance of their

own." ("The Logical Structure of Islamic theology", in *Logic in Classical Islamic Culture*, p. 37).

10. See Louis Couturat, *La loqique de Leibniz d'aprés des ducuments inédit* (Paris, 1901).

11. P.E.B. Journdain in his preface to Louis Couturat, *The Algebra of Logic.*, English translation by L.G. Robinson (London: Open Court, 1914), p. vii.

12. Louis Couturat (*Algebra of Logic,* pp. 52-59) mentions that various attempts were made in Leibniz's time and before him to construct an artificial language. The purpose of such attempts was to make the language more exact and scientific. Descartes also favoured the creation of such a language.

13. See note 8 above.

14. In preface to the translation of the famous debate between Sīrāfī (d. 979) and Matta ibn Yūnus, Muhsin Mahdi shows how Sīrāfī also defended the use of "ordinary language" as against artificial "scientific language' in search of truth. But Mahdi does not seem to distinguish between the scientific/universal language (as understood by Leibniz and others) and "logic", because the reference made by Matta in his debate is to "logic" and not to the "universal or scientific language" nor even to "symbolic logic". See Muhsin Mahdi, "Language and Logic in Classical Islam", pp. 61-62.

15. W.P. Alston (*Philosophy of Language,* Prentice Hall, 1964, pp. 11 - 12) grouped the various theories of meaning into three types, which he calls 'referential', 'ideational', and 'behaviourial'. The referential identifies the meaning of an expression with that to which it refers, the 'ideational' with the ideas with which it is associated and the 'behaviourial' theory with the stimuli that evoke its utterance.

16. J.L. Austin, *How to do Things with Words* (Cambridge, Mass., Harvard Univ. Press, 1967), p. 52.

17. Ludwig Wittgenstein, *Philosophical Investigations*, tr. from German by G.E.M. Anscombe (Oxford: Blackwell, 1965), sections, 2, 3, 48, pp. 10f.

18. Shāṭibī brings out these principles in the sub-sections (*faṣl*) of the main discussion.

19. In this *faṣl*, Shāṭibī mentions that the following sciences were known to Arabs: Astrology, Science of rain, winds, clouds, History, Physiognomy, Fortune-Telling, Medicine, Rhetorics etc.

20. Shāṭibī points out the following salient features of this attitude: (a) conventionally, the Arabs are not bound by words in regard to their being a medium for meaning. (b) The Arabs often deviate from the rules and regulations governing prose and poetry, and it is not considered weakness of speech. (c) They feel free in choosing between synonyms or closer-meaning words and it is not regarded contradictory or disruptive of speech. (d) If it guards against the artificiality in observing rules, it is considered an admirable quality of speech.

21. Khalil 'Athamin, "*Al-Nabiyy al-Umiyy*": An Inquiry into the Meaning of a Qur'anic verse", *Der Islam*, Vol. 69 (1992) 61-80.

CHAPTER SEVEN

TAKLĪF: LEGAL OBLIGATION AND PHYSICAL CAPABILITY

This chapter discusses Shāṭibī's concept of *taklīf*, a term used for legal 'obligation' in *uṣūl*. Etymologically the term has the implication of 'toil', 'pain' and 'hardship'. On the other hand the principle of the voidability of *taklīf mā lā yuṭāq* (obligation which is impossible to fulfil), which is theological in origin, does not accept hardship (literal meaning of *taklīf*) to be part of the concept. The discussion of the term *taklīf*, thus, naturally takes into account both of the above extremes i.e. the literal and theological aspects of obligation.

For a definition of *taklīf*, Shāṭibī proceeds to an analysis of the terms *qudra* (capability) and *mashaqqa* (hardship). According to Shāṭibī *qudra* is an essential element in the concept of legal obligation. He says that the *qudra* (capability to perform) is the *sharṭ* (condition) or *sabab* (cause) of *taklīf* that one is legally obliged to do. Hence, any obligation which is not within the *qudra* of the *mukallaf*, is not valid according to *shar'*, though it may be so rationally (*'aqlan*) (107).[1] The following pages analyse Shāṭibī's discussion of *qudra* and *mashaqqa*.

QUDRA

To define *qudra*, Shāṭibī chooses to analyse *ghayr maqdūr* (unfeasible) which is not within the power of a man to do. Shāṭibī observes that *ghayr maqdūr* is used in four senses.

First, it refers to those acts which are impossible to fulfil (*mā lā yuṭāq*), because they are beyond human capability, as for instance the demand to give up eating or drinking (108-109).

The second sense of *ghayr maqdūr* refers to obligations which cannot be fulfilled because

(a) the obligation concerns acts that cannot be performed without first completing another act. In other words it is a situation where a non-obligated act becomes a means to perform the obligated act (109).

(b) The obligated act is an inevitable consequence of a certain other act. This case is different from (a) because in (a) one has to do a certain act before being able to fulfil the obligatory act, while in (b) one does not perform the obligatory act itself, but only by performing the precedent act does the obligatory act come to occur inevitably. Shāṭibī illustrates it by the example of the obligation to know. Apart from a *priori* knowledge, other kinds of knowing occur inevitably as a result of *naẓar* (observation, reasoning, syllogism) (111).

The third and fourth senses of the term *ghayr maqdūr* are *mashaqqa* (hardship) and *ḥaraj* (impediment). Shāṭibī maintains that strictly speaking *mashaqqa* and *ḥaraj* are not *ghayr maqdūr*, because legal obligations in the *Sharī'a* are related with *mashaqqa* and *ḥaraj*, but not with the above-mentioned first and second senses of *ghayr maqdūr*, and since the *Sharī'a* is not impossible, the *mashaqqa* and *ḥaraj* are not *ghayr maqdūr.*

Shāṭibī does not deny the fact that in *sharī'a* there are occasions where a command is related to a certain apparently *ghayr maqdūr* act, yet he maintains that close examination reveals that the obligation is not actually directed at the *ghayr maqdūr* act. As a principle, he elaborates, the realm of *ghayr maqdūr* is not the object of *taklīf* -, neither in prescription nor in prohibition. If a *shar'ī* command apparently makes a *ghayr maqdūr* obligatory, the command must be understood to refer to a *maqdūr* act which (or the mention of which) either precedes (*sābiq*) this *ghayr maqdūr* as a means or cause, or occurs simultaneously (*qarīn*) with it or succeeds (*lāḥiq*) it. To illustrate, the Qur'anic command: "Do not die but as Muslims (lit. Do not die except if you are Muslims.)" [2:132], literally demands not to die, which is *ghayr maqdūr* to obey. Naturally the obligation must be connected with the phrase that follows the actual command, i.e. to be Muslims (108). This example shows that command may sometimes be related with *ghayr maqdūr* but that *ghayr maqdūr* is not obligatory.

There are further instances in *Sharī'a* where a command is related with a *ghayr maqdūr* and even includes it, yet it does not constitute the actual obligation. In such instances the *ghayr maqdūr* is capable of being the object of either the desire (*ḥubb*) or the detestation (*bughḍ*) of the *Shāri'*. Even though the acts which are *ghayr maqdūr* are neither within the capability of the *mukallaf* nor within his volition, yet they may be desired by the Law-giver. To illustrate, Shāṭibī refers to the example of the obligation to know. If the object of knowing is something *ḍarūrī* (*a priori*), then there is no action involved to fulfil the obligation. but in other cases, knowing is a result of some other act, and even then, as mentioned earlier, it necessarily and immediately follows the act of arranging the premises. In short, the act of knowing itself is *ghayr maqdūr* and yet desired by the *Shāri'* (111).

In the latter category of *ghayr maqdūr*, Shāṭibī refers, in fact, to acts which are involuntary, being *fiṭrī* (natural) and *iḍtirārī* (compulsive) and *musabbab* (caused) (110, 112). Shāṭibī's argument is that such *ghayr maqdūr* acts as mentioned above, are not the objects of obligation, though they are desired by the Lawgiver. The fact that they are desired is proven either in literal expression by the Lawgiver to such effect or by His making it subject to *jazā'* (reward and punishment) (112). On this point Shāṭibī's position rather appears puzzling. How can an act despite being the object of *Shāri*''s desire and subject to *jazā'*, be not the object of obligation?

The jurists are divided in answer to the above question. One view is that the reward and punishment do not concern *ghayr maqdūr* acts. The second view is that reward and punishment both are attached to the *ghayr maqdūr* at the same time. The first view argues that since *ghayr maqdūr* acts are subject to obligation, they are not subject to reward or punishment. When there is no obligation, there can be no reward or punishment (115). Shāṭibī refutes this argument by rejecting the assumption of the necessary relationship of reward and punishment to obligation. He illustrates his view with examples showing that there are obligations which entail no reward or punishment (117-118).

Another argument advanced in favour of the first position proceeds by showing contradiction in the second position. This argument is as follows. Reward and punishment, if their connection with *ghayr maqdūr* acts be accepted, will either concern the acts in question in their essence or in terms of related acts. If reward and punishment concern their essences, then no distinction is possible between one act and another and between reward and punishment. Consequently, both reward and punishment may concern one and the same act at the same time, which is impossible. If reward and punishment concern related acts, instead of essences, then the point is proven that in neither case does reward and punishment concern the *ghayr maqdūr* acts themselves (115).

Shāṭibī refutes this argument saying that by not maintaining a distinction between reward and punishment in respect of one and the same act, the above argument implies that one and the same act can be the object of both desire and detestation of *Sharī'a* at the same time, which is absurd. He argues further that reward and punishment cannot be supposed to concern with related acts, to the exclusion of the act in question. If a connection between *ghayr maqdūr* act and related act is necessary for reward and punishment, it only means that the *ghayr maqdūr* act is certainly effective in determining reward and punishment (118). Shāṭibī, therefore, concludes that an act even though not object of obligation may still earn reward. Also, that rewardability of an act does not make it an obligation. Thus a *ghayr maqdūr* may be desired or rewarded, yet it does not mean that it is obligatory. To be obligatory, an act must be *maqdūr*.

From here, Shāṭibī proceeds to an analysis of *mashaqqa* and *ḥaraj* which, he maintains, are not to be equated with *ghayr maqdūr* in the senses which have been discussed so far. *Mashaqqa* and *ḥaraj* make an act hard and difficult, but they are capable of being object of obligation. Shāṭibī, however, stresses that acts consisting of *mashaqqa* and *ḥaraj* may be object of obligation, yet *mashaqqa* and *ḥaraj* themselves are not objectives of obligation for their own sake. Shāṭibī develops his argument in a detailed analysis of the term *mashaqqa*.

MASHAQQA

Mashaqqa (hardship) is often confused with *ghayr maqdūr* (unfeasible). The discussion below summarising Shāṭibī's views on this point, contends that a distinction between *taklīf mā lā yuṭāq* (impossible) or *ghayr maqdūr* (unfeasible) and *Mashaqqa* (hardship) must be observed. *Sharī'a* aims at none of them *per se*, but it does impose the latter though not the former (119). This discussion calls for an investigation into the meaning of *mashaqqa*.

Literally, *sh-q-q* as in *shaqqa 'alayya al-shay'* (the matter became difficult for me), denotes something "tiresome" and "hard". The Qur'ān says, "You could not reach it save with great trouble to yourselves (*bi shiqq al-anfus*) (17:7). This meaning, when taken in the absolute sense - without reference to its original (*waḍ'ī*) meaning in Arab usage - acquires five particular technical (*iṣṭilaḥiyya*) senses. These five senses, in fact, stem from three considerations: (1) from the general literal sense of the word *mashaqqa*, (2) from the viewpoint of *'āda* (custom, or practice) i.e. whether a certain act is considered *mashaqqa* by *'āda* or not, and (3) from the concept of *taklīf* itself i.e. a *mashaqqa* is so neither in its literal sense nor in its customary sense but is rather derived from the concept of obligation itself. These three viewpoints provide the following five senses of *mashaqqa*:

1. First, in a very general sense, *mashaqqa* applies to all the meanings of "toil" or "trouble", disregarding their being *maqdūr* or not, or being real or metaphorical. It is in this sense that *taklīf mā lā yuṭāq* is also called *mashaqqa*, because in order to fulfil a command which is supposedly *mā lā yuṭāq* man puts himself into vain trouble. For instance if a man tries to fly in the air his attempt will be in vain but it is said that he put himself into hardship. Here a distinction is, however, recognized; "flying in the air" is called *mā lā yuṭāq* not *mashaqqa*; *mashaqqa* is rather the effort made to achieve the end (i.e. to try to fly). Thus it becomes obvious that even linguistic usage associates *mashaqqa*

with *maqdūr* (feasible) only, even if it is used with reference to something impossible.

2. In the second sense *mashaqqa* is applied to those acts which are extraneous to the *mu'tād* (customary). That is to say to perform these acts means to incur hardship upon oneself. For instance, to observe fasting during sickness or a journey is not easy according to *'āda*, and thus it incurs *mashaqqa*. It is here that *Sharī'a* makes certain allowances which are called *rukhṣa* by the *fuqahā'*. These allowances are meant to remove hardship.

3. The third sense of *mashaqqa* is hardship arising from persistence in uninterrupted performance of acts, although they may be initially easy to perform. It creates *mashaqqa* and makes them difficult to carry out. This is an extension of the second sense. While the second concerns particular acts, the third concerns the totality of actions. In such cases *Sharī'a* recognizes the principle of *rifq* (leniency, moderation) by commending the choice of alternative acts which are not tiresome.

4. In the fourth sense of *mashaqqa*, hardship of an act is not extraordinary but rather additional to one's habit and routine. In other words customarily it is not *mashaqqa* but it becomes so because one is obliged to do it. It becomes *mashaqqa* also because it creates responsibility in addition to the acts required by this worldly life.

5. The fifth sense of *mashaqqa* flows from the fact that an act is hard because it is against one's desire. It is different from the fourth sense. Whereas in the fourth sense an act is *mashaqqa* merely because it has to be done as an obligation, there being no additional hardship other than this fact alone. The additional element of hardship comes about because the *taklīf* requires one to oppose (*mukhālafa*) his own desires and it incurs toil and hardship (119-121).

These five senses of *mashaqqa* constitute the framework for investigating whether *mashaqqa* is included under the requirement of obligation or not. Shāṭibī conducts his investigation from three perspectives: (1) by understanding the intention of the Law-giver, (2) by analysing the understanding of the term in *'āda*, and (3) the intention of the *mukallaf*.

The first question is whether the *Shāri'* (Lawgiver) intends *mashaqqa* or not. It is clear that *Shāri'* does not intend *mashaqqa per se*. Firstly, because:

(a) Various statements in the Qur'ān and Ḥadīth categorically deny any intention by the *Shāri'* to impose hardship (121-122).

(b) The existence of well-known allowances (*rukhṣa*) in *shar'* prove the existence of concessions to remove hardship (122).

(c) The consensus on the absence of any intention by *Shāri'* to make *shaqq* (hard) acts obligatory. If it were supposed that *Sharī'a* did such a thing, it would be self-contradiction and hence self-negation; the *Sharī'a* cannot and does not aim at both comfort and hardship at the same time (112-123).

Secondly, from the perspective of *'āda* we also find that not every bit of toil and hardship is called *mashaqqa* in *'āda*. For instance, seeking one's livelihood by following a craft and trade although it involves toil (*kulfa*), is not called *mashaqqa*. Rather a person is reproached if he avoids such toils. All states of the human being in this world are toilsome (*kulfa*), yet they are not called *mashaqqa* (123).

A certain act is not called *mashaqqa* in *'āda* when "it is possible (*mumkin*) habitually (*mu'tād*) and the toil (*kulfa*) entailed by the act does not interrupt the act in general practice (*fi'l-ghālib al-mu'tād*)" (123). In this sense *mashaqqa* in relation to *mu'tād* can be of two kinds: (1) *al-mashaqqa al-mu'tāda*, or the hardship entailed by an act which is possible to bear and within the capacity of a man, although it is, in fact, hard for him; (2) *mashaqqa khārija 'an al-mu'tād*, or "when the perpetuation of a certain act leads to its discontinuation, wholly or partly, or harms (*khalāl*) the doer of the act (*ṣāḥibuhū*) his person, property or his state" (123). Such acts are called *mashaqqa* and are extraneous to *mu'tād* because they are not possible to perform habitually.

Having established this distinction, Shāṭibī points out that the *mashaqqa khārija 'an al-mu'tād* (extraordinary hardship) is obviously not intended by *shar'*. Even *al-mashaqqa al-mu'tāda* (ordinary hardship) is not intended by itself in an obligation. It is required rather because the obligation serves the *maṣlaḥa* of the *mukallaf* (124).

Explaining the relationship between *mashaqqa* and *taklīf*, Shāṭibī clarifies that *taklīf* can be directed to the *mukallaf* in two aspects: (1) Firstly because *taklīf* is itself *mashaqqa* as explained above and (2) secondly because there is an immediate or forthcoming *maṣlaḥa* (good) to be achieved for the *mukallaf*. Shāṭibī obviously favours the second aspect as the only *maqṣūd* of the *Shāri'*. The first cannot be *maqṣūd* because both of these two aspects cannot exist together. The fact of *maṣlaḥa* being the *maqṣūd* has been explained earlier. Hence *mashaqqa per se* cannot be *maqṣūd*.

Why, then, is an obligation called *taklīf*? Shāṭibī answers that, in the usage of Arabs, a thing derives its name from its inseparable attribute, although, in usage, this inseparable attribute is not intended. It is on the basis of this rule of *'ilm al-ishtiqāq* (etymology) that an act is called *taklīf* because it entails *kulfa* and *mashaqqa*, not because *kulfa* is the aim or purpose of this act. The consideration of *kulfa* is possible only when the term *taklīf* is applied in a *majāzī* (metaphorical) sense to a certain act rather than using the term in its *ḥaqīqat al-waḍ' al-lughawī* (the essential original meaning of a word in a language) (125-126) .

(2) The second aspect of this relationship is that the *Shāri'* knows what a *taklīf* is and what it incurs, and since it is known that every *taklīf* incurs *mashaqqa* one may argue that by imposing a *taklīf* the *Shāri'* intends also to impose *mashaqqa* (124-125).

Shāṭibī rejects this argument by refuting the equation of the knowledge of *sabab* and *mashaqqa* with the *qaṣd* (intention). He argues that even in this particular case if knowledge of *sabab* and *mashaqqa* is considered as intention (*qaṣd*) it would be true only as leading to them as a whole; the intention for *mashaqqa* individually is only secondary. But even this supposition is self-contradictory because, the intention for *mafsada* (*mashaqqa*) is posited together with the intention for *manfa'a* (*maṣlaḥa*), which is not acceptable. Hence it is proven that the *Shāri'* does not intend *mafsada* i.e. *mashaqqa* (126-127). Secondly, it is evident from the Qur'ān and other sources that the *Shāri'* intends to remove hardship. How can it be then maintained that the *Shāri'* intends to impose and remove *mashaqqa* at one and the same time?

To sum up the discussion, Shāṭibī concludes that:

> "As explained, the obligation of *mu'tādāt* and the like does not entail *mashaqqa*. Hence what necessarily follows from *taklīf* is not called *mashaqqa*; irrespective of whether the knowledge of its occurrence necessarily requires it or necessitates the intention for it." (127)

Now we come to third perspective of Shāṭibī's investigation, i.e. the obligee's intention. Granted that the *Shāri'* does not intend *mashaqqa* in his imposition of *taklīf*, should a *mukallaf* intend *mashaqqa* while fulfilling his obligations or not? Shāṭibī's general answer is in the negative. The *mukallaf* should not intend *mashaqqa* because the *Shāri'* does not do so and because the *mukallaf's* intention must correspond to that of the *Shāri'*. Consequently the *mukallaf's* intention should be concentrated on act rather than on *mashaqqa* (128).

Shāṭibī investigates this problem further from the point of view of acts themselves. First, the acts are either permissible or prohibited (133). In the latter case, the intention to perform such acts is obviously forbidden. The problematic matter are those acts which are nothing but *mashaqqa* in themselves and which the *Shāri'* imposed as such, as for instance punishments (*'uqūbāt*). Shāṭibī maintains that even here the intention of the *Shāri'* is not to impose *mashaqqa* as such, but to acquire *maṣlaḥa* or to remove *mafsada* by this *mashaqqa*. Accordingly, the *mukallaf*'s intention must also be *maṣlaḥa* and not *mashaqqa* as such. This is the reason why if a *mashaqqa* (e.g. a *ḥalf* (oath) to bequeath all of one's property for charitable purposes) contravenes some *ḍarūrī* or *ḥājī* principle in *dīn* (e.g. the limitation of such a voluntary distribution to only one third of one's property), it will be deemed as void (149).

Mashaqqa contained in the permissible acts, on the other hand, is to be analysed whether this *mashaqqa* is *ikhtiyārī* (by man's own choice) or *iḍṭirārī* (imposed on man without his choice). Further, whether it is called *mashaqqa* in *'āda* or not or whether it is extraneous to all such considerations (133). To simplify, we can divide Shāṭibī's discussion of *mashaqqa* into the following three categories:

(1) *Ikhtiyārī*, where the *mukallaf* intends *mashaqqa* by his own choice.
(2) *Iḍṭirārī*, where *mashaqqa* is an inevitable consequence of a certain act.
(3) *Khārijī*, where the *mashaqqa* is neither of the above but rather falls upon the *mukallaf* without having any connection with them.

Let us analyse these three categories one by one.

(i) *Al-mashaqqat al-ikhtiyāriyya*

As already mentioned, Shāṭibī maintains that since *Shāri'* does not intend *mashaqqa per se*, one must not seek it as an objective. *Al-mashaqqat al-ikhtiyāriyya*, therefore, is condemnable according to him. One may argue that a *mukallaf* may intend *mashaqqa* to augment his reward on the assumption that a reward is enhanced in commensuration with the hardship suffered (125). Shāṭibī rejects this manner of reasoning. To him, the concern of *taklīf* is with action (*'amal*) and that is also at which the *Shāri'* aims. It is, therefore, action and NOT *mashaqqa* which increases reward (127). Secondly seeking *mashaqqa* violates the intentions of *Shāri'*. This violation cannot earn reward (129).

Shāṭibī disregards the *aḥādīth* reporting greater rewards on hardship, saying that all such reports are *al-akhbār al-aḥād* and relate only one matter. They do not constitute *al-istiqrā' al-qaṭ'ī*. Hence these *ẓanniyyāt* cannot invalidate our position (130). Furthermore, in the final analysis these traditions do not prove the intention of *mashaqqa*; rather they stress the acts themselves. The intention to bring about *mashaqqa* is a secondary (*tābi'a*) not the primary (*matbū'a*), concern (130). Finally, there are traditions in which the Prophet reproached those who opted for hardship. His proscription (*nahy*) of hardship (*tashdīd*) is so well known in *Sharī'a* that it has become a definite principle (*al-aṣl al-qaṭ'ī*) (132-133).

Most often opting for hardship by rejecting *rukhṣa* (allowance) is called *'azīma* (determination). The reference is usually made to mystics who disapprove going for allowances. For them *'azīma* is the regular and more praiseworthy manner of performing obligation. Shāṭibī calls the mystics or sufis *arbāb al-aḥwāl* (the people of mystic states). He argues that it is not correct to say that *arbāb al-aḥwāl* intend to bring about *mashaqqa* only. Their purpose is to disregard their own *ḥuẓūẓ* (self-considerations) so as to fulfil their duties toward God. Shāṭibī explains this point more fully by an analysis of *ḥaraj*. *Ḥaraj* is an act which causes an impediment in fulfilling the obligation. The *arbāb al-aḥwāl* regard *ḥuẓūẓ* (self-interest, comforts) as impediment in the performance of their obligation. They prefer to forego their *ḥuẓūẓ* in favour of their duty towards God, because of fear or of love of God (132-148). We shall discuss *ḥuẓūẓ* later, let us now turn to an analysis of *ḥaraj*.

(ii) *Al-mashaqqat al-iḍtirāriyya: Ḥaraj*

In general terms, hardship can be seen in three ways. First, there is the hardship which has become part of daily life and is no more called *mashaqqa* but is rather expressed by terms such as *kulfa* (toil), *ta'b* (exertion) etc. This is called by Shāṭibī *al-mashaqqat al-mu'tāda*. Second, there is the type of hardship which is not habitual. It may not be impossible to bear, but it might be so painful as to be too difficult to endure. This is called by Shāṭibī *mashaqqa ghayr mu'tād.* The third category lies on the fringes of the second one. In itself it may neither be impossible nor painful to bear, but it becomes an impediment to the performance of other acts. This is called *ḥaraj* (133).

According to Shāṭibī *ḥaraj* is revoked in the following two cases:

1. First where one fears being cut off from the Path (*al-khawf min al-inqiṭā' 'an al-ṭarīq*). That is, when inconvenience in performing a certain act amounts to abhorrence to it or it creates a dislike for one's obligation, that inconvenience is called *ḥaraj* and is revokable. The revoked acts include all that may cause any harm to one's body, intellect, property or general condition (136).

2. Second, where the fear of falling short of fulfilling all of one's duties occurs, or, at least, where one's indulgence in one act comes into conflict with his other duties or results in neglecting other duties. In some cases this indulgence prevents one from fulfilling one's duty to others. Thus a persons stands condemned

> because he is required to carry out all his duties without neglecting any one of them (136).

Shāṭibī's argument in favour of the above observations are based on a concept of *Sharī'a* derived from the Qur'ān and Ḥadīth that he describes in the folowing words: "God made this blessed upright *Sharī'a* generous and convenient and by making it so He won people's hearts and evoked in them love for *Sharī'a*. If they had to act in a way against convenience, they could not honestly fulfil their obligations" (136).

There are instances when the Prophet and his companions opted for harder acts. The Prophet is reported frequently permitting seeking of hardship. This poses an apparent contradiction to Shāṭibī's position. Shāṭibī resolves it by analysing the relevant verses of the Qur'ān and *aḥādīth*. He concludes that all the acts in the cited cases are prohibited because they entail the cases of fatigue or an impediment that makes it difficult or tiring to carry on the action further. The *'illa* lies in the fact that the action impedes carrying out other duties or others' duties. The contrary is also true, if an action does not constitute an impediment in the above sense it will not be prohibited even though it may be hard. Shāṭibī thus concludes:

> "In fine, prohibition based on some intelligible *'illa* is the *maqṣūd* of the *Shāri'*... Since this is true, the prohibition depends on their being an *'illa* both for its affirmation and its negation." (138).

There is another situation of hardship worth considering. That is a situation where an obligation involves a risk of losing one's life and yet a person opts for it. Is his option valid? Shāṭibī examines this situation by asking the following question: Did the *Shāri'* remove *mashaqqa* because it is His right (*ḥaqq*) or because it is the right of the *'abd* ? (142). In his answer, Shāṭibī takes into consideration his previous arguments about God's not intending *mashaqqa* and observes that "when someone chooses to see the act as a right of (rather duty towards) God, the act is absolutely forbidden, (because God has removed hardship from religion). But if one regards it as a right of the *'abd*, it is not absolutely forbidden, but rather is left to one's choice." (143).

In this context Shāṭibī reconsiders the case of *arbāb al-aḥwāl* (Ṣufīs) and the people who choose extraordinary hardship in preference to the *shar'ī* allowances or who indulge in certain duties in order to disregard others. Shāṭibī considers the attitude of *arbāb al-aḥwāl* towards *shar'ī* obligations as extraordinary. Shāṭibī explains his view by making a distinction between two kinds of people:

1. *Arbāb al-ḥuẓūẓ* (The people who guard their self interest): They are ordinary people. To them not availing of the *Shar'ī* allowance

means inviting harm and extraordinary hardship. Such people must not carry out an act of this kind and should avail themselves of *shar'ī rukhṣa*. Shāṭibī, however, warns against the other extreme of following one's *ḥuẓūẓ* absolutely so that one departs from the bondage of *'ubūdiyya* (146-147). He concludes:
"The true position according to *sharī'a* is a combination of both aspects with a view of balance (*'adl*); to pursue one's *ḥuẓūẓ* as long as the pursuit does not interfere with an obligatory duty, and to abstain from *ḥuẓūẓ* as long as the abstinence does not lead to prohibition." (146).

2. *Ahl isqāt al-ḥuẓūẓ* also called *arbāb al-aḥwāl* (The people who disregard their self-interests): For whom acts of hardship do not bring about fatigue and harm because they are governed by fear, hope or love. Fear makes hardship feel lesser; hope relaxes the hardness of the act, while love renders the act rather enjoyable. This group is so engrossed in fulfilling their duty to God on the basis of fear, hope and love that they even forget their own *ḥuẓūẓ*. They give up personal considerations (147-148).

(iii) *Al-mashaqqat al-khārija*

There is a third category of *mashaqqa* which falls upon *mukallaf* from without; it is neither intended by the *mukallaf* nor is it a result of any of his actions. In the above discussed categories, *mashaqqa* was a necessary part, or a consequence, of *mukallaf*'s intention or action. In the present category, *mashaqqa* is *khārijī* (external) to his intention as well as to his action.

Shāṭibī maintains that the *Shāri'* does not intend *mashaqqa* because he did not originally intend to impose it. The imposition of *al-mashaqqat al-khārija* when it is known that God intends it, is explained as test and trial of the faith of the *mukallaf*. It is, nevertheless, understood from the totality of *Sharī'a* that it is permissible to remove *mashaqqa* absolutely, to eliminate the related *mashaqqa* and to protect the permissible *ḥuẓūẓ* from being affected by *mashaqqa*. The *Sharī'a* even allows preventing *mashaqqa* before it occurs (150). This permission is known *a priori* (*ḍarūratan*) in *dīn* (151). Shāṭibī illustrates *al-mashaqqat al-khārija* with the examples of hunger, thirst, cold, heat, sickness, bodily harm, etc. Removing all of these *mashaqqa* is allowed (150-151).

Shāṭibī, however, observes an important detail. The obligatory nature of the demand to do away with the *mashaqqa* differs in two kinds of *al-mashaqqat al-khārija*. The first is that where the obligatory nature of the removal of *mashaqqa* is proven, such as in case of an attack upon Muslims to destroy Islam. In such cases the *mashaqqa* consists of an attack or a possible domination of non-Muslims. The obligation to do away with this *mashaqqa* is undoubtedly proven. In the second kind of *al-mashaqqat al-khārija*, for example, an incurable sickness, its elimination is not an irrefutable obligation. In such a case the imposition of hardship and the endurance of trial must be borne. One must submit to such a *mashaqqa* as a *qaḍā'* (decree of destiny).

Shāṭibī sums up the discussion on *taklīf* in reference to *mashaqqa* with the following conclusions:

1. Whether *mashaqqa* falls upon the *mukallaf* particularly and singularly (in such a case, called *al-mashaqqat al-khāṣṣa*), or falls upon others together with him or falls upon others because of him (called *al-mashaqqat al-'amma*), in either case, a *mashaqqa* is not required by *Shāri'*, neither in its essence nor in the act that leads to it. If there be a conflict between two obligations to eliminate two *mashaqqa*, the elimination of a *mashaqqa* which is *'āmma* (general, public) will be given priority over the elimination of *al-mashaqqat al-khāṣṣa* (particular, private) (154-155).

2. *Mashaqqa* may be *mu'tāda* (ordinary) or *khārija 'an al-mu'tād* (extra-ordinary). In case of *mu'tāda*, its removal is not intended by the *Shāri'* just as its imposition was also not intended. Removal of this kind of *mashaqqa* would mean discontinuation of *taklīf*. In case of a *mashaqqa* which is *khārija 'an al-mu'tād*, since it is conducive to disruption in either *dīn* or *dunyā*, its total removal is intended by the *Shāri'*.

There is, however, one consideration. The hardship involved in acts is not the same in all cases; it varies from time to time, place to place and state to state. This is the reason why the same *mashaqqa* may appear to be *khārija 'an al-mu'tād* in certain cases while, in fact, it is *mu'tād*. Shāṭibī explains this difficulty saying that a *mashaqqa* following from a single act has two ends and a middle, the higher end of the *mashaqqa* is such that when something is added to it the *mashaqqa* ceases to be *mu'tād*. This does not, however, exclude *mashaqqa* from being essentially *mu'tād*. The lower end is such that were something subtracted, there would remain no more *mashaqqa* attributable to that act. The *Sharī'a*, according to its requirements, follows precisely the middle way in its obligations, taking both sides equally. Obedience to law comes within the capacity of man without necessitating any *mashaqqa* or any leniency.

Now if *Sharī'a* legislates in view of the *mukallaf*'s deviation from the middle point to one of the above-mentioned ends, the legislation will aim at returning the *mukallaf* to the just middle. But in this process it will lean on the other side so as to restore a balance.

Following this line of argument, it is to be concluded that every *al-kulliyya al-shar'iyya* (universal legal principle) essentially takes the middle position. But if it leans toward one of the extremes, it will do so because of its actual or possible inclination towards the other end. The tendency to *tashdīd* (severity) is brought forward to balance the laxity in a *mukallaf*'s regard for *Dīn*. The tendency to *takhfīf* (laxity) is brought forward to balance hardship and severity.

The departures from the middle position, as reported in traditions, must be understood in the light of the above explanation. This departure is meant to balance the severity or laxity, whichever the case may be, inherent in the act which is the object of obligation. Similarly the stress on piety (*wara'*) and asceticism when they appear to be departures from the middle position, should also be taken as an attempt to balance the laxity in obligation.

NOTE

1. The numbers in the parenthesis in the text in this chapter refer to the pages of *al-Muwāfaqāt*, vol. II (Cairo: Muṣṭafā Muḥammad. n.d.)

CHAPTER EIGHT

TA'ABBUD: STRICT OBEDIENCE

Shāṭibī develops a distinction between moral and legal obligations with reference to the purpose of the Lawgiver in making the *mukallaf* subject to the rules of the *Sharī'a*. For this analysis he proceeds to define the term *ta'abbud* (obedience).

As we have seen in the preceding chapter the distinction between legal and moral obligations was stressed especially under the impact of *ṣūfīs* who considered *maṣlaḥa* as seeking personal desires or interests (*akhdh al-ḥuẓūẓ*) and hence contrary to *ta'abbud* (obedience). According to them, *ta'abbud* meant abandoning of *ḥuẓūẓ* (personal interest). This view had serious implications for the definition of legal obligation. Shāṭibī, therefore, sets out to clarify and analyse the terms of *ta'abbud* and *ḥuẓūẓ* in reference to obligation.

As elaborated earlier, the notions of *zuhd* (asceticism) and *ikhlāṣ*, (integrity) as expounded by Ṣūfīs laid special stress on *tark ḥuẓūẓ al-nafs* (abandoning of personal interests) as a necessary qualification of *'ubūdiyya* (the Ṣūfī understanding of obligation). Shāṭibī maintains that although legal obligation also aims at *ta'abbud* (obedience) yet the *ḥuẓūẓ* are not denied by the notion of *ta'abbud*. It is in fact the conformity of action with the intent of the Lawgiver which constitutes *ta'abbud*. The Ṣūfī sense of *ta'abbud* is further refuted by the limitation of the scope of *ta'abbud* in the sense of absolute obedience. For Shāṭibī, this sense applies only to the *'ibādāt*, while *'ādāt* are governed by *maṣlaḥa*. Since according to him, in the final analysis, the *ta'abbud* in *'ibādāt* is only one aspect of *maṣlaḥa*, and *maṣlaḥa* in *'ādāt* is not opposed to *ta'abbud*, Shāṭibī concludes that legal obligation is motivated by the *maṣlaḥa* of the *mukallaf*.

The discussion of this aspect, arranged by Shāṭibī in twenty problems, deals with the following three main topics: (1) *ta'abbud* and the problem of *ḥuẓūẓ*; (2) *'awā'id*; and (3) the division of obligations into *'ibādāt* and *'ādāt* in accordance with the considerations of *ta'abbud* and *maṣlaḥa*.

TA'ABBUD AND THE *ḤUẒŪẒ*

Shāṭibī opens the discussion saying that "the legal objective in instituting the law is to relieve the *mukallaf* from the dictates of his passions (*hawā*) so that he be a servant of God voluntarily (*ikhtiyāran*) as he is so by nature (*iḍtirāran*, by compulsion)" (168).[1] To prove this point he argues from the Qur'ān and the sayings of the Prophet where following one's passions (*hawā*) is condemned (169). He further contends that human experience in society (*al-tajārib wa'l-'ādāt*) also tells us that the *maṣāliḥ*, be they concerning religious matters or mundane, cannot be achieved by following passions and selfish motives (170). It is therefore necessary that man lives in a society, bound by the laws of society that often force him to give up his personal interests in favour of society.

The above position may appear to deny the interests of the people and may imply a demand for absolute obligation. Shāṭibī makes, here, a significant distinction. He refutes the identification of *maṣāliḥ* with *shahawāt* (desires), *hawā* (passion) and *aghrāḍ* (personal motives). He stresses that the *Sharī'a* aims at the *maṣāliḥ*, and not at realizing *hawā*. He does not accept the idea that *akhdh al-ḥuẓūẓ* (pursuit of self-interest) can be equated with *hawā* (172). In order to distinguish between *hawā* and *ḥuẓūẓ*, Shāṭibī argues in detail that it is condemned to follow passions even in cases where the act concerned is in itself praiseworthy, but this is not so insofar as *ḥuẓūẓ* are concerned (174). The reason is that an action performed in obedience to the stimulus of passion, obviously, pays no attention to the command or prohibition of the law, whereas seeking fulfilment of the *ḥuẓūẓ* and *aghrāḍ* is not opposed to the objectives of *Sharī'a* in the above sense (172, 174). One can seek *ḥuẓūẓ* by making them subservient to the *maṣāliḥ* which are the purpose of law. Referring to the Ṣūfīs' states and experiences, Shāṭibī argues that by denying *ḥuẓūẓ al-nafs* (self-interests) these people aim at something praiseworthy; but by suspending the observance of the legal obligations or by aiming at things which may bring happiness to them, they would merely obey the demand of their passions (175).

On the contrary, Shāṭibī argues that one cannot avoid *ḥuẓūẓ* in fulfilling legal obligations. He says that *ikhlāṣ* (purity), or more specifically *takhlīṣ al-ḥaẓẓ* (clearance from self-indulgence), does not mean denial of *ḥuẓūẓ*, because:

1. Firstly, seeking of *ḥuẓūẓ* is not prohibited by the *sharī'a*. From the standpoint of *ḥaẓẓ*, the *maqāṣid* may be divided into two types: *al-maqāṣid al-aṣliyya* (essential objectives) in which the *mukallaf* has no *ḥaẓẓ*, and *al-maqāṣid al-tābi'a* in which the *ḥaẓẓ* (personal interest) is provided. *Al-maqāṣid al-aṣliyya* means universal necessary obligations consisting of the five *maṣāliḥ* (176) i.e. protection of Life, Faith, Family, Reason and Property. Examples of *tābi'a* are obligations in which the natural desires (*shahawāt*) and pleasures are also satiated (178). Shāṭibī argues

that in *al-maqāṣid al-tābiʻa*, the *shahawāt* are, in fact, a means to achieve *al-maqāṣid al-aṣliyya* and, thus, they no longer remain *ittibā' al-hawā* (self-indulgence). In fact, God knows that *dīn* and *dunyā* are maintained and well preserved by these stimuli in the nature of man which excite him to acquire what he and his fellow beings need. The desire to eat and drink is created so that hunger and thirst motivate him to seek food and drink that are a means to protect his life. There are, however, some desires which one individual cannot fulfil alone; hence he needs the co-operation of others. Thus, although each one fulfils his own desires, in fact, at the same time, he is also working for the benefit of others. Hence his seeking of personal *ḥuẓūẓ* is, in fact not entirely a *hawā* (self-indulgence). On the basis of this consideration seeking of the *ḥuẓūẓ* is made permissible, not prohibited (178-179).

2. Secondly, seeking *ḥuẓūẓ* is an indirect part of legal obligations. Through a detailed analysis of *al-maqāṣid al-aṣliyya* and *al-tābiʻa*, Shāṭibī demonstrates that in obligations where the *ḥaẓẓ* of the *mukallaf* is not the primary goal (*bi'l qaṣd al-awwal*) it is realized indirectly (*bi'l qaṣd al-thānī*). He shows also that where the *ḥaẓẓ* is the primary goal, the act is naturally relieved of *ḥaẓẓ,* because to seek *ḥaẓẓ* in this case becomes part of the obligation (183-186).

3. Thirdly, often the seeking of *ḥuẓūẓ* is a requirement in legal obligations. *Takhlīṣ* (clearance) or *tajrīd* (extrication) from *ḥaẓẓ* refers in fact to those cases where *ḥaẓẓ* is permitted or demanded. If the seeking of *ḥaẓẓ* is qualified by legal provisions and other such conditions, it means not only that *ḥaẓẓ* is required but also that in fact there is no more *ḥaẓẓ* for *mukallaf* (186).

4. Fourthly, seeking of *ḥuẓūẓ* exists even in those cases that are not related to *ḥuẓūẓ*. Legal penalties in which there apparently figures no *ḥaẓẓ* for the *mukallaf*, are, in fact, a means to protect or realize the *ḥaẓẓ* of the *mukallaf*. The penalties are meant to prevent persons from harming other's *maṣlaḥa* so that the *maṣāliḥ* in general are maintained in a better way (190-191).

Shāṭibī maintains that in fulfilling an obligation an act would thus accord either with *al-maqāṣid al-aṣliyya* or with *al-maqāṣid al-tābiʻa*. If it conforms with *al-maqāṣid al-aṣliyya*, its validity cannot be questioned, no matter whether it be free from *ḥaẓẓ* or not In other words the objective is not the abandoning of *ḥuẓūẓ* (196). This conclusion sheds a new light on the notion of *ikhlāṣ* (sincerity, purification). Contrary to the usual Ṣūfī definition of *ikhlāṣ,* which insisted on negation of *ḥuẓūẓ*, Shāṭibī argued that it was conformity with *al-maqāṣid al-aṣliyya* which draws an act closer to *ikhlāṣ al-ʻamal* (purity of action), and the act then becomes an act of *'ibāda*, regrardless of whether it was originally *'āda* or *'ibāda* (202).

In cases where the act accords with *al-maqāṣid al-tābi'a*, the criterion cannot be the *tābi'a*. It must be seen whether the act is connected with *al-maqāṣid al-aṣliyya* or not. If it is connected, even though it seeks *ḥaẓẓ al-nafs*, the act is undoubtedly one of obedience (207). This connection is either actual such as a declaration of intention by the *mukallaf*, or potential such as acts which are means to the permitted act. If this connection with *aṣliyya* is absent, then the act is simply one of *ḥaẓẓ* and *hawā* (207).

Shāṭibī explains the matter further saying that if the seeking of *ḥuẓūẓ* were absolutely opposite to obedience, one would have been allowed to perform an act of *'āda* only if there were no intention and effort to achieve the *ḥaẓẓ al-nafs*. In fact there is no such command in the *Sharī'a*. Nor does the *Sharī'a* prohibt aiming at *ḥuẓūẓ* in *al-a'māl al-'ādiyya* (ordinary acts), even though the Lawgiver always lays stress on *ikhlāṣ* (208).

If the intention to achieve *ḥaẓẓ* is denied in *al-a'māl al-'ādiyya*, any hope for paradise or fear of hell in reference to acts of *'ibādāt* would render them invalid (*'amal bighayr al-ḥaqq*). Such a conclusion is obviously absurd in view of the numerous verses in the Qur'ān and the sayings of the Prophet which promise reward and punishment for such acts. To act in hope of reward or with a fear of punishment is certainly an act of seeking *ḥuẓūẓ* (210).

Shāṭibī defends his conclusion with rational and traditional arguments. He particularly mentions Ghazālī's views on *ḥuẓūẓ* and clarifies his own position by criticizing Ghazālī (214-215). Shāṭibī explains that obligations are divided into two categories. First, there are the *'ibādāt*, by which one seeks closeness to God. They consist of Belief (*īmān*) and all prescribed rituals as fundamentals of Islam. The second category are *'ādāt*. Performance of *'ādāt* obligations means providing *maṣāliḥ* absolutely and opposing these obligations means creating *mafāsid*. The second kind of obligations belongs to this world and aims at the *maṣāliḥ* of the people. The first has to do with the rights of God in this world. It does not aim to yield *maṣāliḥ* in this world but rather in the hereafter (215).

Now in the first category the *ḥaẓẓ* in the hereafter is established. Seeking of *ḥaẓẓ* in this sense cannot be called *shirk* (polytheism), nor is it a denial of *ikhlāṣ*. Furthermore, even according to Ghazālī, the highest aim of *'ubūdiyya* is *naẓar ilā al-maḥbūb* (the vision of the beloved) in the hereafter which is also a *ḥaẓẓ* (216). In fact Ghazālī calls it *al-ḥaẓẓ al-'aẓīm* (greatest interest or pleasure). On the other hand complete negation of *ḥuẓūẓ* is an impossible obligation (216). Seeking *ḥaẓẓ* in this world in *'ibādat* such as to perform *'ibādāt* in order to earn the praise of the people, or for some strictly personal considerations like fasting in order to save money etc., are matters which affect the *ikhlāṣ* of *'ibādāt* (218-219).

As to the second category of obligations, i.e. the *'ādāt* such as *nikāḥ* (marriage), *bay'* (sale), etc., it is well known that the Lawgiver intends through these obligations to maintain the immediate *maṣāliḥ* of the people. Seeking the *ḥaẓẓ* in performing this category of obligations cannot, therefore, be contradictory to the intention of the Lawgiver. Further, if it were wrong to seek these *ḥuẓūẓ*, the Qur'ān and *Sunna* would not have mentioned them as being part of God's Grace and Favour (222).

The distinction in *'ādāt* and *'ibādāt* may be observed in *niyāba* (delegation) as well. *Niyāba* is not allowed in *'ibādāt*, while it is lawful in *'ādāt* with the few exceptions where the obligation is specific and individual. The criterion in this regard is the consideration whether the *ḥaẓẓ* which one aims at can be realized by someone else for him or not. If this obligation can be realized by another person *niyāba* is valid; otherwise, not. For instance, in matters of sale etc. *niyāba* is valid, but it is not so in matters such as eating, drinking, marrying, etc. (227).

Since *ḥaẓẓ* is distinguished from *hawā*, Shāṭibī enumerates three characteristics of the obligation which assure that the effort to achieve *ḥaẓẓ* in obedience to the Lawgiver will not reduce one's act to *hawā*. These characteristics are *dawām* (constancy) (242), *kulliyya* (totality) and the *'umūm* (generality) of the obligation. It is a test of one's obedience when one has to carry out an obligation constantly (243). The characteristic of *kullī* (total) requires that all obligations, and each obligation in its entirety, must be met without there being any possibility of getting exemption from some, or part of an, obligation. All particulars and parts of an obligation are obligatory without preference of one above the others (244). Being *'āmm*, the obligations are obligatory upon each *mukallaf* without distinction.

The only exception to *'umūm* is the Prophet, in respect to his regular obligations as well as to his special distinctive privileges (*mazāyā*). This case is unique, partly because *khawāriq al-'ādāt* (deviation from regular habits) are often equal to *'ādāt* in the case of the prophets. Since as a general rule the acts of the Prophet are obligatory, as models to be followed, and the cases of *khawāriq al-'ādāt* are impossible to emulate, the latter must be considered as special to the Prophets. They are not obligatory unless the *Sharī'a* explicitly demands so (249-266). The main argument that underlies this discussion is that the extraordinary acts of the Prophet where he appears to be abandoning *ḥuẓūẓ* are in fact *khawāriq al-'ādāt* in the case of a common man (269). Since the *Sharī'a* is universal, it cannot oblige all men with things which are *khawāriq* (275). Invalidity of the *khawāriq*, however, does not mean that law does not or cannot be changed. What Shāṭibī is stressing is the fact that the *khawāriq* do not convey the sense of legal change; they are rather exceptions to laws of nature. In addition to Prophetic revelation, Shāṭibī includes *kashf* (mystic revelation) and *ru'yā* (dreams) of the *awliyā'* in *khawāriq* (266-269). In order that it may be understood fully, this discussion requires a rather detailed analysis of the notions of *'ādāt* and *khawāriq*, and their relationship to the rules of the *sharī'a*. A fuller analysis of *'āda* is presented in a subsequent chapter, as it is more suited to the discussion there.

Briefly, Shāṭibī uses *'ādāt* both in the sense of habits, customs and human behaviour and as opposed to *'ibādāt*. Essentially, *'āda* belongs to the physical world. *'Ādāt* are constant; and when some event happens contrary to *'ādāt* it is called *kharq al-'āda*. Not all of the *'ādāt* are constant, however. It is, in fact, only the universals of being which are constant. Shāṭibī calls them *al-'awā'id al-mustamirra*. Some of these *'awā'id* (pl. of *'āda*) are either introduced or sanctioned by *Sharī'a*, hence called *al-'awā'id al-shar'iyya*. Others are current in the practice of the people, hence called *al-'awā'id al-jāriya*. *Sharī'a* does not oppose *al-'awā'id al-jāriya*; in fact, it shows a constant regard for them. There are, however, variations in the practice of these *'ādāt*. Also, they change with time and place.

A detailed analysis of *al-'awā'id al-shar'iyya* by Shāṭibī reveals that *maṣlaḥa* is the basic consideration both in the change and the continuity of these *'awā'id*. In the light of this view it may be seen that *ta'abbud* toward *al-'awā'id al-shar'iyya* is not devoid of *ḥuẓūẓ* and *maṣlaḥa*.

TA'ABBUD AND *MAṢLAḤA*

From the above analysis Shāṭibī concludes that the essential consideration in *'ibādāt*, insofar as the *mukallaf* is concerned, is *ta'abbud* without regard for *ma'ānī* (inner meanings). In *'ādāt*, on the other hand, the essential consideration is that of *ma'ānī* (300). This conclusion is further demonstrated by the following points of argument. First, from a survey of *Sharī'a* it may be inductively known that provisions such as *ṭahāra* (ritual cleanliness) and *tayammum* (ablution with dust) in the realm of the *'ibādāt* are difficult to explain, except in terms of *ta'abbud* (301). In the realm of *'ādāt*, it is obvious that such provisions are based on the *maṣlaḥa* of the people. It is thus inductively discoverable that the Lawgiver relies on a regard for *maṣlaḥa* in *'ādāt* (305).

Secondly, in *'ibādāt* the extension of the scope of *ta'abbud* is not intended (301). In other words, the obligation is limited to the specific commands comprised in the *'ibādāt*. This is why no explicit reason is given for promulgating such commands. In the case of *'ādāt*, on the contrary, the objective of the law is to extend the rules to other cases. Hence the Lawgiver generously explains the rules of law relating to *'ādāt* providing their *'ilal* (reasons) and *ḥikam* (wisdom) (306).

Ta'abbud and *ma'nā/maṣlaḥa*, however, are not opposite terms for Shāṭibī. He characterized *ta'abbud* by various statements: "*al-rujū' ilā mujarrad mā ḥaddahū al-Shāri'*" (recourse only to what the Lawgiver has determined) (304); "*al-inqiyād li awāmir Allāh*" (being bound by the commands of God) (301); "*mā huwa ḥaqqun lillāh khāṣṣatan*" (that which is the exclusive right of God) (315); "*rāji'un ilā 'adami ma'quliyat al-ma'nā* (that which refers to the nonintelligibility of its reason) (318). Shāṭibī defines *ma'nā* in this context as follows: "*ḍabtu wujūh al-maṣāliḥ*" (to define the scope of *maṣāliḥ*) (308).

The distinction between *ta'abbud* and *ma'nā* or *maṣlaḥa* occurs initially in reference to the question whether the reason for a command is intelligible or not. If the reason is intelligible, the command is based on *ma'nā*: otherwise, it is *ta'abbud* (314). This explanation is still insufficient, however, because the "intelligibility" needs to be qualified further. Shāṭibī explains that "intelligibility" obtains where the *ma'nā* or *maṣlaḥa* can be extended as an *'illa* to other similar cases. To illustrate:

> We know that the required conditions in marriage such as that of the guardian and the dower, etc., are laid down to distinguish marriage from fornication (*sifāḥ*)... But (if they are considered the *'illa* of marriage) they are but general principles just as humility and submission to the Sublime are the reasons for the obligation of *'ibādāt*. This amount (of *'illa*) is not sufficient to establish an analogy, to extend the above rule to further cases; so that one might say that were a distinction between marriage and fornication to be established by some other factors, the above conditions would no more be required (308).

This explanation implies at least two things; one, that *ta'abbud* according to Shāṭibī, is absolute in obligations in the sense that they must be fulfilled without asking for reason, and second, that *ta'abbud* cannot be made the basis of analogy. Shāṭibī seems to be stressing the second implication, rather than the first. In other words, he is implicitly arguing that the absoluteness of obligation in matters of *ta'abbud* is maintained only in the sense that it is not to be extended. There is no denial of *'illa*; in fact it is only after the search for an *'illa* in the command that one can decide whether the *'illa* given or implied is general or specific. What is denied is the extension by *ta'līl* and *qiyās*. The denial of *ta'līl* amounts to placing a limitation on the scope of the application of these commands. It is in the sense of specifically limited command that *ta'abbud* is spoken about in this context. As Shāṭibī himself says, "In all those matters where a consideration of *ta'abbud* is established, there can be no *tafrī'* (deduction, extension by analogy) from them" (310).

Shāṭibī, however, also accepts that even matters, where the consideration of meaning without *ta'abbud* (in the sense mentioned above) is established, are not free from *ta'abbud* (in the general sense of the term) (315). This general sense of *ta'abbud* is demonstrated by the following considerations. First a *mukallaf* is bound to obey a command because of the sense of demand (*iqtiḍā'*) and option (*takhyīr*) imposed by the command, not because he finds in it a certain *maṣlaḥa* (311). Second, even if a decision about an *'illa* is taken, this process does not assure us that the *'illa* decided upon is the only *'illa* of that command or that it is the only *maṣlaḥa* to be realized. This state of indecisiveness (by the *wāqifīn*) is removed by recourse to *ta'abbud* (312). Shāṭibī further explains that *qiyās* means a search for an *'illa* only insofar as it is ordinarily possible. The method of *qiyās* does not exhaust all the *'ilal;* it is rather based on the most probable (*ghalabat al-ẓann*) *'illa*. On this basis *'qaḍā' bi'l ta'addī'* (judicial decision by extension of the original ruling) is not contrary to *ta'abbud* which, here, means 'not based on reason' (312).

The legal obligations are known to us in two ways: either through well-known methods such as *ijmā'* (consensus), *naṣṣ* (text), *ishāra* (indication), *munāsaba* (affinity), etc., or through instances where none of these methods can be applied. The obligations of the latter kind are known only by *waḥy* (revelation). In this category of obligation the absence of *'illa* and *ta'addī* (extension) within command demands *ta'abbud* only. This *ta'abbud* means to stop at the point where the *Shāri'* has defined the limit; if the *'illa* is not given, *ta'abbud* demands that the command must not be extended by *qiyās* (313). "A *maṣlaḥa* is so from God in such a manner that it is verifiable (*yaṣdiqu*) by human reason (*'aql*) and reassuring (*taṭma'inn*) to the soul (*nafs*)" (315).

The *taklīf* can also be viewed as rights of God. In this sense they become *ta'abbudī*. Shāṭibī, however, regards *ta'abbud* as a general sense of the rights of God. He divides these rights into three categories. First are those rights which belong exclusively to God, such as the *'ibādāt*. Second are those rights of God which involve the rights of men as well, but the consideration of the former dominates. The third category consists of those rights of God in which consideration for the rights of men dominates. It is to the last category that *maṣlaḥa/ma'nā* belongs directly, and hence this category is not essentially *ta'abbudī* (318-320).

Shāṭibī further clarifies the distinction between *ta'abbud* and *maṣlaḥa*, and between *'ibādāt* and *'ādāt* from the point of view of *ḥuqūq* (rights). He says that the right of God means a situation "where it is understood from *shar'* (law) that the *mukallaf* has no option (*khiyara*), whether the *ma'nā* is intelligible or not" (318). The right of man is defined as "what refers to his (man's) *maṣāliḥ* in this world" (318). The *maṣāliḥ* in the hereafter are generally rights of God. Thus *ta'abbud* means something "the meaning of which cannot be specifically understood" (318). In view of these definitions Shāṭibī concludes that *'ibādāt* essentially refer to the rights of God and *'ādāt* to the rights of men (318).

To conclude, Shāṭibī's discussion of *ta'abbud* refines the concept of legal obligation that is either what is defined by the lawgiver and that cannot be extended by reasoning, or what is given by the lawgiver in such a way that legal reasoning can extricate the cause or basis of the rule and it can be extended further. It underlines the fact that a legal obligation can be defined only by law and its methodology, not by pure reason, mystic experience, moral considerations, or theological arguments.

NOTE

1. The numbers in the parenthesis in the text of this chapter refer to the pages of *al-Muwāfaqāt,* Vol. II (Cairo: Muṣṭafa Muḥammad, n.d.)

CHAPTER NINE

NIYYA: INTENT

So far the discussion in the preceding chapters has been concerned with the objectives of the *Sharī'a* from the perspective of the Lawgiver. The present chapter discusses the objectives of the *mukallaf* or what is the purpose and intent of the obligee in a legal act. On the whole these objectives have to do with the intention of the *mukallaf* and its effect on the validity or utility of the act. In this regard Shāṭibī analyses the following terms: *niyya* (intention), *maqāṣid, takalīf,* and *jalb al-maṣāliḥ* (acquisition of *maṣlaḥa*) and *taḥayyul* (recourse to legal devices to escape the severity of the law).

Shāṭibī begins with an analyses of the principle that "acts are (judged) by *niyya* (intentions)" (323),[1] to establish an interrelation between 'act' and 'intention'. He raises some questions. Does it mean that intention without an act and an act without intention are not legally valid? Further, what is intention? Does it mean 'the correspondence with the intention of the lawgiver in a particular act' or something else? It may be noted here that Shāṭibī uses the terms *niyya, qaṣd, maqṣid, ibtighā'* interchangeably, all of which have the sense of the English word "intention".

To analyse the relationship between *niyya* and act, Shāṭibī observes that these are *maqāṣid* that mark the distinction between *'āda* and *'ibāda*. The same act, such as the act of prostration, is *'ibāda* according to one intention i.e. purely dedicated to God, but it is no more *'ibāda* according to the other, i.e. prostrating oneself before idols (324). Thus acts are judged by the intention of their authors. Shāṭibī maintains a distinction at this point between *al-aḥkām al-waḍ'iyya* (Declaratory rules) and *al-aḥkām al-taklīfiyya* (Obligation-defining rules). Obligation-defining rules are those rules of law which come into effect by the declaration of the Lawgiver in the form of *amr* (command), or *nahy* (prohibition), on which bases they are divided into five well-known values of obligatory, commendable, permissible, reprehensible and forbidden. Since *al-aḥkām al-taklīfiyya* create obligations directly, a necessary condition for their performance is the intention of the *mukallaf* to do so. *Al-aḥkām al-waḍ'iyya* are those rules which are not the effect of a direct command but which become effective because they are positioned besides a direct command either as a means or a cause, or a condition or a impediment. Hence the legal validity of acts commanded by Oblidation-defining rules will be judged by the intent of the author of the act.

One possible objection to this position may be drawn from the cases of acts done under *ikrāh* (duress) and *hazl* (joke) where the intention of the *mukallaf* is not connected with the acts in question, yet juridically the acts are considered to be valid (325). Shāṭibī's answer to this objection entails very significant points of philosophical interest. In brief, he seems to maintain a distinction between two standpoints of deciding the validity of an act; from the standpoint of religion and morality the act is subject to *al-aḥkām al-taklīfiyya* and here the intention must correspond explicitly with the act, otherwise the act is not valid. From the juridical standpoint, in cases other than *'ibādāt*, expression of intention and its correspondence with the said act is not a necessary requirement; an act is valid and subject to juridical consequences even if a corresponding *niyya* is absent.

The source of confusion on this matter is the assumption that *niyya* is absent in the cases of duress and joke. In fact here the *niyya*, is not lacking in an absolute sense. Shāṭibī, therefore, begins his answer by explaining various senses of the considerations of *niyya*. In its general sense, *niyya* (in the sense of volition) is a necessity (*ḍarūra*) for the validity of an action. This is so because the doer of an action insofar as he is *mukhtār* (one who has a choice, freedom of will), necessarily has an implicit intention in his action, whether his intention is to obey the command of the Lawgiver or not. From this standpoint intention is absent only in such cases as, for instance, when a certain action is performed by a *nā'im* (a person in sleep) or by a *majnūn* (an insane person). Having no *ikhtiyār,* individuals in these states, are not *mukallafīn*. Those acts which are done with *ikhtiyār*, however, cannot be considered as lacking *niyya*. Hence acts performed under duress or as joke will be judged, juridically, by such intentions. This sense of the consideration of *niyya* is from the standpoint of *al-aḥkām al-waḍ'iyya*. As has been explained earlier, from the standpoint of *al-waḍ'iyya*, an act becomes valid and its juridical consequences are effective if the necessary conditions of the said acts are fulfilled, even though a corresponding *niyya* be absent in that act. For instance, if a person returns a deposit to its owner, even though unwillingly, juridically his act of returning the deposit is valid and effective (327); the act itself is deemed to constitute intent.

Unlike the above-mentioned general sense, the consideration of *niyya*, in the special sense means the intention to obey law. In this special sense *niyya* becomes a necessary condition for the validity of an act in cases of *'ibādāt*. It is also necessary when one wants to transform all his acts, *'ibādāt* as well as *'ādāt*, into *ta'abbudāt*. Free actions (*al-a'māl al-dākhila taḥt al-ikhtiyār*) can be changed into *ta'abbudī* if the intention of obedience accompanies them. This sense of *niyya* pertains to *al-aḥkām al-taklīfiyya*. As discussed earlier, from the standpoint of *al-taklīfiyya* an act becomes valid, and the *jazā'* becomes effective, only if the act is accompanied by the intention to obey the *Shāri'*.

The *niyya* of obedience is understood to mean that the intention of the *mukallaf* performing an act will be in conformity with the intention of the Lawgiver in instituting the law, i.e. with the *maṣāliḥ* of the people (331). From this standpoint any act by which one intends for what is unlawful, becomes void (*bāṭil*). The reason for this judgement is that laws aim at achieving *maṣlaḥa* and removing *mafsada*. A contrary intention in the lawful acts would be equivalent to seeking *mafsada* and preventing *maṣlaḥa* which is against human interest as well as the *Sharī'a* (333).

In the light of the above discussion, human acts are classified into the following four types. First, those acts where the act and the intention both conform with the objectives of the Lawgiver. Second, where both do not conform. Third, where the act conforms, but the intention does not. Fourth, where the intention conforms, but the act does not (337). The legal value of the act in the first and second type is obvious i.e. lawful and unlawful respectively. In the third type the doer will be considered disobedient only in his intention but not in his act. In other words, he has violated the right of God, but not the right of men (338). If a man knows, however, that his intentions do not conform to the objectives of the Lawgiver, although his act does, then he is to be blamed more because he is taking advantage of his act for some other objectives (339).

In the fourth type, if the doer of the act knows that his act is contrary to the objectives of the Lawgiver then his conduct is similar to *ibtidā'* (*bid'a*, innovation in a religious matter). *Bid'a* as such is *madhmūm* (condemned) according to Shāṭibī. *Al-bid'a al-muḥarrama* or *al-bid'a al-madhmūma* is understood by Shāṭibī in reference to the second type of acts where intention and act both are contrary to the objectives of the Lawgiver (340). In *bid'a per se* the intention conforms but the act does not. Shāṭibī, however, excludes those cases where the doer does not know that his act does not conform. In such a case he will not be regarded as disobedient, but his act will still not be considered as compliance (*imtithāl*) (342).

Now, the question is: What is *imtithāl*? Obviously, *imtithāl* is that the intention of the author of an act must accord with the intent of the Lawgiver. This is conceivable only if an obligee intends acquisition (*jalb*) *maṣlaḥa* because that also constitutes the intent of the Lawgiver.

JALB AL-MAṢLAḤA: ACQUISITION OF COMMON GOOD

The *jalb* (seeking for) *al-maṣlaḥa* within the limits of the *Sharī'a* is a necessary requirement of *niyya*. The act of seeking *maṣlaḥa* does not, however, occur always in isolation; often it is connected with other acts as well. Hence the questions that need to be considered in regard to *jalb al-maṣlaḥa* have to do with the following situations; striving for *maṣlaḥa* when the result will be harmful to others, and secondly, striving for the *maṣlaḥa* of someone else (348).

Shāṭibī considers eight types of situations where one's own *maṣlaḥa* may be harmful to others. Harm may be general to the whole community or may be specific to someone; it may be inevitable; it may be avoidable, etc. (349-362). The main principle upheld in these discussions is that if there is an alternative to harm, harm must be avoided. Disregarding an alternative would mean that harm becomes the only purpose of one's action (349). Furthermore, striving for *maṣlaḥa* even though it may be harmful to others will be allowed if there is *maṣlaḥa* for more people than are harmed. The right of striving for *maṣlaḥa* will be given preference to the consideration of avoiding harm if it is well known that a prohibition to strive for *maṣlaḥa* will cause harm to the seeker. In cases where the seeker himself does not meet any harm but engages in efforts to achieve *maṣlaḥa* that customarily leads to harm, it must be seen whether this potential harm is *qaṭ'ī* (definie), *nādir* (rare) or *ẓannī* (probable). A man will be prevented from striving for *maṣlaḥa* only if the harm done to others is *qaṭ'ī* (348).

The second question in regard to *jalb al-maṣlaḥa* is that of seeking the *maṣlaḥa* of others. As a general rule Shāṭibī states that if someone is obliged to seek his *maṣāliḥ*, it is no longer obligatory for others also to seek his *maṣāliḥ* (364). This rule is similar to the rule of *niyāba*. The main points that Shāṭibī brings forth in this discussion serve to show that no man is under obligation to fulfil the specific obligations of others. We are not concerned here with the obligations of *'ibādāt*, because *'ibādāt* cannot be fulfilled by proxy. The obligations under discussion concern this world. Such obligations, however, become binding upon others when the original *mukallaf* is unable to fulfil them, although they are his personal needs. For instance, the following obligations aim at striving for the *maṣāliḥ* of others: *zakāt*, lending money, burying the dead body, looking after the affairs of minors and the insane, etc. Among these obligations some are general (or public, *kifā'iyya*) and some are specific (*'alā al-ta'yīn*) and individual obligations. A specific obligation cannot be fulfilled by proxy. An individual is required to seek the *maṣāliḥ* of others, only if his own *maṣāliḥ* are not affected and if he is capable of fulfilling his own as well as others' obligations, or if other people are looking after his personal *maṣāliḥ*. If he cannot fulfil both his and others' obligations at the same time, his obligation to others will give way and his own *maṣlaḥa* will be preferred to others'. If the matter at issue is a general obligation to others, then others must look after that individual's obligations while he fulfills his duty (364-368).

Shāṭibī's conclusions regarding the above two questions of striving for *maṣlaḥa* are very significant to his legal philosophy. He seems to admit that by doing good, or trying to do good, i.e. to strive for one's *maṣlaḥa*, one may also actually do evil, i.e. to harm others. This would make the *Sharī'a* in some instances result in evil deeds. To rectify such a consequence, Shāṭibī stresses that obligations be undertaken after considering their ends and consequences, and not on their appearance as good or bad. Furthermore, the goodness of obligations, or the ultimate criterion of *maṣlaḥa*, is good of the larger number of people and harm to less of them. If the good of the few is harmful to many, it no longer remains good.

The above conclusion shows that in Shāṭibī's legal thinking definition of law implies consideration for society as a whole. This consideration is too strong to allow a legal obligation to be defined as an individual's commitment towards the Lawgiver. In fact, Shāṭibī even implies that by disregarding the social implications of a legal obligation, one's individual commitment to do good may result in evil.

Shāṭibī views legal obligation also as a social obligation. If a person has devoted himself to look after the *maṣāliḥ* of the society it becomes a kind of societal obligation for others to look after the *maṣāliḥ* of that individual. Shāṭibī states that this is why the obligation to pay *zakāt* is prescribed, mutual lending of money is allowed, and looking after the maintenance of wife and children is required. In all the above cases the affected individuals is unable to look after his interests. For instance wife and children are unable to look after their own *maṣālīh*. Wife is fully occupied serving the *maṣāliḥ* of others and children are simply incapable of looking after themselves. That is why husband and parent are obliged to take care of the needs of wife and children respectively.

The intention of seeking one's own *maṣlaḥa* in legal obligation sometimes leads to the circumvention of one's obligation by legal devices. With the exception of the Ḥanafis, jurists mostly regard legal devices (*ḥīla, taḥayyul*) as contrary to legal obedience. Shāṭibī explains that such a general view of legal devices is debatable.

TAḤAYYUL: LEGAL DEVICE

Shāṭibī defines *ḥīla* and *taḥayyul* as follows:

> "When a *mukallaf* uses certain means in order to escape an obligation or to make some forbidden thing permissible for him, this use of means which causes an obligatory thing to become apparently non-obligatory and a forbidden thing apparently to become permissible, is called *ḥīla* or *taḥayyul*" (379).

These means are either apparently permitted in *Sharī'a*, or are not permitted. These devices render a rule inapplicable or transfer the consideration of the matter at issue to some other act (378).

Taḥayyul, according to Shāṭibī, operates on two premises:

(1) It strives to transfer the value of one legal act to another legal act externally, i.e. merely on the basis of apparent similarity between the two acts.

2) It disregards the inner meaning (i.e. *maṣlaḥa*) of the acts on the basis of which the acts were primarily intended by the *Shāri'*, and by doing so reduces the value of these acts to become means to certain other acts, whereas they were meant to be the end.

Shāṭibī illustrates it with the following example: Someone wishes to sell ten dirhams in cash for twenty on credit. Because of the prohibition on usury, such a transaction is not allowed. This person evades this prohibition by the following *ḥīla*. He buys a piece of cloth for ten dirhams and sells it for twenty on credit. To refer to the above premises, he transferred the value of selling of dirhams (which is prohibited) to the act of selling the cloth (which is permitted) only on the basis of their external similarity (both are acts of selling). But he disregarded the *maṣlaḥa* in both acts; he rather used the *maṣlaḥa* of one act, i.e. to earn profit in selling cloth, as means to achieve his own end.

In the light of the above explanation Shāṭibī regards *taḥayyul* as unlawful in principle (380). He supports his argument from the Qur'ān and Ḥadīth. He contends that rules of law are made for the *maṣāliḥ* of the people; hence acts will be judged according to their relation to *maṣāliḥ* because that is the objective of the Lawgiver. If an act is based externally and internally on lawful grounds, it is evidently a valid act. On the other hand, if it is externally lawful but the intention of that act is repugnant to a legal principle it is not lawful (385).

Shāṭibī stresses that legal acts are not intended (*maqṣūda*) for their own sake, but for their *ma'ānī* which are the *maṣāliḥ*. The *maṣāliḥ* in *'ibādāt* are closeness to God, devotion to Him alone with submission and humility and conformation of the heart and other parts of body in obedience to Him. If these *maṣāliḥ* are not sought, even the *'ibādāt* become unlawful. There is a clear instance in the case of *ṣalāt* done for the sake of *ri'ā' al-nās* (to put up a show for the people). Such *ṣalāt* is not valid (385).

In view of the above explanation *ḥiyal* (plural of *ḥīla*) are of three types. First, the *ḥiyal* of the hypocrites which are unanimously regarded as void and illegal (387). Second, *ḥiyal* which are unanimously held to be lawful such as uttering phrases of unbelief under duress. Shāṭibī, here, however, excepts from this rule the case of one who uses the confession of Islam to save his life. In their motives both cases are similar, for both aim at *al-maṣlaḥa al-dunyawiyya* (worldly good). In the latter case, however, since the real intention is different from that of a *ḥīla*, i.e. one confesses but does not believe in Islam he is seeking a *mafsada* in the hereafter, and hence the use of the confession is not lawful (387).

The third type of *ḥiyal* are those whose legal validity or invalidity cannot be decided as clearly as in the above types. Neither is it clear that such *ḥiyal* agree with the intentions of the Lawgiver nor can it be said that they oppose it. Hence they have been controversial. Shāṭibī illustrates that type with two cases; *nikāḥ al-muḥallil* (marriage of a divorcee with a second husband in order to make remarriage with the first husband lawful) and *buyū' al-ājāl* (sales on credit). Shāṭibī finds it impossible to decide in favour of or against the practice of these two *ḥiyal*. He is of the opinion that those who regard this type as forbidden, find it against the *maṣlaḥa*. In other words, it is an intentional violation of *sharī'a*. He disagrees with this conclusion (388). Shāṭibī only provides the arguments of those who are in favour of these two *ḥiyal*, but does not give his opinion in favour of or against them (391). He recommends caution on this point because Ḥanafī books were not available to him.

NOTE

1. The numbers in the parenthesis in the text of this chapter refer to the pages of *al-Muwāfaqāt*, Vol. II (Cairo: Muṣṭafā Muḥammad, n.d.)

CHAPTER TEN

'ĀDA AND *BID'A*: CONTINUITY AND CHANGE

In the preceding chapters we have studied Shāṭibī's doctrine of the *maqāṣid* according to his own formulation and to the structure of his own presentation. We are now in a better position to appreciate how the concept of *maṣlaḥa* enjoys pivotal significance in Shāṭibī's legal philosophy.

In the framework of Shāṭibī's terminology, the problem of continuity and change can be discussed with reference to the concepts of *'āda* and *bid'a*. The concept of *'āda* explicates the notion of social change and its relation to law. *Bid'a* presents a concept of change which is generally linked with change on social practices.

'ĀDA

Shāṭibī's discussion of *'āda* turns around three problems: the constancy of *'ādāt*, the possibility of their change and their relationship with the *Sharī'a*. According to Shāṭibī, "*'Āda* only means that a given act, if it is supposed to take place without any impediment, takes place only in a certain manner which is known by other similar acts." (2:281)[1] Shāṭibī's definition partially resembles the theory of determinism. This deterministic element is the constancy of the occurrence of *'ādāt* which Shāṭibī calls *istiqrār* (persistence) and *istimrār* (continuity) (2:279).

The continuity of *'ādāt* is a necessary condition without which the fulfilment of a legal obligation cannot be conceived. The other element is the certainty and predictability of the *'āda*, as Shāṭibī says, "the occurrence of *'āda* in the world of existence is a known (*ma'lūm*) matter, not a conjecture (*maẓnūn*)" (2:279). Both the elements are such that their absence makes any law impossible.

> If a divergence (*ikhtilāf*) is presumed in *'awā'id*,[2] it would necessitate a divergence in law-making (*tashrī'*); in the

classification of law (*tartīb*) and in its declaration (*khiṭāb*), and the *Sharī'a* would not be the same as it is now (2:280).

Shāṭibī's concept of *'āda* includes various referents: sometimes he means simply habits and human behaviour (2:297)[3], on other occasions it is equivalent to custom.[4] It is also contrasted with *'ibādāt* so as to mean what the other jurists generally call *mu'āmalāt* (2:307-308). In fact Shāṭibī's use of the term is inclusive of all these senses. This interpretation is admissible if we recall that Shāṭibī contrasts *Sharī'a* or *amr* (command) with *kawn* (creation) (3:121 f.). The *'āda*, then, would be related to *kawn* or the physical world as the counterpart of *aḥkām al-sharī'a*.

Shāṭibī's concept of the continuity of *'āda* is questioned on two points, first on the ground that the continuity of a certain thing in this world is equivalent to the beginning of its existence, because for its continuity as for its existence it also requires an agent who, however, may possibly become non-existent. During the first period the continuity of the non-existence of that thing was possible, but when it was brought into existence, one of the two possibilities was achieved, i.e. its existence; the other possibility i.e. its non-existence still remains to be actualised. When it is possible to conceive the possibility of its discontinuity, how can one talk with certainty about its continuity?

The second objection is that very often events occur contrary to *'āda* (*khawāriq al-'āda*). This fact of actual occurrence supplements the above argument about the potential possibility of non-continuity of *'ādat*. How, then, can it be maintained that the occurrence of *'ādāt* is known with certainty?

Shāṭibī replies by analysing the notion of possibility. He argues that the notion of possibility is logical (*al-jawāz al-'aqlī*), while tradition is not concerned with possibility but with occurrence (*wuqū'*). Many a thing happens although logically it is possible that it does not happen. In fact the term "possibility" (*jawāz*) refers to the "possible" itself, while "necessary" (*wujūb*) and impossible (*imtinā'*) imply some external factor. Thus the latter cannot be contradictory to the former.

Second, the certainty and predictability in *'ādāt* do not concern each and every *'āda*. Essentially they concern the universals of being (*kulliyāt al-wujūd*), not the individuals. Hence if an individual deviates, this does not refute the universal. The argument from *khawāriq al-'āda* refers to individuals. Furthermore, it is the occurrence of *khawāriq al-'āda* that assures our knowledge about the universal *'ādāt* and *vice versa* (2:281-282).

From the above it can be seen that Shāṭibī speaks about the continuity of only those *'awā'id* which are universal. Their continuity is not only an actual fact, but it is also necessitated by the requirement of a stable base for law.

Kharq al-'āda is not a proper example of changing *'ādāt* ; in fact, *kharq al-'āda* is a breach of a universal *'āda*, and hence it happens seldom. Shāṭibī, therefore, dismisses *kharq al-'āda* as a serious objection to the continuity of *'ādāt*, as well as an example of change.

Shāṭibī classifies *al-'awā'id al-mustamirra* (constant habits), in reference to *Shāri'* into two kinds: *shar'iyya*, which are introduced or sanctioned by *Sharī'a* and *al-'awā'id al-jāriya bayn al-khalq*, (2:283 f.) those which are current among the people. These two categories are not exclusive of each other; the first category also belongs to the habits and customs of the people. *Shar'* necessarily gives consideration to *al-'awā'id al-jāriya*, because in fact Divine law (*Sunnat Allāh*) corresponds with the *'awā'id* in general; hence the *Sharī'a* was instituted commensurate with the institution of *'awā'id* (3:265).

Shāṭibī believes in the relationship between *Sharī'a* and *'āda* more than between *Sharī'a* and *'aql*. As mentioned earlier, it was in the periods of *fatra* (hiatus between Divine Revelations) that the philosophers (*'uqalā'*) claimed to know good and evil by reason alone (2:307). According to Shāṭibī, this was possible, in fact, only because the values of good and evil already posited in human nature existed as instituted in *'ādāt*. This is why Shāṭibī finds that the *Sharī'a* has not rejected *'ādāt* entirely. In the case of the *Sharī'a* of Prophet Muḥammad, indeed, the *Sharī'a* confirmed most of the *'ādāt* that were practiced by the people in the pre-Islamic period. Examples of such laws are the following *'ādāt* which were regarded good in the pre-Islamic period and were also adopted by Islam: *diya* (blood money), *qasāma* (compurgation), gathering on the day of *'arūba* (the ancient Arabic name for Friday) for sermons, and *qirāḍ* (loan) etc. (2:307).

Shāṭibī illustrates the relation of the *Sharī'a* and *'āda* by the case of *khamr* (intoxicant). "It was habitually used in pre-Islamic days. Islam came, and left it intact in the period before migration and a few years after. The *shar'* did not pronounce any law regarding *khamr* until the verse "They ask you about *khamr* and *maysir*..." was revealed. Shāṭibī explains that the fundamental rule of *Sharī'a* is that when an evil (*mafsada*) in a thing transgresses its goodness (*maṣlaḥa*), it is valued as evil. The evils are prohibited, hence the reason for its prohibition is clear. In cases where *Sharī'a* has not pronounced the prohibition, even though this aspect of its evaluation is apparent, the people will act upon the supposition that the original law established by the continuity of practice (*'āda*) remains intact (1:174).

Shāṭibī's discussion of the relation of *Sharī'a* and *'āda* implies the aspect of change as well. *'Āda* can change in certain cases, but more important is the fact that when a change takes place within an *'āda*, it also effects a change in the rule of the *Sharī'a*. A thing which was relatively good when it becomes evil it is evaluated by *Sharī'a* accordingly. This takes us to Shāṭibī's view of legal and social change. First we will discuss the aspect of change in *'āda*, then the problem of legal change will be dealt with.

Beside *al-'awā'id al-shar'iyya* (legalised customs) which do not change, there are *al-'awā'id al-jāriya* (current customs) whom Shāṭibī divides into two: first, *al-'awā'id al-'āmma* (general customs), which do not change with the change of time, place or state; and second, those which change. In the first category, Shāṭibī mentions the *'awā'id* of eating, drinking, joy, sorrow, acquiring nice things, etc. The evaluation in these categories has been established on the basis of the *'awā'id* of past generations; they have never changed. In fact they are based on the Divine law in Creation [law of nature]. In the second category are the *'awā'id* such as the forms of dress, styles of dwelling, etc., which change with time, place, and states. In this category, therefore, it is not correct to evaluate *'awā'id* in absolute terms on the basis of past experience. Even if there is some external evidence to prove the continuity of such an evaluation, it must be kept in mind that this evaluation was made in view of some external factor, not because of *'āda* itself. Similarly the evaluation in the present cannot be carried on into the future, or to the past. The reason for this temporal limitation is again the probability of change (2:297-298).

It should be noted here that in the usage of the term "change", Shāṭibī includes both 'horizontal' and 'vertical' senses of change. The former is the change which we observe in a certain social practice among various societies and countries. The latter is the change in social practices over time, replacement of old *'ādāt* by additions or modifications. For the 'horizontal' change Shāṭibī uses the term *ikhtilāf* and for the 'vertical' the terms "*taghyīr*" and "*tabdīl*".

Shāṭibī discusses five senses of change in customs (2:284-285). (1) The first is exemplified by the difference of social values, good (*ḥusn*) and evil (*qubḥ*). For example, keeping the head uncovered is regarded as impudent in eastern countries but not so in western countries (e.g. Andalus, Morocco, etc.). (2) The second change results from the linguistic usage due to the difference of technological (*ṣanā'i'*) levels. This change usually takes place among various peoples (*umam*), but it also occurs within one people, e.g. the differences of the technical vocabularies among men of various trades and professions. (3) The third, is the difference in *mu'āmalāt* (dealing with each other), like the *'āda* (custom) of receiving a dowry (*ṣadāq*) before the consummation of a marriage. (4) The fourth change results from the difference of considerations which are external to the acts in question, for example, the difference in the criterion of maturity (*bulūgh*) among various people, whether on the basis of puberty or on the basis of age. (5) The fifth change is the case of irregular *'awā'id* which become regular *'ādāt* for some peoples or individuals, for instance a person who, due to certain injuries, can no more urinate in the regular manner. The irregular manner of his urinating becomes an *'āda* for him. The illustrations of changing *'awā'id* show that Shāṭibī admitted the possibility of change in *'āda* in both 'horizontal' and 'vertical' senses. This would then imply that *Sharī'a* insofar as it is connected with an *'āda* must also admit change. It may also be noted that Shātibī's term *'āda* includes usage of language, habits, customs and social practices. All of these are called *al-'awā'id al-jāriyya bayn al-nās* to distinguish them from *al-'awā'id al-shar'iyya.*

Shāṭibī discusses six aspects of the problem of change with reference to *Sharī'a*. Firstly there are immutable universal principles on which the *Sharī'a* is based and which underlie the Meccan part of the Qur'ān. These principles are also called *maqāṣid al-sharī'a*, and they never change. The second are *al-'awā'id al-shar'iyya* (legalised customs). As mentioned earlier, they are the *'awā'id* introduced or sanctioned by the *Sharī'a*. In contrast to the universal principles, they are more specific and concrete rules of law. According to Shāṭibī, they also do not change. "Because," Shāṭibī explains, "they are among the rules of the *Sharī'a*. Even if the views of the *mukallafīn* (subjects of law) differ about them, it is not correct to change good into evil... For instance witness by a slave cannot be allowed on the ground that custom is no longer apposed to it or that such evidence has become acceptable in practice... If this change were permitted it would constitute abrogation of the rules which are constant and continuous, whereas abrogation after the death of the Prophet is void (*bāṭil*)" (2: 283-284).

Thirdly, there are *'awā'id* which are either a means or a mediate cause (*sabab*) to the fulfilment of certain rules of the *Sharī'a*, like the physical capability to perform an act, the *'awā'id* about maturity, etc. "Since they are mediate causes (*sabab*) for the effect, i.e. 'caused act' (*musabbab*), they are also commanded by the Lawgiver. Hence there is no difficulty in giving them due consideration and accepting them as the basis of rules" (2:284). The problem then is to ask whether the rules of the *Sharī'a* would change if this basis changed. Shāṭibī replied in the affirmative, saying "The rule of the *Sharī'a* will always be in consonance with these *'awā'id*" (2:284).

Fourthly, there are *al-'awā'id al-mutabaddila* (changing customs) the five senses of which have been mentioned above. Shāṭibī explicitly argues that the rules of *Sharī'a* must accord with the changes in this category of *'awā'id.*

The fifth aspect concerns the legal changes which imply that certain matters are not covered by *Sharī'a* and hence additional rules are required. Shāṭibī stresses here the need for further investigation. A certain *ḥadīth* lays down the rule that 'the matters on which the Lawgiver is silent, are *'afw* (not obligtory, the word literally means forgiven). This *ḥadīth* makes it clear that *Sharī'a* does not cover everything. The *ḥadīth*, however, renders the position of those jurists questionable who maintain that there is nothing *maskūt 'anhu* (where the Lawgiver is silent), because they claim that every case is either covered by the text (*manṣūṣ*) or is coverable by an analogy based on the text. To avoid the conflict with the above *ḥadīth*, they explain that *Shārī*''s silence can be removed in a number of ways; for instance, by way of *istiṣḥāb*, or by referring back to the *Shāri*''s explicit proclamations in laws revealed before Prophet Muḥammad, or by confining the interpretation of the text to the generality of a specific ruling by disregarding its modifications if they are not mentioned immediately after the ruling (1:173).

Shāṭibī goes into a detailed analysis of the nature of this silence (i.e. *'afw*). He finds that this silence has two types. First is the type of silence where there was no immediate cause for issuing a command and hence the Lawgiver did not say anything. Second is the type where such a cause existed and required change in the existing rule but the Lawgiver still kept silent. To Shāṭibī, this second type of silence is a form of textual confirmation of the existing rules; there can be no addition or amendment in the rule (2:410). To interpret this silence as absence of ruling would thus lead to introducing a *bid'a*.

The first type is what can be properly called "silence". Because of its obvious significance, Shāṭibī's explanation on this point needs to be quoted in his own words.

> One of them [the aspects of silence] is, that He is [found] silent because there was no motive (*dā'iya*) that necessitated any [ruling]... For instance the events that occurred after the (death of the) Prophet. They certainly did not occur in his lifetime and hence none can say that the Lawgiver said nothing about them, even though they occurred. They took place later and hence the people of *Sharī'a* were obliged to examine those events and to execute them according to what had been established as universal principles.
>
> The new things that the righteous ancestors introduced in Islamic law belong to this type. The examples of this type are *al-maṣāliḥ al-mursala* such as the collection of the Qur'ān etc... These are some of those things that were not discussed in Prophet's days, nor were they enquired about. Nor did they find place in social practice so that a cause for such an enquiry might arise (2:409-410).

The category of *'afw*, according to Shāṭibī falls between the *ḥalāl* (lawful) and the *ḥarām* (forbidden). This category not only admits the possibility of matters not covered by *Sharī'a*, but also the fact that they are subject of further interpretation. (1:161).

The sixth aspect of change is what Shāṭibī calls *iḥdāth fī al-sharī'a* (innovation). Shāṭibī does not believe in the unlawfulness of every *iḥdāth*. He argues that *iḥdāth* occurs in *Sharī'a* in three ways. It happens first because of ignorance or neglect of the objectives of law. This is either ignorance of the means of understanding the objectives, such as ignorance of the Arabic language and its grammar, or it is ignorance of the objectives themselves. A second reason for *iḥdāth* is *taḥsīn al-ẓann bi'l 'aql* (evaluating the goodness of a thing by reason), to decide the value of a thing on the basis of merely rational speculation. Here it must be noted that Shāṭibī is not speaking against the use of reason. His comment should be understood in the context of legal interpretation. A legal system has its own criteria or fundamental rules according to which the legal validity of an action is judged. Legal acts cannot be judged valid on the criteria of reason and ethics. A third cause is following one's own desires in seeking the truth. In such a case the desire dominates and even conceals the true evidences and leads to false conclusions.[5]

Bid'a is one aspect of *iḥdāth*. *Iḥdāth* can occur in all subject matters of *Sharī'a*, while *bid'a*, according to Shāṭibī, is limited to certain areas of law. This distinction requires a rather detailed analysis of Shāṭibī's concept of *bid'a*.

BID'A

Shāṭibī's book *al-I'tiṣām* is specifically designed to discuss the problem of *bid'a*. We need not go into the details of his arguments; what concerns us here is to discuss *bid'a* and its legitimacy. Shāṭibī vehemently condemns *bid'a* on more than nine grounds.[6] His reasons for condemnation can be summed up by saying that since *Sharī'a* in religious matters is complete and final, anyone who innovates commits, among other sins, two grave errors. One is the implication of equality with or rather superiority to God, the Lawgiver. Because the promulgation of *bid'a* implies that the innovator knows more than God about the *Sharī'a*. Second, that he relies more on human reason and personal desires than on the intent of the Lawgiver.[7]

Shāṭibī's condemnation of *bid'a* cannot, however, be taken as condemnation of all legal changes. Not only would such a conclusion not conform with his views discussed above, but it would also give a wrong idea about Shāṭibī's understanding of the concepts of *bid'a* and *ijtihād*.

Shāṭibī explains that etymologically *bid'a* comes from *bada'a* which means to invent something new, the like of which has not existed. In a technical sense, however, this "new-ness" and "invention" is only in reference to *Sharī'a*.[8] In reference to *Sharī'a* human acts can be of three kinds: required, prohibited, or optional. The category of prohibited actions is governed by two considerations, either simply because it is prohibited by law, or, that it literally opposes the rules of *Sharī'a*. It is the latter consideration to which the technical sense of *bid'a* pertains.[9]

Shāṭibī gives two definitions of *bid'a*. The first is a definition that does not include *'ādāt*; the second includes both *'ibādāt* and *'ādāt*. The first definition is as follows:

> A way (*ṭarīqa*) of innovation in religion (*dīn*) that resembles the way of the *Sharī'a* (*tuḍāhī al-ṭarīqat al-shar'iyya*) and which is intended to be followed in order to strive in the utmost toward obedience (*ta'abbud*) to Allah.[10]

The second definition replaces the phrase 'in order to strive...' with the following qualifying clause: "with the same intentions that *Sharī'* aims at."[11]

Shāṭibī even goes further to clarify the qualifications included in the definition. It is relevant to note some of these qualifications. The qualification of 'religion' (*dīn*) is significant because according to Shāṭibī "if this way of innovation belongs to *dunyā* (mundane matters) exclusively, it would not be a *bid'a*". Examples cited are innovations in crafts, in plans of cities, etc.[12] The qualification of 'innovation' excludes those matters which have their bases in *shar'*.

The qualification of ''intention of similarity with the *Sharī'a*'' is also very important. Shāṭibī admits that the intentions of the innovators are not bad in themselves, but he implies that they misunderstood the purpose of the *Sharī'a*. Shāṭibī does not equate *bid'a* with heresy only because it is a new thing. The key terms in this respect are 'intention' and the 'right understanding of the purpose of the *Sharī'a*. How is this right understanding to be judged?

In one respect right understanding means correspondence of both intention and acts with the purpose of *Sharī'a*. Shāṭibī analyses the relationship between intention and act to the purpose of *Sharī'a*. We have discussed it in a preceding chapter on *niyya*. To recapitulate it briefly, if the intention of an act and the act itself conform with the purpose of the *Sharī'a*, the act certainly is valid. The act is not valid if the act and the intention both do not conform with the *Sharī'a*. If the intention conforms and the act does not, it is called *bid'a*. If the act conforms but the intention does not the act belongs to the category of *ri'ā'* and hypocrisy (2:337).

According to Shāṭibī, *al-maṣāliḥ al-mursala* illustrate the cases where the intention and the act both conform to the purpose of the *Sharī'a*, (2:341-342) for example levying of new taxes in addition to those prescribed in the texts. The conformity of the act with the purpose of the *Sharī'a* and the intention in this case show the right understanding of the *Sharī'a*. Further, the intention does not conflict with the objectives of the *Sharī'a*. In fact it is this conformity of *al-maṣāliḥ al-mursala* with the *maqāṣid al-sharī'a* that distinguishes them from *bid'a*. Shāṭibī disagrees with the jurists who equated *al-maṣlaḥa al-mursala* with *bid'a*.[13] To him the two were completely opposed to each other.[14] He argued that first of all the jurists are not agreed upon an exact definition of *al-maṣlaḥa al-mursala*. Even Ghazālī expressed two different views on this point.[15] Secondly, Shāṭibī explains, *al-munāsib al-mursal* (synonymous with *al-maṣlaḥa al-mursala* in Ghazālī's terminology) which is neither specifically supported by the legal text nor is it rejected, is not a *bid'a*. On the contrary it is supported by the existence of the genus which is common between *al-sharī'a* and *al-maṣlaḥa al-mursala*, and, furthermore, this genus is considered valid by the *Sharī'a*. Its validity is not based on any specific evidence but on its consideration as a whole.[16]

Shāṭibī illustrates *al-maṣāliḥ al-mursala* with ten examples. Among them are the following events from Islamic legal history: the collection of the Qur'ān; determining the penalty for using intoxicants; allegiance to a less qualified person appointed for an office in the presence of a better qualified one.[17] He finds three elements common in all the ten examples. First is the element of suitability with the objectives (*maqāṣid*) of *Sharī'a*,[18] *al-maṣāliḥ al-mursala* do not conflict with the fundamentals or with the evidences of the *Sharī'a*. Second, they are rationally intelligible. *Al-maṣāliḥ al-mrsala* do not fall under the category of *ta'abbud* because the latter are not rationally intelligible in detail. Shāṭibī gives more than ten examples to prove this point.[19] Thirdly, *al-maṣāliḥ al-mursala* refer to the following principles: protection of (human) necessities; removal of impediments which are harmful to religion; and protection of an indispensable means to the end of law.[20]

Shāṭibī, thus, shows that the acceptable *maṣāliḥ* cannot be equated with *bid'a* and that they are not limited to the category of *ḍarūrī*, as some jurists have maintained; they cover other categories as well. In fact, the above explanation of *al-maṣlaḥa al-mursala* conforms to Shāṭibī's concept of *maṣlaḥa* which is of fundamental significance to his doctrine of *maqāṣid al-sharī'a*.

In case of *'ibādāt* the intention of similarity with *Sharī'a* leads to an extension of the sense of *ta'abbud*. For instance, in Shāṭibī's period the practice of chanting the names of God (*al-dhikr*) in congregation was considered by some Ṣūfīs obligatory.[21] Such an intention does not exist in the innovations in *'ādāt*. Nevertheless wherever this intention (of similarity with religious obligation) is absent in a new thing, even though there be similarity in actuality, such a new thing will not be regarded as *bid'a*.[22] Shāṭibī illustrates it with the following examples: taxes levied on property in a specific proportion and amount that resemble *zakāt*; use of sieves; washing hands with *'ushna* (potash); erecting lofty buildings, etc.[23]

Lack of such distinctions as above, in various types of 'new things' in Islamic law, had made the concept of *bid'a* confusing as well as controversial. The jurists who would accept nothing new in Islamic law rejected *bid'a* absolutely. Some jurists maintained a broad distinction between good and bad *bid'a*. Scholars such as Ibn 'Abd al-Salām and Qarāfī even divided *bid'a* into five categories corresponding to the five categories of legal valuation: obligatory, recommended, indifferent, reprehensible and forbidden.[24] Shāṭibī regards such a division meaningless and irrelevant. In his view, with the exception of the *bid'a* mentioned by these scholars in the categories of 'reprehensible' and 'forbidden' the others are not *bid'a* at all.

Shāṭibī refined the meaning of the concept of *bid'a* and made it more precise by clarifying his terminology and fitting it into a proper framework of legal philosophy. He showed that the *bid'a* are of two kinds only, *ḥaqīqiyya* (absolute) and, *'iḍāfiyya* (relative). *Al-bid'a al-ḥaqīqiyya* is that which is not proven by any *Shar'ī* evidence like the Qur'ān, *Sunna*, *ijmā'* or a reliable basis of reasoning, neither in general nor in particular. *Al-bid'a al-iḍāfiyya* is that which touches upon both aspects. In one aspect it is connected with some *Shar'ī* evidence; in the other, it is not. It is only in the latter aspect that it is *bid'a*.[25]

The common point in the two above definitions of *bid'a* given by Shāṭibī is the intention of the innovator to compete with the Lawgiver. Obviously this common point can be taken as the essence in Shāṭibī's concept of *bid'a*. Real *bid'a*, according to Shāṭibī, however, are only those which belong to *'ibādāt*. Shāṭibī argues this point in two ways. First he refutes the thesis of his opponents who argue that if innovations are possible in *'ibādāt*, they should also be possible in *'ādāt*. Furthermore, there are a large number of *aḥādīth* which predict the occurrence of new things in later periods which proves the possibility of *bid'āt*.

Shāṭibī dispels this objection saying that the dispute is not about the possibility but about the actual occurrence of *bid'a* in *'ādāt*; hence the argument of 'possibility' is not valid. As for predictions in *aḥādīth*, the argument is misleading. These particular *aḥādīth* do not call all of these new things *bid'a*, and moreover, these matters are not condemned there because they are innovations. Shāṭibī continues by saying that were every new thing in *'ādāt* regarded as *bid'a*, then every change in matters such as eating, clothing, speaking, etc., would stand condemned.[26] He sums up his argument in the following fashion:

> There are *'awā'id* which change with time, place and persons. If every change is condemned then everyone who differs in this respect with those Arabs who were in contact with the companions of the Prophet... will be considered as not

following them and hence deviating from the right path. This is quite difficult to accept.[27]

The implications of the above statement are fundamentally important for the question of legal change. Shāṭibī, here, is saying that there are large areas of life — in fact everything except *'ibādāt* — where the concept of *bid'a* does not apply. The implication is that the *Sharī'a* does not control these areas of life or at least does not control them in the same sense as it controls the relations between man and God.

Shāṭibī's second manner of argument against including *'ādāt* among *bid'āt* is the consideration of *ta'abbud* (obedience). As mentioned earlier, from the view point of *shar'*, acts of the *mukallafīn* are of two kinds; *'ādāt* and *'ibādāt*. It is generally agreed that *'ibādāt* are *ta'abbudī* (non-extendible), but there is disagreement whether *'ādāt* are also *ta'abbudī*. Shāṭibī defines *ta'abbudī* as "that the meaning of which cannot be rationally understood from the act itself". Matters such as ritual cleanliness, prayers, fasting and pilgrimage are all *ta'abbudī*. Matters such as those whose meanings can be rationally understood and whose goodness or badness can be known are *'ādī*. Examples are acts relating to sale, marriage, lease and punishment for crimes. It is in this sense that *'ādāt* are not *ta'abbudī*, and hence the term *bid'a* is not applicable.[28]

In the light of what has been said so far, it is possible to reconstruct Shāṭibī's theory of social and legal change as follows.

One finds a significantly elaborate conception of social as well as legal system in Shāṭibī's thought. The conceptions of these systems emerge from Shāṭibī's analyses of *'awā'id* and *Sharī'a*. It must, however, be noted that Shāṭibī sees both of these systems originating from one source, God. Yet as they represent two different levels of Divine Will, they do not function in the same way. *'Āda* as physical law, instituted in human habits such as hunger, thirst, etc., represents the level of *al-irādat al-takwīniyya* (The Divine Creative will), where man has no choice but to obey the rules. In the *Sharī'a*, obedience depends on man's choice. Human acts insofar as they belong to *al-irādat al-takwīniyya*, obey the laws of *takwīn* (creation) necessarily, but those acts which belong to *al-irādat al-tashrī'iyya* (Divine Legislative Will) necessarily need man's intention and volition for obedience. The *'awā'id* (customs), the habits of individuals and social practices of the community that are in conformity with the laws of nature (*kulliyāt al-wujūd*) are products of *al-irādat takwīniyya*. They provide the deterministic element to stabilizes the function of a social as well as a legal system. There are, of course, some deviations (*khawāriq*) from this continuity of *'awā'id*, but these deviations establish (rather than refute) the factor of stability. Those *'awā'id* that continue to occur are called *al-'awā'id al-mustamirra* and the rules of the *Sharī'a* have their basis in this type of *'awā'id*.

The connection of the *Sharī'a* with the recurring *'awā'id* makes possible for the *Sharī'a* to be certain, eternal and continuing. The eternity of the *Sharī'a* does not originate from the continuity of *'awā'id*, in the sense that the concepts and rules of *Sharī'a* become eternal because of these *'awā'id*. In fact the *Sharī'a* forms the ultimate bases which are abstract, universal and general and, thus, believed to be unchanging. The continuity of *'awā'id* makes the actualization of these ultimate bases possible.

Shāṭibī clarifies that human reason alone could not discover these ultimate bases, hence this knowledge was revealea in two ways: on the one hand it was instituted in *'awā'id*, and on the other, it was revealed through the *Sharā'i'*. Human reason tended either to total laxity or to sheer determinism in its attempt to discover these ultimate bases. Consequently revelation of the *Sharā'i'* was necessary to save man from such extremes. Leaving aside the question of how the revelation of the *Sharī'a* differed from human reason in this respect or how far it is a denial of any role to human reason, what is notable here is Shāṭibī's attempt to explain that the *Sharī'a* aims at the good of mankind. And that this good is judged in relation to and on the basis of *'awā'id*.

With the exception of universal physical habits, the *'awā'id* are, however, subject to change. The *Sharī'a* is based on the unchanging principles of *'awā'id*, which are thus called *al-'awā'id al-shar'iyya*. Nevertheless the *'awā'id* which belong to human beings (*al-'awā'id al-jāriya bayn al-khalq*) may change. Since *Sharī'a* governs these *'awā'id* as well, it must respond to these changes. The mechanism of this response to social practices gives birth to legal systems.

Shāṭibī illustrates some such changes. The legal system faces one type of change when an individual, coming from a different social system, becomes the subject of another legal system, or a legal system is introduced where a different social system is in operation. Obviously, this change does not affect the fundamentals because the *'awā'id* on which *Sharī'a* is based are universal. Nevertheless this change requires to be accommodated in order to maintain the stability of the legal system. The second type of change occurs where the old custom no longer satisfies human needs, or when some new elements either from without or from within are introduced. Yet another type of change is introduced when social practices or institutions come into conflict with each other or with the purpose of law; this conflict may arise from a clash of personal interests or because of certain new developments in society. Whatever the cause, the change in a social system takes place in such manner that it requires the legal system to respond to those changes.

The need to respond to social changes is essentially the result of the aim of the legal system at its own as well as at the stability of the social system. Since the possibility of change is unending and the rules of law are limited, it is out of this necessity that the legal system is organized on a rational basis both in its principles and methods, so that it is manageable by human reason. According to Shāṭibī, since human reason alone cannot achieve such organization, the *Sharī'a* has provided mankind with general guidelines. Among these guidelines some can be tested in social practice and some cannot. Those which cannot be tested are *'ibādāt* and they are to be obeyed as such. Of those which can be tested and are rationally intelligible are *'ādāt*. The latter constitute the major area of human acts. Since it is possible to rationally organize the *'ādāt,* the *Sharī'a* has left the details to be worked out by legal reasoning. As discussed above, this area of *'ādāt* belongs to the category of *'afw*.

The decision about the situations not covered by the *Sharī'a* may mean application of established rules or it may mean extension of these rules. Shāṭibī does not accept any extension of *'ibādāt* by analogy or other means, such extension is allowed only in *'ādāt*.

While *'ibādāt* are not rationally intelligible, the *'ādāt* are. Moreover, often in the Qur'ān, an *'illa* is mentioned in case of *'ādāt* which means that the *Sharī'a* not only considers them intelligible, but also extendible. The method and process of extending this *'illa* to other cases is called *ijtihād* to which we shall turn in the next chapter.

NOTES

1. The numbers in the parenthesis in the text refer respectively to volume and page numbers of *al-Muwāfaqāt* (Cairo: Muṣṭafā Muḥammad, n.d.).
2. Shāṭibī uses both *'ādāt* and *'awā'id* as plurals of *'āda*. Etymologically, some linguists claim that *'awā'id* is the plural of *'ā'id* and *'ā'ida* (something that re-occurs), and *'ādāt* is plural of *'āda*. This distinction is, however, generally disregarded. In Shāṭibī's use of *'awā'id* there is some indication that he uses *'ādāt* for those legal acts which are opposite to *'ibādāt*, and *'awā'id* for habits, customs, etc. But this distinction is not consistently maintained by him.
3. Examples of eating, drinking, etc., are given to illusturate *'āda*.
4. Shāṭibī gives the examples of the variety of *'āda* in different forms of human dwellings; on p. 307, he gives the examples of customs in the pre-Islamic period to illustrate *'āda*.
5. *Al-I'tiṣām*, Vol. II, 293ff.
6. *Ibid.*, Vol. I, 26-111.
7. *Ibid*, 82.
8. *Ibid.*, 18f.
9. *Ibid.*, 18.
10. *Ibid.*, 19.
11. *Ibid.*
12. *Ibid.*
13. Shāṭibī here refers to Mālik whose reliance on *al-maṣāliḥ al-mursala* is strongly criticised by other jurists. Shāṭibī defends Mālik in the following manner.

    > Mālik's opinions, adhering to the principle of not applying rational explanations in matters of *'ibādāt,* revolves entirely around his [approach to]

stop at the limits prescribed by the *Sharī'a*, [and thus] disregarding what *munāsib* requires... [This is] in contradiction to *'ādāt* which are governed according to suitable reason (*al-ma'nā al-munāsib*) which is evident to human reason (*'aql*). He employed laxity (*istirsāl*) with self-confidence and with deep insight in reasoning by *maṣlaḥa* ... [He employed this laxity so frequently] that the scholars often criticise him for this laxity. They imagined that Mālik threw off the yoke [of *Sharī'a*] and opened the gate of law-making. How far is it [from truth]!" *Al-I'tiṣām*, p. 113.

14. *Ibid.*, p. 115.
15. *Ibid.*, 96.
16. *Ibid.*, 98.
17. *Ibid.*, pp. 99-110.
18. *Ibid.*, p. 111.
19. *Ibid.* For instance, Shāṭibī explains that the *Shārī'a*'s prescriptions about cleanliness from human excretions are not rationally uniform. In case of urine and stool one is obliged only to wash certain parts of one's body, (i.e. ablution), but in case of noctural discharge, washing of the whole body is obligatory.
20. *Ibid.*, p. III, pp. 113-115.
21. *Al-I'tiṣām*, Vol. II, 24.
22. *Ibid.*, Vol. I, 22. *"Fa kullu mā 'ukhturi'a fi'l-dīni mimmā yuḍāhī al-mashrū' wa lam yuqṣad bihī al-ta'abbud, fa qad kharaja 'an hādhihī al-tasmiya"*.
23. *Ibid.*, pp. 22-23.
24. *Ibid.*, 147ff.
25. *Ibid.*, 232ff.
26. *Ibid.*, Vol. II, 63-67.
27. *Ibid.*, 67.
28. *Ibid.*, 68.

CHAPTER ELEVEN

IJTIHĀD

Shāṭibī discusses the doctrine of *ijtihād* quite comprehensively at the end of the fourth volume of *al-Muwāfaqāt*, dealing with its three aspects:

(1) The doctrine and the various critical problems related with it;
(2) *Fatwā* as a form of *ijtihād;* and
(3) *Istiftā'* or the formulation of the question and the process of legal enquiry.

The present chapter is an anlysis of these three aspects of *ijtihād* as discussed by Shāṭibī.

1. THE DOCTRINE OF *IJTIHĀD*

Shāṭibī's analysis of the doctrine of *ijtihād* cannot be properly understood without reference to his legal philosophy and to his view of the history of the *Sharī'a* and the development of Islamic law. For his legal philosophy we may refer to the discussion in the preceding chapters. Presently we may recapitulate it briefly that in his legal philosophy God provides knowledge of good and bad to man through Divine laws, natural instinct and social experience. Human reason discovers *maṣlaḥa*, welfare of man, by an inductive analysis of the data known through these sources that have one common origin, God. The role of human reason is to discover this *maṣlaḥa* and apply it to a given case. This interaction of reason with revelation provides dynamism to Islamic law in the form of *ijtihād*.

This role of human reason in the development of Islamic law has been made possible by the fact that Divine laws are not in conflict with, rather they are indeed closer to, human social experience of good and bad. Humans define good what they have found mostly useful in their social experience. The *Sharī'a* generally affirms the same as *maṣlaḥa* (2:27).[1]

Shāṭibī observes this principle operating in the development of Islamic law, the morally good customs of the people are approved by the *Sharī'a* as fundamentals of Islamic law. This becomes clear from the brief history of Islamic law as overviewed by Shāṭibī.

Two Phases of the *Sharī'a*

Shāṭibī notes two distinctive phases in the history of the revelation of Islamic law: the Meccan phase and the Medinan phase. The *Sharī'a* in the Meccan phase was very close to the customs and morals of the people and was therefore easily comprehensible to the wise of the society. They could easily discover the universal principles of good by exercising simple *ijtihād* (4:236). The laws relating to prayers, expending wealth on the needy, helping the poor, caring for relatives, protecting the rights of the neighbour were all such as were easily comrehensible to the human reason (4:233).

In Medina substantive laws were given. They were in fact further qualifications and clarifications of those general principles that were revealed in Mecca. For instance, the injunction about *jihād* was revealed in Madina when the Muslims were strong enough to carry out with force the Meccan injunction of enjoining good and forbidding evil and inviting people to the fold of Islam. The general principles revealed in Mecca were explained more specifically sometimes in the Qur'ān, and sometimes by the *Sunna*. The process of clarification, specification, qualification, abrogation, etc., in Medina assured that the Meccan injunctions continued to be operative in principle. The Madani amendments actually affirmed the residual Meccan rules as continuing legal (*qānūn*) principles (4:237). Comparing the Meccan laws with the Medinan laws one finds that the former deal with justice and with the rights of God and man. The Medinan laws deal mostly with actual situations, spelling out concessions and penalties relating to conflicts and disputes in specific cases, but only as details of the universal principles that were revealed in Mecca. The Meccan verses of the Qur'ān therefore, form the primary principles and source and the Medinese verses constitute the secondary principles.

Shāṭibī's views can perhaps be summarised by saying that the Meccan part of the Qur'anic revelation dealt with the moral and ethical principles which constituted the primary rules of the *Sharī'a*. They were universally known moral truths and no great amount of scholarship was required to discover them. The Madani part of revealtion, on the other hand, dealt with legal matters which constituted applied exemplification of the primary ethical principles. Ideally, one should not forget the ethical side of law in practice, but unfortunately, indulgence in legal details led later Muslim societies to relegate their moral aspect to a consideration of secondary significance. Shāṭibī observes that as long as the scholars spoke about the first principles, i.e. the universal moral laws, they shared common ground with the common man. The gap between them widened only when it came to work out detailed laws. It became more and more a special field for the jurists (4:238).

Customs and Morals

While the jurists worked more with reference to the secondary principles there were some groups of Muslims who adhered instead to the first principles alone. Shāṭibī refers to Ṣūfīs as an example of this group.

People often claim that Ṣūfīs opted for hardship in obligations and thus deviated from the *Sharī'a*. Refuting this view, Shāṭibī explains that the Ṣūfīs in fact followed the Sunna, because the Prophet and his companions continued to follow Meccan injunctions in Madina as primary principles where no concession or qualification was considered necessary. Quoting an instance from the Ṣūfī literature, Shāṭibī says that a Ṣūfī was enquired how much *zakāt* was due on the amount of two hundred dirhams. The Ṣūfī replied: "According to our school of law, all belongs to Allah (i.e. the whole amount of 200 dirhams should be paid as *zakāt*), but according to your school of law, the amount of *zakāt* is five dirhams" (4:240). Shāṭibī explains that the Ṣūfī's reference was to the fact that the Meccan verses prescribed expending one's wealth in the path of God without going into details about the limits on which the *zakāt* was due and how much it was to be paid. It was left to the *ijtihād* of the individual. It was in Medina that the obligation of *zakāt* was defined and its limits were determined (4:240). The Medina laws, therefore, provided concessions to the general laws of Mecca.

To Shāṭibī, the Ṣūfīs excelled others in their following the Prophet and his companions by abiding by the Meccan primary principles of the *Sharī'a*. The jurists felt a need to examine the primary as well as the secondary principles to find out details and developments in the dealings between human beings. They abided by the primary principles as ideals. Subsequently, however, the first principles were forgotten, particularly in the later periods when non-Arab customs were subjected to the primary principles of Islamic law (4:238).

Change and continuity

When the boundaries of Islam expanded and other nations flocked to its fold, disputes also arose due to varying perceptions of law. Conflicting opinions abounded. People with different cultural backgrounds and customs understood the laws differently. The reason is probably that the customs provide people the primary rules of ethics by which they evaluate laws. The definition of "right" differed in specific cases where specific rulings were needed. Some groups of people violated the laws and opposed legal prescriptions. There was thus a need to define penalties for such persons. It was necessary to distinguish between a moral and a legal duty. Finer distinctions needed to be developed between obligatory and commendable, and between prohibition and reprehension. As particular cases multiplied, judgements on the basis of common sense alone were no longer feasible (4:234).

It was particularly difficult as all persons, Arabs or not, who were not trained intellectually, or who were accustomed to some pre-Islamic customs, or who considered some pre-Islamic customs more beneficial. The jurists therefore attended to the task of defining limits and penalties and to work out detailed laws in matters where opinions conflicted or could do so. They also defined specific rights and actions in unforeseen situations. They maintained a line of distinction between the lawful and the prohibited for the people so that they do not trespass those limits. They determined the anchor points on which the rules were fixed in specific cases. They showed the way out in each case from the legal perspective. They defended the check posts on the defence line, sometimes harshly and sometimes leniently. That was the manner of the jurists' *ijtihād* (4:237).

The crucial question that came before Islamic jurisprudence time and again was how the matters lying in the area between the lines of lawful and prohibited could be defined. Should they be left to the moral conscience of the individual or should it be legally determined? Do they fall within the scope or not?

Shāṭibī elaborated that in this regard two trends developed in the legal interpretation among the Muslim jurists. *Aṣḥāb al-ra'y* (the rationalists) believed that the Divine law aimed at the protection of human welfare. They allowed human reason to discover *maṣlaḥa* in the lawful and the prohibited and to extend its application to other subjects. The *Ẓāhirīs* (the literalists) argued that the purpose of Divine law was to try mankind in this world. The welfare was not the objective as such, but it was so because it was the Grace of the Lawgiver. The former abstracted laws paying more attention to the meaning while the latter abided by the letter and deduced laws from the literal senses (4:230).

DEFINITION OF *IJTIHĀD*

The Divine law has not provided a ruling for each and every individual case that would occur ever. It has prescribed only universal principles, general statements and a number of examples that provide guidance in an infinite number of cases. In Shāṭibī's view, legal cases do not happen in this world in abstract. They occur in specific situations with distinguishable facts. Each individual case differs from the other in details and facts. The *qāḍī* or *muftī* distinguishes these cases from each other. (4:92). Two institutions, *futyā* (juris-consultation) and *ḥukm* (*qaḍā*, court of law), were developed by the Muslim society to deal with legal cases. A *qāḍī* or a *muftī* finds out which general or abstract principle governs a specific case. Sometimes this knowledge is easily available and often it requires a great effort. This whole process is called *ijtihād* (4:93).

It is in this particular context that Shāṭibī defines *ijtihad* as a process in which one exhausts one's efforts to one's full capacity in order to acquire exact or probable knowledge to reach judgement in a given case (4:113).

FOUR TYPES OF *IJTIHĀD*

Experience tells us that the number of such cases is very small that are entirely new and that have no bearing on the preceding cases. Due to extensive activity of the jurists in the field most legal matters have already been examined. Hence a judge or a *muftī* need not exercise *ijtihād* in each and every case. *Taqlīd* (following the precedent) may suffice in most matters (4:100). This is in this perspective that Shāṭibī discovers following four types of *ijtihād*.

(1) ***Taḥqīq al-Manāṭ al-'Āmm*** (Identification of general anchor point[2])

In this type, the rule, a *shar'ī* precept (*mudrak*), is already established. The function of the *mujtahid* is to identify the anchor point of law in general terms in a given case (4:91). In other words the basis of the legal provisions are examined so as they are applicable to all the *mukallafīn*. The generality, here, is further explained by Shāṭibī to mean that this type concerns *anwā'* (types) of *mukallafīn,* and not the *ashkhāṣ* (individuals) (4:97).

Shāṭibī illustrates this point by an example of the *shar'ī* ruling that requires a witness to be *'adl* (just). The general and broad meanings of *'adl* are known, but to determine the characteristics and qualifications on the basis of which a witness can be typically described as *'adl* is the function of a *mujtahid*. There are two levels of inquiry here. First, to define the characteristics of *'adl* and the second, to verify whether the witness in question possesses those charecteristics. The first level belongs to this type (4:91)

(2) ***Taḥqīq al-Manāṭ al-Khāṣṣ*** (Identification of particular anchor point)

Whereas the above type aimed at the identification of general charecteristics of a legal value or concept, the present type focuses on identification of the persons, acts or facts in a given case that correspond with these charateristics. For instance the term *faqīr* covers a wide range of persons as its referents. To define *faqīr* with particular reference to a specific point of law is *taḥqīq al-manāṭ al-'āmm*, because the inquiry is still general. However, to identify a particular person whether he answers that definition is called *taḥqīq al-manāṭ al-khāṣṣ* (4:91). For this a *mujtahid* relies more on *taqwā* (piety, care, and prudence) and *ḥikma* (wisdom, inner reason) (4:97-98). *Taqlīd* cannot solve this problem, becuase this process of evaluation can never end. Every new case is unique in itself in this respect (4:91). Furthermore, the *Sharī'a* does not pronounce its rulings to cover all particular cases individually. The rulings of the *Sharī'a* are general and abstract so that they can cover new cases whose number is infinite (4:92).

Shāṭibī regards the first and second types of *ijtihād* ever-continuing. The discontinuity of this *ijtihād* would make the application and extension of the rules of the *Sharī'a* impossible (4:105). If this type of *ijtihād* discontinues, the obligations of *Sharī'a* will exist only in man's minds, and not in practice (4:93).

(3) ***Tanqīḥ al-Manāṭ*** (Distinguishing between two anchor points)

This type concerns those cases where the proper qualification (*wasf*) is mentioned in the text of the ruling but in conjunction with another matter; the task of separating and distinguishing this qualification is done by *ijtihād* (4:95). Shāṭibī further explains that this type does not concern with the method of *qiyās*, but is rather a type of *ta'wīl al-ẓawāhir* (interpretation of the literal sense) (4:96). In a certain sense it also belongs to what Shāṭibī calls *al-ijtihād bi'l-istinbāṭ* (reasoning by inference) (4:162 f.). Other jurisprudence texts discuss this type under *masālik al-'illa* (the methods of finding the legal cause).

(4) ***Takhrīj al-Manāṭ*** (Locating the anchor point)

This type refers to the text of a ruling where *manāṭ* are not mentioned. The *manāṭ* are found through the process of deduction. This method is also called *al-ijtihād al-qiyāsī* or reasoning by analogy (4:96).

Shāṭibī maintains that among these four types, the first two are ever continuing (4:89) but the continuity of the other two depends on their need. The reasons for the continuity of the first two types have already been noted. Shāṭibī explains the need of continuing the other two as follows:

> The new events which were not known in the past are very few, in proportion to those which have occurred in the past, because of the expansion of the body of rules due to the investigation and *ijtihād* of the preceding jurists. It is therefore possible to accept their decisions (*taqlīd*) in the major part of the *Sharī'a* (4: 105).

Shāṭibī finds in *ijtihād* three processes. One that depends on inference and deduction and hence is connected with the written legal material. The second process of *ijtihād* is that where it is not directly concerned with the text, but with the law itself. In reference to the above-mentioned four types of *ijtihād*, these two processes are particularly relevant to *taḥqīq al-manāṭ* and *takhrīj al-manāṭ*. The third relates to deductions which require neither of the above types of knowledge (4:165 f). This process is, in fact, the application of the verified *manāṭ* to specific cases.

Consequently, in *ijtihād* two steps are inolved; first *taḥaqquq al-manāṭ* (investigation of the basis of ruling or anchor points) and second *taḥakkum* (judgement) (4:334). Shāṭibī explains further that the method of deduction of conclusion in *ijtihād* is quite different from what is followed by logicians. The premises here do not mean the formulation of propositions in accordance with the figures (*ashkāl*) of syllogism known in logic. Nor does *ijtihād* depend upon considerations of syllogism, such as *tanāquḍ* (contradiction) and *'aks* (conversion). If there is found any similarity, it must not be confused with the technical terms of logicians.

The closest logical figures of syllogism to the method of *ijtihād* are *qiyās iqtirānī* (syllogism by coupling or combining two propositions) or *istithnā'ī* (syllogism by exclusion) (4:337). Shāṭibī quotes the Māliki jurist Abu'l Walīd al-Bājī (d. 1081) who rejected logicians' claims that there cannot be a conclusion without two premises, and, referring to *fiqh*, argued that it is possible to conclude from one premise only (4:339).

It is in the light of this explanation that Shāṭibī rejects the requirement of a knowledge of the rules of logic for *shar'ī* purpose, (4:339) whereas knowledge of the Arabic language and that of the objectives of law is considered *sine qua non*. As for other sciences such as the science of the readings of the Qur'ān, or that of *ḥadīth*, or *kalām*, they are not considered absolutely necessary. In fact, a *mujtahid* can justifiably accept the conclusions reached by these sciences as *muqaddimāt* (premises, foundations) in *ijtihād* (4:110-111). For Shāṭibī's views on this subject let us analyse the qualifications he prescribes for a *mujtahid*.

QUALIFICATIONS FOR *IJTIHĀD*

With reference to the above four types, Shāṭibī explains that there are two levels of *ijtihād* activity: Simple and specialised (4:233).

SIMPLE *IJTIHĀD*

Simple *ijtihād*, mostly relating to the type of *taḥqīq al-manāṭ*, may be exercised by any one. In this type original *ijtihād* is not necessary. *Taqlīd* also suffices (4:93). That is mostly in cases where identification of an anchor point relates to genus, and not to an individual. For instance the question of determining of puberty. The general principles are already fixed by the jurists. What is left is only application of this principle to a specific case. According to Shāṭibī, simple *ijtihād* does not require any special qualifications, only the knowledge of the subject matter, even on secondary level, is sufficient.

Simple *ijtihād*, according to Shāṭibī, refers to the universal principles which are commonly understood by a specialist and a common man (4:238).

Shāṭibī explains that laws revealed in Mecca were general, universal and simple. They, however, continue to be the first principles of Islamic law. The process of *ijtihād* is simple as long as it is a question of general principles and their application.

That is why Shāṭibī argues that even a non-believer can participate in the exercise of *ijtihad* as long as it belongs to the category of simple *ijtihād*, because it is only a mechanical activity. However, when a case requires examination in detail, and determination of the value of a genus, then it becomes the case of specialised *ijtihād* (4:111).

SPECIALISED *IJTIHĀD*

With reference to the above categories, *tanqīḥ al-manāṭ, takhrīj al-manāṭ, taḥqīq al-manāṭ al-'āmm* are called specialised *ijtihād* and would require an expert to exercise it.

According to Shāṭibī an *ijtihād* in these categories is valid only if exercised by those who are qualified to do so and have attained the required skills (4:167). Essentially there are two basic requirements for a qualified *mujtahid* (a person who exercises *ijtihād*): (1) perfect understanding of the purpose of law (*maqāṣid al-sharī'a*), and (2) command on the skill of deduction on the basis of this understanding. What is the purpose of law? How is it established? What is its scope? These are the questions that have been elaborated in detail in earlier chapters. When a person attains a level of understanding where he can perceive the intent of the Lawgiver in each of the rulings of Divine law and in its various classes, he acquires the qualification to be a deputy of the Prophet in his functions of *ta'līm* (teaching), *futyā* and *ḥukm* (4:107).

The second requirement, i.e. the skill to deduce rules is in fact subservient to the first. The understanding of the purpose of law is truly demonstrated in this skill. However, there are three levels of attaining this skill: (1) *mujtahid*, (2) *ḥāfiẓ* (master of the sources), (3) *'ālim* (who can consult others). *Ijtihād* is validly exercised only by the scholars at first two levels (4:108). It is not necessary to attain the level of *ijtihād* in each relevant science. *Ijtihād* is itself an independent science and hence the premises and postulates taken from other sciences are assumed to be true in this science as they are not its subject matter (4:110). As we have mentioned earlier, Shāṭibī argues that *ijtihād* can be exercised by a non-believer in God, in Prophethood and in Divine law because *ijtihād* is based on postulates that are assumed to be valid *a priori* regardless whether he believes them to be actually so (4:111).

The science on which the validity of *ijtihād* depends and which must be acquired is that of Arabic language. It does not mean grammar, syntax, lexicology, and semantics or other branches of linguistics. It rather refers to the general knowledge about language. The level of attainment in this science is like that of experts such as Khalīl, Sībawayh and others (4:115). It means that a person must attain a level where he understands the Arab usage like an Arab (4:115). Shāṭibī distinguishes between two types of requirement for the knowledge of Arabic language. If *ijtihād* refers to deduction from the texts, the knowledge of Arabic language is essential, but if it relates to meaning, concepts and ideas in abstract without reference to text, the knowledge of Arabic is not essential (4:162).

In cases of *taḥqīq al-manāṭ*, knowledge of the purpose of law is not required, nor the knowledge of Arabic language. For instance, where a case requires the expertise of *ḥadīth*, a *mujtahid* may rely on a *muḥaddith* regardless whether the latter knows about the purpose of law or Arabic language. What is relevant is his skill to distinguish between a sound and a weak *ḥadīth* (4:165).

In addition to the above, the knowledge of conflicting opinions and the basis of their conflict is also essential for the exercise of *ijtihād* (4:161-162).

Shāṭibī also discusses different levels in the attainment of knowledge and their relevance to the exercise of *ijtihād*. He explains that a seeker of knowledge passes through three stages in the attainment of knowledge:Firstly, as a student, he reaches a stage where his mind stimulates him to examine what he has learnt and to investigate the causes. This state arises due to perception of some meanings and principles behind certain rules, but it is vague and partial. He has still some doubts and questions for which he turns to his teacher. In this state a student often wavers between conflicting views and is not clear. At this stage therefore he should withhold himself from exercising *ijtihād* and adhere to *taqlīd* (4:225).

Secondly, a scholar reaches a clearer understanding of the meaning in his learning by examination and by means of legal proofs. He achieves certainty. If there are doubts, he finds himself capable to dispel them by arguing against them. Is this scholar qualified to exercise *ijtihad*? Shāṭibī examines arguments from both sides without resolving the conflict. It appears that Shāṭibī is not sure about the ability of the scholar at this stage.

Thirdly, a scholar investigates both sides of the case and determines legal meaning in the specific case quite objectively, inclining to neither side. From this position he decides in favour of the view that is more appropriate considering the act of the obligees (4:232). Shāṭibī regards this stage as that of a wise jurist, and a philosopher who is par excellence qualified to exercise *ijtihād*. His *ijtihād* is undoubtedly valid. He has the required ability and the command. A scholar in this stage is capable of issuing a *fatwā* that is appropriate to the inquirer's particular conditions, whereas a scholar in the second stage responds on the basis of universals, not in view of specifics of the case. A scholar in the third stage examines the consequences before answering the question, whereas a scholar in the second position does not concern himself with consequences (4:233).

Consideration of consequences of a judgement is quite essential to Shāṭibī in exercising *ijtihād*. He elaborates that a *mujtahid* should judge an act committed by a person in favour or against, only after examining its consequences (4:194). An act may be lawful in itself but it may have consequences that are contrary to the goals of the law. Similarly, an act may be unlawful itself, but its effects may be lawful. It is therefore necessary to take effects of a legal act or judgement into consideration. According to Shāṭibī the following juridical rules are based on this principle: (1) *ḥiyal* (Legal Devices) (3) *murā'āt al-khilāf* (consideration of conflicting opinions), (4) *istiḥsān* (juristic preference). He mentions here another rule: allowing the pursuit of a *maṣlaḥa* which is surrounded by unlawful matters. For instance marriage makes it obligatory to earn livelihood for the family, but the legality of most means of earning is doubtful, or one may be compelled to follow an unlawful trade. Seeking livelihood in these cases would be allowed in view of this principle with the condition that the person avoids the unlawful as much as possible (4:210).

Shāṭibī quotes Mālik's following code for the exercise of *ijtihād*, spelling out the various steps of the process:

> The rule is that you examine the given case in the light of the *Sharī'a*. If it is correct according to the *Sharī'a* then consider its consequences in the context of the conditions of its time and its people. If by its mention your mind does not recall any evil then submit it to reason. If you feel that it will be accepted by reasonable people, then you may give your opinion in general terms if the case relates to a matter that is generally acceptable. If it cannot be generalised then give specific opinion. If the case in question does not accept this process, then it is better to keep silent that would be more in conformity with the welfare of the people, legal as well as rational (4:191).

INVALID *IJTIHĀD*

The requirement in the above principle to consider particular circumstances of the individual does not, however, warrant arbitrary interpretation of Islamic law. That would render *ijtihād* invalid (4:167). There may, however, be cases where error is not intentional, for example when some evidence was not known or was not obvious to the scholar at the time of judgement. In such cases, the judgement becomes invalid if it was repugnant to the *Sharī'a* (4:170). It shall not even be counted as a difference of opinion because it does not constitute *ijtihād* at all.

Another type of invalid *ijtihād* is when it is motivated by a hidden desire leading the scholar to ignore clear facts and evidence. His opinion is sometimes in conflict partially and sometimes totally with the universals and general principles of the *Sharī'a*. This situation may arise when a scholar considers himself a mujtahid or others believe him to be so and his opinion is counted as such. An *ijtihād* based on hasty judgements and interpretation does not exhaust all the meanings and implications of a text (4:175).

The discussion so far has been concerned with the process of *ijtihād* common to both a *qāḍī* and a *muftī*. Shāṭibī distinguishes *fatwā* as a separate form of *ijtihād* which we discuss in the next section.

2. *FATWĀ*

Shāṭibī discusses *fatwā* as a form of *ijtihād*, to distinguish it from *qaḍā* or *ḥukm*. He argues that *muftī* succeeds Prophet Muḥammad in his capacities of the transmitter of laws and legislator (4:245). A *mufti* conveys the laws to society either exactly as he has received them from the Prophet or by interpretation of the transmitted texts. The latter capacity is that of a legislator.

A *fatwā* is expressed by a *muftī* in the following three manners:

1) Verbal: An opinion expressed verbally or in writing;

2) Action: An answer given to a question by bodily gesture such as by nodding his head or waving his hand, or by some signs. A *muftī*'s view may also be known by his action or practice (4:247). Shāṭibī explains that psychologically human beings tend to imitate actions of others, especially those of the leaders of the community, particularly when they have a feeling of love and respect for the leader.

3) Approval/confirmation. The silence of a *muftī* in response to a question regarding a certain act or practice also constitutes *fatwā*. This amounts in fact to his approval.

Discussing validity and legitimacy of a *fatwā*, Shāṭibī distinguishes between legal and actual authority. Since a *muftī* is a successor of the Prophet, his action should not be contrary to the *fatwā*. In this sense if the *fatwā* is contrary to the dictates of knowledge i.e. he gives an opinion contrary to law, or his actions are contrary to the men of religion, his *fatwā* will have no legitimacy. Contradiction of one's words by his deeds affects the validity of a *fatwā*. He loses the right of authority (4:256), as people do not respect him.

If a *muftī*'s actions are openly violative of ethical norms, his *fatwā* is not binding. His *fatwā* may be in strict accordance with the evidence and principles, but since his own conduct is contrary an inquirer cannot be certain whether the muftī is reliable. Hence he is not bound to abide by the *fatwā*. But if *muftī*'s conduct is not openly contrary then his *fatwā* is acceptable, and an inquirer is exonerated of his obligation if he follows the *fatwā* (4:258).

In Shāṭibī's estimation a *muftī* at the highest level is the one who deals with people on the scale of an average of the well known rules that is suitable for the majority, neither leading to hardship nor to leniency amounting to anarchy and disintegration of society. He keep a balance between the two extremes (4:259).

Shāṭibī distinguishes on this point between a *mujtahid* and a *muftī* saying that as a *mujtahid* he may opt for himself an obligation which is harder than the average. However, as a *muftī* he should not make this option known because people follow him and it may not be convenient for them (4:260).

3. *ISTIFTĀ'*: PROCESS OF LEGAL INQUIRY

When a person faces a religious question and he is not well versed to find an answer himself, he is obliged to make an inquiry. This inquiry is called *istiftā'* and the inquirer a *mustaftī*. Shāṭibī says that God has not obliged men to remain ignorant. Therefore it is one's duty to seek knowledge by inquiry. But this inquiry must be addressed to a person who is expert in that matter (4:262). If there are more than one persons, he should follow a process of legal enquiry called *al-takhyīr wa'l tarjīḥ* (choice and preference). Preference should be given to a muftī who fulfils all the conditions required for his appointment for this position and whose words and deeds agree with his *fatāwā*. In short he is a person who you can follow even without posing a question because his personal practice provides answers to most of such questions (4:271). The reason is that such a person commands respect and authority and his *fatwā* appeals to the heart of the people. If such a person is not obviously available as the *muftī*s vary in their level of conformity between their words and deeds, preference may be given to the one who is better than others in this regard (4:271).

Shāṭibī stresses this point because he considers *muftī* to be a person whom people obey. Obedience to a religious authority is justified on two grounds. Firstly, infallibility as in the case of the Prophet or his companions or consensus. Secondly, official position as in case of judges and other officials. In these two cases the question of choice or preference does not arise. It is in cases other than these that obedience will not be justified before enquiry (4:283). We have spoken above about the three stages of attainment of knowledge. Only a *muftī* whose *ijtihād* is considered valid merits obedience. According to Shāṭibī, a true *muftī* does not hasten to issue *fatwā*, and takes utmost care in giving his opinion (4:286), because a *fatwā* has same value for a layman as a revealed text has for a *mujtahid* (4:282).

Shāṭibī then proceeds to discuss certain rules for the legal inquiry. The following is a brief summary.

1. A *muftī* is not bound to answer every question posed to him. He is obliged to answer in the following situations: (a) when he knows the specific subject matter in question in a given case or there is a clear legal ruling in the matter. (b) The inquirer can understand his answer. (c) The question does not lead to affectation. (d) The question relates to a legal act. On the contrary, a *muftī* is not bound to answer a question (a) that is not specific, (b) that needs further investigation, or (c) when there is no clear legal text available (4:313).

2. Excess of questions is objectionable. According to Shāṭibī, asking too many questions and indulging in inquiries on pure imaginary and theoretical probabilities is not approved particularly when the question is not religiously useful, and is hypothetical, unreal, and polemical (4:320).

Finally, Shāṭibī makes a very significant observation by noting that legal inquiry is quite distinct from logic. Legal reasoning is not necessarily based on the logical format of two premises yielding to the conclusion. In logic, an analogy can be established and a conclusion can be drawn only from two premises. In legal reasoning it is not necessary. There is, therefore, no need to follow rules of logic in discovering legal meaning. Often the conclusion is drawn from one premise alone (4:339).

The need for *ijtihad* was often justified by the jurists by arguing on the basis of *khilāf*. In other words if the opinion of scholars differed on a certain point, the case was considered open for *ijtihād*. For Shāṭibī this implied *khilāf* in the *Sharī'a,* which he vehemently rejected. He maintained that in its basis *Sharī'a* has unity; *khilāf* is neither intended to exist nor to perpetuate (4:118). What justifies *ijtihād* is the absence of rules to cover new cases. Hence *khilāf* in this technical sense is not sufficient to justify continuity of *ijtihād* (4:128). Let us analyse Shāṭibī's views on *khilāf* in the next chapter.

NOTES

1. Numbers in parenthesis refer to the volume and page number of *Al-Muwāfaqāt* (Cairo: Muṣṭafā Muḥammad, N.D.)

2. We have translated *manāṭ* as anchor point because it suits to Shāṭibī's discussion. *Manāṭ*'s root *n-w-ṭ*, literally means to hang or attach something, and *manāṭ* means a place on which a thing is hung or attached for security. In its secondary meaning *nāṭa* means to make something heavy by attaching it to something else, and thus placing it at a distance from other things. It also means to cut or separate a thing from others by one's own judgement without consulting others. It is spoken for tying a camel for security, for a fixed point in heaven for a star and for anchor to secure a boat in water.

   It is significant that Shāṭibī uses this term in place of *'illa* (cause) which is generally used by the jurists in the context of *qiyās*. Shāṭibī's use of this term avoids the question of causality and also the presumed infallibility of syllogistic method of reasoning.

   The use of the term *manāṭ* stresses that the relationship between the rule of law and this point is not that of cause and effect, i.e. the rule does not come into existence or its compliance does not take place necessarily by the existence or occurrance of this point. It only means that a rule is hung, suspended or attached to this point to secure it. The act of attaching or suspending is not attributable to the jurist. His effort only consists of identifying, distinguishing and locating this anchor point.

CHAPTER TWELVE

AL-KHILĀF: DIVERSITY

It has been stated earlier that the aspect of disagreement in Mālikī *fiqh* was the problem that struck Shāṭibī's mind early in his career and continued to perplex him even later. Often *khilāf* was argued as a valid justification for further *ijtihād*. Shāṭibī maintained that the *Sharī'a* is a unity, *khilāf* is neither intended to exist nor to perpetuate (4:118).[1] *Khilāf* cannot constitute justification for *ijtihād* (4: 128). He wrote to many scholars and disputed with them on the many facets of this matter.

Because of various historical reasons which do not concern us here, Mālikī *fiqh* abounded with disagreement on a number of cases. This was a very perplexing phenomenon for a tradition which upheld the consensus of scholars and the unity of the practice. Consequently scholars were occupied in a perennial discussion on this issue.

Very broadly speaking, in the course of time, during the development of the Maliki tradition in Spain, four positions were taken on this issue. First, some scholars, foremost among them Ibn 'Abd al-Barr (d. 463/1079), denied the existence of "disagreement" in Mālikī *fiqh*. This position was taken generally by some other ancient scholars also (4:151). It was essentially this position that Shāṭibī came to adopt after lengthy discussion.

The second position in this respect was taken under the influence of the *taṣawwuf*.[2] Since Ṣūfī-oriented jurists feared that an indulgence in cases where disagreement existed might lead someone astray in seeking for lenient options, they regarded it an obligation to avoid the cases of disagreement. They considered these lenient options as instances of *rukhṣa* (concession) in contrast to *'azīma* (regular) cases which were the only path to be followed by a resolute person (4:144-45). Shāṭibī traced this trend to the teachings of Qushayrī on the basis of which in a later period upholders of the position had adopted the following formulation: "*al-wara' bi'l khurūj 'an al-khilāf*" (piety consists in avoiding the cases of disagreement). Under the impact of *taṣawwuf*, this position had been accepted by a number of *fuqahā'* as well.

Shāṭibī regarded the Ṣūfīs' renunciation of *rukhṣa* as an attitude appropriate to the *khawāṣṣ* (special, elite) and *arbāb al-aḥwāl* (the people of mystical states). He questioned this trend when it meant imposition of an impossible obligation for common people. He took this stand because the ṣūfī-oriented jurists had gone as far as to consider *wara'* obligatory for every one (4:104). Shāṭibī wrote to scholars in Spain and North Africa. Among the replies to his query, Ibn 'Arafa's *fatwā* is available to us as preserved by Wansharīsī.[3] In his question, Shāṭibī states that scholars such as Ghazālī, Ibn Rushd and Qarāfī maintained that piety consisted in avoiding "disagreement". The basis of their argument was that the cases of disagreement in the details (*furū'*) of *shar'* were like *mutashābihāt* (equivocal statements) which the Prophet urged to avoid. Shāṭibī found it logically impossible to maintain such a position. Ibn 'Arafa's answer can be summarized as follows. He explained that the cases of disagreement were very few and that to avoid them was not only possible but obligatory. The reason was that these cases, being equivocal, had equally forceful arguments in favour and against; such a situation would then be conducive only to an arbitrary decision. Ibn 'Arafa insisted that to opt for the less convenient was the result of the fear of severe punishments from Allah. This fear was the reason why Ibn Ḥazm condemned those who sought for convenience in the *Sharī'a*. Ibn 'Abd al-Salām also condemned the trend to choose the more convenient of any two *fatāwā*.[4]

The third position considered the existence of "disagreement" a proof of permissibility. Shāṭibī stated this position in the following words:

> Often where scholars' views on a certain matter differed, a *fatwā* recommended abstention (from the matter in question). It was said, "Why do you recommend abstention whereas the problem is disagreed upon?" Thus the disagreement became the proof of permissibility, simply because it was disagreed upon; neither was there any evidence in favour of its possibility, nor was it based on a worthier authority to be followed than the one which demanded abstention (4:141).

MURĀ'ĀT AL-KHILĀF

The fourth position was that of *murā'āt al-khilāf*. This principle not only admitted the existence of conflicting opinions of jurists but also regarded all the conflicting opinions equally valid. This principle in some cases led to free permissibility, in some to a hardship and in others to mere impossibility. Although it was a commonly accepted position, Shāṭibī differed and disputed it with a number of scholars. Among them the names of Ibn Qabbāb, Fishtālī, Ibn 'Arafa and Sharīf Tilimsānī are known to us.[5] To help appreciate the problem, this discussion is summarised below.

In Granada there arose a certain issue in which different opinions were attributed to Mālik. According to the *Uṣul al-fiqh*, every one of these contradictory opinions had to be rejected. It was further realized that such disagreement existed in the major part of the Mālikī tradition. If the rules of contradiction were applied, most of the Mālikī tradition would have to be rejected. As a measure of necessity (*ḍarūra*), Mālikī *fuqahā'* adopted the principle of *murā'āt al-khilāf* saying that all of those opinions were equally valid. The application of this principle, however, posed a number of problems.[6]

Shāṭibī illustrated the difficulty in the application of this principle by citing a number of cases. If in a particular case of marriage scholars disagreed on the validity of that marriage, it was to be considered void. Yet in reference to its effects an allowance was to be made for the opinion that favoured its validity. Hence rules such as inheritance remained effective as if the marriage were valid. The problems that this position raised for Shāṭibī were the following:

(i) It disregarded the established principle of *Uṣul al-fiqh*, that the consideration of time could declare one of those opinions as 'later' and hence more reliable.

Another principle relevant to cases of contradictory opinions was also discarded. It stated that if two contradictory opinions were attributed to a *mujtahid* both of them should be suspended until one of the two could be established with certainty.

(ii) The Mālikī scholars were not consistent in applying this "allowance" (*murā'āt al-khilāf*). In some cases they denied the "allowance", while in other cases they insisted on it. This inconsistency made the soundness of this principle doubtful. On the other hand, it rendered its application arbitrary.

(iii) Thirdly, assuming the soundness of this principle, its basis in the *Sharī'a* as a principle of *fiqh* is not known. Apparently this problem refers to evidence (*dalīl*). The difference between two statements (*qawl*) must inevitably be so because they are based on two different pieces of evidence which are contradictory to each other in the sense that the opposite of one is the requirement of the other.[7] Thus *murā'āt al-khilāf* would mean granting each one of such statements what is required by the other, entirely or partially.

Sharīf Tilimsānī answered the question[8] by refuting Shāṭibī's argument that among two statements of an *imām* or a *mujtahid*, the later in time eliminated the earlier. Tilimsānī questioned the consideration of time factor in such cases, and argued that this consideration implied the principle of abrogation (*naskh*) which was applicable only to statements originating from the Lawgiver (*Shāri'*). He distinguished between the three: *Shāri', al-mujtahid al-muṭlaq* and *mujtahid fi'l madhhab*. Since it was the *Shāri'* alone who could institute laws and who could withdraw them, it was, therefore, in his statements alone, that in case of contradiction the later would abrogate the earlier. The *mujtahid*, whether "*muṭlaq*" or "*fi'l-madhhab*," did not make laws but rather sought and decided in favour of one of the pieces of evidence. *Al-mujtahid al-muṭlaq* sought evidence in the commands of the *Sharī'a*; the *mujtahid fi'l-madhhab* sought evidence in the statements of *al-mujtahid al-muṭlaq* whom he considered the *imām* for his *madhhab*. The differences of opinion in the case of *mujtahids* was, therefore, based on the difference in choice of evidence. The evidence, derived from the *Sharī'a*, in the instance of each of the opinions could not be invalid. Hence the question of later and earlier, with the effect of one eliminating the other, could not arise in the case of opinions by a *mujtahid*.

Tilimsānī did not oppose the principle of *murā'āt al-khilāf*. If one follows his argument more closely, one may see that he regarded this principle as necessary. Since all the different opinions of *mujtahids* are supposed to be based on certain evidence from the *sharī'*, by neglecting any of them one would be committing the wrong of rejecting a *shar'ī* evidence.

Tilimsānī's elaboration, however, did not answer Shāṭibī's question. It admitted that the basis of difference lay in the legal evidence itself, but it did not explain how one could claim the existence of two or more contradictory pieces of evidence in the *Sharī'a* on the same case.

Ibn 'Arafa's answer[9] was longer than others. His answer consisted partly of the arguments already seen in Tilimsānī's reply and partly of whittling down Shāṭibī's arguments to contradictions. He explained the principle of *murā'āt al-khilāf* from a different perspective. He defined *murā'āt* as abiding by the implications of the *Sharī'a* evidence not only in a given case (*madlūl*) but also its implications in other cases. In other words, as a matter of fact, the principle of *murā'āt* implied abiding by the implications of evidence in those aspects in which a *mujtahid* prefers one piece of evidence to another. In this way, he was neglecting neither of them but was rather abiding by the both at the same time.

Abū 'Abd Allāh al-Fishtālī adopted Ibn 'Abd al-Salām's view in his answer. In reference to an action which was considered wrong by one *mujtahid* and was regarded as sound by the other, Fishtālī distinguished between two situations; one before the occurrence of the action and the other after its occurrence. According to him, the prohibition was absolute in the former situation, but once the action had taken place, an allowance may be given to the opposite opinion for the sake of public convenience.[10] For instance in case of a void marriage, implications of voidability differ before and after the consummation.

Ibn al-Qabbāb's answer was very succinct and brief. He regarded *murā'āt al-khilāf* as one of the best principles of Mālikī *fiqh*. He defined it as granting to each one of the two pieces of evidence its value (*ḥukm*). He, however, distinguished between two situations; one was a case of disagreement where it was inevitable to prefer one opinion over the other. Of this type are the cases of *ta'āruḍ* (conflict) and *tarjīḥ* (preponderance). Second was the situation where both pieces of evidence led to the same conclusion or in some sense complemented each other. Such an instance was a case of *murā'āt al-khilāf.*[11]

UNITY OF *SHARĪ'A*

Shāṭibī was not satisfied with these answers. They were either irrelevant or they tried to explain away the evident meaning. The only point on which Shāṭibī and Ibn al-Qabbāb agreed was that the problem was really very abstruse.[12] Shāṭibī believed that there was no place for "disagreement" in the *Sharī'a* such as that would constitute the basis of *murā'āt al-khilāf*. Hence the principle of *murā'āt* was false. The main conclusion that Shāṭibī reached was the unity of the origins of *Sharī'a*. He maintained that, "all rules of *Sharī'a* originate from one root, even though there may be a diversity of rules" (4:118).

The basis of this conclusion were the following five points (4:118-132):

(i) A large number of Qur'ānic verses stress the original unity of the *Sharī'a* and, further, they condemn "disagreement".

(ii) If disagreement were permissible, there would be no place for the question of abrogation. The need for the discussion of abrogation means only that two statements are so contradictory to one another that one has to be replaced by the other.

(iii) If the existence of disagreement were permitted, it would imply the imposition of an impossible obligation. In other words, to command someone to obey two mutually contradictory commands at the same time is to put him under an impossible obligation.

(iv) The legal theorists (*uṣūliyyīn*) recommend a decision in favour of rejection of one of the contradictory evidences over the other. This fact implies the non-permissibility of "disagreement".

(v) It would be absurd to maintain that both of the contradictory commands are simultaneously intended by the Lawgiver because one would negate the other.

Apart from the linguistic, geographical and historical causes of "disagreement", it was claimed that there were certain factors in the *Sharī'a* itself that seemed to favour disagreement. Among these, three factors are worth noting (4:211-214).

First, the existence of *mutashābihāt* (equivocations) in the Qur'ān. These equivocations make allowance for the disagreement of opinions, expressed either in interpretation or in suspension of the judgement. Further, it cannot be denied that the *mutashābihāt* were intended to be equivocal by the Lawgiver. Shāṭibī discussed the problem of *mutashābihāt* in detail in *al-Muwāfaqāt*. He maintained that there was no *tashābuh* in the fundamentals of the *Sharī'a* (3:96).

Shāṭibī also disputed the assertion that *tashābuh* was the intention of the Lawgiver. Dealing with the matter in detail, he distinguished between two intentions (*irādāt*) of the Lawgiver: *al-khalqiyya al-qadriyya* (creational predestined intention) (3:119), and *al-amriyya al-tashrī'iyya* (imperative legal intention). Shāṭibī argued that *mutashābihāt* belong to the second category of Divine intention because here human will was free. There, disagreement is not intended by the Lawgiver, because the Qur'ān states that only one of the interpretations is correct. If disagreement were allowed, then every interpretation would have to be regarded as correct.

Second, justification for *khilāf* is drawn from the *Shar'ī* permission for *ijtihād* (legal reasoning). It is maintained that *ijtihād* naturally leads to disagreement. Shāṭibī refuted this argument. He maintained that every conclusion reached by a *mujtahid* was not correct. Its correctness or error depended on its correspondence with the intention of the Lawgiver who does not favour disagreement (4:127).

Third, *khilāf* was made analogous to the existence of the principle of *rukhṣa* in the *Sharī'a*. This principle, which means to opt for a concession from regular rules in special cases, allows for the existence of disagreement. Shāṭibī refuted this argument stressing that *rukhṣa* does not mean to opt for one of the two equally applicable rules in a case. If it were arbitrary, it would not be allowed in the *Sharī'a*. The principle of *rukhṣa* is applicable only in those cases where regular rules become hard or impossible to abide by. Thus, in fact, *rukhṣa* means two different rules in two different cases, not two different rules in a single case, which is the meaning of disagreement (4:144).

To summarise Shāṭibī's arguments, it may be said that he understood *khilāf* (disagreement) essentially as *ta'āruḍ al-adilla* (contradiction of evidences).

Hence, for Shāṭibī *khilāf* involved the problem of *tarjīḥ al-adilla* (preponderance) while for others it involved only the problem of *jam'* (combining) or *murā'āt* (making allowance).

Shāṭibī's methodological objection concerned the distinction made by Maliki scholars between *muttafaq 'alayh* (agreed upon) and *mukhtalaf fīh* (disagreed upon). They stressed that in case of the former, consideration could be given only to that evidence on which it was decided to be "agreed". In case of *mukhtalaf fīh*, however, the evidence on which the opposing decisions were based must also be considered. To Shāṭibī the above standpoint was inconsistent. If it were *shar'ī* evidence which provided the basis of a decision, then why was it opposed to a *muttafaq 'alayh*? Why should a decision be considered as *mukhtalaf fīh* when it was based on a *shar'ī* evidence? To agree with the upholders of *khilāf* would mean, for Shāṭibī, to believe in the existence of contradictions or diversity in the principles of the *Sharī'a*. This belief negates the unity of the origins of the *Sharī'a*.

To conclude this discussion, it may be said that Shāṭibī was not against difference of opinion and interpretation. What he was stressing was that every differing opinion was not correct and final. *Ijtihād*, though producing differing opinions, did not imply finality, because that would not only mean imposing one's opinion on others, but would also negate the unity of the *Sharī'a*, because all divergent opinions based on *ijtihād* would claim to be correct.

NOTES

1. Numbers in parenthesis in this chapter refer to the volume and page number of *Al-Muwāfaqāt* (Cairo: Muṣtafā Muḥammad, N.D.).
2. Ṣūfīs' views on *rukhṣa* are discussed in Shāṭibī, *al-I'tiṣām* (Cairo, 1915), Vol. 1, p. 169.
3. Al-Wansharīsi, *al-Mi'yār*, (Fas, 1314 H), vol. VI, p. 254-270.
4. *Ibid.*, p. 267.
5. *Al-Mi'yār*, pp. 254-280.
6. *Ibid.*, p. 254.
7. *Ibid.*
8. *Ibid.*, and Aḥmad Bāba, *Nayl al-Ibtihaj* (Cairo, 1351 H.), p. 262.
9. *Al-Mi'yār*, p. 262.
10. *Ibid.*, p. 274.
11. *Ibid.*
12. *Ibid.*, p. 271.

CHAPTER THIRTEEN

SHARĪ'A: THE SOURCE OF ISLAMIC LAW

Shāṭibī has defined most of the essential terms which he uses, but he does not give a definition of *Sharī'a*. An understanding of a term can, however, be obtained from other words used as its opposites or used in association with it.[1] Accordingly, we find that Shāṭibī's concept of *Sharī'a* is associated essentially with the notion of 'revelation'.

On the epistemological level the terms *'aql* (human reason) and *hawā* (desire)[2] are used as terms opposed to *Sharī'a*. Ontologically, *Sharī'a* is contrasted with *kawn* (being) (3:121).[3] Shāṭibī distinguishes between *kawn* and *Sharī'a* also as two different aspects of Divine Will. *Kawn* is the expression of the creative aspect of Divine Will, and *Sharī'a* is the expression of the legislative aspect. This distinction implies that in the first aspect there is no lapse of time between will (command) and the occurrence of an event. In other words when God wills creation of a thing it is created/occurs immediately. This immediate compliance is not implied, however, in the Legislative Will. For instance, God commands Muslims to pray, the event of performance of prayer does not occur automatically.

The term *Sharī'a* is also used as synonymous with *waḥy* (revelation) (2:169; 1:35). Since *waḥy* is a process and *Sharī'a* is not, the synonymous use of the two makes sense only if we understand *Sharī'a* as the substance and *waḥy* as a process of conveying it.

As for an explanation of the term through synonyms or substitutes in Shāṭibī's text, the Qur'ān is equated with the *Sharī'a* (3:369). The application of the term is also extended to *ḥadīth* of the Prophet, the *sunna* of the Prophet and that of his companions (1:46-47); but whereas the rulings in the Qur'ān are exact (*qaṭ'ī*) in general and in detail, the *sunna* is exact only in general, but probable (*ẓannī*) in detail (4:7). The absolute and original *Shāri'* is Allāh only. The Prophet, *muftī*s and *mujtahid*s are also considered to be *sharī'* by Shāṭibī, but they function on God's behalf (4:245), and not in their own right.

The characteristics of the *Sharī'a* that Shāṭibī has enumerated are the following: blessed (*mubāraka*), Arabic (2:64), general, accessible to a common unlettered person (*ummiyya*)[4], universal (*'āmma; kulliya*)[5], liberal (*samḥa*)[6], convenient (*sahla*)[7], protected (*ma'ṣūma*)[8]. We have already explained most of these terms in the preceding chapters.

FIQH, UṢŪL AL-FIQH AND *SHARĪ'A*

The other terms that are associated with the term '*Sharī'a*' are *fiqh* and *Uṣūl al-fiqh*. The term *fiqh* is used by Shāṭibī more in its literal and essential meanings than in the technical sense. The phrase *fiqh al-sharī'a* (2:59) as used by Shāṭibī may mean "understanding of the *Sharī'a*", "investigation of the *Sharī'a*" or "establishing the meaning of *Sharī'a*".

Shāṭibī, however, uses the term '*Uṣūl al-fiqh*' more often in a certain technical sense. In *al-I'tiṣām*, he defines it as follows:

> "*Uṣūl al-fiqh* means [to infer, by method of] induction of universal [principles] from the evidence [of *Sharī'a*] until the *mujtahid* finds them conspicuous (*nuṣb 'ayn*), and the searcher finds them easy to apply".

The equations he uses to explain the term *uṣūl* show that his concept of *Uṣūl al-fiqh* is very closely connected with that of *Sharī'a*. He argues that *Uṣūl al-fiqh* have the same relationship to *Sharī'a* that the *uṣūl al-dīn* (the principles of religion; *kalām*) have with *dīn*. (1:131) He explains that to *Qāḍī* Ibn al-Ṭayyib *Uṣūl al-fiqh* meant the principles of the science of the *Sharī'a* (in the epistemological sense), whereas to Imām al-Juwaynī they were the proofs (*adilla*) of the *Sharī'a*[9] (1:131). Shāṭibī did not consider them either as proofs or directives for the *Sharī'a*, but as the principles derived inductively from the underlying universal laws in the *Sharī'a* (1:29 ff).

An analysis of Shāṭibī's views of the origins of the *Sharī'a* reflects his concept of *Sharī'a* closely associated with 'revelation'. According to Shāṭibī, the *Sharī'a* is the light of knowledge.

> In their pre-*Sharī'a* state, mankind sought their ends at random. Because of its inclination to passions and desires (*hawā*), human reason is unable to discover the *maṣāliḥ* (good) of all mankind. It goes after personal and individual intersts. Its efforts, therefore, lead only to confusion. It drew conclusions with defective analogies; it sought health from a sick body. Mankind was walking in reverse yet it believed that it was on the right path. This state of self-assurance led to sheer determinism (*ijbār*) in the very concepts of freedom, power, and choice (*aqdār*). Necessitarianist values (*ḥukm al-iḍṭirār*) were attached to acquired acts (*al-af'āl al-muktasaba*). Men were in this plight, when

God showed His Grace and sent prophets to every people with *sharā'i'* (pl. of *Sharī'a*). The prophets explained to the peoples in their own languages what was the true right path (1:19-20).

This account of the origin of the *Sharī'a* is difficult to interpret in terms of time because Shāṭibī on other occasions argues that there never was a time without the *Sharī'a*. This account then can be understood either in an allegorical sense or in the sense that Shāṭibī was referring to what he calls the *fatra*, the period of interval in between periods of revelations of *sharā'i'*.

THE QUR'ĀN

The last *Sharī'a* in these series of revelations was sent to Prophet Muḥammad b. 'Abd Allah. God revealed to him His Book, the Qur'ān. This book established the criterion of distinguishing certitude from doubt (1:19-20).

The Qur'ān is the totality (*kulliya*) of the *Sharī'a*, the fountain-head of wisdom. It is the source of the *Sharī'a* (3:345). The Qur'ān began to be revealed first in Mecca and was continued in Medina. The universal principles were revealed in Mecca; they included, among other things, belief in God, the Prophet and the Hereafter, general rules such as prayer, alms, and general ethical rules about justice, virtue, patience, etc. These rules generally concerned religious and social practices in the pre-Islamic period. The general principles revealed in Mecca were complemented with additional particular rulings pertaining to contracts, prohibition of intoxicants, prescription of penal punishments, etc. (3:103-104).

The above account indicates that the *Sharī'a* insofar as it is a revelation of laws by God, was completed in the days of the Prophet. As to the question of change in the days of the Prophet, Shāṭibī maintains that the fundamental principles revealed in Mecca were permanent; they were never changed or repealed, because they were the necessary and essential matters. Abrogation (*naskh*) occurred only in particular details, not in universals (4:236).

In other words, the finality and immutability of Islamic law in the days of the Prophet meant the non-changeability of fundamentals of the *Sharī'a* only. Legal change is, however, possible in individual cases. Two legal institutions are involved in this matter, *futyā* and *qaḍā*.

LEGAL INSTITUTIONS

Shāṭibī considers *qaḍā* and *futyā* both as *wilāyāt* (administrative offices) (2:247). Like establishing a government, they are also *kifā'iyya* (societal obligations). In Shāṭibī's structure of *maqāṣid*, *kifā'iyya* (2:180) in contradistinction to *'ayniyya* which are specifically individual obligations of each person, are an obligation for the society as a whole, somehow to be fulfilled though each individual may not be involved. *Kifā'iyya* are still essential and necessary as they are among the *maqāṣid* of the *Sharī'a*. They are indeed complementary to *'ayniyya* because they make the fulfilment of the latter possible. The *kifā'iyya* aim at achieving the common good (*al-maṣāliḥ al-'āmma*) for all the people, because one individual by himself cannot take care of his interests or his family. How can he attend to the good of the whole society? One necessarily needs co-operation with others. Consequently one works for his own benefit but also toward the interests of others; thus the benefit of all is achieved by all. Such is the manner in which general (public) institutions such as *khilāfa, wazāra, niqāba, qaḍā* and *futyā* came into being. They were recognized by *Sharī'a* in the public interests because were they to be abandoned, the social order would be destroyed (2:177-179).

This clarification was necessary to show that *futyā* and *qaḍā* being societal obligations are functions performed on behalf of the whole society. Consequently the interests of the society as a whole are required to be considered.

AUTHORITY

Shātibī's concept of the *Sharī'a*'s authority is based on two notions: *'iṣma* and *qaṭ'iyya*. Though *'iṣma* implies freedom from error, yet it cannot be understood in the sense of infallibility in Shāṭibī's terminology. To him *'isma* is equivalent to *ḥifẓ* (safety, protection, assurance) from error or loss. He explains that the *'isma* of the Qur'ān has been attained through its wider study, preservation and the development of sciences relating to the Qur'ān. The *'iṣma* of the *Sharī'a* in the hands of the generation succeeding Prophet Muḥammad came to be as they inferred the rules of *Sharī'a* by seeking its objective from the Qur'ān and *Sunna*, sometimes literally, sometimes from its implications and sometimes by deducing the 'cause' (*'illa*) of the command. They applied these rules to cases that were unprecedented. In this way they made matters convenient for their successors. "This is the exact meaning of *ḥifẓ*..." (2:58-61).

Another serious problem in connection with the concept of *Sharī'a* was the wide differences of opinion among the jurists. Since *Sharī'a* found expression in *fiqh* in the post-Qur'anic period mostly through jurists' interpretations, the agreement or disagreement of jurists on a certain point acquired fundamental importance. Their consensus constituted *ijmā'*, a source of law next only to the Qur'ān and *Sunna*. Their disagreement too could not be underrated. The paradoxical problem of *murā'āt al-khilāf* that we have analysed earlier was very consequential for the doctrine of the unity of the *Sharī'a*. Shātibī's analysis of the problem shows that disagreement is not in *Sharī'a*, it is in *fiqh*.

In the preceding discussion of Shāṭibī's views on the nature of Islamic law we have seen that he does not regard law-making essentially an abstract intellectual exercise. Law is not known through intellect. For Shāṭibī the essential source of the knowledge of law is "revelation". The revelation makes the intention and will of Allah known to man. Shāṭibī develops the doctrine of the two aspects of Divine Will which was advanced by Ibn Taymiyya as well, a doctrine we have already discussed in the preceding chapters.

We have also seen in a preceding chapter that Shāṭibī explains the role of reason in his analysis of the definitions of *maṣlaḥa* and *taklīf*. He argues that since the realm of *kawn* is observable and measurable, *Sharī'a* has taken care that its laws conform to the laws of *kawn*, so that they become conveniently knowable to man. Shāṭibī has made it clear that in order to be abidable, a legal injunction must be physically possible. In other words a rule of *Sharī'a* must essentially conform to the laws of human physical nature. In his analysis of the *shar'ī* definition of *maṣlaḥa*, Shāṭibī observes that the *Sharī'a* has regularized as legal good what is considered to be good in social experience. Further, when in social experience a certain 'legal good' begins to harm the fabric of human society or even an individual, it loses its quality of being legally good.

To conclude, Shāṭibī distinguishes between *fiqh* and *Sharī'a*. *Fiqh* stands for substantive law. Islamic law (*fiqh*) has its source in *Sharī'a* (revelation) that aims at the protection of basic needs of mankind. Islamic law has developed through the process of *ijtihād* of the jurists. *Ijtihād* requires proper understanding of the objectives of the *Sharī'a* and the intent of the Lawgiver. A *mujtahid* must distinguish between two areas of *Sharī'a*: *'Ibādāt* where he cannot make any changes, and *'ādāt* where legal change is possible.

NOTES

1. For the validity of this method, we refer to the following work which has used this method in a highly successful manner: T. Izutsu, *God and Man in the Koran* (Tokyo, 1964).
2. *Al-Muwāfaqāt*, comm. 'Abd Allāh Dirāz (Cairo, n.d.), Vol. II, 169. Shāṭibī argues that the Qur'ān uses *waḥy* (revelation), which is the opposite of *hawā*. Elsewhere (Vol. I, 35), he contrasts the terms *'aqliyya* and *shar'iyya*.
3. Numbers in parenthesis refer to the above mentioned edition of *al-Muwāfaqāt*.
4. *Al-Muwāfaqāt*, vol.II, 69. Here the term *ummiyya* has not been translated in the usual literal sense, but in what it means in Shāṭibī's system of thought, especially in his theory of meaning.
5. *Ibid.*, 274-275.
6. *Ibid.*, 136.
7. *Ibid.*
8. *Ibid.*, 58. *Ma'ṣūm* is usually translated as "infallible", but in Shāṭibī's terminology, as he himself has explained, it means "protected", not "infallible".
9. *Al-I'tiṣām*, Vol. I, 19.

CONCLUSION

Shāṭibī's impact on modern Muslim legal thought is evident from frequent references to his works in almost all recent books on Islamic law. Notwithstanding this fact, few exclusive studies of Shāṭibī have appeared in European languages. Recent studies in Arabic language have also failed to bring out the originality in his thought. Not only this, but as we have noted, scholars like Goldziher, Margoliouth, Brockelmann, Rudi Paret, Malcolm Kerr and Asin Palacios have committed serious errors about Shāṭibī's name, origins, works and his date of death.

There could be many reasons for this state of affairs, but three of them stand out very prominently. First, until lately Islamic legal theory was not taken seriously by the Western scholarship. The situation has, however, improved in recent years. Second, Shāṭibī was presented by several modern scholars, like Goldziher and Rashīd Riḍā, as a crusader against *bid'a* and consequently his legal doctrines were studied in a reformist framework. Third, the concept of *maṣlaḥa* which was the fundamental principle of his philosophy did not enjoy the esteem that it actually deserved.

Muslim scholarship generally adhered to Ghazālī who examined *maṣlaḥa* within the framework of the theory of four sources and regarded it as an extra source and arbitrary principle. It was acceptable only if it was supported by the four sources. Ghazālī identified it with *maṣlaḥa mursala* or *istiṣlāḥ*, i.e. not based on *nuṣūṣ* and hence rejected like *istiḥsān*. Consequently, the legal validity of *maṣlaḥa* was questioned because it did not conform to the method of *qiyās*, which according to the theory of *uṣūl* was the only method that provided certainty. *Maṣlaḥa* was not also acceptable on theological grounds. Ash'arīs and Shāfi'īs argued that it attributed causality to God's commands. Consequently, *maṣlaḥa* as a legal theory suffered from the following weaknesses: arbitrariness, lack of support by the *nuṣūṣ* and uncertainty. Modern scholarship also regarded *maṣlaḥa* as a doctrine of expediency. Discussing *maṣlaḥa,* traditional as well as modern scholarship has usually focussed on jurists who were critical of *maṣlaḥa*. They did not study scholars like Shāṭibī, Ibn Qayyim, and Ibn 'Abd al-Salām.

Shāṭibī took interest in *maslaha* for various reasons. Firstly, because *maṣlaḥa* was essentially a Mālikī principle. Being a Mālikī, Shāṭibī was naturally inclined to this concept. Secondly, in contradistinction to Shāfi'īs who were interested more in theory of law and theological issues, Mālikī and Ḥanafī jurists both developed their jurisprudence closely connected with actual local practices and with substantive laws of their respective schools. Shāṭibī sought a synthesis between the methods of Ḥanafī and Mālikī schools, analysing *istihsān* and *istiṣlāḥ*. Thirdly, Shāṭibī found that the political, social, commercial and legal changes in Granada in fourteenth century posed problems that could not be solved by the deductive methods of *qiyās*. Consequently a principle more comprehensive than *qiyās* was required. Shāṭibī found this principle in *maṣlaḥa* that argues on the basis of the purposes of law defined by an inductive analysis of the *Sharī'a*.

Besides the factors mentioned above, Shāṭibī also responded to the Ṣūfī criticism of the morality of obligation as defined in *fiqh*. Ibn 'Aṭā' Allāh, Ibn 'Abd al-Salām and others questioned the moral validity of the *fiqhī* doctrines. They denied the consideration of personal interest and benifit in religious obligations, describing piety as giving up all personal interests. Shāṭibī rejected this criticism and argued that a Ṣūfī could give up personal interests but that could not be made a measure for all human beings in setting standards for legal obligation. He regarded such considerations as innovation of religious duties. Defining innovations in religious matters as *bid'a*, he distinguished *maslaha* from a *bid'a*, the former applied only to *mu'āmalāt* or *'ādāt* and the latter to *'ibādāt*.

Refuting the argument about the uncertainty of *maslaha,* Shātibī elaborated that *Uṣūl al-fiqh* or *Uṣūl al-Sharī'a*,—as he prefers to use the latter term in the title of the book—were certain because they conformed with the universally accepted principles. Further, since they were derived by a method of inductive reasoning that takes into consideration the totality of the Qur'anic verses and *aḥādīth*, contrary to *qiyās* that relies on individual verses or *aḥādīth*, these principles were more certain than those derived by *qiyās* because the latter was a method of deduction from one specific text.

In the introductory chapter of *al-Mawāfaqāt*, Shāṭibī deals specifically with this question of the certainty of the *Uṣūl al-fiqh*. He argues that laws in any human society are based on the following three universals: *Ḍarūriyāt*, *Ḥājiyāt*, and *Taḥsīniyāt*. These three universals are certain in Islam as well, because they conform not only with the laws of reason but also because they are derived by induction from the primary sources of Islamic law. He explains further that certainty and exactness in Islam are judged from the following three perspectives: (1) reason, (2) social practice, and (3) tradition. It is clear that by reason Shāṭibī means logic because he says that according to laws of reason there could be only three categories of values: necessary, possible and impossible. Similarly, in social practice also actions are divided into three categories: obligatory, permissible and forbidden. Traditionally, a transmitted text or practice is also classified into three categories: it is either continually reported exactly in the same words, or in the same meaning and thus producing exact indication in these two categories, or exactness may be derived on the basis of induction of the textual sources.

Shāṭibī observes that exactness is further judged in terms of validity and proof. The above three perspectives can only determine validity of a certain word, concept or action in view of their respected criteria. In order to describe anything as proven, however, one has to look beyond validity. The proof is established only by the occurrence of the concerned action in actual existence. Reason (i.e. logic) alone cannot provide proof of exactness. A thing defined to be rationally good may not be exactly so in actual existence. Similarly, a solitary report of a textual source cannot provide exactness. Exactness in this case can be achieved only by the method of induction. Thus, according to Shāṭibī, the exactness of the *Uṣūl al-fiqh* is based on a combined force of reason (logic), induction, and correspondence of these two with their actual occurrence in the world of existence, practice.

This is the framework in which Shāṭibī explains the exactness of *maṣlaḥa* or *al-Istidlāl al-mursal*. He says that a juristic principle like *maṣlaḥa*, even though not supported by a specific text, gains certainty and exactness by its conformity with the totality of legal commands and by its correspondence with the general and total meaning of textual sources. This principle is not only valid according to the criterion of reason and logic but is also proven by practice.

Shāṭibī explains further that even though principles of language and theology are discussed in *Uṣūl al-fiqh,* they are neither its subject matter nor they can provide exactness to it, because they cannot govern the interpretation of Islamic law. The basic criterion in Islamic Law is that the issue under consideration must be actual, useful and related with action and practice. Abstract and imaginative issues are regarded as irrelevant in Islamic law. Shāṭibī rejects abstract approach to legal problems. First, law must deal with the problems on the level that is comprehensible for a common man. Second, law must deal with actual conditions of society.

Shāṭibī is very critical of philosophical approach to *Uṣūl al-fiqh*. His criticism, however, should be understood in view of his apprehension against abstract and arbitrary opinions. He was not in favour of allowing a decisive role to reason (logic) in legal matters. According to him syllogistic reasoning is not sufficient in legal arguments. It must be ratified by inductive reasoning. Secondly, legal values cannot be determined by logic alone. They are informed by the tradition and practice of a society. A certain thing may be considered rational but it will be called legal only after it is declared so by a legislating process in a society. Thus an individual may find a certain law irrational, but he cannot call it illegal. In Shāṭibī's legal theory *'āda* (custom and nature) play a more positive role than reason.

Historians of Islamic law have noted two basic difficulties in its development as a law. First, its religious origins and early theological framework that led to its confusion with theology and did not allow its growth as law. Second, although the rulers, judges and government officials recognized *Sharī'a* as a source of law, yet they often differed with jurists in their interpretation of law. The jurists did not recognize legislation by rulers, judgements of courts and customary laws as part of Islamic law. Consequently, Islamic law developed into two parallel systems: Jurists' books (*fiqh*) and judicial practice (*'amal*). The difference of actual judicial practice from *fiqh* was considered a deviation from Islamic law. *Fiqh* became more and more isolated from law in practice and came closer to theology.

Separating *mu'āmalat/'ādāt* from *'ibādāt* in the subject matters of Islamic law, and restricting the application of *ta'abbud* to *'ibādāt* only, Shāṭibī tried to distinguish law from theology. His criticism of the concept of Ṣūfī piety (*'ibāda, ta'abbud*) and distinction of law from Ṣūfī concept of religion and morality, implied a positivistic approach to law. His emphasis on exactness by way of inductive method of reasoning, in contradistinction to the deductive method of *qiyās,* also indicated his positivistic philosophy.

We find that the main difficulty in Shāṭibī's philosophy of law lies nevertheless in his ambiguous treatment of the distinction between *'ibāda* and *'āda* at some places. Shāṭibī distinguishes *'āda* from *'ibāda*, saying that an *'āda* is subject to legal reasoning, whereas an *'ibāda* is not, and a change is allowed in *'āda* but not in *'ibāda*. It suggests that *'āda* is not immutable. Shāṭibī however, does not apply this distinction in case of *al-'awā'id al-Shar'iyya*, the social practices adopted by *Sharī'a*. He illustrates this point with several examples, including the law of non-admissibility of a slave's testimony. Although this law has its origins in the social practice, yet Shāṭibī regards it immutable because it is endorsed by the Qur'anic text. He, therefore, argues that even if a certain society begins to allow such testimony, Islamic law would not permit it.

The question is: Does a custom or social practice lose its status of *'ada* when adopted by *Sharī'a*? Does it transform into an *'ibāda*? Or is there a third category between *'āda* and *'ibāda*? What is the criterion for this categorization? Is it the textual mention of a law that makes it immutable? These questions need to be explored further, in the light of Shāṭibī's discussion of *'āda* and *'ibāda*. They need to be examined also with reference to Shāṭibī's views on the Qur'anic legislation that Meccan as containing universal principles. We shall examine these questions in our next study on Shāṭibī's concept of *'āda*.

BIBLIOGRAPHY

I. AL-SHĀṬIBĪ'S WORKS

Fatāwā al-Imām al-Shāṭibī. Edited by Abu'l Ajfān. Tunis: Author, 1987.

Al-Ifādāt wa'l inshādāt. Edited by Abū'l Ajfān. Beirut: Al-Risāla, 1983.

Al-I'tiṣām. Edited by Rashīd Rida. Cairo: Muṣṭafā Muḥammad. N.d. [1915]; 1332 A.H.

Al-Muwāfaqāt. 4 Vols.
Editions:
(i) Edited by Ṣaliḥ al-Qā'ijī and others. Tunis: Matba'a Dawlatiyya, 1884.
(ii) Edited and introduced by Musā Jārullāh. Kāzan, 1909;
(iii) Edited and commented by M. Al-Khiḍr Husayn. Cairo: Salafiyya, 1923;
(iv) Edited and commented by 'Abd Allah Dirāz. Cairo: Matba'a Tijāriya Muṣṭafā Muḥammad, n.d;
(v) Cairo: Raḥmāniyya. n.d.;
(vi) Edited by M. M. 'Abd al-Ḥamīd. Cairo: Muḥammad 'Alī, 1969;
(vii) Reprint of Dirāz edition. Bayrut: Dār al-Ma'rifa [1970].

Translations:

Turkish: Erdoğan, Mehmed (Translator). *Şâtibî el-Muvâfakât, Islâmî ilmiler metodoligisi*.
Istanbul: Iz Yayincilic, 1990.

Urdu: Kīlāni, 'Abd al-Raḥmān (Translator). *Al-Muwāfaqāt li'l-Shāṭibī*. Lahore: Diyal Singh Trust Library, 1992.

2. OTHER WORKS

'Abbādī, Aḥmad Mukhtār (ed.). *Mushāhadāt Lisān al-Dīn Ibn al-Khaṭīb fī bilād al-Maghrib wa'l-Andalus*. Iskandariyya: Jāmi'a Iskandariyya, 1958.

'Abbās, Iḥsān. Introduction to Ibn al-Khaṭib, *al-Katībat al-Kāmina* ... see Ibn al-Khaṭīb.

'Abd Allāh, 'Umar. *Sullam al-wuṣūl li 'ilm al-uṣūl*. Cairo: Dār al-Ma'ārif, 1956.

'Abduh, Muftī Muḥammad. "Taqrīr muftī al-diyār al-miṣriyya fī iṣlāḥ al-maḥākim al-shar'iyya". *Al-Manār* 2 (1899): 577-82, 593-8, 609-12, 625-28, 648-51, 663-66, 759-764.

'Abdullāh, 'Umar. *Malik's Concept of 'Amal in the light of Maliki Legal Theory*. Ph.D Dissertation. Chicago: University of Chicago, 1978.

Abu'l Naṣr, Jamīl, M. *A History of the Maghrib*. Cambridge: Cambridge University Press, 1971.

Abū Sinna, Aḥmad. *Madkhal al-fiqh al-Islāmī*. Cairo: Maṭba'a Lajnat al-Bayān al-'Arabī, Jāmi'a al-Azhar, 1965.

Abū Zuhra, Muḥammad. *Mālik*. Cairo: Maṭba'a Aḥmad 'Alī, 1946; Maktabat al-Anjalū al-Miṣriyya [1952].

_____. *Al-Shāfi'ī*. Cairo: Dār al-Fikr al-'Arabī, 1978.

Aghnides, N.P. *Mohammedan Theories of Finance*. New York: Columbia University; Longmans, 1916.

'Ajlān, Muḥammad 'Abd Allāh. "Adillat al-aḥkām al-shar'iyya fī uṣūl al-Shāṭibī". M.A. Thesis at Jāmi'at al-Imām Muḥammad bin Sa'ūd al-Islāmiyya, Riyāḍ, 1398 H.

Alston, W.P. *Philosophy of Language*. Prentice Hall, 1964.

Āmidī, Sayf al-Dīn. *Al-Iḥkām fī uṣūl al-aḥkām*. Cairo: Maṭba'a Ma'ārif, 1914.

Anderson, J.N.D. *Islamic Law in the Modern World*. New York: New York University Press, 1959.

Arnaldez, R. "Ibn Rushd". *The Encyclopaedia of Islam*. 2nd ed. vol. 3: 909-920. Leiden: Brill, 1971.

'Athamin, Khalil. "*Al-Nabiyy al-Umiyy*": An Inquiry into the Meaning of a Qur'ānic verse". *Der Islam*. Vol. 69 (1992) pp. 61-80.

Austin, J.L. *How To Do Things With Words*. Cambridge, M.A.: Harward Univ. Press, 1967.

A'ẓamī, Muḥammad Muṣṭafā. *On Schacht's Origins of Muhammadan Jurisprudence*. Riadh, 1985.

_____. *Studies in Early Ḥadīth Literature: With a critical Edition of some Early Texts*. Indianapolis: American Trust Publications, 1978.

Azhar. *Fihris Maktabat al-Azhariyya*. Cairo, 1946.

Bābā, Aḥmad. *Nayl al-ibtihaj* [on the margin of Ibn Farḥūn's *al-Dībāj al-mudhahhab*]. Cairo: 'Abbās b. 'Abd al-Salām, 1351 A.H.

Baghdādī, Ismā'īl Pāshā. *Īḍāḥ al-maknūn*. Cairo: Bahiyya, 1945.

Baṣrī, Abu'l Ḥusayn. *Al-Mu'tamad fī uṣūl al-fiqh*. Dimashq: Al-ma'had al-'ilmī al-firansī, 1964.

Batsieva, S.M. "Ibn Khaldūn et son milieu social". *Atti del Terzo Congresso di Studi Arabi e Islamici*. Napoli, 1967. Pp.133-144.

Bel, A. "Abd al-Wāḥid al-Rāshid". *The Encyclopaedia of Islam*. Ist ed. Leiden: Brill, 1913. I:66.

_____. "Almohades". *The Encyclopaedia of Islam*. Ist ed. Leiden: Brill 1913. I:314-318.

Bellefonds, Y. Linant de. "Immutabilité du droit musulman et réformes législatives en Égypte". *Revue internationale de droit comparé*. 7 (1955): 5-35.

_____. *Traité de droit musulman comparé*. Vol. I. Paris: Mouton, 1964.

Bercher, Leon. (Ed. Transl. Comm.) Ibn 'Acim. *Al-Acimiyya ou tuhfat al-h'ukkam fi nukat al-uqoud wa'l ah'kam*. Alger: Institute d'études orientales, 1958.

Bergsträsser, G. *Grundzüge des islamischen Rechts*. Berlin: J. Schacht, 1935.

Berque, J. "'Amal". *The Encyclopaedia of Islam*. 2nd ed. Leiden: Brill, 1960. I:427-28.

Bertrand, Louis and Charles Petrie. *The History of Spain*. Translated by W.B. Wells. New York: Appleton, 1934.

Birişik, Abd al-Hamid. "Al-Muwāfaqāt kī ishā'at ké muta'alliq chand bātén". Urdu translation of Mūsā Jārullāh's Turkish Introduction to Shāṭibī's *al-Muwāfaqāt* (1909 Edition). *Fikr-o Naẓar*. October - December, 1993.

Bousquet, G.H. *Précise de droit musulman*. Alger: Maison des Livres, 1947.

Bousquet, G.H. and J. Schacht (editors). *Selected Works of C. Snouck Hurgronje*. Leiden, 1957.

Brockelmann, Carl. *Geschichte der arabischen Litteratur*. Leiden: Brill, 1943-49.

_____. *Zweiter Supplementband*. Leiden: Brill, 1938.

Brunschvig, R. "Logic and Law in Classical Islam". Von. Grunebaum (editor). *Logic in Classical Islamic Culture*. Wiesbaden: Harrassowitz, 1970. Pp. 9-20.

_____. "Polémique medievals autour du rite de Malik". *Al-Andalus*, XV (1950). Pp. 377-435.

Būṭī, Sa'īd Ramadān. *Ḍawābit al-maslaha fī al-Sharī'a al-Islāmiyya*. Damascus: Umawiyya, 1966-67.

Cahen, Claude. "Body Politic". Von Grunebaum (editor). *Unity and Variety in Muslim Civilization*. Chicago: University of Chicago Press, 1955. Pp.132-158.

Cairns, Huntington. *Legal Philosophy from Plato to Hegel*. Baltimore: John Hopkins, 1967.

Chehata, Chafik. "Logique juridique et droit musulman". *Studia Islamica*. 13 (1965): 5-25.

_____. "L'équité en tant que sources du droit hanafite". *Studia Islamica*. Vol. XXV (1966): 123-138.

Cheneb, M. "Ahmed Baba". *The Encyclopaedia of Islam*. Ist ed. Leiden: Brill, 1913. I: 191-2.

Cherbonneau, M.A. "Lettre à M. Defremery sur Ahmad Baba le tombouctien, auteur du *Tekmilet ed-Dibadj*". *Journal Asiatique*. 5e Serie. I (1853): 93-100.

Codera, D.G., and Zaidin. *Tratado de numismatica arabigo-española*. Madrid: Murillo, 1879.

Coulson, N.J. "Doctrine and Practice in Islamic Law". *Bulletin of the School of Oriental and African Studies*. XVIII/2 (1956): 211-226.

_____. *A History of Islamic Law*. Edinburgh: Edinburgh University Press, 1964.

Couturat, Louis. *La logique de Leibniz d'aprés des documents inédit*. Paris, 1901.

_____. *The Algebra of Logic*. English translation by L.G. Robinson. London: Open Court, 1914.

Dawālībī, Ma'rūf. *Al-Madkhal ilā 'ilm uṣūl al-fiqh*. Beirut: Dār al-'ilm l'il Mala'īn, 1965.

Demombynes, M. Gaudefroy-. "Histoire des Benoul Ahmar". Translation from Ibn Khaldūn's *Kitāb al 'Ibar*. *Journal Asiatique*. 9th series. Vol. XII. Paris, 1898. 309-340; 407-462.

Dirāz, Muḥammad 'Abd Allāh. Introduction to Shāṭibī's *al-Muwāfaqāt*. Cairo: Muṣṭafā Muḥammad; Raḥmāniyya, n.d.

Dozy, R. P. A. *Histoire des musulmans d'Espagne*. Leiden, 1932.

_____. *Supplement aux dictionnaires arabes*. Vol. II. Paris: Maisonneuve, 1967.

Emilia, A.D'. "Roman Law and Muslim Law, a Comparative Outline". In *East and West*. Vol. IV/2 (1953).

Erdoğan, Mehmed. *Şâtibî el-Muvâfakât, islâmî ilimler metodoligisi*. Istanbul: iz Yayincilik, 1990.

Etzioni, Amitai. *Social Change, Sources, Patterns and Consequences*. New York: Basic Books, 1964.

Fagnan, E. "Les tabaqat Malikites". D.F. Saavedra. (Editor). *Homenajea D.F. Codera*. Zaragoza: Mariano Escar, 1904. Pp.105-113.

Fierro, Maribel. "The Treatises against Innovations (*Kutub al-bid'a*)". In *Der Islam*. Vol. 69 (1992). Pp. 204-246.

Fitzgerald, S.G.V. "The Alleged Debt of Islamic Law to Roman Law". *Law Quarterly Review*. Jan. 1951. 81-102.

_____. "Nature and Soruces of Shari'a". M. Khadduri and H.J. Liebesny (editors). *Law in the Middle East*". Washington: Middle East Institute, 1955. Pp.85-112.

Friedmann, W. *Law in a Changing Soceity*. London: Pelican, 1964.

Fuller, Lone L. *The Morality of Law*. New Haven: Yale, 1970.

Gayangos, Pascual de. *The History of the Mohammedan Dynasties in Spain*. [Translation of Maqqarī's *Nafḥ al-ṭīb*]. Johnson Reprint, 1964 of Cairo 1902 edition.

Ghazālī. *Al-Mustasfā min 'ilm al-uṣūl*. Baghdād: Muthannā, 1970.

Gibb, H.A.R. "Constitutional Organization". Khadduri, M. and H.J. Liebesny (editors). *Law in the Middle East*. Washington: Middle East Institute, 1955. Pp.3-27.

______. and H. Bowen. *Islamic Society and the West*. Vol. I, Part 2. Toronto: Oxford University Press, 1957.

_____. *Mohammedanism*. New York: Oxford University Press, 1962.

_____. *Studies on the Civilization of Islam*. Boston: Beacon, 1968.

_____. *Travels in Asia and Africa* 1325-1354 [by] *Ibn Baṭṭuṭa*. London: Kegan Paul, 1963.

Goitein, S.D. "The Birth-Hour of Muslim Law?" *Muslim World* L(1960).

Goldziher, I. "Das Prinzip des Istiṣḥâb in der Muhammedanischen Gesetzwissenschaft". *Weiner Zeitschrift für die Kunde des Morgenlandes*. Summary in French by G.H. Bousquet. *Arabica* VII (1960): 12-15.

_____. *Muslim Studies*. [Transl. S.M. Stern from *Muhammedanische Studien*]. Vol. II. London: George Allen and Unwin, 1971.

_____. "The Spanish Arabs and Islam". Translated by Joseph de Semogyi. *Muslim World*. LIII (1963): 5-18; 91-105; 178-184; 281-286.

_____. *Streitschrift des Gazali gegen die Batinijja-Sekte*. Leiden: Brill, 1916.

Granja, F. De la. "Ibn Zamrak". *The Encyclopaedia of Islam*. 2nd ed. III: 972-973. Leiden: Brill, 1971.

Ḥajwī, Muḥammad b. Ḥasan al-. *Al-Fikr al-sāmī fī tārīkh al-fiqh al-islāmī*. First and Second volumes Rabāt: Idārat al-ma'ārif, 1345 A.H.; Third Vol.; Tūnis: Nahḍa, n.d.,; Fourth Vol.; Fās: Jadīda, n.d. [1931]

Ḥakīm, Abu'l Ḥasan 'Alī b. Yūsuf. *Al-Dawḥat al-mushtabika fī ḍawābiṭ dār al-sikka*. Edited by Ḥusayn Mu'nis. Madrid: Ma'had al-Dirāsāt al-Islāmiyya, 1960.

Hamidullah, Muhammad. "Influence of Roman Law on Muslim Law". *Hyderabad Academy Journal,* 6 (1943).

Hart, H.L.A. *The Concept of Law*. Oxford: Clarendon, 1965.

_____. *Law, Liberty and Morality*. New York: Vintage, 1963.

Ḥassān, Ḥusayn Ḥāmid. *Naẓariyyat al-maṣlaḥa fi'l-fiqh al-Islāmī*. Cairo: Maktabat al-Mutanabbī, 1981.

Hazard, H.W. *The Numismatic History of Late Medieval North Africa*. New York: American Numismatics Society, 1952.

Heckscher, E.F. "Mercantilism". H.W. Spiegel, (ed). *The Development of Economic Thought*. New York: Science Books, 1966. Pp.32-41.

Hourani, Albert. *Arabic Thought in the Liberal Age, 1798-1939*. London: Oxford, 1962.

Hourani, G.F. *Islamic Rationalism, The Ethics of 'Abd al-Jabbār*. Oxford: Clarendon, 1971.

_____. "Two Theories of Value in Medieval Islam". *Muslim Wrold* L(1960), 269-278.

Hunwick, J.O. "Aḥmad Bābā and the Moroccan Invasion of the Sudan (1591)". *Journal of Historical Society of Nigeria*. Vol. II (1962): 311-28.

_____. "A New Source for the Biography of Ahmad Bābā al-Tinbuktī" (1556-1627)". *Bulletin of the School of Oriental and African Studies*. Vol. XXVII (1964): 568-593.

Hurgronje, C.S. *Selected Works of C. Snouck Hurgronje*. Edited and Translated by G.H. Bousquet and J. Schacht. Leiden: Brill, 1957.

Ibn 'Abbād. *Ar-Rasā'il al-ṣugrā*. Edited by Paul Nwiya. Beiruth: Imprimérie Catholique, 1958.

_____. *Sharḥ matn al-ḥikam l'il-imām Abī'l-Faḍl Aḥmad b. 'Aṭā Allāh al-Iskandarī*. Cairo: Muṣṭafa Āfandī, 1320 A.H.

Ibn 'Abd al-Salām. *Qawā'id al-aḥkām fī maṣāliḥ al-anām*. Cairo: Istiqāma, n.d.

Ibn Aḥmar, Ismā'īl. *Nathīr farā'id al-jumān fī naẓm fuḥūl al-zamān*. Edited by Muhamad Riḍwān al-Dāya. Bayrut: Dār al-Thaqāfa, 1967.

Ibn 'Arafa. *Ḥudūd fiqhiyya*. Comment. Muḥammad al-Raṣa' *Sharḥ al-Ḥudūd al-Fiqhiyya*. Tūnis: Maṭba'a Tūnisiyya, 1305 A.H.

Ibn 'Āshūr, Fāḍil. *A'lām al-fikr al-Islāmī fī tārīkh al-maghrib al-'arabī*. Tunis: Najāḥ, n.d.

Ibn 'Āṣim. *Tuḥfa*. See Bercher.

Ibn Baṭṭūṭa. *Tuḥfat al-nuẓẓār fī gharā'ib al-amṣār wa 'ajā'ib al-asfār*. Edited by 'Awamirī Bek and Jād al-Mawlā. Cairo: Amīriyya, 1935.

Ibn Farḥūn. *Al-Dībāj al-mudhahhab*. Cairo: 'Abbās b. 'Abd al-Salām, 1351 A.H.

Ibn Ḥājib. *Muktaṣar muntahā al-uṣūlī*. Cairo: Būlāq, 1317 A.H.

Ibn Khaldūn. *Muqaddima*. Cairo: Būlāq Amīriyya, 1320 A.H.

_____. *Shifā' al-sā'il li tahdhib al-masā'il*. Edited by Muḥamad b. Ṭavīt al-Ṭanji. Ankara: Ankara University, 1958. [Istanbul, 1957].

_____. *Šifa as-sā'il litahzīb al-masā'il*. Edited and translated by I.A. Khalife. Beyrouth: Imprimérie Catholique, 1958.

_____. *Kitāb al-'ibar*. Bayrūt: Maktabat al-Madrasa wa dār al-Kitāb al-Lubnānī, 1959.

Ibn al-Khaṭīb, Lisān al-Dīn. *Al-katībat al-kāmina fī man laqaynāhu bi al-Andalus min shu'arā' mi'at al-thāmina*. Edited by Iḥsān 'Abbās. Bayrūt: Dār al-thaqāfa, 1963.

_____. *A'māl al-a'lām fī man būyi'a qabl al-iḥtilām min mulūk al-Islām*. Edited by Lévi-Provençal. Bayrūt: Dār al-Makshūf, 1956.

_____. *Al-iḥāṭa fī akhbār al-Gharnāṭa*. Cairo: Maṭba'a Mawsū'āt, 1901.

_____. *Khaṭrāt al-ṭayf wa riḥlat al-shitā' wa'l-ṣayf*. Edited by 'Abbādī in *Mushāhadāt*... See 'Abbādī.

_____. *Mi'yār al-ikhtibār*. (*Mushāhadāt Lisān al-Dīn Ibn al-Khaṭīb fī bilād al-maghrib wa'l Andalus*. Iskandariya, 1958.

_____. *Mufākharāt Mālaqa wa Salā*. Edited by 'Abbādī in *Mushāhadāt*... See 'Abbādī.

Ibn Maryam. *Al-Bustān fī dhikr al-awliyā' wa'l 'ulamā' bi Tilimsān*. Edited by Ibn Cheneb. Algiers: Tha'ālibiyya, 1326 A.H.

Ibn Qayyim. *I'lām al-muwaqqi'īn*. Cairo: Sa'āda, 1955.

Ibn Sa'īd. *Al-mughrib fī ḥulā al-Maghrib*. Cairo: Dār al-Ma'ārif, 1953.

Ibn Taymiyya. *Qā'ida fi'l-mu'jizāt wa'l karāmāt wa anwā' khawāriq al-'ādāt*. In *Majmū' al-rasā'il wa'l-masā'il*. Vol. V. Cairo: Maṭba'a Manār, 1349 A.H.

Idris, Roger. "Réflexions sur le Malikism sous les Umayyades d'Espagne". *Atti del Terzo Congresso di Studi Arabi e Islamici*. Napoli, 1967. Pp.397-414.

Imamuddin. *Political History of Spain*. Dacca: Najma, 1969.

'Inān, Muḥammad 'Abd Allāh. *Al-āthār al-andalusiyya al-bāqiyya fī Isbāniyya wa'l Burtughāl*. Cairo: Shirka Musāhama Miṣriyya, 1956.

_____. *Nihāyat al-Andalus*. Cairo: Maṭba'a al-Miṣr, 1958.

Iqbal, Muḥammad. *Reconstruction of Religious Thought in Islam*. Lahore: Ashraf, 1965.

Isfahānī, Rāghib. *Al-Mufradāt fī gharīb al-Qur'ān*. Karachi: Tijārat Kutub, 1961.

Isnawī, Jamāl al-Dīn. *Nihāyat al-su'l*. Printed on the margin of Ibn Amīr al-Ḥājj. *Al-taqrīr wa'l-taḥbir*. Cairo: Būlāq, 1317 A.H.

Izutsu, T. *God and Man in the Koran: Semantics of the Koranic Weltanschauung*. Tokyo: Keio Institute of Cultural and Linguistic Studies, 1964.

Jārullah, Mūsā. Introduction. See Birişik.

Jeffery, Arthur. *The Foreign Vocabulary of the Qur'ān*. Barodan, 1938.

Juwaynī, Imām al-Ḥaramayn al-. *"Al-Burhān fī uṣūl al-fiqh"*. M.S. III Ahmet 1321, photo I.R.I. no: 219. *Al-Burhān fī uṣūl al-fiqh*. Edited by 'Abd al-'Aẓīm Dīb. Qaṭar, 1399 H.

Juynboll, Th. W. *Handbuch des Islamischen Gasetzes*. Leiden: Brill, 1910.

_____. "Hadith". *Shorter Encyclopaedia of Islam*. Leiden: Brill, 1961. Pp.116-21.

Kaḥḥāla, 'Umar Riḍā. *Mu'jam al-mu'allifīn*. Damascus: Maktaba 'Arabiyya, 1957.

Kalābādhī, Abū Bakr al-. *Al-ta'arruf li madhhab ahl al-taṣawwuf*. Cairo: 'Īsā al-Bābī, 1960.

Kerr, Malcolm H. *Islamic Reform, The Political and Legal Theories of Muḥammad 'Abduh and Rashīd Riḍā*. California: University of California Press, 1966.

_____. "Rashid Rida and Legal Reform". *Muslim World*. Vol. L (1960). Pp. 99-108; 170-181.

Khadduri, M. "From Religion to National Law". J.H. Thompson an R.D. Reischauer (editors). *Modernization of the Arab World*. Princeton: Nostrand, 1966. Pp.37-51.

Khallāf, 'Abd al-Wahhāb. *Maṣādir al-tashrī' al-Islāmī fī mā lā naṣṣa fīh*. Cairo: Dār al-Kutub al-'Arabī, 1955.

Khuḍrī, Muḥammad. *Uṣūl al-fiqh*. Cairo: Maṭba'a al-Istiqāma, 1938; Muṣṭafā Muḥammad, 1933.

Kramers, J.H. "Droit de l'Islam et droit islamique". *Analecta Orientalia, Posthumous Writings and Selected Minor Works of J.H. Karmers*. II:63-74. Leiden: Brill, 1956.

Krenkow, F. "Al-Shāṭibī" [Abul Qāsim]. *The Encyclopaedia of Islam*. Ist ed. Leiden: Brill, 1934. IV: 337-8.

Kubrā, Najm al-Dīn. *Fawā'iḥ al-jamāl wa fawātiḥ al-jalāl*. Edited by Fritz Meier. Wiesbaden: Steiner, 1957.

Lacerte, Henry. *The Nature of Canon Law According to Suárez*. Ottawa: University of Ottawa, 1964.

Lammens, H. *Islam, Beliefs and Institutions*. London: Methuen, 1929.

Lane, E.W. *An Arabic-English Lexicon*. London: William Norgate, 1863-93.

Laoust, Henri. *Contribution à une étude de la méthodologie canonique de Taki-d-Din Ahmad b. Taimiya*. Cairo: Imprimérie de l'institut français d'archéologie orientale, 1939.

_____. *Le Califat dans la doctrine de Rashid Rida*. Beirut: Institut Français à Damas, 1938.

_____. *Essai sur les doctrines sociales et politiques de Taki-d-Din Ahmad b. Taimiya*. Cairo: Imprimérie de l'institut français d'archéologie orientale,. 1939.

Lavoix, M.H. *Catalogue des monnaies musulmanes de la Bibliothéque Nationale*. Paris: Imprimérie Nationale, 1891.

Levy, R. *The Social Structure of Islam*. Cambridge: Cambridge University Press, 1957.

Liebesny, H.J. "Religious Law and Westernization in the Moslem Near East". *American Journal of Comparative Law*. Vol. II (1953). Pp. 492-504.

López-Ortiz, J. "Fatwas granadinas de los siglos XIV y XV". *Al-Andalus*. Vol. VII (1941). Pp. 73-127.

MacDonald, D.B. "Ḥizb". *The Encyclopaedia of Islam*. 2nd ed. III: 513-4. Leiden: Brill, 1971.

Mackeen, A.M.M. "The Early History of Sufism in the Maghrib prior to Al-Shādhilī (d. 650/1256)". In the *Journal of the American Oriental Society*, Vol. 91 (1971).

Maḥbūbī, Ṣadr al-Sharī'a. *Sharḥ al-tawḍīḥ wa'l-tanqīḥ*. Istānbul: Maṭba'a Bosanawi, 1304 A.H.

Mahdi, Muhsin. *Ibn Khaldūn's Philosophy of History*. Chicago: Phoenix, 1964.

_____. "Language and Logic in Classical Islam". In G.E. Von Grunebaum (Ed.). *Logic in Classical Islamic Culture*. Wiesbaden, 1970.

Maḥmaṣānī Ṣubḥī. *Falsafat al-tashrī' fī' al-Islām*. Beirut, 1952. Translated by F.J. Ziadeh. *The Philosophy of Jurisprudence in Islam*. Leiden: Brill, 1961.

_____. *Muqaddima fī iḥyā 'ulūm al-sharī'a.* Beirut: Dār al-'ilm l'il-mala'īn, 1962.

_____. "Transactions in the Sharī'a". M. Khadduri and H.J. Liebesny (editors). *Law in the Middle East.* Washington: Middle East Institue, 1955. Pp. 179-202.

Maḥmud, 'A. Ḥalīm. *Al-madrasat al-Shādhiliyya wa imāmuha Abu'l Ḥasan al-Shādhilī.* Cairo: Dār al-Kutub al-Ḥadītha, 1387 A.H.

Makdisi, George. "The Juridical Theology of Shāfi'ī: Origins and Signifcance of Uṣūl al-fiqh". In *Religion, Law and Learning in Classical Islam.* Hampshire: Variorum, 1991.

_____. "Remarks on Traditionalism in Islamic Religious History". Carl Leiden, (editor). *The Conflict of Traditionalism and Modernism in the Muslim Middle East.* Austin: University of Texas, 1966. Pp.77-78.

Makhlūf, Muḥammad. *Shajarat al-nūr al-zakiyya.* Cairo: Salafiyya, 1930-31.

Mālik. *Al-Mudawwanat al-kubrā.* Baghdad: Muthannā, 1970.

Manṣūr, 'Abd al-Ḥafīẓ. *Fihris makhṭūṭāt al-maktabat al-Aḥmadiyya bi Tūnis.* Bayrūt: Dār al-Fatḥ, 1969.

Maqqarī, Shihāb al-Dīn. *Azhār al-riyāḍ fī akhbār 'Iyāḍ.* Cairo: Lajnat al-Tālīf, 1939.

Maqqarī, Abū'l 'Abbās. *Nafḥ al-ṭīb.* Edited by Muḥammad Muḥy al-Dīn 'Abd al-Ḥamīd. Cairo: Maṭba'a Sa'āda, 1949.

Marçais, G. "Note sur les ribats en Berbérie". *Mélange René Basset.* II: 395-430. Paris: Edition Ernest Leroux, 1925.

_____. "Ribat". *The Encyclopaedia of Islam.* First Edition. Leiden: Brill, 1936. III:1150-52.

Margoliouth, D.S. "Recent Arabic Literature". *Journal of Royal Asiatic Society.* London. 1916. Pp.397-98.

Mawdūdī, Abū'l A'lā. *The Islamic Law and Constitution.* Edited and Translated by K. Ahmad. Lahore: Islamic Publications, 1960.

Mīkhāl, 'Umar Sulaymān al-. "al-Aḥādīth al-I'tiṣām l'il Shāṭibī". M.A. Thesis, at the University of Imām Muḥammad b. Sa'ūd, 1405 H.

Miranda, Ambroxio Huici. "Gharnāṭa". *The Encyclopaedia of Islam*. 2nd Edition. Leiden: Brill, 1965. II: 1012-14.

_____. "The Iberian Peninsula and Sicily". P.M. Holt and others (editors). *The Cambridge History of Islam*. II:406-439. Cambridge: Cambridge University Press, 1970.

Monés, Hussain. "Le role des hommes de religion dans l'histoire de l'Espagne musulmane jusqu'à la fin du Califat". *Studia Islamica*. Vol. XX (1964): 47-88.

Monroe, J.T. *Islam and the Arabs in Spanish Scholarship*. Leiden: Brill. 1970.

Morand, M. *Introduction à l'étude du droit musulman algérien*. Alger: J. Carbonel; Ancien Maison, 1921.

Mūsa, M. Yūsuf. *Al-madkhal li dirāsāt al-fiqh al-Islāmī*. Cairo: Dār al-Fikr al-Arabi, 1961.

Nadwī, Riḍwān 'Alī. *Al-'Izz bin 'Abd al-Salām*. Damascus: Dār al-Fikr, 1960.

_____. "Two Great Contemporaries of Thirteenth Century A.D. Sulṭān al-'ulamā al-'Izz ibn al-Salām and Ibn 'Arabī". *Islamic Culture* XLV (1971). Pp. 193-201.

Nakamura, Hajime. "The Indian and Buddhist Concept of Law". E.J. Jurji (editor). *Religious Pluralism and World Community*. Leiden: Brill, 1969. Pp.131-174.

Nallino, C.A. "The Impossibility of the Influence of Roman Law on Muslim Law". trans. Hamidullah. *Voice of Islam*. Karachi, 1963. 1/2, 63-67.

Niyazi, Nadhir, "Istiṣlāḥ". *Urdū dā'ira ma'ārif Islāmiyya*. II: 586-91. Lahore: Danishgah Panjab, 1965.

Nubāhī, Qāḍī Abū'l Ḥasan al-. *Al-Marqabat al-'ulyā fī man yastaḥiqq al-qaḍā' wa'l futyā*. Edited by Lévi-Provençal. Cairo: Dār al-Kātib al-Miṣrī, 1948.

Nwiya, Paul. *Ibn 'Abbād de Ronda*. Beyrouth: Imprimérie Catholique, 1961.

Ostrorog, Leon. *The Angora Reform*. London: University of London, 1927.

Palacios, Asin. "Un précurseur Hispano-Musulman de san Juan de la cruz". Translation by M.L. de Celigny. *Étude Carmelitaines*. Paris. 1932.

Paret, Rudi. "Istiḥsān and Istiṣlāḥ". *Shorter Encyclopaedia of Islam.* Leiden: Brill, 1961. Pp.184-86. In *E.I.* New edition. Leiden: Brill, 1978. Vol. IV, 225-259.

Powers, David. S. *Studies in Qur'ān and Hadith, The Formation of the Islamic Law of Inheritance.* Berkeley, 1986.

Prieto, Antonio y Vives. "Indicacion del valor en las monedas Arabigo Espagnolas". D.F. Saavedra (editor). *Homenaje à D.F. Codera*, Zaragoza: Mariano Escar, 1904. Pp. 105-113.

Provençal, Lévi E. "Aḥmad Bābā". *The Encyclopaedia of Islam.* 2nd ed. Leiden: Brill, 1960. I: 279-80.

_____. "Al-Andalus". *The Encyclopaedia of Islam.* 2nd ed. Leiden: Brill, 1960. I: 486-92.

_____. *Histoire de l'Espagne musulmane.* Paris: Maisonneuve, 1950.

_____. *Inscriptions arabes d'Espagne.* Leyde: Brill, 1930.

_____. "Naṣrids". *The Encyclopaedia of Islam.* Ist ed. III:878-81. Leiden: Brill. 1936.

_____. "Shāṭiba". *The Encyclopaedia of Islam.* Ist ed. Leiden: Brill, 1938. IV: 337.

Qarāfī, Shihāb al-Dīn. *Al-furūq.* Cairo: Dār Iḥyā Kutub al-'Arabiyya, 1346 A.H.

_____. *Al-iḥkām fī tamyīz al-fatāwā 'an al-aḥkām wa taṣarrufāt al-qāḍī wa'l imām.* Edited by 'Abd al-Fattāḥ Abū Ghudda. Ḥalab: Maṭba'a Islāmiyya. 1967.

_____. *Tanqīḥ al-fuṣūl fī 'ilm al-uṣūl.* In *al-Dhakhīra.* Cairo: Maṭba'a Kulliyat al-Sharī'a, 1961.

Qushayrī, Abu'l Qāsim al-. *Al-risāla fī 'ilm al-taṣawwuf.* Cairo: Muḥammad 'Alī, 1948.

Rahman, F. *Islam.* London: Weidenfeld, 1966.

_____. *Islamic Methodology in Hisotry.* Karachi: Central Institute of Islamic Research, 1965.

Rāzī, Fakhr al-Din. *Al-maḥṣūl fī uṣūl al-fiqh*. MS. Yale University. Nemoy, A-1039 (L-643). Also *Al-Maḥṣūl fī 'Ilm uṣūl al-fiqh*, edited by Ṭāhā Jābir Fayyāḍ al-'Alwānī. Riyāḍ: Jāmi'at al-Imām Muḥammad b. Sa'ūd, 1980.

Renaud, H.P.J. "Deux Ouvrages perdus d'Ibn al-Ḥaṭîb: Identifiés dans des manusscrits de Fes -- Conclusion sur Ibn al-Ḥaṭîb medecín". *Hesperis*. Vol. XXX (1946): 214-225.

_____. "Un medecín du royaume de Granade: Muhammad aš-Šaqûrî". *Hesperis*. Vol. XXX (1946): 31.64.

Riḍā, Rashīd. *Tārīkh al-ustādh al-Imām al-Shaykh Muḥammad 'Abduh*. Cairo: Dār al-Manār, 1350/1931.

_____. *Yusr al-Islām*. Cairo: Nahḍa, 1956.

Rīsūnī, Aḥmad al-. *Naẓariyyat al-maqāṣid 'ind al-Imām al-Shāṭibī*. Riyāḍ: Al-Dār al-'Ilmiyya l'il-Kitāb al-Islāmī, 1992.

Robertson, A.J. *The Principles of Mohammedan Law*. Rangoon: Myles Standish, 1911.

Rosenthal, E.I.J. *Political Thought in Medieval Islam*. Cambridge: Cambridge University Press, 1962.

Ṣa'īdī, 'Abd al-Muta' āl-. *Al-Mujaddidūn fī'l-Islām*. Cairo: Adab, Namūdhajiya n.d.

Salāwī, Aḥmad b. Khālid. *Al-istiqṣā' fī akhbār duwal al-maghrib al-aqṣā*. Cairo: Dār al-Kitāb, 1954-56. Dār al-Bayḍā, 1954.

Ṣanhūrī, Abd al-Razzāq. "Wujūb tanqīḥ al-qānūn al-madanī al-Miṣrī. *Majallat al-Qānūn wa'l Iqtiṣād*. 6(1963).

Santillana, D. *Istituzioni di diritto musulmano malichita*. Roma: Istituto per l'Oriente, 1938.

Sarkīs, Yūsuf I. *Mu'jam al-maṭbū'āt al-'arabiyya wa'l-mu'arraba*. Cairo: Sarkīs, 1928.

Sarrāj, Abū Naṣr. *Kitāb al-luma' fī al-taṣawwuf*. Edited and commented by R.A. Nicholson. London: Luzac, 1964.

Schacht, J. "Classicisme traditionalisme et ankylose dans la loi religieuse de l'Islam". R. Brunschvig (editor). *Classicisme et déclin culturel dans l'histoire de l'Islam.* Paris: Besson et Chantemerle, 1957. Pp.141-166.

_____. "Fiḳh". *The Encyclopaedia of Islam.* 2nd ed. Leiden: Brill, 1965. II: 886-91.

_____. "Foreign Elements in Ancient Islamic law". *Journal of Comparative Law.* 1950, 3-4, 9-16;

_____. *Introduction to Islamic Law.* Oxford: Clarendon, 1966.

_____. "Islamic Law". *Encyclopaedia of Social Sciences.* New York: MacMillan, 1932. VIII: 344-49.

_____. "Muḥammad 'Abduh". *Shorter Encyclopaedia of Islam.* Leiden: Brill, 1961. Pp.405-407.

______. *The Origins of Muhammadan Jurisprudence.* Oxford: Clarendon, 1959.

______. "The Present State of Studies in Islamic Law". In *Atti del Terzo Congresso di Studi Arabi e Islamici.* Naples, 1967.

______. "Theology and Law in Islam". Von Grunebaum (editor). *Theology and Law in Islam.* Wiesbaden: Harrassowitz, 1971. Pp. 3-23.

Seco de Lucena, Luis. *Documentos Arabigo-Granadinos.* Madrid: Instituto des Estudios Islamicos, 1961.

Seybold, G.F. "Granada". *The Encyclopaedia of Islam.* Ist ed. Leiden: Brill, 1927. II: 175-7.

Shabāna, Muḥammad Kamāl. "Al-ḥālat al-iqtiṣādiyya bi'l-Andalus khilāl al-qarn al-thāmin al-hijrī". *Al-Baḥth al-'Ilmī*, III (1966).

Shabāna, Muḥammad Kamāl. "Shuyūkh Ghuzāt al-maghāriba fī'l Andalus kamā arrakha lahum Ibn al-Khaṭīb fī *al-Iḥāṭa*". *Al-Baḥth al-'Ilmī. V* (1968). Pp.134-136.

Shāfi'ī al-. *al-Risāla*, ed. Aḥmad Muḥammad Shākir. Cairo: Muṣṭafā al-Bābī, 1940.

Shalabī, Muṣṭafā. *Ta'līl al-aḥkām 'ārḍ wa taḥlīl li ṭarīqat al-taḥlīl wa taṭawwurātihā fī uṣur al-ijtihād wa al-taqlīd.* Cairo: Azhar, 1949.

Sharqawi, E. *Religion and Philosophy in the Thought of Fakhr al-Dīn al-Rāzī. The Problem of God's Existence.* Unpublished Thesis. McGill University, Montreal, 1970.

Slane, De. *Histoire des Berberes*. [Translation of Ibn Khaldūn's *Kitāb al-'ibar*]. Paris: Geuthner, 1927.

Smith, Margaret. *Al-Ghazali, The Mystic*. London: Luzac, 1944.

Subkī, Tāj al-Dīn. *Jam' al-jawāmi'*. Printed on the margin of 'Abd al-Raḥmān Bannānī, *Ḥāshiya... 'alā matn Jam' al-jawāmi'*. Cairo: Muṣṭafā Bābī, 1937.

Suyūṭī, Jalāl al-Dīn al-. *Al-Itqān fī 'ulūm al-Qur'ān*. Cairo: Muṣṭafā Muḥammad, H 1368.

Taftāzānī, Sa'd al-Dīn. *Sharḥ al-tawḍīḥ wa'l tanqīḥ*. See Maḥbūbī.

Ṭalbī, M. "Ibn Khaldūn". *The Encyclopaedia of Islam*. 2nd ed. Leiden: Brill, 1971. III: 825-31.

Toledano, H. *The Chapter on Marriage from Sijilmāsī's Al-'Amal al-Muṭlaq: A Study in Moroccan Judicial Practice*. Unpublished Ph.D. Thesis. Columbia University, 1969.

Tonkī, Maḥmūd Ḥasan. *Mu'jam al-muṣannifīn*. Beirut: Wazankoghraf Ṭabbāra, 1344 A.H.

Toy, C.H. "The Semetic Conception of Absolute Law". Carl Bezold (editor). *Orientalische Studien Theodor Nöldeke*. Giessen: Ricker, 1906.

Trimingham, J. Spencer. *The Sufi Orders in Islam*. Oxford: Clarendon, 1971.

Ṭūfī, Najm al-Dīn. *Sharḥ al-arba'īn*. Printed as appendix in Muṣṭafā Zayd, *Al-maṣlaḥa fi'l-tashrī' al-islāmī wa Najm al-Dīn al-Ṭūfī*. Cairo: Dār al-Fikr al-'Arabī, 1954.

Turki, Abdel Magid. "Lisān al-Dīn Ibn al-Ḥaṭīb (713-76/131-74), juriste d'après son oeuvre inédité: Muṯlā al-ṭarīqa fī ḏamm al-waṯīqa [Muthlā al-ṭarīqa fī dhamm al-wathīqa]. *Arabica* XVI (1969). Pp. 155-211, 280-311.

Tyan, É. "Méthodologie et sources du droit en Islam". *Studia Islamica*. X (1959): 79-109.

Udovitch, Abraham L. *Partnership and Profit in Medieval Islam*. Princeton: Princeton University Press, 1970.

Van Ess, Josef. *Die Erkenntnislehre des 'Aḍudaddîn al-Îcî: Übersetzung und Kommentar des ersten Buches seiner Mawâqif.* Wiesbaden: Steiner, 1966.

Van Kleffens, E.N. *Hispanic Law Until the End of the Middle Ages.* Edinburgh: University Press, 1968.

Von Grunebaum, G.E. "Concept and Function of Reason in Islamic Ethics". *Oriens.* Vol. XV (1962): 1-17.

Voorhoeve, P. *Handlist of Arabic Manuscripts: Library of University Leiden.* Lugundi: Batavorum, 1957.

Wansharīsī, Abu'l 'Abbās Aḥmad al-. *Al-Mi'yār al-mu'rib wa'l-jāmi' al-mughrib 'an fatāwā 'ahl Ifrīqiya wa'l-Andalus wa'l-Maghrib.* Fas: n.p., 1314/1941. [New edition: 1401/1981].

Wittgenstein, Ludwig. *Philosophical Investigations.* Translation from German by G.E.M. Anscombe. Oxford: Blackwell, 1965.

Zabīdī, Muḥamad Al-Murtaḍā. *Itḥāf sādat al-muttaqīn.* Cairo: Maṭba'a Maymaniyya, 1893.

Zarqā, Muṣṭafā Aḥmad. *Al-madkhal al-fiqhī al-'āmm.* Dimashq: Maṭba'a Jâmi'a, 1961.

Zayd, Muṣṭafā. *Al-Maṣlaḥa fī al-tashrī al-Islāmī wa Najm al-Dīn al-Ṭūfī.* Cairo: Dār al-Fikr al-'Arabī, 1954.

Ziriklī, Khayr al-Dīn. *al-A'lām.* Cairo: Muallif, 1954.

GLOSSARY
of Technical Terms*

abadī: eternal, continuous 158 [M,2:37]

'abd: servant [M,2:168]

'āda: custom, or practice 186 [M,2: 121]; custom 215 [M,2: 284]; habits 152 [M,2:11]; "A given act that, if it is supposed to take place without any impediment, takes place only in a certain manner which is known by other similar acts." 212 [M,2: 281]

'adam ta'yīn: non-specification 93 [F:165]

'ādāt: (pl. of *'āda*). "Acts which aim at the protection of human life, intellectual faculty and other things in this world". 152 [M,2:9]

adilla: sources 120, 122 [M,3:5,27]; proofs 248 [M,1:35]; sources [M,3:41]

'adl: balance 193 [M,2:146; 4:90]

'afw: silence 217 [M,1: 166]; not obligatory; "between lawful and forbidden" 216 [M,1:161]

aḥbās: (pl. of *ḥabs*). trust properties 93 [F:168]

al-aḥkām al-laṭīfa: subtle rules, niceties of a language 178 [M,2:84]

al-aḥkām al-taklīfiyya: obligation-defining rules 205 [M,1:109]

al-aḥkām al-waḍ'iyya: declaratory rules 205 [M,1: 187].

ahl isqāṭ al-ḥuẓūẓ: The people who disregard their self-interests in an obligation, Ṣūfīs 193 [M,2: 147]

aḥwāl: (pl. of *ḥāl*). conditions, circumstances 158 [M,2:37]; mystic state [M,1: 30]

a'imma: the rulers 74 [IT,1: 28]

akhbār: (pl. of *khabar*) predicate [M,2:67]

'aks: reverse 232 [M,4:337]

ālām: (pl. of *alam*). pain 159 [M,2:42]

alfāẓ: (pl. of *lafẓ*). words 169 [M,2:66]

'ālim: a knowledgeable person, a *mujtahid*, or the one who at least knows the objectives of law and can consult others for details 233 [M,4:107]

'amal: custom, practice [M,3:66]; (pl. *a'māl*). action [M,2:323]

---

* This is a select list of technical terms used by Shāṭibī in his works, along with their contextual meanings. The numbers without parenthesis refer to the present book and those in parenthesis refer to the volume and page numbers of Shāṭibī's works abbreviated as follows: M = *al-Muwafāqāt*, IT = *al-I'tiṣām*, IF = *al-Ifādāt*, F = *Fatāwā*

amr: command, "demanding someone to do something and to will to bring it into existence" 213 [M,3:119]

anqāḍ: the demolished and unused parts of an estate 93 [F:168]

'aql: human reason 247 [M,1:35]; logic, [M, 1:34] intellect, intellectual faculty 152 [M,2:10]

'aqlī: rational, logical, speculative 159 [M,1:29]

arbāb al-aḥwāl/aṣḥāb al-aḥwāl: the people of mystical state, Ṣūfīs 241 [M,2:132]; friends, saints [M, 2:130]; friends of God [M,1: 306]

arbāb al-ḥudūd: logicians, essentialists 174 [M,1:58]

arbāb al-ḥuẓūẓ: the people who guard their self interests 192 [M,2:146]

'arūba: the ancient Arabic name for Friday 214 [M,2:307]

aṣḥāb al-ra'y: the rationalists 229 [M,4:230]

aṣl: principle, textual base 191 [M,3:16]

al-aṣl al-qaṭ'ī: definite principle 191 [M,2:133]

asrār: (pl. of *sirr*). explanation 81 [M,1:24]

al-'awā'id al-'āmma: general customs 215 [M,2:297]

al-'awā'id al-jāriya: current customs 215 [M,2:286]

al-'awā'id al-jāriya bayan al-khalq: current social practices 214 [M,2:283]

al-'awā'id al-mustamirra: constant habits/customs, 214 [M,2:283]

al-'awā'id al-mutabaddila: changing habits/customs 216 [M,2:284]

al-'awā'id al-shar'iyya: legalised customs, "practices approved by Sharī'a" 215, 216 [M,2:283]

al-'awā'id al-thābita: unchanging, established practices/habits [M,2:284]

awāmir: (pl. of *amr*). modes of imperative injunctions 122 [M,3:119]

awliyā' Allāh: friends of God 74 [IT,1:11]

'azīma: regular, fixed 191, 240; "Originally, a general rule" [M,1:300]; not opting for a lenient view of law [M:1:287]

bā'ina: irrevocable divorce 91 [F:142]

bāṭil: void, ineffective 216 [M,2:284]

bayān: exposition, explanation, expansion 122 [M,3:311,321]

bid'a: innovation; "A way of innovation in religion that resembles the way of *Sharī'a*, and which is intended to be followed in order to strive in the utmost toward obedience to Allah" 219 [IT,1:19]

al-bid'a al-ḥaqīqiyya: True innovation, "an innovation not proven by a *shar'ī* evidence, Qur'ān, Sunna, ijmā' or a reliable basis of reasoning, neither in general nor in particular" 221 [IT,2: 232).

al-bid'a al-iḍāfiyya: Relative innovation, "a pious innovation in religion connected with some *shar'ī* evidence only partially" 221 [IT,2:232]

burhān: demonstrative proof, 157 [M,2:32]

al-burhān al-qaṭ'ī. definite proof [M,1:77]

al-burhān al-'aqlī: rational proof [M,3:52]

buyū' al-ājāl: sales on credit, a legal device 211 [M,2:389]

dalāla: indication, signification leading to the meaning of a word 171 [M,2:95] *al-dalāla al-aṣliyya*: indication of essential meaning, primary meaning 122 [M,2:66]

al-dalāla al-tābī'a: subsidiary indication, indicator of secondary meaning 122 [M,2:66]

dalīl: evidence, proof 242 [M,2:82]

ḍarūra: necessity, requirement 206 [M,2:327]

ḍarūratan: *a priori*, necessarily 193 [M,2:151]

ḍarūrī: "A legal objective which is indispensible for sustaining religious and worldly interests, neglect of which may disrupt the worldly interests or may corrupt, impede or destroy life in this world and salvation and rewards in the hereafter" 151 [M,2:8]

dawām: constancy, perseverance 200 [M,2:242]

dawr: arguing in a circle [M,2:43]

dharā'i': the rule of preventive measures 123 [M,4:198]

al-dhatī al-khāṣṣ: particular essential 174 [M,1:58]

dīn: religion 219 [M,2:10]; religion and the hereafter 151, 152 [M, 2:8]; matters relating with *'ibādāt* [IT,1:37], The basic principles taught by the Qur'ān and Sunna, originally revealed in Meccan verses of the Qur'ān [M,3:47].

dunyā: mundane matters, matters relating to *'ādāt* 219 [IT,1:37]

far': (pl. *furū'*), branch, a particular case for which an analogy is sought from a general principle, details 241 [M,2:31].

fasād: corruption, confusion 100 [F:137]

fatwā: legal opinion, "an answer to a legal question given by an expert, by way of words, action or approval" 123 [M,4:246]

fiqh al-sharī'a: understanding of the Sharī'a 248 [M,2:59]

fiqh: law 72 [IT,1:25]

fiṭra: nature, innate characteristic, without compulsion or acquisition 185 [M,2:110]

furū': see *far'*

fuṣūl: differentia 174 [M,1:57]

futyā: the institution of juris-consultation 229 [M,2:155; M,4:107]

ghalabat al-ẓann: most probable 203 [M,2:313]

al-ghālib al-aktharī: the major dominant factor 159 [M,2:53]

gharaḍ: selfish motive, individual interest 197 [M,2:172]

gharar: hazard, risk 97 [F:158]

ghashsh: adulteration 96 [F:149]

ghayr maqdūr: unfeasible 186 [M,2:118], impossible [M,2:117]

ḥabs: *waqf*, trust 93 [F:168]

hādin: the inhabitant of a country on truce terms with another 95 [F:145]

ḥāfiẓ: a scholar who is master of the sources of the objectives of law, but not a *mujtahid*, 233 [M,4:107]

ḥāja: general need 152 [M,2:12]

ḥājī: needed 151 [M,2:8]; "A legal objective aiming at the expansion of the meaning of a law in order to remove the strictness of the literal sense the application of which may cause impediments or hardships, and may eventually disrupt the objectives of law 152 [M,2:10-11]

ḥākim: judge 229 [M,4:90, 93]

ḥalāl: lawful, permitted 94 [M,1:161]

ḥaqīqat al-waḍ' al-lughawī: an original, essential and literal meaning of a word, in contrast to metaphorical sense 189 [M,2:126]

ḥaqq: right, due [M,2:318]

ḥaraj: impediment, a type of hardship 184 [M,2:159; F:159]

ḥarām: forbidden 94, 217 [M,1:161]

ḥarbī: a person at war, enemy 95 [F:145]

hawā: passion 197 [M,2:170]; desire, lust 248 [M,2:172]; self-indulgence 198 [M,2:170]; opposite to *waḥy* (revelation) 251 [M,2:169]

hazl: joke 206 [M,2:230]

ḥaẓẓ: personal interest, share 197 [M,2:176]; self-indulgence [M,2:180]

ḥimā: fence, protective zone 154 [M,2:16]

ḥiyal: (pl. of *ḥīla*). legal devices, "An apparently lawful device, but which is employed in order to evade or change a rule of law" 235 [M,2:378]

ḥukm: the institution of *qaḍā*, court of law, 229 [M,4:106]; judgement 175 [M,1:45]; rule [M,1:78], practice [M,1:139]; value, category 244 [M,1:137]

ḥuẓūẓ: (pl. of *ḥaẓẓ*). comforts 191 [M,2:146,180]; personal benefit, self-interest 196 [M,2:147-148, 181-182]

'ibāda: *ta'abbud*, a rule of law which is not extendible rationally (analogically) 255 [M,2:300,310]; purely a right of God [M,2:318]; rituals, worship 152 [M,2:10]

'ibādāt: (pl. of *'ibāda*). "Obligations which aim at the protection of religion (dīn)" 152 [M,2:8]

ibtidā': *bid'a*, innovation in a religious matter, "When the intention for an action is in coformity with *Sharī'a* but the action or its omission itself is contrary to *Sharī'a* and the person knows about this contradiction" 207 [M,2:340]

iḍṭirārī: compulsive 185 [M,2:110]

iḥkām: clarification, unequivocation, established, opposite to *tashābuh* in one sense and *naskh* in another 122 [M,3:85]

ijbār: determinism 248 [M,1:19]

ijmā': consensus 203 [M,2:313; 3:5)

ijmāl: concision, general, vague, unclear 122 [M,3:342]

ijtihād bī'l-istinbāṭ: reasoning by inference, 231 [M,4:167]; "A process of reasoning in which one exhausts one's efforts to one's full capacity in order to acquire exact or probable knowledge to reach judgement in a given case" 230 [M,4:113]

al-ijtihād al-qiyāsī: reasoning by analogy 123 [M,4:96,163]

ikhbār: communication, proposition 173 [M,2:66,67,280]

ikhlāṣ: purity, abandoning selfish motives 197 [M,2:202]; sincerity, 198 [M,2:201]

ikhtilāf: divergence, 212 [M,2:280]; difference of opinion, 123 [M,4:125]; horizontal change 215 [M,2:284]

ikhtiyār: choice, volition 197 [M,2:168]

ikrāh: compulsion, imposition, duress 206 [M,2:325]

'ilal: (pl. of *'illa*). reasons 202 [M,2:306]; *maṣlaḥa* [M,2:313]; *manāṭ 239* [M,4:92f]; "The reason or the purpose attached to a command or a permission" [M,1:265]

'ilm al-kalām: philosophical theology 122 [M,1:45]

'ilm al-jadal: disputation, the science of framing questions and answers 124 [M,4:311]

'ilm al-ishtiqāq: etymology 189 [M,2:126]

imāma: leading the prayers 73 [IT,1:25; F: 172],

al-imāmat al-kubrā. political leadership, headship, government [M,1:176]

imtinā': impossibility 213 [M,2:282]

imtithāl: compliance 207 [M,2:337]

iqtidā': authority 123 [M,4:261]; followig, adherence, *taqlīd* [M,24:283];

iqtidā bī'l-af'āl, emulation, imitation [M,4:272]

iqtiḍā': demand 203 [M,2:311]

irāda: will 156 [M,4:119]

al-irāda al-amriyya: Ordering Will [M,3:120]

al-irādat al-khalqiyya al-qadriyya: the Divine Determinist Creative Will [M,3:119]

al-irādat al-takwīniyya: The Divine Creative Will 222 [M,3:121]

al-iradat al-tashrī'iyya: Divine Legislative Will 222 [M,3:121]

ishāra: textual indication 203 [M,2:313]

al-istidlāl al-mursal: a process of reasoning that overrides analogical deduction, same as *istiḥsān* 124 [M,1:39;4:206] same as *al-maṣlaḥa al-mursala*, [IT,2:115]

istiḥsān: juristic preference 123 [M,4:205]; to accept the better of the two pieces of evidence [M,4:208]; To abandon what an evidence requires in favour of some other argument by way of exception or allowance [M,2:207]; to adopt a particular *maṣlaḥa* in preference to a general evidence [M,2:206]

iṣṭilāḥiyya: particular, technical meaning 186 [M,2:119]

istimrār: continuity 212 [M,2:283]

Istiqrā': induction [M,3:10]

istiqrār: persistence 212 [M,2:279]

istirsāl: laxity 225 [IT,2:132]

istiṣḥāb: principle of the presumption of the continuity of the legal validity of a rule or practice 217 [M,1:173, M,2:396]

istithnā: exception [M,4:339],

i'tiqādiyyāt: matters relating to beliefs and creeds, opposite of *'amaliyyāt* 180 [M,2:88]

al-i'tiyād al-kasbī: acquired habitude 155 [M,2:27]

al-jam': combining, integration of divergent views 246 [M,4:294]

jawāhir: (pl. of *jawhar*) essence 174 [M,1:57]

jawāz: possibility 213 [M, 1:34]

al-jawāz al-'aqlī: logical possibility 213 [M,2:281]

jazā': reward and punishment 185 [M,2:110]

al-jihat al-ghāliba: *Predominant side 157 [M,2:32]*

al-jihat al-marjūḥa: *the dominated aspect*

al-jihat al-rājiḥa: the dominating aspect

jināyat: penalties, the laws aiming at the protection of the five *maṣāliḥ* in a preventive negative manner 152 [M,2:9]

kaffāra: penalty, penance, atonement, expiation 91 [F:142]

kashf: mystic revelation, 201 [M,2:266]

khawāriq: deviations, beyond ordinary 222 [M,2:268]

khawāriq al-'āda: extraordinary, irregular habit, unusual event or act, contrary to *'āda*, 213 [M,2:281]; miracles, supernatural [M,2:269]

khawāṣṣ al-khāṣṣ: very special, elite, refers to the Ṣūfīs 241 [M,2:216]

khilāf: disputation 123 [M,4:222]; conflict of laws, conflict of opinions 173 [M,4:133]; disagreement 173 [M,4:141]

khiṭāb: proclamation 155 [M,2:26]; mode of proclamation 213 [M,1:109]

khiṭāb al-taklīf: Obligation defining mode of proclamation [M,1:109]

khiṭāb al-waḍ': declaratory mode of proclamation [M,1:109]

khiṭāba: preaching, delivering Friday sermon 73 [IT,1:25]

khiyara: option 203 [M,2:318]

khuṭaṭ: professions 73 [IT,1:25]

khuṭba: Friday sermon 74 [IT,1:27]

kifā'iyya: public offices, societal duties or functions 208 [M,2:177,180]

kirā' al-arḍ: lease of land 97 [F:154]

al-Kitāb/al-kitāb al-'azīz: Qur'ān 122 [M,3:345,346]

kulfa: toil 188, 191 [M,2:123, 124]; "An act which is hard but does not harm the person or property if continued" [M,2:123]

kullī: universal 158 [M,1:33]; total 249 [M,2:37]

al-kulliyāt al-'aqliyyah: laws of reason [M,1:78; 2:53]

al-kulliyāt al-'Arabiyya: rules of Arabic language [M,2:53]

al-kulliyāt al-istiqrā'iyya: universal rules known inductively 159 [M,2:53]

kulliyāt al-Sharī'a: universal principles inductively derived from the Qur'ān [M,1:29] same as *uṣūl al-Sharī'a* [M,1:77]

al-kulliyāt al-shar'iyya: universal legal principles 195 [M,1:78]

kulliyāt al-wujūd: laws of nature 222 [M,2:282]

lafẓ: word 169 [M 2:84] "a medium to reach the intended idea" [M,2:87]

lawāḥiq: (pl. of *lāḥiq*) succeeding 184 [M,2:108]; annexes, related matters [M,4:294]

lawth: incomplete, circumstantial, evidence leading to presumption of guilt in case of homicide 100 [F:173]

maḍārr: (pl. of *maḍarra*). opposite of *manfa'a*, harmful things 159 [M,2:40]

madhmūm: condemned, blameworthy 207 [M,2:340]

mafsada: evil, opposite of *maṣlaḥa* 214 [M,2:174], hardship 159 [M,2:42]

māhiya: quiddity, entity 174 [M,1:57]

ma'hūd: general and apparent understanding 176 [M,2:65]

majāz: metaphorical use of a word 189 [M,2:126]

māl: property 152 [M,2:10]

ma'lūm: known, established, exact 212 [M,2:279]

man': abstention, prohibition 159 [M,2:40]

ma'nā: meaning 169 [M,2:66]; reason 169 [M,2:300]

al-ma'nā al-aṣlī: primary meaning 174 [M,2:95]

al-ma'nā al-ifrādī: individual meaning, non-contextual 174 [M,2:87]

al-ma'nā al-maqṣūd: target meaning 177 [M,2:83]

al-ma'nā al-munāsib: proper idea, rationally apparent meaning 225 [IT,2:132; M,1:89]

al-ma'nā al-tab'ī, secondary meaning 174 [M,2:95]

al-ma'nā al-tarkībī: contextual meaning 174 [M,1:53]

ma'ānī: inner meaning 201

al-ma'ānī al-mabthūtha: scattered meaning [M,2:87]

ma'ānī mujarrada: meaning separated from the peculiar characteristics of a word 174 [M,4:230]; concepts [M,4:163]

al-ma'ānī al-muṭlaqa: simple meaning, abstract meaning 174 [M,2:66]

manāfi': (pl. of *manfa'a*, opposite of *maḍarra*). benefits, uses, advantages 159 [M,2:40]

manāṭ: anchor, basis of a rule 230, 239 [M,4:90]

māni': restrictive, preventive; "A reason required by an *'illa* which negates the *'illa* of an act" 121 [M,1:285]; opponent, [M,2: 99]

manṣūṣ: rules or reasons mentioned in the text 217 [M,1:173]

maqāṣid: objectives, goal, end, 152 [M,2:8], intention [M,2:54]

al-maqāṣid al-aṣliyya: primary objectives 197 [M,2:100, 176]

al-maqāṣid al-shar'iyya: legal objectives 233 [M,2:100, 176]

maqāṣid al-shar': purpose of law, ends of law [M,4:106]

maqdūr: feasible, within human capacity 187 [M,2:119]

maqṣūd: intended 210 [M,2:385]

maṣālih: good 248 see *maslaḥa*

maṣālaik al-'illa: the methods of finding the legal cause 231, modes of determining or distinguishing the reason (*'illa, ratio decidendi*) of a rule of law or judgement [M,2:306]

mashaqqa: hardship 122 [M,2:119], "The hardship of an act which is customary and possible to bear and this hardship does not cause a person to discontinue the act" [M,2:123]

al-mashaqqat al-'amma: general hardship, "the hardship which is so for everyone" [M,2:154]

al-mashaqqa ghayr mu'tāda: extra-ordinary hardship [M,2:135]

mashaqqa khārija 'an al-mu'tād: extra-ordinary hardship 188 [M,2:156]; "An act which cannot be continued perpetually, wholly or partly, without disruption or harm to the person, property or to the conditions of the perpetrator 188 [M,2:123]

al-mashaqqa al-khāṣṣa: particular, specific, individual hardship 194 [M,2:154]

mashhūr: popular practice, well-known, better known 91 [F:127]

maskūt 'anhu: where the Lawgiver is silent, matters not covered in the Qur'ān 216 [M,1:173]

maṣlaḥa: good, goodness, opposite to *mafsada* (evil) 188 [M,2:125]; advantage, benefit, opposite to *maḍarra* [harm] 214 [M,1: 174]; interest [M,2:9]; public weal 94 [F:137]; public interest 100 [F:187]; "A matter that concerns the subsistence of human life, the completion of man's livelihood, and the acquisition of what his emotional and intellectual qualities require of him in an absolute sense" 151 [M,2:25]

al-maṣāliḥ al-'āmma: public interest, public offices 250 [M.2:17]

al-maṣlaḥa al-maghlūba: the good which is dominated by evil in an act [M.2:27]

al-maṣlaḥa al-mashūba: the good mixed with disadvantages and harms 155 [M.2:27]

al-maṣlaḥa al-mursala: a reason, cause or benefit not explicitly supported by the text 220 [IT.2:115] [F:188]

al-maṣlaḥa al-ukhrawiya: the benefit in the Hereafter [M.2:32]

al-maṣlaḥa al-dunyawiyya: worldly good, the benefits in this world, 211 [M.2:26]

ma'ṣūma: protected 248 [M.2:58]

ma'tam: mourning 90 [F:209]

mazāyā: special distinctive features, privileges of the Prophet 200 [M.2:249]

maẓnūn: conjecture, imagined, inexact 212 [M.2:279]

al-milk: ordinary property 93 [F:171]

mu'āṭāt: silent transaction, offer and acceptance without words [F:147]

mu'āmalāt: dealing with each other, contracts, transactions 215 [M.2: 284]

muftī: jurist exercising *ijtihād* 123 [M.4:245]

mujtahad fīh: a matter requiring *ijtihād* [M.4:113] matters which are open to difference of opinion [M.4:123]

mujtahid: a jurist who is expert in *Sharī'a* reasoning 123 [M.4:108], see *ijtihād*

mukallafīn: subjects of law 158 [M.2:37]

mukhtār: one who has a choice, freedom of will, free agent 206 [M.2:327]

munāsaba: affinity, one of the methods of determining a *maṣlaḥa* 203 [M.2:313]

al-munāsib: a legal evidence or reason not supported by a specific text, synonymous with *al-maslaḥah al-mursala* 220 [IT.2:111]

muqaddima: pre-requisite 155 [M.2:24]

muqaddimāt: postulates, premises 232 [M.4:111]; first premises in syllogystic reasoning [M.4:339]

muqallid: follower, a person who is not qualified to exercise *ijtihād* [M.4:132]

murā'āt al-khilāf: allowance or consideration of conflicting opinions 235 [M.4:204]; where regard for the opposite view is maintained 242 [M.4:150]

murattab: salary [F:167]

murū'a: manliness, civility 153 [M.2:14]

musāqat: an irregular, but allowed as an exception, lease of a plantation of fruit trees; agrarian association 97 [M.2:46]

mutashābihāt: open for debate [M.4:123]; equivocal statements 241 [M.4:157]; opposite to *muḥkamāt*, unclear [M.4:176]

muṭlaq: absolute/simple 172 [M.2:66]

muzābana: a contract for barter of dried dates for fresh dates 99 [F:157]

muzāra'a: the lease of a field for cultivation 97 [F:155]

nafs: soul 203 [M.2:315] self, life 152 [M.2:10]

nahy: prohibition 205 [M.2:391]; "demanding to abondon a certain act and to will for its non-occurence" [M.3:119]; proscription 191 [M.3:48]

najāsa: dirt, filth 90 [F:125; 2:11]

naskh: abrogation 242 [M,4:236]; repealing, amendment, qualifying a simple or general statement, clarification, "Removal of an earlier divine rule by a later divine evidence" [M,3:108]; opposite to *iḥkām* [M,3:85]

nasl: family 152 [M,2:10]

naṣṣ: clear text 203 [M,2:313]; mostly refers to the Qur'ānic text, but often used for the texts of *ḥadīth* as well [M,3:342] opposite to *maskūt 'anhu* [M,1:144]; opposite to *tashābuh* [M,3:86]

nawāhī: (pl. of *nahiy*), modes of prohibitive injuctions 122 [M,3:119]

naẓar: examination, ivestigation 157 [M,2:110]; reasoning, syllogism, argument by arranging premises to yield conclusion 184 [M,2:111]

nāẓir: assessor, examiner [M,4:93], [F:174]

nikāḥ al-muḥallīl: marriage of a divorcee with a second husband in order to make remarriage with the first husband lawful 211 [M,2:388]

niyāba: delegation, substitution, proxy 200 [M,2:227]

niyya: intent in the sense of volition 206 [M,2:326]; intention, 205 [M,2:327]

qaḍā': decree of destiny 194 [M,2:151]; judgement [M,4:92]; judgeship [M,2:80]

qaḍā bi'l ta'addī: judicial decision by extending the meaning of the original ruling 203 [M,2:312]

qaḍāyā' al-'uqūl: rational propositions, laws of reason [M,3:27]

qāḍī: judge [M,4:92]

qasāma: compurgation, a pre-Islamic custom adopted in Islamic law 214 [M,2:307]; declaration on oath by several persons 101 [F:173]

qaṣd: intention 189 [M,2:126, 326]; motive [M,2:373]

al-qaṣd al-khalqī al-takwīnī: intention of creation, Creative Divine Will 156 [M,2:29]

al-qaṣd al-tashrī'ī: intention of Legislation, Legislative Divine Will 156 [M,2:29]

qaṭ'ī: definite, opposite to *ẓannī* 208 [M,1:29]

qawā'id: (pl. of *qā'ida*), basic principle [M,2:89; 4:198]; fundamentals 180 [M,2:91]

qirāḍ: an irregular, but allowed as an exception, contract of money lending, commenda, a pre-Islamic practice adopted in Islamic law 152 [M,2:46]

qiṣāṣ: lex talionis 154 [M,2:10; F:173]

al-qiyās: analogy [M,2:102]; one of the four aspects of the evidence in *Sharī'a* [M,3:5]

al-qiyās al-iqtirānī: syllogistic reasoning by coupling or combining two propositions 232 [M,4:337]

al-qiyās al-istithnā'ī: syllogistic reasoning by exclusion 232 [M,4:33]

al-qiyās al-naẓarī: syllogistic reasoning by arranging propositions in a particular form 178 [M,2:84]

al-qiyās al-sharṭī: syllogistic reasoning by conditional exclusion [M,4:337]

qubḥ: evil, opposite of *ḥusn* 215 [M,2:284]

qudra: capability, power, ability 183 [M,2:108]

quwwa: potential [M,3:176]

raf' al-ḥaraj: removal of hardship 99 [F:159]

rafḍ: extreme Shī'ism 74 [IT,1:11]

raj'a: return, revocation 91 [F:142]

al-ra'y: human reason, a synonym or substitute for *qiyās* [M,3:245]; legal opinion, view [M,1:40]; personal discretion, whim [M,3:393]

rifq: leniency, moderation 187 [M,2:123]

riyāsa: political office, government, political power [M,1:179]

rukhṣa: allowance, exemption, "A lenient view of law based on a legal excuse for hardship" 188 [M,1:301]

ru'yā: dreams 201 [M,2:266]

sabab: cause, mediate cause 183, 216 [M,2:107]; "A matter that has been declared by law to be the reason for a command as its requirement" 216 [M,1:265]

sadd al-dharā'i': to block the ways possibly leading to undesired consequences [M,4:198; 3:257]

ṣaḥīḥ: valid 121 [M,1:291]; effective [M,1:292]

sahla: convenient 248 [M,2:136]

samḥa: liberal 248 [M,2:136]

ṣanā'i': technologies, crafts 215 [M,2:284]

satr: covering, *satr al-'awra*, covering private parts of body 152 [M,2:11]

al-sawād al-a'ẓam: the majority 72 [IT,1:25]

shahwa: lust [M,2:174], [M,2:214]

shahawāt: pl. of *shahwa*) natural desires 197 [M,2:108,178]; desires 197 [M,2:169]

shāqq: hard 188 [M,2:121]

al-shar': Law [M,1:38]

Shāri': Lawgiver 243, 187 [M,2:121]

Sharī'a: (pl. *sharā'i'*), law [M,2:38] revealed law, Qur'ān [M,1:77]

Shar'iyya: legal, 156 *shar'iyyat al-aḥkām*: legality of rules [M,2:27]

sharṭ: condition 121, "A quality that completes the requirement of a thing or a rule" [M,1:262]

shawār: marriage gift 92 [F:140]

shiqq: hardship, severity [M,2:119]

ṣiḥḥa: soundness, opposite of *buṭlān* [M,1:291]

sirr: inner self, a mystic term 75 [M,1:102]

al-siyāsa al-shar'iyya: punishment of crimes, public law executed according to Islamic laws, [M,4:147]

Sunna: original tradition, opposite to *bid'a* 73 [M,4:4]; "Laws conveyed by the Prophet especially in matters where no Qur'ānic text existed" [M,4:3]; practice of the companions of the Prophet; words, actions and approval of the Prophet [M, 4:4,6]

Sunnat Allah: Divine Law, way of God 214 [M,3:265]

ta'abbud: recourse only to what the Lawgiver has determined 202 [M,2:304]; "To stop at a point where the *Shāri'* has defined the limit" 203 [M,2:313]; "to define the scope of *maṣāliḥ* in obligations", 202 [M,2:308]; strict obedience, 222 [M,2:300]; "without looking for reason" [M,2:304]; bondage to God, [M,2:301] "Non-intelligibility of meaning or reason of an obligation" 202 [M,2:318]; "compliance of the commands of God; 202 [M,2:301] that which is the exclusive right of God 202 [M,2:318]

ta'abbudī: non-extendible, "where meaning of the command or prohibition cannot be specifically understood 222 [IT, 2:79]

ta'addī: extension 203 [M,2:304]

ta'āruḍ: contradiction, conflict 244 [M,4:294]

ta'āruḍ al-adilla: contradictory or conflicting evidences 245 [M.4:299]

tabaddul: change from good to bad [M.2:284]

tabdīl: change [M.2:280]

taḥaqquq al-manāṭ: investigation of the basis of ruling or anchor points 232 [M.4:334]

taḥayyul: recourse to legal devices (*ḥīla*) to escape the severity of the law 205. 209 [M.2:378; 4:201]

taḥqīq al-manāṭ: identification of the anchor point [M.4:89]

taḥqīq al-manāṭ al-'āmm: identification of general anchor points 230 [M.4:97]

taḥqīq al-manāṭ al-khāṣṣ: identification of particular anchor points 230 [M.4:97]

taḥsīnī: commendable 151 [M.2:8]; (pl. *taḥsīnāt*). a grade of *maṣlaḥa;* "To adopt what conforms to the best of customs, to avoid manners that are disliked by the wise people 152 [M.2:11].

tajārib wa'l-'ādāt: social experience and practice 197. [M.2:170]

tajarrud 'an al-ḥaẓẓ: disregard of personal benefit 198. [M.2:186]

takālīf: (pl. of *taklīf*). obligations 158 [M.2:107]

al-takālīf al-shar'iyya: legal obligations 160 [M.2:172]

takhfīf: laxity 195 [M.2:159]

takhlīṣ min al-ḥaẓẓ: liberation from self-indulgence 197 [M.2:186]

takhrīj al-manāṭ: locating the anchor point 231 [M.4:96]

takhṣīṣ: particularization, restriction, [M.3:273]

takhyīr: option 203 [M.2:311]

ta'līl: (pl. *ta'ālīl*). determination of the cause of Divine commands by logical and linguistic analysis [M.2:7]

tamāthul: parallel evaluation. comparable equality 153 [M.2:12]

tanāquḍ: contradiction 232 [M.4:337]

tanqīḥ al-manāṭ: distinguishing between various anchor points 231 [M.4:95]

taqlīd: accepting other's opinion 231 [M.4:91]; strict adherence to a school of law 104 [M.4:118]

taqwā: peity. care and prudence 230 [M.4:97]

tarjīḥ: preponderence 244 [M.4:294]

tartīb: system 213 [M.2:280] classification. arrangement [M,3:366. 369]

taṣbīḥ al-qabr: vigil at the grave until morning. a mourning rite 90 [F:209]

tashābuh: equivocation. incomprehensibility. opposite to *iḥkām* [M,3:85]

tashdīd: hardship. severity 191 [M. 2:132; F:158]

tashīl: convenience 99 [F:158]

tashrī': law-making. legislation 212 [M.2:280]

ta'wassu': expansion. removal of difficulty. openness. laxity 152 [M.2:10]

tawīl al-ẓawāhir: interpretation of the apparent and evident meaning 231 [M.4:96]

ta'yīn: specification 93 [F:166; M.4:261]

taysīr: facility [F:158]

'ubūdiyya: servitude without personal interest. the Ṣūfī understanding of obligation 196 [M.2:179]

ummī: derived from *umm* (mother), original state, unlettered; not acquainted with the sciences of the ancient [M,2:69]

ummiyya: general, accessible to a common unlettered person 248 [M,2:69]

'umūm: general and absolute sense of a word, applicable to all the refrents of a word 122 [M,3:260]

'uqalā': philosophers, wise men 214 [M,2:307]

'uqūbāt: punishments 190 [M,2:149]

'urf: custom [F:168]

uṣūl al-dīn: principles of religion, *'ilm al-kalām*, theology, 72, 248 [IT,1:38; M,1:31]

uṣūl al-fiqh: "induction of the universal principles of the evidence" 248 [IT,1:38], universal laws of *Sharī'a* [M,1:30]

uṣūliyyīn: theorists 244 [M,4:122]

waḍ'ī: posited, assigning 175 [M,2:89, 107], original usage, opposite to *iṣṭilāḥī* [M,2:119] declaratory, opposite to *taklīfī* 120 [M,1:187]; conventional, opposite to rational, logical [M,2:53]

waḥy: revelation 247, 251, 203 [M,2:313] prophethood, prophecy [M,2:250]

wāqifīn: the people in the state of indecisiveness 203 [M,2:312]

wara': piety 195 [M,2:92]

al-wara' bī'l khurūj 'an al-khilāf: piety of avoiding the cases of disagreement 240 [M,1:103]

wilāyāt: administrative offices 249 [M,2:247]

wujūb: necessity, obligation 213 [M,2:282]

wuqū': occurrence actuality 213 [M,1:34]

ẓāhir: evident, apparent, literal meaning 174 [M,2:392]

al-Ẓāhiriyya: the literalists, opposite to *aṣḥāb al-ra'y* 229 [M,4:230]

ẓannī: probable, opposite to *qaṭ'ī*, 247 [M,1:29]

zuhd: asceticism 196 [M,2:168]

INDEX